The Ethics of Conditional Confidentiality

The Ethics of Conditional Confidentiality

A PRACTICE MODEL FOR MENTAL HEALTH PROFESSIONALS

Mary Alice Fisher

Oxford University Press is a department of the University of Oxford.
It furthers the University's objective of excellence in research, scholarship,
and education by publishing worldwide.

Oxford New York
Auckland Cape Town Dar es Salaam Hong Kong Karachi
Kuala Lumpur Madrid Melbourne Mexico City Nairobi
New Delhi Shanghai Taipei Toronto

With offices in
Argentina Austria Brazil Chile Czech Republic France Greece
Guatemala Hungary Italy Japan Poland Portugal Singapore
South Korea Switzerland Thailand Turkey Ukraine Vietnam

Published in the United States of America by
Oxford University Press
198 Madison Avenue, New York, NY 10016

Library of Congress Cataloging-in-Publication Data

Fisher, Mary Alice.
The ethics of conditional confidentiality : a practice model for mental health professionals /
Mary Alice Fisher.
p. cm.
Includes bibliographical references and index.
ISBN 978-0-19-975220-1
1. Psychotherapist and patient–Moral and ethical aspects. 2. Psychoanalysis–Moral and ethical aspects. 3. Confidential communications. I. Title.
RC480.8.F57 2013
174.2'9689–dc23
2012024750

Printed in the United States of America
on acid-free paper

CONTENTS

PART III Practical Considerations

ACKNOWLEDGMENTS

I wish to thank the many mental health professionals who have shared their ethical and ethical/legal dilemmas in private consultation. Their identity is protected, because those consultations were conducted in confidence, but learning about their problems helped me make this book more practical. I also thank the many workshop participants whose questions have prompted important changes in my own thinking across the years. And I especially thank the therapy patients who have helped me learn to practice what I preach.

This book represents the third step in a progression of publications on this topic. The first was a 2008 article in *American Psychologist*, which introduced an Ethical Practice Model for protecting confidentiality rights. The second was an invited chapter, Confidentiality and Record Keeping, in the 2012 *APA Handbook of Ethics in Psychology*. I am grateful for the support and encouragement extended by Samuel Knapp, the editor-in-chief of that volume, because that chapter provided an opportunity to expand the original article into a much broader discussion of confidentiality ethics. Finally, in publishing this book, Oxford University Press has allowed me to build on those previous publications and to extend that discussion even further, thereby offering what I hope will be a practical and comprehensive confidentiality resource for mental health service providers of all professions.

I thank my colleague and former professor, Sherry Kraft, for invaluable suggestions, personal encouragement, and editorial assistance across the years. And I wish to thank Ken Pope, a clinical psychologist whom I have never met, whose website at kspope.com, as well as his articles and ethics texts, have long provided much valuable information for my teaching, writing, and consultation on this and other topics.

My special thanks and gratitude go to Richard Redding, J.D., Ph.D., whose expertise combines the perspectives of mental health and law. He served as consulting editor for Chapter 7 and other legal sections of this book, and he helped make them more accurate and more intelligible. On his advice, I added a legal Appendix that should be very useful for those who are unfamiliar with the legal categories.

Sarah Harrington, my editor at Oxford University Press, was patient with my delays, welcoming of requests and suggestions, and thoughtful about readers' needs. At her suggestion, the legal Appendix III is duplicated online on the website of the Center for Ethical Practice, allowing readers to link directly to the current version of the relevant statutes. My further appreciation goes to Gerald Koocher who reviewed the manuscript and offered helpful suggestions, and to the other reviewers who remain anonymous. Finally, I thank the many at Oxford who shepherded this book along its way, including Jodi Narde, Andrea Zekus, Susan Lee, Jaimee Biggins, and Annie Grace, at Newgen.

In many respects, this project has been a family affair. Linda Fisher Thornton has read and edited my manuscripts for many years, beginning with early writings on the topic of confidentiality. The Center for Ethical Practice, Inc., under whose auspices this work was completed, owes its name to Joseph Thornton. Robert Fisher has provided ongoing technical assistance and personal support, without which this book and its predecessors would never have gotten off the ground. Hannah Fisher Barton spent countless hours establishing an Endnote library, and Rebekah Fisher Keathley conducted annual reviews of statutes to ensure that the Center's legal library remained up to date. This writing project was possible only after Edith Huff Fisher became managing director of the Center for Ethical Practice, lightening my load and keeping me on track. And finally, without the support, encouragement, and intellectual stimulation provided by Curtis Crawford, I would never even have begun to write.

Mary Alice Fisher, August 2012

INTRODUCTION

It is no longer a secret that therapists sometimes disclose their patients' secrets. At one level, this is simply a statement of fact—an acknowledgment that therapeutic confidentiality, once considered absolute, now has some very severe limits. Therapists, whose ethical rule was once "Disclose *nothing* without the patient's consent," now have a professional ethic that permits disclosure of confidential information in certain circumstances, even if the patient objects. This new "conditional confidentiality" ethic arose because court decisions and reporting laws began to legally require therapists to breach confidentiality. But the fact that a breach of confidentiality is legally required (and therefore now ethically permitted) does not reduce its impact on the patient.

It is precisely because of this potential for harm that the ethical freedom to place patients' confidences at risk comes with a clinical price: Instead of beginning therapy relationships with the old promise – "Everything you tell me will remain in this room" – therapists must now begin each new relationship by telling prospective patients exactly when they might disclose information without their consent. In other words, therapists are not ethically or legally free to "keep secret" the fact that they do not always keep secrets.

Why was it *ever* a secret? The fact that this information was ever withheld from patients raises some embarrassing questions. Why do therapists have a history of being less than completely honest with prospective patients about the fact that confidentiality will be limited—or about exactly what those limits might be? Why have therapists often treated even the most foreseeable disclosures of confidential information as if they were "professional secrets"—as if patients had no right to know their therapist's intentions in advance, or even to know about all of their disclosures after the fact? The ethics codes of most mental health professions have always required therapists to discuss the "limits of confidentiality" with prospective patients before providing services. Yet, when the Health Insurance Privacy and Accountability Act (HIPAA) was enacted in 1996, many treated its required "Notice of Privacy Practices" as a frightening new mandate—therapists were now legally required to describe the limits of confidentiality *in writing*.

Why were therapists so confused for so long about whose secrets to protect and whose to disclose? By what path did mental health professionals travel from *yesterday* (when all therapists were bound by that familiar one-sentence rule) to *today* (when each therapist places slightly different limits on the protection of patient confidences)? When did the ethical and legal complexities become so confusing that just hearing the word "confidentiality" provokes anxiety in many therapists?

Was HIPAA upsetting to therapists because they were unprepared to describe their own intentions—perhaps because they had not yet decided exactly what their intentions really *are* about confidentiality? Why are so many therapists still using a cookie-cutter "Notice of Privacy Practices" that does not accurately describe their own policies? Why do therapists' conversations with prospective patients about the "limits of confidentiality" often lack the specificity patients need for exercising their right to protect *themselves*? Why is conversation about confidentiality often difficult, even among trusted clinical colleagues?

Tentative answers to such questions were suggested in my 2008 *American Psychologist* article entitled, "Protecting Confidentiality Rights: The Need for an Ethical Practice Model." That explanation goes something like this: Over 40 years ago, rapidly changing laws began to collide with slowly changing ethics codes, leaving therapists with no clear ethical guidance about how to respond to the new laws that required them to disclose confidential information. Left to their own devices, clinicians evolved some creative solutions—and also some maladaptive patterns—in their attempt to cope with the new legal demands.

That is the *shorthand* answer. Therapists' personal answers vary. This book is an attempt to help mental health professionals be clear about what their professions require, about what their own personal position about confidentiality really is, and about which confidentiality promises they are ready to make and to keep—clear both for themselves and with their patients.

Four recurring themes are at the heart of this book.

- *First, therapists must be honest with themselves.* As clinicians, they have some difficult decisions to make about confidentiality, and, at the most basic level, their freedom of choice is quite limited. They are still ethically free to offer patients *unconditional confidentiality* and make the promise that "Everything you tell me stays in this room," but only if they are prepared to disobey the law, eschew managed care, and protect confidences in every circumstance, no matter how severe the legal, financial, and personal risks to themselves. The alternative is to offer patients only *conditional confidentiality* instead; but since this transfers the risks to their patients, therapists have an ethical duty to explain in advance exactly when they intend *not* to protect confidences, regardless of the clinical implications of that conversation. Perhaps because they dislike both options, some therapists try to "straddle the fence," seeking a middle-ground compromise in their attempt to avoid both extremes. But, ethically speaking, there are no other basic options—only these two. Therapists who believe otherwise—who believe there can be some ethical middle ground in which they can breach confidentiality sometimes, case by case, without knowing in advance exactly when they might do that—are misleading themselves. Delaying the decision about which road to take has not helped matters; it has simply left patients at risk.

- *Second, therapists have an ethical and clinical imperative to be fully honest with their patients.* They are not ethically free to conduct intakes in a posture that promises (or, by silence, implies) more protection of confidences than they will actually provide. In other words, they are not ethically free to place patients at risk by eliciting their personal secrets without first explaining very clearly when they might later disclose those secrets to others (which therapists sometimes do if protecting patients' confidences places *them* at too much risk). So, in behalf of therapy patients, the opening statement in this Introduction can be read as an admonition to mental health professionals: We must stop "posing" as better secret-keepers than we actually are. We must be clear and specific. We must not presume that an unintelligible five-page HIPAA form is a sufficient substitute for obtaining truly informed consent about confidentiality's limits.
- *Third, therapists have an ethical responsibility not to succumb to figure–ground confusion.* The more often therapists are legally required to disclose information without the patient's consent, the more they are at risk for treating breaches of confidentiality as if they were the rule rather than the exception to the rule. The more often third-party payers demand information for reimbursement purposes, the more therapists are at risk for providing it without obtaining informed consent—without informing patients about exactly what will be disclosed (and the implications of disclosing it) and obtaining consent from the informed patient before sending it. In other words, there is still a confidentiality rule, and therapists have an ethical obligation not to allow its exceptions to overshadow that ethical rule. This applies to both legally imposed exceptions and voluntary exceptions. Therapists who have made a basic choice to offer only "conditional" confidentiality now must decide what "conditions" they will impose voluntarily; and this decision must be made in advance so that it can be explained to patients in advance.
- *Fourth, patients are best protected if therapists uphold the confidentiality rule to the extent legally possible.* This is a supererogatory position that goes beyond the requirements of most ethics codes and definitely goes beyond the requirements of the law. Many laws (including both state laws and HIPAA) now allow therapists to disclose information without the patient's consent in many circumstances; but the fact that a disclosure is legally allowed does not necessarily make it ethical. In this book, we therefore take the position that, unless legally *required* to breach confidentiality, therapists should obtain consent before disclosing anything about their patients. When might such consent be obtained? First, it can be obtained in advance: As a condition of receiving mental health services, prospective patients can give their consent to accept the "routine" disclosures that will apply to all patients. Subsequently, consent for patient-specific disclosures (e.g., to their personal physician or prescribing psychiatrist) can be obtained as needed in each case.

This book presents the topic of confidentiality from an ethical perspective, not a risk management perspective. In other words, it presents the topic of confidentiality from the point of view of protecting patients and their rights—the ethical point of view—not from the perspective of therapist self-protection—the risk management point of view. Many risk management resources are already available; and besides, one of the best risk management strategies is to protect patients and their rights by practicing within the ethical standards of one's own profession. When it comes to confidentiality, however, therapists' ethical standards can be complicated and confusing; and when we add the laws that can limit confidentiality, it becomes even more difficult to clarify what is ethical to do and what is not.

This book therefore will focus on the "practical ethics" of confidentiality—the "how to" of ethical practice that protects patients' rights about it. The goal is to outline a set of ethical practices that will reduce the risk that patients' secrets will be betrayed unexpectedly. Toward that end, this book begins with a review of the ABCs of "conditional confidentiality," providing an ethical framework that will hopefully lessen the confusion and help therapists clarify their responsibilities.

This book does not focus on legal compliance. However, mental health professionals must understand the relevant laws well enough to be prepared to respond ethically if they arise. Therapists often face situations in which laws conflict with their formal ethical standards or with their personal ethical position about confidentiality. Although we do not advocate breaking the law to protect patient confidentiality, we do applaud and support those therapists who choose to engage in civil disobedience, placing themselves at personal, financial, and legal risk in order to protect a patient's confidentiality. Their actions sometimes lead to more protective laws. But much can be done to protect patients' rights short of taking the step of engaging in civil disobedience. This can include always protecting confidentiality to the extent legally possible. Toward that end, this book contains a detailed chapter about responding ethically to legal demands, as well as sections emphasizing the distinction between those disclosures that are merely legally allowed and those that are actually legally required.

Finally, and most importantly, this book is an attempt to begin a conversation. It is unfortunately true that, on some professional topics, the various mental health professions part company or have conflicting interests. On the topic of confidentiality ethics, however, there are few professional dividing lines or turf battles. The ethics codes of all the mental health professions describe similar duties about confidentiality because they all protect patients' rights about it, and, for the most part, they define those rights in similar ways. This made it possible to construct a multidisciplinary ethics-based practice model—a six-step outline of "The Ethics of Conditional Confidentiality "—that applies to all of the mental health professions. The final step in that model suggests how the conversation begun here might be continued.

Part I of this book summarizes the ethical mandates that define therapists' choices about confidentiality, as well as the legal mandates that limit those choices. It begins with ethics, to stress the importance of upholding the standards that have been established by the mental health professions themselves. The ethical standards in the respective ethics codes define the "ethical floor" about confidentiality—the minimum professional standards with which mental health professionals must comply. Then, with that ethical baseline in place, we consider how laws can affect therapists' behavior about confidentiality. Finally, we consider the interactions between ethics and laws—the ways they can overlap or can conflict—and we simplify that discussion with the Ethical Practice Model that places laws into ethical context.

In Part II, that six-step model becomes the outline for a six-chapter discussion of how to practice ethically about confidentiality. Throughout, we advocate that therapists not "settle for the ethical floor" about confidentiality, but instead "reach for the ethical ceiling" by protecting their patients' confidentiality rights to the extent legally possible.[1] The model helps place laws into ethical context and provides an ethical language that can be shared by all mental health professionals in their discussions about confidentiality and its limits.

Part III addresses record keeping issues that affect confidentiality. It also contains discussion of confidentiality issues with specific patient populations and in certain settings. Finally, there is a chapter punctuating the importance of providing ethics-based training so that all staff—clinical and nonclinical—will be clear about the confidentiality standards they must uphold in mental health settings.

The appendices contain ethical information and other resources for easy reference when reading these chapters. The first two appendices contain selected confidentiality-related ethical standards from the ethics codes of some national associations of mental health professions: clinical social work, counseling, marriage and family therapy, psychiatry, and psychology. Appendix VII gives sources for obtaining the ethics codes for these and other mental health professions and their sub-specialties. *These appendices are not a substitute for being familiar with the entire ethics code of one's profession, and it is recommended that all therapists and other mental health professionals obtain and keep handy a copy of the ethics code(s) that will govern their own work.*

Throughout this book, the term "therapy" is used generically to describe all therapeutic mental health services, including counseling, psychotherapy, or psychoanalysis, whether provided by counselors, psychiatrists, psychologists, clinical social workers, psychiatric nurse practitioners, or others. The term "patient" is used to describe all those who receive these direct clinical services, except when quoting someone else who has used the term "client" instead; otherwise, the term "client" will be used here only to describe individuals, groups, or agencies receiving other services provided by mental health professionals (e.g., consultation, evaluation, education).

The term "counselor" is used broadly to apply to all those who describe their services as counseling, including marriage and family counselors, general mental health counselors, substance abuse and alcoholism counselors, and any other group that defines its services as "counseling."[2]

The concepts in this book should be useful not only to therapists and counselors, but to mental health professionals who provide other services, such as psychological assessment, clinical consultation, or coaching, or who lead helping groups, such as weight loss groups, habit control groups, or support groups. Part III includes discussions of some of these services and the confidentiality implications of the settings in which they might be provided.

The Ethical Practice Model can be very useful to those who teach clinical ethics or supervise others. This would include not only those who serve in clinical training programs as program directors, professors, supervisors, or administrators, but also those clinicians who provide supervision to trainees within their own setting or who participate in peer consultation. Since it applies across professional lines, the model should be useful to multidisciplinary practice groups or clinical agencies, and it can facilitate conversations about confidentiality in interdisciplinary ethics training and continuing education workshops for all mental health professionals.

In 1995, Bollas and Sundelson suggested that those mental health professionals who wish to provide *absolute* confidentiality should band together to support each other as they face the severe legal and financial consequences of that choice. Most have avoided those consequences by choosing to offer only *conditional* confidentiality instead. But they, too, need each others' support, because it is easy to become very confused about *its* responsibilities and unprepared for *its* consequences. Since we are all struggling with the same dilemmas and making the same mistakes, we can be learning together. We have nothing to lose. Those who receive our services have everything to gain.

PART I

The ABCs of "Conditional Confidentiality": An Ethical, Legal, and Ethical/Legal Review

1

Ethical Responsibilities About Confidentiality

There is a profound confusion, among even well-qualified clinicians, about confidentiality. Bollas, C., & Sundelson, D. (1995),
The New Informants: The Betrayal of Confidentiality in Psychoanalysis and Psychotherapy, p. xii

Can you keep a secret? If you are a therapist, the correct answer is not just "Yes, I can." It is "Yes, I *must*."

Confidentiality is an ethical duty for all mental health professionals. Ethics codes emphasize its importance. Therapists have long described it as their most important professional duty.[1]

Confidentiality is also a legal duty. Many laws protect confidentiality, and some of them impose penalties for therapists who breach it. But other laws can severely limit a therapist's ability to protect patients' confidences, and this has created a great deal of confusion.

Faced with increasing numbers of laws that required therapists to disclose information without the patient's consent, the mental health professions gradually changed their ethics codes to allow those legally required disclosures. In other words, once laws began placing conditions on confidentiality, the professions began giving therapists ethical permission to do the same.[2]

Ethically speaking, this "conditional confidentiality" can become very complicated to practice. On the surface, confidentiality might seem to be an easy concept; but in actual practice, it becomes quite complex. Even experienced clinicians are sometimes profoundly confused about their confidentiality obligations and are anxious and despairing about the impact of laws on patient privacy and confidentiality.[3]

The confusion is exacerbated by the fact that although ethical standards about confidentiality apply to therapists nationwide, each state imposes very different legal limitations on therapists' ability to protect patients' confidences. Furthermore, legally imposed exceptions to confidentiality not only differ from state to state, but also from setting to setting and from circumstance to circumstance within each state.[4]

Adding to the confusion is the fact that laws can go in several directions at once: Some laws protect confidentiality (e.g., nondisclosure laws and privileged communications laws); other laws require clinicians to disclose confidential information (e.g., mandated reporting laws); and some laws actually do *both*. Finally, it doesn't help matters that confidentiality is one of the broadest of all the ethical principles, which means that it arises across virtually every facet of a clinician's professional life.[5]

It is not surprising, then, that therapists themselves name confidentiality as the aspect of practice most likely to create ethical dilemmas.[6] Regrettably, some now believe that, on balance, "the porousness of confidentiality seems to be increasing," and that young therapists are tending to seek ways of making exceptions to confidentiality in order to serve other social or personal interests, rather than seeking ways to protect confidentiality in the patient's best interest.[7]

Finally, as legally imposed exceptions to confidentiality have multiplied, the possible ways of dealing with the exceptions have increased in number and complexity. Bollas argues that there have been so many qualifications to confidentiality that "it exists only in name and not in fact."[8] Beck earlier worried that "disclosure without consent" was fast becoming the rule rather than the exception. "What occurs is a kind of *figure–ground reversal*. When there are too many exceptions, the exceptions become prominent and the rule fades into the background."[9] Some would say that this time has already arrived.

If therapists and other mental health professionals are to avoid this confusion and learn how to maintain ethical practices in this climate of conditional confidentiality, they must address four concepts that are frequently misunderstood:[10]

- *First,* there are ethical standards about confidentiality, and there are laws about confidentiality: They are two entirely different things. They do sometimes overlap, but it is ethically essential that therapists not confuse them.
- *Second,* no law can change a profession's own ethical standards: Laws can require therapists to make exceptions to their profession's confidentiality rule, but laws do not change or "erase" the ethical rule itself.
- *Third,* ethically speaking, a *legally required* disclosure is very different from a *legally allowed* disclosure: The latter is a "voluntary" disclosure (meaning that the patient remains free not to give consent and the therapist remains free not to disclose), and, strictly speaking, any voluntary disclosure requires the patient's informed consent.
- *Fourth* (and related to the first), when laws or organizational policies about confidentiality conflict with ethical standards, therapists must notice the conflict because they have an ethical duty to try to resolve it in a direction consistent with professional ethics.

It is difficult to have clear conversations about confidentiality ethics with each other, with patients, or with others unless we share a common definition of terms. The definitions in Box 1.1 are used throughout this book.

BOX 1.1 Definitions

Perspectives About Professional Behavior

Ethical focus. Attention to the practices that are most protective of patients and their rights (including following or exceeding the standards described in one' professional ethics code).

Legal focus. Attention to what the relevant laws and regulations might require, permit, or prohibit.

Risk management focus. Attention on minimizing the legal risks to oneself (e.g., identifying ways in which patients can be harmed—or perceive themselves to be harmed—in order to protect oneself from allegations of misconduct, whether founded or frivolous). (Definition adapted from Knapp & VandeCreek [2006], pp. 11, 35.)

Terms describing ethical behavior

Ethically required. Behavior explicitly required by a professional ethics code (e.g., therapists must inform prospective patients about the limits of confidentiality before providing services).

Ethically allowed or ethically permitted. Behavior explicitly allowed (but not required) by an ethics code (e.g., therapists are ethically free to disclose confidential information in certain specific circumstances).

Ethically prohibited. Behavior explicitly disallowed by an ethics code (e.g., therapists may not audio-tape patients without their consent).

"Ethical floor." A standard of behavior that complies with the letter of the ethics code (i.e., the minimum standards required by the profession).

"Ethical ceiling." A standard of behavior chosen by the therapist that is more patient-protective than the ethics code requires (e.g., following personally imposed supererogatory duties, such as never disclosing anything without a patient's informed consent unless legally required to do so, not disclosing confidential information simply because some law allows it, etc.).

Terms Describing Differential Legal Circumstances

Legally required. Behavior explicitly mandated by state or federal statute, regulation, or case law (e.g., most states have laws legally requiring therapists to report child abuse).

Legally allowed or legally permitted. Behavior allowed by law or regulation (e.g., the Health Insurance Portability and Accountability Act [HIPAA] legally permits (but does not legally require) therapists to disclose patient information for certain treatment, payment, or health care operations without patient authorization).

Legally prohibited. Behavior explicitly disallowed by some law or regulation (e.g., most state licensing boards legally prohibit sexual relationships with current patients).

Note that the first three terms are not mutually exclusive, but it is ethically important to understand the distinctions among them. In their ethics text, *Ethics in Psychotherapy and Counseling,* Pope and Vasquez (2011) differentiate between the ethical, legal, and risk management perspectives:

> Awareness of relevant legislation, case law, and other legal standards is critical, but legal standards should not be confused with ethical responsibilities. A risk in the emphasis on legal standards is that adherence to minimal legal standards ... can become a substitute for ethical behavior ... An overly exclusive focus on legal standards can discourage ethical awareness and sensitivity. It is crucial to realize that ethical behavior is more than simply avoiding violation of legal standards, and that one's ethical and legal duties may, in certain instances, be in conflict. Practicing "defensive therapy"—making risk management our main focus—can cause us to lose sight of our ethical responsibilities and the ethical consequences of what we say and do. Ethical awareness avoids the comfortable trap of aiming low, of striving only to get by without breaking any law. Though often compatible, the legal framework is different from the ethical framework. Ethical awareness requires clearly distinguishing the two and alertness to when they stand in conflict. (p. xiii)

When the terms from Box 1.1 are applied to various ethics codes, it becomes apparent that each mental health profession has slightly different standards about what is ethically required and what is ethically permitted about confidentiality. Therefore, although we can learn from each others' ethics codes, it is important that therapists take responsibility for knowing what their own ethics code actually requires.[11]

The distinctions in Figure 1.1 are also important for communicating clearly about the concepts described throughout this book. As indicated, the terms "confidentiality" and "privacy" should not be used interchangeably, because they are not synonymous. Similarly, the term "privilege" should not be used as a substitute for the word "confidentiality."[12] Privilege is a small subcategory of confidentiality—a legal term used only in a limited context: to indicate whether or not information might be available as evidence in court.

An understanding of ethical responsibilities begins with professional ethics codes.[13] There, one finds both aspirational underlying principles and enforceable ethical standards. Supplementing these ethics codes, ethicists within each mental health profession have published guidebooks and casebooks that explain and interpret the ethical standards, and some national professional associations also provide guidelines that elaborate upon them. Ethics texts provide further guidance, and these often contain helpful vignettes about confidentiality.

Underlying Principles

Few therapists read the introductory sections of their ethics code. But this is where the professions recognize the moral concepts that underlie their ethical standards.

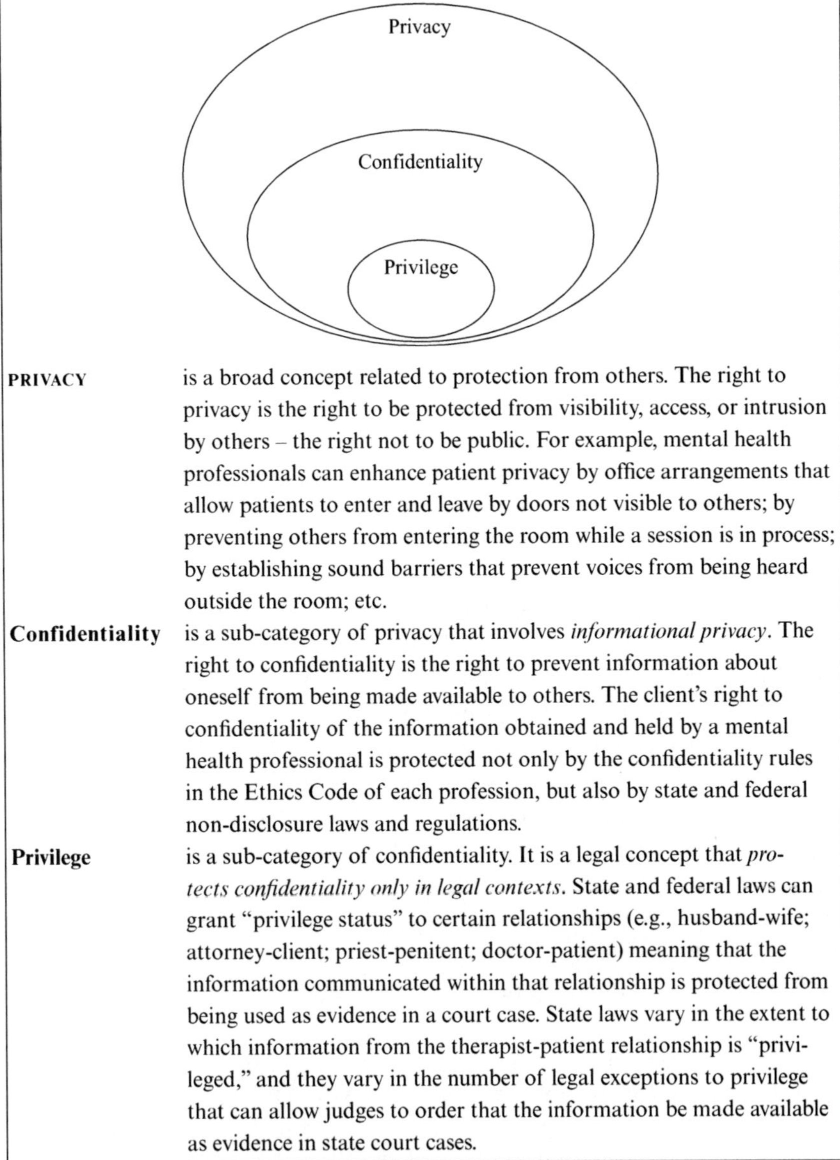

PRIVACY	is a broad concept related to protection from others. The right to privacy is the right to be protected from visibility, access, or intrusion by others – the right not to be public. For example, mental health professionals can enhance patient privacy by office arrangements that allow patients to enter and leave by doors not visible to others; by preventing others from entering the room while a session is in process; by establishing sound barriers that prevent voices from being heard outside the room; etc.
Confidentiality	is a sub-category of privacy that involves *informational privacy*. The right to confidentiality is the right to prevent information about oneself from being made available to others. The client's right to confidentiality of the information obtained and held by a mental health professional is protected not only by the confidentiality rules in the Ethics Code of each profession, but also by state and federal non-disclosure laws and regulations.
Privilege	is a sub-category of confidentiality. It is a legal concept that *protects confidentiality only in legal contexts*. State and federal laws can grant "privilege status" to certain relationships (e.g., husband-wife; attorney-client; priest-penitent; doctor-patient) meaning that the information communicated within that relationship is protected from being used as evidence in a court case. State laws vary in the extent to which information from the therapist-patient relationship is "privileged," and they vary in the number of legal exceptions to privilege that can allow judges to order that the information be made available as evidence in state court cases.

FIGURE 1.1 Distinguishing among privacy, confidentiality and privilege. Figure and definitions adapted from Koocher, G.P., & Spiegel, P.K. (2009). "What should I do?: 38 Ethical dilemmas involving confidentiality." A continuing education module available online at http://www.continuingedcourses.net/active/courses/course049.php

These include such principles as beneficence and nonmaleficence (i.e., doing good without doing harm), fidelity, responsibility, integrity, justice, and respect for people's rights and dignity.

> Confidentiality rules are based on the moral principles of *beneficence*, in that therapists act to promote patient welfare; *nonmaleficence*, in that therapists avoid actions that could harm patients; *integrity* (i.e., fidelity), in that therapists keep their promises; and *respect for patient autonomy*, to the extent that patients have control over the release of the information generated from patient services.[14]

In addition to such moral principles, there are practical and clinical considerations that also underlie the emphasis on confidentiality. For example, assurance of confidentiality is considered "critical for the provision of many psychological services";[15] and confidentiality has sometimes been described as "a cornerstone of the helping relationship."[16] Maintaining confidentiality has long been considered "an essential ingredient in the work of psychologists,"[17] and it helps therapists of all professions to create a "culture of safety" that fosters patient trust.[18]

The ethical requirement to protect confidentiality applies to mental health professionals in all their professional relationships, but it is considered especially important in therapy relationships. Many consider confidentiality essential to effective psychotherapy;[19] and prospective therapy patients often arrive with the expectation that confidentiality will be absolute.[20] "It seems reasonable to assume that for many people, trust that their privacy will not be intruded upon beyond the confines of the clinical relationship is an important element in permitting unguarded exchanges during treatment."[21] If patients enter therapy believing their secrets will be safe there, they will naturally feel betrayed if confidentiality is breached unexpectedly.

Several of the mental health professions have filed *amicus* (friend of the court) briefs in court cases, stressing the importance of confidentiality and arguing for its protection. The American Psychological Association (APA) argued that since a therapy patient "must expose his most intimate thoughts, feelings, and fantasies," therapists must be able to create "an atmosphere in which patients can reveal sensitive and potentially embarrassing confidences without fear that they will be disclosed to others."[22] The American Psychiatric Association (APsyA) warned of "adverse consequences that flow readily from the breach of privacy."[23] These perspectives received legal backing from the U. S. Supreme Court in its 1996 *Jaffee v. Redmond* decision.[24] In a later court case, the National Association of Social Workers (NASW), joined by others, argued that "but for assurances of confidentiality, many existing psychotherapeutic relationships would be impaired or would cease altogether, and fear of disclosure may prevent those in need from seeking help in the first place."[25]

Confidentiality also serves some broad social purposes. In addition to protecting the confidences of individual therapy patients, it promotes public trust in the therapy professions.[26] Confidentiality can also be an important factor in helping patients avoid the stigma that is sometimes an impediment to seeking needed mental health care; confidentiality not only protects confidences, but it also protects the fact that an individual has sought treatment.[27]

Considerations such as these can be cited by therapists who are contesting subpoenas or other legal demands for disclosure. Such factors can also be noted in discussing the importance of confidentiality and advocating for its protection when teaching or supervising students, when conversing with colleagues, when educating attorneys or the public, or when lobbying for legislative reform to provide better confidentiality protections for patients (see Chapter 9).

Formal Ethical Standards

Each ethics code contains not only aspirational principles but also enforceable ethical standards that require therapists to behave in certain ways about confidentiality. These ethical standards describe the minimum standards of behavior—the "ethical floor"—concerning confidentiality. Mental health professionals can also create their own supererogatory ethical standards about confidentiality—personally imposed standards of behavior that rise above the minimum standards imposed by their profession—in order to provide their patients with even better protections.[28] In other words, they can choose to reach for their "ethical ceiling" rather than settling for the "ethical floor" described in their ethics code.

ETHICAL STANDARDS ABOUT CONFIDENTIALITY

Ethics codes are not organized as confidentiality manuals, so the ethical standards relevant to confidentiality are not always easy to find. Although many are located in the confidentiality section of an ethics code, many other relevant ethical standards are scattered throughout the document. For psychologists, the APA Ethics Code contains 31 ethical standards related to confidentiality, of which only seven are in the section "Privacy and Confidentiality." For counselors,[29] the American Counseling Association (ACA) Ethics Code contains 36 separate standards bearing on confidentiality, only 14 of which are in a section called "Confidentiality, Privileged Communication, and Privacy." For marriage and family therapists, the American Association of Marriage and Family Therapists (AAMFT) Ethics Code contains at least 32 relevant Ethical Standards, only seven of which are in the "Confidentiality" section. For social workers, most of the relevant ethical standards do appear in the NASW Ethics Code section "Privacy and Confidentiality," but a few others are scattered throughout the document.

In Appendix I, the ethical standards affecting confidentiality are listed numerically. This is useful for seeing them within the structure of one's ethics code, but this type of list is not helpful for understanding their interrelated implications. The ethical responsibilities become clearer when the ethical standards are organized as in Appendix II, using the three principle-based categories suggested by Knapp and VandeCreek: (1) "key standard"; (2) "clarifying, amplifying, and application standards"; and (3) "exceptions to the key standard."[30] Using this system also makes it easier to separate the confidentiality rule from its ethically allowed exceptions, which vary slightly across the professions.

The "Key Standard"

This ethical standard contains the confidentiality rule. For most professions, the rule itself is written in simple terms, but it usually makes reference to the fact that there can be legal exceptions to the rule:

- *Counselors.* According to the ACA, counselors "do not share confidential information without client consent or without sound legal or ethical justification."[31]
- *Marriage and family therapists.* According to the AAMFT, "client confidences" may not be disclosed "except by written authorization or waiver, or where mandated or permitted by law."[32]
- *Psychiatrists.* According to the APsyA, psychiatrists "safeguard patient confidences and privacy within the constraints of the law."[33]
- *Psychologists.* According to the APA, psychologists "have a primary obligation and take reasonable precautions to protect confidential information obtained through or stored in any medium, recognizing that the extent and limits of confidentiality may be regulated by law or established by institutional rules or professional or scientific relationship."[34]
- *Social workers.* According to the NASW, social workers "should respect clients' right to privacy ... ; protect the confidentiality of all information obtained in the course of professional service, except for compelling professional reasons; [and] protect the confidentiality of clients during legal proceedings to the extent permitted by law."[35]

The Clarification, Amplification, and Application Standards

Ethical standards that expand on the confidentiality rule vary across professions. These standards can require therapists to do such things as obtain patient consent before electronically recording therapy sessions, minimize disclosures when providing oral or written reports, and avoid disclosing identifiable patient information when writing or teaching. Some ethical standards allow therapists to consider confidentiality when deciding how to respond to ethical violations by colleagues. Other standards require therapists to respect confidentiality when obtaining consultation with other professionals, and to obtain the patient's informed consent before submitting claims for third-party reimbursement. Finally, confidentiality mandates include the requirement to develop record keeping policies that ensure confidentiality and to prepare for therapist absences or unexpected endings that might place patient records or confidentiality at risk.

Therapists are also responsible for ensuring that employees, supervisees, and others to whom they delegate responsibility will perform their duties competently.[36] Although most ethics codes do not explicitly require that staff be trained about the ethics of confidentiality, this seems essential for ensuring that patients' confidentiality rights will be protected in the setting[37] (see Chapter 13, "Ethics-Based Staff Training About Confidentiality").

Exceptions to the Key Standard

Each profession has a different list of ethically allowed exceptions to the confidentiality rule. These can be compared across professions in Appendix II. Note that these exceptions ethically permit (but do not ethically require) breaches of confidentiality.

Psychologists have only three ethically permitted bases for disclosing patient information: patient consent, legal requirement, and legal permission.[38] Their confidentiality rule and its exceptions might therefore be stated this way: Psychologists are ethically free to disclose confidential information only with the patient's consent unless the disclosure is either legally required or legally permitted.

Social workers have an ethics code that allows few exceptions to confidentiality. They are ethically free to disclose confidential information without patient consent "for compelling professional reasons" or "to prevent serious, foreseeable and imminent harm to a client or other identifiable person."[39] Psychiatrists may also reveal confidential information disclosed by the patient when this is legally required, or "when, in their clinical judgment, the risk of danger is deemed to be significant."[40]

Counselors have a slightly longer list of ethically allowed exceptions to confidentiality. In addition to disclosing with patient consent, counselors are ethically allowed to disclose with sound legal or ethical justification, for protecting the patient or another from serious harm, if a patient with a communicable life-threatening disease is placing an identifiable third party at high risk, or if a terminally ill patient plans to hasten death.[41]

ETHICAL STANDARDS ABOUT INFORMED CONSENT

Ethical practice about confidentiality requires more than just protecting confidential information. As reflected in Appendix II, it also involves protecting patients' rights about informed consent. This is sometimes discussed in ways that make it sound very complicated, but the concept is actually very simple: *Informed consent simply means "consent from an informed person."*

> Informed consent is an essential aspect of the establishment of every professional relationship in which [mental health professionals] participate. When done effectively, it helps promote other individuals' autonomy, engages them in a collaborative process, and helps to reduce the likelihood of exploitation or harm, among a number of potential benefits.[42]

As it relates to confidentiality, informed consent takes two different forms. First, informed consent involves protecting the right to be informed about the potential risks before giving consent to receive services. This includes informing

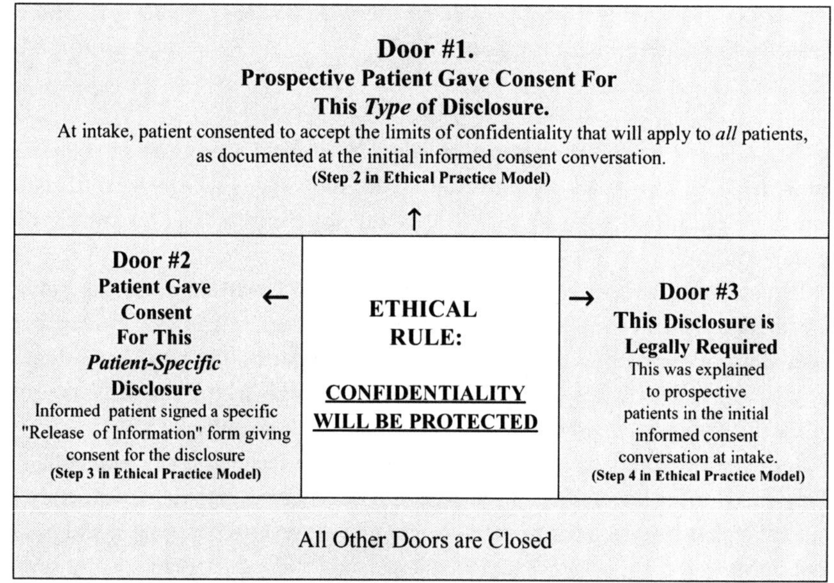

FIGURE 1.2 Ethically permitted "doors" to disclosure of confidential information. Adapted from the disclosure metaphor in Behnke, S. (2004, September). Disclosures of confidential information under the new APA Ethics Code: A process for deciding when and how. *Monitor on Psychology, 35*, 78–79.

prospective patients about the limits of confidentiality that will apply to all patients and obtaining their consent to accept these limits as a condition of receiving services. Second, a subsequent informed consent responsibility protects the patient's right to be informed before giving consent for voluntary client-specific disclosures. This involves protecting their right to be informed about the nature of the information that will be disclosed about them, as well as the foreseeable implications of disclosing it, before being asked to give consent for it to be disclosed.[43] These informed consent protections are reflected in multiple ethical standards (see Appendix II).

These two situations are different enough that some have questioned whether it is even appropriate to use the term "informed consent" to describe the initial conversation that takes place before services are provided.[44] When confidentiality will be conditional, therapists have an initial requirement "to inform prospective clients about the foreseeable *conditions* in advance, before obtaining their consent to receive services. In other words, it would be ethically appropriate to begin a professional relationship without discussing the limits of confidentiality only if confidentiality had no limits."[45] However, this conversation meets the criteria for "informed consent" only if the therapist (1) informs the prospective patient about the times when information may be disclosed without the patient's further consent, then (2) obtains the *informed* patient's voluntary *consent* to accept those described limits of confidentiality as a condition of receiving therapy services, and (3) documents the patient's consent.[46] (For a detailed discussion of this process that informs the prospective patient's consent to receive services, see Chapter 5, "Telling Prospective Patients the Truth About Confidentiality's Limits.")

Figure 1.2 metaphorically illustrates how patients' confidentiality rights can best be protected—by disclosing without patient consent only if required by law. This is a variation on the metaphor suggested by Stephen Behnke, Director of the Ethics Office of the APA, when he described the three exceptions to confidentiality allowed by the APA Ethics Code as the only three ethically available "doors" to disclosure: "Other than these three doors, there is no other way of ... communicating with anyone" about the patient.[47] Figure 1.2 reflects the central importance of the informed consent process in the protection of confidentiality rights.

Door 1 is opened at intake through the initial informed consent conversation, and that door then remains open throughout the relationship. Note that a therapist who intends to exercise any of the ethically allowed breaches of confidentiality described in the previous section must explain that plan to prospective patients at intake and obtain the informed patient's consent to accept those limits of confidentiality as a condition of receiving services. In other words, Door 1 is open only if the therapist explained during the initial informed consent interview that this disclosure might be made without the patient's further consent. This includes disclosures the therapist can be legally required to make, or disclosures the therapist might make voluntarily without further patient consent. This conversation therefore covers the foreseeable "limits of confidentiality." In this way, when informed patients give consent to receive services, they are giving informed consent to accept the described limits of confidentiality as a condition of receiving those services. This protects their right to give "informed refusal" of services instead.

Door 2 is opened when the therapist obtains consent for disclosures that are specific to the particular patient. Whereas the initial informed consent conversation describes the limits of confidentiality that will apply to *all* patients, this conversation obtains consent for a voluntary disclosure that is specific to *this* patient. This can include obtaining patient consent to discuss information with another professional (e.g., primary care provider, medical specialist), with a family member (e.g., parent, spouse, adult child), or with an agency (Social Services, mental health clinic, school, etc.). This informed consent process can take place at intake or at any time thereafter during the therapy relationship. It involves (1) informing the patient about what information will be disclosed and to whom, as well as about the foreseeable implications of disclosing or not disclosing it; (2) obtaining the *informed* patient's voluntary *consent* to disclose it under those circumstances; and (3) documenting this process by obtaining the patient's signature on a "Consent for Release of Information" form. The patient's consent to this particular disclosure opens Door 2 for a specific period of time that can be documented on the form.

Legally speaking, Door 3 is automatically open if a particular disclosure is required by some law. Ethically speaking, however, consent for these disclosures is actually obtained in advance through Door 1, by informing prospective patients about the possibility of these potential legally imposed breaches of confidentiality. The therapist will then be ethically free to walk through Door 3 if there is no legal alternative; but this ethical freedom arises not because the disclosure is legally required but because the patient was informed about and gave consent in advance to accept such a disclosure as a condition of receiving services.

Note that Door 3 is *not* open for disclosures that are merely "legally allowed" (but not legally required).[48] The most ethically appropriate path for such disclosures is through Door 1, which allows the patient's informed consent to be obtained in advance. Otherwise, therapists should obtain the patient's explicit consent for such disclosures at the time they are made, thereby opening Door 2.

ETHICAL STANDARDS ABOUT CONFLICTS BETWEEN ETHICAL DUTIES AND OTHER OBLIGATIONS

Mental health professionals have certain ethical standards that apply when legal or organizational requirements come into conflict with their ethical duties. These conflicts arise most often around issues of confidentiality. It is ethically important to notice such conflicts and to respond in a way that is protective of patients (see Appendix II, sections 2, E).

The summaries below are brief because this topic will be discussed in more detail in Part II (see Chapter 7, "Responding Ethically to Legal Demands," and Chapter 8, "Avoiding Preventable Breaches of Confidentiality").

Psychologists, when faced with a conflict between an ethical standard and a legal requirement or an organizational policy must "clarify the nature of the conflict, make known their commitment to the Ethics Code, and take reasonable steps to resolve the conflict consistent with the General Principles and Ethical Standards of the Ethics Code."[49] In other words, when faced with a conflict between ethical standards and other requirements, psychologists are ethically required to attempt resolution in the direction most protective of the patient.

Counselors faced with a conflict between ethical standards and laws must also make known their commitment to their ethics code and take steps to resolve the conflict. If the conflict cannot be resolved, counselors "may adhere to the requirements of law, regulations, or other governing legal authority." However, if the conflict is between the ethics code and one's organizational requirements, counselors must "specify the nature of such conflicts and express to their supervisors or other responsible officials their commitment to the *ACA Code of Ethics*. When possible, counselors work toward change within the organization to allow full adherence to the *ACA Code of Ethics*. In doing so, they address any confidentiality issues."[50]

Social workers have no ethical standard that addresses ethical–legal conflicts generally, but, if faced with demands for information during a legal proceeding, they have an ethical responsibility to protect confidentiality to the extent permitted by law. The introductory Statement of Purpose to the NASW Code of Ethics also includes the following aspirational statement: "Instances may arise when social workers' ethical obligations conflict with agency policies or relevant laws or regulations. When such conflicts occur, social workers must make a responsible effort to resolve the conflict in a manner that is consistent with the values, principles, and standards expressed in this *Code*. If a reasonable resolution of the conflict does not appear possible, social workers should seek proper consultation before making a decision."[51]

Psychiatrists have no ethical standards about ethical–legal conflicts generally, but they do have one that applies in a specific circumstance related to confidentiality: If ordered by the court to reveal the confidences entrusted to them by patients, psychiatrists may comply or "may ethically hold the right to dissent within the framework of the law. When the psychiatrist is in doubt, the right of the patient to confidentiality and, by extension, to unimpaired treatment should be given priority."[52]

Other Professional Guidelines and Recommendations

Confidentiality issues are addressed in numerous professional guidelines that are published by the national offices of therapists' professional associations. These sometimes include casebooks that elaborate on the profession's ethics code. Other recommendations and guidelines appear in ethics texts and published articles. Unlike the ethical standards, such guidelines are aspirational, not enforceable, but they can be very useful in providing more detailed practical guidance than can be included in an ethics code.

For psychologists, the most extensive confidentiality recommendations are available in the APA Record Keeping Guidelines.[53] Other APA resources cover confidentiality issues in child protection matters, custody proceedings, and other legal contexts; guidelines for responding to subpoenas; and confidentiality issues with specific patient populations.[54] The APA has also recently published a two-volume *Handbook of Ethics in Psychology*, which contains an extensive chapter on confidentiality and record keeping.[55]

For counselors, guidelines in the ACA Legal Series included monographs about confidentiality and its exceptions, preparing for court appearances, and special issues in marriage and family counseling.[56] For social workers, relevant guidelines are available to members of the NASW through its website. These include ethics casebooks and record keeping recommendations.[57]

Some national professions provide recommendations that are available online only for members of their respective clinical organizations. For example, information about record keeping in private practice is available to members of the APA Practice Organization (see www.APAPractice.org) and to members of the NASW

Private Practice Specialty Section (see www.socialworkers.org/sections). For school psychologists, ethical recommendations are available through the National Association of School Psychologists (NASP) (www.nasponline.org). For school counselors, recommendations are available through an ACA division, the American School Counselor Association (ASCA) (www.schoolcounselor.org).

Ethical Decision Making About Confidentiality

Although an understanding of the relevant ethical standards is essential, often these alone are not sufficient when faced with an ethical dilemma. Ethical conflicts can arise when two ethical principles come into conflict (as when one must choose between protecting patient autonomy and breaching confidentiality to involuntarily hospitalize a patient who is at risk for self-harm). Ethical–legal conflicts can arise when an ethical responsibility conflicts with a legal requirement. Such conflicts can be difficult to resolve.

> All mental health professionals should internalize a *decision-making strategy* to assist in coping with every ethical matter as it arises… Those who can document a sustained, reasoned effort to deal with the dilemma will have a distinct advantage should their decisions and actions ever be challenged.[58]

In considering how to resolve an ethical dilemma involving confidentiality, it can be useful to follow the steps of a formal ethical decision-making model. This can provide a structure for the process of considering the options and weighing the potential consequences of various possible actions. When the ethical dilemma involves confidentiality, using a structured process can be important for protecting the patient's rights. Most professional ethics texts include a chapter on ethical decision making, and many such ethical decision-making models are available.[59]

2

Laws Affecting Confidentiality

Awareness of relevant legislation, case law, and other legal standards is critical, but legal standards should not be confused with ethical responsibilities. A risk in the emphasis on legal standards is that adherence to minimal legal standards . . . can become a substitute for ethical behavior.

Pope, K. S., & Vasquez, M. J. T. (2011),
Ethics in Psychotherapy and Counseling, p. xiii

Confidentiality is first and foremost an ethical duty, but many laws recognize its importance. It does complicate matters, however, that while some laws support the ethical goal of protecting confidentiality, other laws can require therapists to disclose confidential information. Some laws actually do both: Their underlying goal is the protection of patients' confidentiality rights, but they contain exceptions that impose legal limits on that protection.[1]

Both state laws and federal laws can affect patient confidentiality, and the relevant legal information is not always easy to find. As noted in the epigraph above, the relevant information might be in the form of statutory law, regulatory law, or case law. At the state level, there are wide variations in these laws. Mental health professionals are responsible for knowing the relevant laws in their own state,[2] keeping in mind that all three kinds of laws—statutes, legal regulations, and case law—can affect a mental health professional's ability to protect confidences.

Underlying Legal Concepts

Laws that *protect* patient confidentiality reflect the fact that society has an interest in preserving the relationship between patient and therapist. These include laws that prevent therapists from disclosing information without the patient's consent (i.e., nondisclosure laws), as well as privileged communications laws, which protect the information communicated to a therapist from being available as evidence in a court case.

In contrast, laws that *limit* confidentiality are enacted on the basis that certain societal interests are more important than the confidentiality of mental health patients. Some such laws are designed to protect vulnerable members of society, such as laws requiring the reporting of child or elder abuse or imposing a duty to protect a potential victim from harm by a patient. Other laws that create exceptions to therapist–patient privilege in court cases are enacted on the basis that the proper administration of justice requires that mental health evidence sometimes be made available as evidence in court cases.

Appendix III provides examples of each type of law described below, and an online version of this Appendix provides links to example statutes. Many of the laws that protect confidentiality also contain exceptions that limit the protection; laws that have both protective and limiting functions are discussed in both of the categories below. Laws that limit confidentiality will also be discussed in more detail later, in Chapter 7, "Responding Ethically to Legal Demands."

Laws Protecting Confidentiality

Laws protective of confidentiality include nondisclosure laws (which protect confidentiality generally) and privileged communications laws (which protect confidentiality only in legal proceedings). As reflected in Figure 1.1, it is ethically important that therapists not confuse the concepts of "confidentiality" and "privilege." Confidentiality is a broad ethical and professional duty; within that wide domain of confidentiality, privilege is a specialized legal concept that protects patient information only in the context of a court case. Understanding this difference has "critical implications for understanding a variety of ethical problems" related to confidentiality."[3]

NONDISCLOSURE LAWS

Nondisclosure laws protect the confidentiality rights of therapy patients by legally prohibiting therapists and others from disclosing confidential information without first obtaining the patient's explicit consent. These laws provide legal support for the confidentiality rights that are protected by the professions in their ethics codes. Failure to comply with these laws can have legal consequences for therapists, including tort liability and/or professional discipline.

At the state level, laws and regulations that govern the licensing of mental health professionals usually include nondisclosure provisions, some of which contain (or mirror) the confidentiality and nondisclosure requirements in the licensee's own ethical standards. Most states also have general statutes that legally prohibit disclosure of confidential information by mental health professionals in any setting, as well as regulations that protect patients' confidentiality rights in state mental health facilities. Such laws vary widely from state to state. Therapists are responsible for knowing the laws that prohibit disclosure in their own state and setting.

At the federal level, some laws and regulations that contain nondisclosure provisions give special confidentiality protections to patients receiving services in federally funded substance abuse treatment facilities.[4] Not only do these provide special confidentiality protections and expanded privilege protections for these patients, but they contain few exceptions to that protection. Therapists who provide services in these settings must be familiar with these laws because they grant special confidentiality and privilege rights that are available only to these patients.

However, the most prominent federal nondisclosure mandates are found in the extensive legal regulations under the Health Insurance Portability and Accountability Act (HIPAA), which protect the privacy and confidentiality rights of all health care patients. These are comprised of several separate rules, and they are among the legal requirements that both protect and limit confidentiality.[5] In this section, we briefly summarize the legal protections they provide; the next section will address the limitations of that protection. (See Appendix IV for a more complete summary of the HIPAA regulations.)

The *HIPPA Transaction Rule* (45CFR, § 162.900ff) standardizes the electronic transmission of patient information and requires computer safeguards such as encryption and passwords. Any health care provider who electronically transmits patient information must not only comply with the Transaction Rule itself, but must also comply with all other HIPAA Rules.

The *HIPAA Security Rule* (45CFR, § 164) protects the confidentiality of electronically stored patient information. Its security requirements, which include administrative, physical, and technical safeguards, exceed those found in any ethics code. For example, therapists covered under this rule are required to implement policies concerning employee access to patient information, security of workstations, and transporting of patient data; to provide for security of patient data in emergencies; and to train all workplace personnel in security awareness.

The *HIPAA Privacy Rule* contains nondisclosure provisions. It also requires that therapists give prospective patients a "Notice of Privacy Practices" (45 C.F.R. § 164.520) that explains when information about them might be disclosed. This rule also created new federal rights about which each patient must be notified: the legal right to inspect, copy, and request amendments to their official records; the right to receive an accounting of all disclosures; the right to request that communications to them be made by certain means or directed only to specific locations; and the right to request restrictions on certain uses and disclosures to others involved in their care or related to payment.

The *HIPAA Enforcement Rule* (45CFR § 160) stipulates that both the Transaction Rule and the Security Rule are enforced by the Center for Medicaid and Medicare Services, while the Privacy Rule is enforced by the U. S. Office of Civil Rights. Civil penalties for violation of any HIPAA Rule can reach $100 per violation (capped at $25,000 for each individual requirement violated). Ongoing violations are treated as a separate violation for each day they occur. Although enforcement of HIPAA's Privacy Rule was lax for years, this changed with the enactment of the Health Information Technology for Economic and Clinical Health Act (HITECH) in 2009. "HIPAA enforcement has gone HITECH—literally—and the changes could be expensive for providers found non-compliant, with fines of $100 to $50,000 per violation up to an annual maximum of $1.5 million."[6]

The *Security Breach Notification Rule* (45CFR § 164, Subpart D), the newest HIPAA Rule, stipulates that any confidentiality breach must be reported to the patient(s) whose confidentiality was violated. Breaches involving 500 or more patients must be reported immediately to the Secretary of Health and Human Services and to the media; unauthorized disclosures involving fewer patients must be reported annually.[7] Other recent amendments broadened the Privacy and Security Rules to give patients the right to obtain access not only to records held by their provider, but also to any records of electronic transactions related to their treatment that are held by the provider's business associates (e.g., billing agents, answering services, and others who provide contracted services).

In educational settings, federal nondisclosure regulations include those found in the Family Educational Rights and Privacy Act (FERPA) and the Individual Disability Education Act (IDEA). Like HIPAA, both have an underlying goal of protecting confidentiality rights, but they also contain broad exceptions that legally allow certain disclosures.

PRIVILEGED COMMUNICATIONS LAWS

Privileged communications laws treat the communications held in certain "privileged" relationships as deserving of special protections that prevent them from being available as evidence in court proceedings. Privileged relationships can include husband–wife, attorney–client, priest–penitent, and physician–patient, as well as various therapist–patient relationships. Privileged communications laws make it less likely that the information generated in these relationships will be subpoenaed, and make it more likely that if a subpoena is issued, a judge will quash it or issue a protective order. The privileged communications laws that apply in state courts can be quite different from those in federal courts. As noted below, however, all privilege laws contain exceptions that limit their protections.

Ordinarily, it is the patient, not the therapist, who holds the right to invoke the privilege.[8] Patients involved in a court proceeding can (1) invoke the privilege, objecting to the use of therapy information as evidence in a court proceeding; or can (2) waive the privilege by giving consent for the therapist to disclose confidential information. However, patients are usually not legally permitted to exercise a partial waiver; once a patient waives therapist–patient privilege in any respect, it can lead to disclosure of all material relevant to the case.[9]

In state courts, the degree of privilege protection varies widely across states and sometimes across professions within a single state. Some states have therapist–patient privilege statutes that are modeled after attorney–client privilege; other states have privilege statutes with broad exceptions that leave patient information unprotected, especially in child custody cases.[10]

In federal courts, Rule 501 of the Federal Rules of Evidence governs the initial presentation of evidence, but it does not list specific categories of privilege. Instead, it simply stipulates that, in determining whether the potential evidence is privileged, federal courts are "governed by the principles of the common law as they may be interpreted by the courts of the United States in the light of reason and experience."[11] However, the U.S. Supreme Court strengthened therapist–patient privilege protections in 1996 in their *Jaffee v. Redmond* decision:

> Like the spousal and attorney client privileges, the psychotherapist patient privilege is "rooted in the imperative need for confidence and trust"... Treatment by a physician for physical ailments can often proceed successfully on the basis of a physical examination, objective information supplied by the patient, and the results of diagnostic tests. Effective psychotherapy, by contrast, depends upon an atmosphere of confidence and trust in which the patient is willing to make a frank and complete disclosure of facts, emotions, memories, and fears. Because of the sensitive nature of the problems for which individuals consult psychotherapists, disclosure of confidential communications made during counseling sessions may cause embarrassment or disgrace. For this reason, the mere possibility of disclosure may impede development of the confidential relationship necessary for successful treatment.[12]

Legally speaking, this decision was important because it confirmed and expanded therapist–patient privilege in federal court cases. Ethically speaking, however, the important thing about the *Jaffee* case is that it reached the Supreme Court only because a therapist refused to disclose patient information, even when she was confronted with a subpoena and faced possible incarceration for contempt of court.[13] Her action was important because it protected the confidentiality of the therapist–patient relationship, "a fragile and perishable commodity."[14] Although the *Jaffee* decision applies only in federal court cases, it is often cited by those who are seeking protection of patient information in a state court, and it is quoted by those who are lobbying for better privilege law protections in their own state.

Laws Limiting Confidentiality

Most of the laws limiting confidentiality would apply to mental health professionals regardless of their roles, but therapists are the most likely to be affected by these laws, because they are the ones most likely to receive legal demands for information. "By virtue of the special relationship that develops in psychotherapy, . . . confidential information communicated in that setting is more often the subject of struggles between psychologists and outside individuals or entities."[15]

Laws that limit confidentiality can be divided into three basic types. First, laws can require therapists to report certain information, or to initiate some other disclosure. Second, laws can grant others the legal right to obtain access to patient information or records, or to redisclose it without the patient's consent. Third, privilege laws contain exceptions that allow patient information or records to be used as evidence in a court case in certain circumstances.

These are not formal legal categories, but they are useful in several respects. First, they reflect where the action originates: Laws in the first category require therapists to *initiate* a breach of confidentiality (by taking confidential information out of the therapy room on their own initiative), whereas the other two categories begin with actions initiated by others, to which therapists must then *respond* (for example, to a subpoena). Second, these categories reflect ethical response possibilities: They separate the non-negotiable legal requirements (such as the laws in the first category that require therapists to report specific information to specific others) from contestable legal requests (which include most of the laws in the second and third categories). Finally, using such categories can make it easier for therapists to stay current about their laws and easier for them to understand the implications of legal changes: After each legislative session, the new laws affecting confidentiality can easily be placed into ethical context, because all new reporting laws belong in category one, amendments to privilege law go into category three, and almost everything else goes into category two.

It is important for therapists to become familiar with all three types of legally imposed limits on confidentiality. "A lack of respect for and a lack of familiarity with the significance of these exceptions could have dire professional consequences."[16] Later sections of this book will describe how therapists can prepare to respond ethically to these laws that limit patients' confidentiality rights. (For example, see Chapter 3, "Placing Laws Into Ethical Context," Chapter 4, "Preparing," and Chapter 7, "Responding Ethically to Legal Demands.")

LAWS MANDATING SPECIFIC DISCLOSURES

Laws that mandate specific disclosures can require a therapist to *initiate* a disclosure of confidential information, even if the patient objects. Therapists have long been among those legally mandated to report suspected abuse or neglect of children,[17] and most states require similar reports about elderly or disabled adults. Some states require reports of domestic abuse in certain circumstances. Some states have laws or licensure regulations requiring therapists to report to their licensing boards if they know that a colleague of their own profession has engaged in unprofessional conduct, or if their therapy patient has a condition that places the public at risk, even if those reports require them to breach confidentiality.

A patient's threat to seriously harm someone else may or may not trigger a disclosure mandate. After the 1975 *Tarasoff* case in California, many other states took legal action to protect the potential victim of a patient's planned violence. The resulting laws are often inaccurately referred to as "duty to warn" laws, even though almost all states actually have enacted "duty to protect" laws instead. They allow several possible protective responses, not all of which require the therapist to warn a potential victim or even to disclose confidential patient information.[18] (See further discussion of this issue in Chapters 4, 7, and 8.)

Finally, cases of potential harm to self are addressed in most states as exceptions to the nondisclosure laws, but not as legally mandated reporting requirements. In other words, most states legally *allow* (rather than legally require) therapists to disclose confidential information if necessary to protect a patient from self-harm. However, "legal regulations governing state agencies and institutions, as well as policies voluntarily adopted by private agencies or groups, sometimes do require disclosure without patient consent if that is deemed necessary for protecting the patient's own safety."[19]

LAWS ALLOWING ACCESS TO OR REDISCLOSURE OF PATIENT INFORMATION

Some laws grant others access to confidential patient information in certain circumstances. As in the previous category, these laws give priority to the protection of others' rights or others' safety, rather than to the protection of a patient's right to confidentiality.

At the federal level, the Patriot Act gives priority to gathering information about possible terrorists. As originally enacted, it allowed Federal Bureau of Investigation (FBI) agents to demand patient information and to order a therapist not to tell anyone (including the patient) that the information had been surrendered. However, as amended in 2006, the Patriot Act now includes better protections, and therapists have the right to inform patients of the request before relinquishing the information.[20]

Some states have statutes that grant others access to patient information for use in civil commitment proceedings. "For example, statutes governing hearings for involuntary commitment may require that the records of current or former mental health treatment be made available immediately without patient consent if requested by the hearing officer, attorneys, guardians ad litem, or others."[21] In custody cases involving children or in guardianship cases involving incapacitated adults, state laws can give the court-appointed guardian *ad litem* access to therapy records without consent. Similarly, in cases involving child abuse, some state laws established to govern Court Appointed Special Advocate (CASA) programs can allow court-appointed lay volunteers to obtain access to a child's therapy records without child or parent consent.

Other state laws can allow those who receive confidential patient information to redisclose it to someone else without the patient's further consent. These include statutes allowing third-party payers to disclose certain information to certain others (e.g., to an employer who purchased an employee's health plan), regulations allowing state agencies to exchange information (e.g., exchanges between a psychiatric hospital and community clinic for treatment planning or discharge planning), or statutes allowing CASA volunteers to testify in court about the information obtained from a child's therapist.

EXCEPTIONS TO THERAPIST–PATIENT PRIVILEGE

All privilege statutes contain exceptions. "These exceptions arise from the perspective that the proper administration of justice sometimes requires that information confided to a therapist be made available as evidence" in a court case.[22]

Exceptions to privilege vary widely.[23] "The most common statutory exceptions to therapist–patient privilege are child abuse cases, involuntary commitment proceedings, and cases in which patients place their own mental health into issue."[24] In most states, these exceptions will apply. In some states, however, there are also other very broad exceptions to privilege that leave patient information poorly protected. For example, two states (North Carolina and Virginia) have a judicial-discretion exception to therapist–patient privilege. This is the broadest and least predictable exception, because it allows any judge, in any case, to order information held by a therapist to be disclosed as evidence.[25]

Such exceptions can increase the likelihood that therapists will receive subpoenas, because attorneys presume that the judge might consider the information admissible as evidence. In states where this is likely to happen, it is important to understand the distinction between a discovery subpoena and a judge's order or "court order." A subpoena can often be contested successfully, thereby preventing access to the patient information that is being sought. (See a detailed discussion of responding ethically to subpoenas in Chapter 7, "Responding Ethically to Legal Demands.")

Finally, privilege will ordinarily not apply if the mental health professional is serving in certain forensic specialist roles, rather than as a therapist. For example, a mental health professional who is conducting a court-ordered psychological evaluation must begin by informing everyone involved that privilege will not apply and that the information obtained in the process of the evaluation may be made available as evidence in a court case. Because the confidentiality protections for clients in forensic cases will not be the same as those for patients in therapy cases, mental health professionals are admonished not to try to serve in both roles with the same client/patient.[26] (For more details about this issue, see Chapter 8, "Avoiding Preventable Breaches of Confidentiality," and, in Chapter 12 see the section, "Legal Settings.")

Laws Allowing Therapists to Disclose Information Without Patient Consent

Some laws *allow* therapists to disclose information without patient consent, but do not *require* therapists to disclose anything. They therefore create no true ethical-legal conflict, because they impose no actual legal limits on confidentiality. However, some mistakenly treat the fact that a disclosure is *legally* allowed as if that were synonymous with being *ethically* allowed. In fact, these are voluntary disclosures, and, as such, they require consent. (See, in Chapter 3, the discussion of the important distinction between voluntary and "involuntary" (legally compelled) disclosures.)

Such laws can appear either as legal exceptions to a nondisclosure law or as a free-standing statute or regulation that allows certain disclosures without patient consent. Examples include the HIPAA Privacy Rule, whose underlying purpose is ostensibly "nondisclosure," but which nevertheless contains exceptions that allow information to be disclosed without patient authorization for numerous broad purposes, including disclosure of information for "treatment, payment, and health care operations."[27] Other examples include state laws with confidentiality protection as the primary purpose, but which contain legal exceptions allowing therapists to disclose information for similarly broad purposes without patient authorization (see examples in Appendix III).

Ethically, it is very important to remember that although such exceptions legally *allow* disclosure, they do not *require* it. Making such disclosures without patient consent would ordinarily be considered unethical, but some ethics codes do technically give therapists ethical permission to treat these legally allowed disclosures as exceptions to confidentiality. Such laws nevertheless raise important informed-consent implications and other ethical questions.[28] (For a further discussion of this issue, see, in Chapter 6, the section on "Legal Considerations" and in Chapter 8, the section on "Abusing Legally Allowed Exceptions to Confidentiality.")

These laws provide therapists with an opportunity to offer the best protections to patients by reaching for the "ethical ceiling" rather than settling for the minimum standard or "ethical floor." Therapists who intend to make disclosures that are allowed by such laws can devise clear policies about this in advance, so that prospective patients can give their consent at the initial interview for this type of disclosure to be made without further authorization. In other words, since these disclosures are *not legally required,* the most patient-protective practice for the therapist who intends to make such disclosures is to inform prospective patients about these potential limits of confidentiality at intake, and to obtain their consent to receive services under those conditions. As reflected in the discussion about Figure 1.2, this makes such disclosures ethical not because they are legally allowed, but because the client gave prior consent at intake. (For other examples of such laws and a more detailed discussion of their implications, see, in Chapter 3, the section on "Distinguishing Between Voluntary and "Involuntary" Disclosures." Also see Chapter 8, "Avoiding Preventable Disclosures.")

3

Placing Laws Into Ethical Context

All psychologists must uphold the same ethical standards about confidentiality even though each state imposes different legal limits on their ability to protect clients' confidences. The resulting ethical-legal confusion is exacerbated by legally based confidentiality training that treats legal exceptions as if they were the rule and fosters the impression that attorneys are now the only real experts about this aspect of practice.

Fisher, M. A. (2008b). Protecting confidentiality rights:
The need for an ethical practice model. *American Psychologist, 63*, 1–13

Much of the confusion about confidentiality has resulted from the partial overlap between ethical standards and laws. If they sometimes agree with each other, is there really any important difference between the two? If so, does it matter?

From an ethical point of view, there is a very large difference between ethical standards and laws. It therefore matters a great deal to patients that therapists understand the difference and that they not focus on laws to the exclusion of their profession's ethical standards. "It is crucial to realize that ethical behavior is more than simply avoiding violation of legal standards."[1]

Making Ethically Important Distinctions

The first step out of the ethical-legal confusion involves making some important distinctions. This requires (1) recognizing the difference between ethical standards and laws and (2) making a distinction between voluntary and legally compelled ("involuntary") disclosures of patient information. Only with those two distinctions in mind is it possible to learn how to maintain an ethical posture when responding to laws that demand a breach of confidentiality.

DISTINGUISHING BETWEEN ETHICAL STANDARDS AND LAWS

The ethical standards of a profession are formulated by members of that profession. The ethics code of a national professional association must be followed by members of that professional association, and courts sometimes hold it to be the community standard of practice even for those who are not members. The ethics code applies regardless of the state or setting in which the professional practices. If a mental health professional violates his or her code of ethics, a state or national professional association can censure and/or revoke membership.

In contrast, legal standards can be created by legislators (who enact statutory laws), administrators (who promulgate regulatory laws), and judges (through decisions that make case law), and all of these vary from state to state and sometimes vary from setting to setting within a state. Most laws affecting confidentiality occur at the state level and therefore apply only to the professionals within that state. If a mental health professional violates the law, this can lead to legal penalties or revocation of a license to practice, financial penalties, and tort liability for civil damages if the legal infraction caused injury or harm.

At the risk of insulting those who are sophisticated about such matters, the following summary begins at the very beginning, because these concepts can confuse mental health professionals everywhere, regardless of their state's laws:

- *"Professional ethical standards about confidentiality" and "legal requirements about confidentiality" are two very different things.* This may seem too obvious to need repeating. But much of the confusion about confidentiality actually begins here, with therapists tending to confuse legal standards with professional ethical standards. "The mistake is to move from a premise that some action is legally required to a conclusion that it is ethically required. The unhappy truth is that ethical obligations can conflict with legal ones."[2] For example, in seeking consultation, the two questions, "What am I ethically required to do here?" and "What am I legally required to do here?" are sometimes treated as if they were interchangeable—as if asking either question would elicit the same "right" answer. In fact, each may refer to the other (i.e., ethics codes mention laws, and some laws refer to professional ethics). But the answers to the two questions are sometimes very different, so equating the two is an ethical mistake that can have unfortunate consequences for therapists and patients, because …
- *Professional ethics must be treated as the baseline.* The first task is to learn the ethical responsibilities, as defined by the mental health professions. The same ethics codes apply everywhere, regardless of the state or setting in which someone practices their profession. This is evidence that (1) there are certain rights that all patients have about confidentiality, regardless of the laws of the state in which they seek treatment. Our ethics codes are also reminders that (2) therapists are ethically responsible for protecting certain of those rights more carefully now, precisely because

confidentiality itself is no longer always legally protectable. Laws can limit a therapist's ability to protect confidences by requiring confidential information to be disclosed, but this does not mean therapists are free to focus on these legal requirements and ignore their profession's ethical standards about such laws. In other words, the ethical standards of one's profession may be only half of the story, but it must always be treated as the *first* half because ...

- *Ethical standards require therapists to behave in certain ways in response to laws that can limit confidentiality.* Professional ethics codes acknowledge that state laws can limit the ability to protect confidences (which is the old news), and most now also emphasize the ethical responsibilities that therapists incur precisely because those laws exist (which is the "newer news" that some mental health professionals have been slow to hear!). Laws vary from state to state and are always subject to change, so ethics codes address them only in very general terms. But this does not mean that therapists are ethically free to ignore the legal details.
- *Therapists in each state are ethically responsible for filling in the relevant legal details for themselves.* Therapists have always been responsible for knowing about state laws and regulations that affect the practice of their own profession.[3] The legal obligation to understand the laws arises because the state expects therapists to practice "legally," regardless of profession or setting. The ethical obligation to learn the legal details, especially about confidentiality, arises because therapists can practice ethically (i.e., can protect their patients' rights) only if they (1) understand how their state's laws define those rights and (2) learn the legal options for responding to laws that limit the patient's rights about confidentiality.
- *State laws can have a direct impact on how ethical standards must be applied.* For those therapists unfamiliar with legal categories and legal language, this can become confusing, because ...
- *Each law that limits confidentiality can have different ethical implications (i.e., different implications for patients' rights) and can have different legal options for responding protectively.* Most ethics codes now contain exceptions to the confidentiality rule that allow disclosure whenever that is legally required, but they also impose ethical responsibilities when laws conflict with ethical standards. (See, in Chapter 1, the section, "Ethical Standards About Conflicts Between Ethical Duties and Other Obligations.") We advocate that mental health professionals protect confidences to the extent legally possible. This means learning the legal options available for responding to each type of law in the most protective manner legally available. (This is the subject of Chapter 7.)

The ability to understand these six concepts can be essential at the level of "practical ethics" about confidentiality For example, therapists who make careful distinctions between ethics and laws can reap several practical advantages that help them protect both their patients and themselves:[4]

- The laws that protect patient information can become important tools when carrying out one's ethical duty to defend patient confidentiality. For example, when therapists are responding ethically to a demand for disclosure, it can be useful to cite relevant nondisclosure laws; and, when in receipt of a subpoena, it can be ethically important to know the legal process for contesting it if the patient does not want the information to be used as evidence.
- Ethical duties are sometimes incorporated into legal requirements, in which case failure to conform to an ethical standard can become a legal liability. For example, professional ethical standards are sometimes included within state licensure regulations and thereby become the basis for responding to complaints against providers. In a malpractice case, the ethical standards are sometimes cited as the "community standard of care," and therefore are treated as the legal standard of care.
- Ethical responsibilities and legal responsibilities sometimes come into conflict. When that happens, therapists have an ethical obligation to notice the conflict, because they have an ethical responsibility to try to resolve it.[5] When faced with an ethical-legal conflict about confidentiality, therapists can best protect their patients if they have made some important ethical and personal decisions in advance. The therapist who understands the distinctions can predict the ethical-legal conflicts and can make some difficult decisions before they arise, preferably using a structured decision-making process that takes into account both ethical duties and laws.[6] "At times, therapists may decide to follow the law despite their ethical concerns. At other times, they may determine that a conscientious objection is warranted."[7]
- Knowing the difference between ethical standards and laws is important because "if obeying the Ethics Code would result in disobeying the law, then legal advice is critical."[8] It can be important to find an attorney who is an expert about mental health law, but therapists must be the experts about their own ethical duties, and they should be prepared to present that ethical perspective when obtaining legal consultation.

One of the easiest ways to illustrate the difference between laws and ethical duties is to compare the Health Insurance Portability and Accountability Act (HIPAA) regulations with the confidentiality mandates in professional ethics codes. On the one hand, there is a significant overlap between the two: The HIPAA Privacy Rule contains some nondisclosure provisions that support the ethical confidentiality rule, and the HIPAA requirement to provide a "Notice of Privacy Practices" (45 C.F.R § 164.520) overlaps with ethical standards that require therapists to inform prospective patients about the limits of confidentiality.

> In some respects, the HIPAA protections exceed therapists' ethical requirements. For example, HIPAA legally requires that information about limits of confidentiality be presented to patients in writing, and requires each setting to appoint a Privacy Officer and a Security Officer to ensure compliance. Patients are given the legal right to inspect, copy, and request amendments to their records; to request that confidential communications be made by alternative means or directed to alternative locations; to request restrictions on certain uses of information; and to receive an accounting of all disclosures. Finally, whereas Ethics Codes contain no explicit requirement for staff training about confidentiality, HIPAA requires "workforce training" that teaches everyone in the setting how to protect patient privacy and confidentiality (45CFR 184 530(b) (1).[9]

In other respects, however, HIPAA is comparatively *unprotective* of patients' confidentiality rights. As implied by its name, "Health Insurance Privacy and Accountability Act," the primary legal purpose was supposedly the protection of privacy rights in a climate of electronic transmission of identifiable patient data. Yet, in reality, the HIPAA regulations introduced broad new legally allowed exceptions to confidentiality. This means that HIPAA legally allows therapists to make much broader disclosures without patient consent than those ethically allowed by professional ethics codes. Furthermore, unlike ethics codes, the HIPAA Privacy Rule contains no true informed consent provision: Under HIPAA, the patient's signature on a "Notice of Privacy Practices" serves merely as an acknowledgment that the form was received. This does not meet the ethical criteria for the informed consent process that is required by ethics codes (see Chapter 1), described in the Ethical Practice Model (See Chapters 5 and 6), and outlined in detail in later discussions of staff training (see, in Chapter 13, the section on "Advantages of Ethics-Based Training").

Regrettably, such distinctions between ethics and laws are not usually made in the confidentiality training that is conducted as attorney-led HIPAA training. Attorneys are experts about the law, but most are not experts about therapists' ethical standards. Unless it is combined with ethics-based training, law-based training can therefore have some important ethical disadvantages.

> First, it fosters the impression that attorneys—not clinicians—have become the only "real" experts about this aspect of practice. Second, it creates a legal language about confidentiality that threatens to usurp psychologists' own clinical or ethical language about it: Laws take center stage, when what is needed is a language for placing them into ethical context. Third, it exacerbates the figure–ground confusion (by substituting legal rules for ethical rules) and often takes a risk-management perspective that raises anxiety: It encourages psychologists to focus on obeying laws in order to avoid risks to *themselves*, when what they need is a clearer focus on their ethical obligations

> and the potential risks to *clients*. Finally, the legal emphasis obscures an important fact about risk management: Understanding and following the relevant ethical principles is an essential ingredient in avoiding a malpractice suit.[10]

Even risk management manuals advise therapists to begin by grounding their thinking about confidentiality not in laws but in their own ethical standards: "First, good risk management principles are based on ethical principles… Second, ethical principles help guide behavior in situations in which laws or disciplinary codes do not give direction."[11]

DISTINGUISHING BETWEEN VOLUNTARY AND "INVOLUNTARY" (LEGALLY REQUIRED) DISCLOSURES

The terms "legally required" and "legally allowed" are used throughout this book and were defined in Box 1.1. To understand the implications of that distinction, one must be aware of the ethical differences between voluntary and "involuntary" disclosures.

Most ethics codes explicitly allow therapists to disclose confidential patient information if legally compelled to do so.[12] Such disclosures are "involuntary" in the sense that, legally speaking, they must be made whether or not the therapist wants to disclose and even if the patient objects. However, therapists do have an ethical obligation to inform prospective patients in advance about such potential limits of confidentiality. Thus, when patients give their consent to receive therapy services, they have already been informed that confidentiality will be "conditional" to the extent that disclosures can be legally *required*.

In contrast, any disclosure of information that is not legally required is a "voluntary" disclosure in the sense that the therapist is legally free not to disclose the information, and the patient is legally free to withhold consent for it to be disclosed. This "voluntary" category therefore includes disclosures which, although not legally required, are *legally allowed*.

It is ethically important to distinguish voluntary disclosures from legally required (or "involuntary") disclosures because, from an ethical perspective, the patient's informed consent should be obtained before any voluntary disclosure is made.[13] Using the metaphor in Figure 1.2, this means that unless this potential limit to confidentiality was discussed at intake (thereby opening Door 1), disclosure is ethical only through Door 2 (i.e., with the patient's explicit consent). Except in emergencies or when clinically contraindicated, when obtaining this consent, the therapist should first inform the patient about the nature of the information that will be disclosed, then obtain the *informed* patient's *consent* to disclose it. (The fact that obtaining a signature on a consent form does not suffice as "informed consent" is discussed in detail in Chapter 6.)

By far, most of the disclosures made by therapists fall into this "voluntary" category, including disclosures that provide identifiable patient information to other treating professionals and disclosures to third-party payers for reimbursement purposes, both of which are legally allowed without patient authorization by HIPAA and by some state laws. Therapists themselves may sometimes experience disclosures to third-party payers as "involuntary" (perhaps because they feel financially coerced), but, ethically speaking, they are voluntary and therefore require the patient's informed consent. Since it is not possible at the initial informed consent interview for the therapist to inform the patient about exactly what may later need to be disclosed for reimbursement purposes, patients are best protected if they are given the opportunity to provide consent for specific reimbursement disclosures at the time they are made.[14] (This issue is explored in further detail in Chapter 6, "Obtaining Truly Informed Consent Before Disclosing Confidential Information Voluntarily," and in Chapter 8, "Avoiding Preventable Disclosures.")

Using an Ethical Practice Model to Integrate Ethical Duties and Legal Requirements

When ethical standards about confidentiality are listed in numerical order (as in Appendix I), there are no visible clues about their relationship to each other, or about the relationship between ethical duties and legal demands. A more coherent and integrated picture of therapists' ethical obligations in behalf of patients' confidentiality rights is visible in Appendix II, but even this system of organization does not reflect how laws fit into the ethical picture. Yet, "without a comprehensive organizing schema, professional therapists cannot be expected to grasp intuitively the conflicting demands."[15]

This absence of a coherent picture of the relationship between ethics and laws has created difficulties both in practice and in training. Without a shared framework for integrating ethics and laws, conversations about confidentiality can become complicated, whether in teaching ethics, supervising students, conducting peer case consultations, or obtaining formal advice from ethics offices or legal consultants. Part II of this book is therefore organized around the six steps of an ethics-based practice model that helps place laws into ethical context (see Box 3.1).

This model is built upon therapists' collective ethical standards. It clarifies the interrelationship among the many ethical duties about confidentiality,[16] but, more importantly, it provides an ethical context into which therapists can integrate both the laws that protect confidentiality and the laws that limit it. This enables therapists to predict potential conflicts between ethics and laws, to discuss them with patients, and to be prepared to respond ethically when they arise.

This six-step Ethical Practice Model thus provides a structure for integrating ethical and legal responsibilities. The six chapters in Part II provide the structure

BOX 3.1 Ethical Practice Model for Protecting Confidentiality Rights

Step 1: Prepare

A. Understand patients' rights and therapists' ethical responsibilities in behalf of those rights.
B. Decide what voluntary limits will be imposed on confidentiality in the practice setting.
C. Learn the laws that can affect therapists' ability to protect confidential information.
D. Clarify your own personal ethical position about confidentiality and its legal limits.
E. Develop a plan for ethical response to each law requiring therapists to disclose "involuntarily."
F. Choose reliable ethics consultants and legal consultants and use as needed.
G. Devise informed consent forms that reflect these actual policies and intentions.
H. Prepare to discuss confidentiality and its limits in understandable language.

Step 2: Tell Prospective Patients the Truth (Inform Their Consent)

A. Inform prospective patients about potential limits that may be imposed on confidentiality.
B. Explain any roles or potential conflicts of interest that might affect confidentiality.
C. Obtain informed patient's consent to accept limits as a condition of receiving services.
D. Reopen the conversation if patient's consent circumstances, laws, or therapist's intentions change.

Step 3: Obtain Informed Consent Before Disclosing Voluntarily

A. Disclose without patient consent only if legally unavoidable.
B. *Inform* patient adequately about the content and implications of potential disclosures.
C. Obtain and document the patient's *consent* before disclosing.

Step 4: Respond Ethically to Legal Demands for Disclosure

A. Notify patient of pending legal requirement for a disclosure without patient's consent.
B. Respond ethically to legal obligations according to plan (from Step 1,E above):
   1. Laws requiring therapists to initiate disclosures (e.g., reporting laws)
   2. Laws granting others access to patient information without patient consent
   3. Laws allowing recipients of information to redisclose without further patient consent
   4. Exceptions to privilege in court cases
C. Limit disclosure to the extent legally possible, using protective laws when available.

Step 5: Avoid Preventable Breaches of Confidentiality

A. Establish and maintain protective policies and procedures.
B. Conduct staff training.
C. Monitor note taking and record keeping practices.
D. Avoid dual roles that might create conflicts of interest about confidentiality.
E. Anticipate legal demands; empower patients to act protectively in their own behalf.
F. Protect patient identity in presentations, research, consultations.
G. Prepare a professional will to protect patient confidentiality in event of illness or death.

Step 6: Talk About Confidentiality

A. Model ethical practices about confidentiality; confront others' unethical practices.
B. Provide peer consultation about confidentiality ethics.
C. Teach ethical practices to students, supervisees, employees.
D. Educate attorneys, judges, consumers, and the public.
E. Lobby for legislative reform toward better legal protections of confidentiality.

Adapted from Fisher, M.A. (2008). Protecting confidentiality rights: The need for an ethical practice model. *American Psychologist*, *63*, 1–13. DOI: 10.1037/0003-066X.63.1.1

---

for discussing, step-by-step, the ethical responsibilities that arise from placing limits and conditions on confidentiality.

The model might therefore be described as an outline of "The Ethics of Conditional Confidentiality." It would apply to all mental health professionals, regardless of whether their basic position is one of offering absolute confidentiality or conditional confidentiality. However, it is especially useful for those who have decided to place some conditions on confidentiality, because it provides step-by-step details to help them navigate the ethical-legal maze when confidentiality is conditional.

PART II

Protecting Patients' Confidentiality Rights With an Ethics-Based Practice Model

Introduction to Part II: The Ethics of Conditional Confidentiality

The Ethical Practice Model (Box 3.1) provides the structure for the following six-chapter discussion of confidentiality ethics. To include practical advice about protecting patients' confidentiality rights at each step along the way, an entire chapter is devoted to each of the six steps in the model.

Throughout, we advocate that mental health professionals not "settle for the ethical floor" about confidentiality, but instead "reach for the ethical ceiling" by protecting their patients' confidentiality rights to the extent legally possible.[1] Toward that end, this model is designed to help mental health professionals place laws into ethical context and keep them there, and the discussion in the next six chapters maintains that perspective.

It is easy to see how the steps of this model reflect the categories of ethical standards described in Appendix II. For example, the "key standard" (or confidentiality rule) is represented in Step 3, and some of the "clarification, amplification, and application standards" are represented in Step 5. Regarding the category of "exceptions to confidentiality," Step 2 reflects the ethical requirement to inform prospective patients about these exceptions, Step 4 deals with the complications of responding ethically to legally imposed exceptions, and Step 5 warns against making unethical exceptions to confidentiality. Finally, Step 6 emphasizes the importance of teaching and supporting each other—and of educating others—about confidentiality issues.

The model is also consistent with the metaphor in Figure 1.2 about the ethically available doors to disclosure—the three ethical routes to the release of confidential information:

- *Door 1, the "initial informed-consent" door*. Step 2 of the model involves obtaining a prospective patient's consent to accept the general limits of confidentiality that apply to all patients in that setting, as a condition of receiving services, as discussed in Chapter 5.

- *Door 2, the "consent for patient-specific disclosures" door.* Step 3 of the model involves obtaining the patient's informed consent before disclosing confidential information voluntarily, as described in Chapter 6.
- *Door 3, the "legal mandate" door.* Step 4 of the model involves responding ethically to legal demands, a complicated process that is described in Chapter 7.

Note that there is no separate "legal permission" door, even though some ethics codes allow one. Step 5 of the model serves as a caution that those disclosures require either an informed consent discussion at intake or explicit consent from the patient at the time of the disclosure, thereby opening either Door 1 or Door 2. Other "preventable" disclosures that therapists sometimes make, but which are unethical if there is no ethical "door" to such a disclosure, are also covered by Step 5 and are discussed in Chapter 8.

> Like the Ethics Codes on which it is based, this model gives therapists the ethical freedom to create setting-specific limits on confidentiality, as long as patients are informed about these policies in advance and consent to accept them as a condition of receiving services. The overall ethical framework of this model would apply in any setting, but the legal details will vary from state to state, and sometimes from setting to setting within a state.[2]

How do legal demands fit into confidentiality ethics? One advantage of the Ethical Practice Model is that it *helps mental health professionals place laws into ethical context and keep them there.* Step 1 reflects the importance of learning the relevant laws and regulations, including both those that protect confidentiality as well as those that limit it. Thus prepared, the therapist is ready to initiate the informed consent conversation at Step 2. For legally allowed disclosures, Step 3 provides a way of obtaining patient consent for disclosures not discussed at Step 2. State laws that limit confidentiality take center stage at Step 4, with an emphasis on responding ethically to legal demands. Finally, Step 5 describes ways of avoiding the ethical risks that arise from ignoring protective laws, failing to anticipate unprotective laws, or making legally unnecessary disclosures based upon misunderstanding the law.

For reference, the Ethical Practice Model presented in Box 3.1 is also available in Appendix V in a form that reflects this integration of legal material into the ethical structure. A color-coded version of the model, which more clearly indicates how state laws and Health Insurance Portability and Accountability Act (HIPAA) regulations fit into the ethical structure, is available online.[3]

This model can be used by mental health professionals in any role or setting. In the chapters that follow, the ethical details will be discussed as they would apply in clinical settings, but mental health professionals in other roles or settings can incorporate into the model details from other ethical standards specific to their work.[4]

The outline of the model may appear simple, but carrying out these ethically required tasks can become very complicated. "This model systematizes therapists' *ongoing* responsibilities about confidentiality, but if faced with a specific ethical dilemma at any Step along the way, therapists are strongly advised to use a structured ethical decision-making model."[5]

The Ethical Practice Model is not a substitute for familiarity with the relevant ethical standards themselves. Ethics codes do not always provide a clear answer to a confidentiality dilemma, but an early step in any professional decision-making process involves determining which ethical standards or moral principles might apply in the situation.[6] When a confidentiality dilemma involves both ethical and legal issues, using a structured decision-making process is especially important. The discussion concerning Step 4 in this model describes therapists' ethical options in response to some of those legal circumstances. However, "deciding how to respond to an ethical-legal conflict can require difficult personal soul-searching as well as careful decision making."[7] Hansen and Goldberg have provided a matrix for separating the many relevant variables into seven categories: moral principles and personal values; clinical and cultural considerations; ethics codes; agency or employer policies; federal, state, and local statutes; rules and regulations; and case law.[8] Knapp and colleagues have provided a specific decision-making model that can facilitate the process of resolving ethical-legal conflicts.[9]

In Part II, the chapter titles reflect the subject matter of each step in the model, but the titles and subtitles below more clearly capture their spirit and reflect the frustrations reported by many therapists:

Step 1. Figuring Out How You Intend to Behave About Confidentiality
(or *"Scrambling to Come Up With a Clear Plan Before the Next Intake")*

Step 2. Telling Prospective Patients Your Real Intentions About Their Secrets
(or "*Now That I Know What I Will Do, Dare I Say So*?")

Step 3. Ensuring That Each Patient's Consent Is Properly Informed
(or "*When Is a Signed Consent Form Not Informed Consent*?")

Step 4. Withstanding the Vicissitudes of Practicing Ethically Under My State's Laws
(or *"What Can I Do About Those *** Reporting Laws and Subpoenas?"*)

Step 5. Preventing the Preventable Disclosures
(or *"Talking Less and Wearing Fewer Hats")*

Step 6. Refusing to Keep Confidentiality Problems a Secret
(or *"Talking More About Confidentiality and Trying on Some New Hats"*

4

Step 1: Preparing

In hindsight, the proper decision or path is often stunningly clear. However, it is important for us to nurture the objectivity that will strengthen our foresight and allow us to make correct decisions before the fact… A little forethought can affect the outcome of almost any situation. Bennett, B. E., Bryant, B. K., VandenBos, G. R., & Greenwood, A. (1990).

Professional Liability and Risk Management, p. 1

This chapter walks therapists through some of the preparation that is required for protecting patients' confidentiality rights. This is presented as the first Step in the Confidentiality Practice Model (Box 3.1) because some of the most important decisions a therapist makes about confidentiality must be made before the patient arrives. "Ordinarily, a therapist's ethical obligations toward a client do not begin until the relationship begins. In a 21st-century legal climate, however, protection of confidentiality rights may need to begin before the prospective client ever enters the consulting room."[1]

Like it or not, it has become impossible to practice ethically about confidentiality without spending time preparing to practice ethically. "Unless they first inform themselves, therapists will be unable to accurately inform prospective patients about what confidentiality's limits will be; and, unless they have made some important personal decisions in advance, they could easily find themselves unable to live up to some of the confidentiality promises they make at intake."[2]

Regrettably, this aspect of confidentiality ethics is often neglected, both in training and in practice. Ethics codes never mention the need for "preparation" related to confidentiality. Journal articles about confidentiality never begin here, and continuing education workshops rarely mention the importance of "forethought" about confidentiality. Until very recently, ethics texts offered little or no advice about the scope of planning required for the protection of patients' rights about confidentiality. The ethical implications of this chronic lack of preparation are therefore rarely discussed even in theory, much less in practical terms.[3]

In this chapter, forethought about confidentiality is discussed as it relates to protection of patients and their confidentiality rights, which is an *ethical* perspective. However, forethought is also important for therapists' self-protection, and many of the available discussions of forethought are written from a risk management perspective.[4] Without adequate preparation, today's therapists are not only unable to protect patients from the harm that can result when personal information that they believed would be kept confidential is disclosed to others unexpectedly; they are also thereby unable to protect themselves from the potential ethical and legal liabilities that arise from disclosing such information without the patient's consent when it legally could—and therefore ethically should—have been protected. Malpractice insurers therefore remind therapists that, when unprepared, they may place not only their patients, but also themselves, at risk.

> The three most important aspects of risk management are *forethought* (anticipation of problematic events), *thought* (mindfulness of relevant factors when resolving an immediate issue), and *afterthought* (learning from experience)... Through forethought you can anticipate, prevent, or mitigate many problems. Through thought you can respond carefully and prudently when problems occur. By afterthought you can reflect back on what happened and modify future responses accordingly.[5]

This chapter is about the first of those—forethought and planning. The entire six-step model is designed to help therapists be more mindful and planful in creating policies and making decisions about confidentiality. This first step is about organizing the planning process.

Forethought about confidentiality begins with becoming fully informed, both about the relevant ethical standards and about the laws that can affect patient confidentiality. Once ethically and legally informed, the therapist can establish clear policies that are ethically based, but which also take into account the relevant laws. This involves making some difficult personal decisions in advance, in order to be ready to describe the potential limits of confidentiality to prospective patients and ready to answer their questions honestly.

Learning Ethical Standards That Define Patients' Rights About Confidentiality

For easy reference, selected ethical standards relevant to confidentiality are listed in numerical order in Appendix I, and then listed by category in Appendix II. These form the "ethical floor" about confidentiality—the minimum standards of behavior mandated by the respective mental health professions.[6] Although it is important to consider all of one's ethical standards when developing policies, the final column in these appendices suggests those that are especially important to consider here, during Step 1.

Two important things about confidentiality ethics become visible in Appendix II. First, the ethical standards relevant to confidentiality include not only those about confidentiality itself, but also those about informed consent: Every profession requires that prospective patients be *informed* about confidentiality's limits before giving *consent* to receive services. Second, the ethical standards about ethical-legal conflicts are also very relevant to confidentiality, even though they may not contain that word. Although these ethical standards are slightly different for each profession, all therapists do have certain ethical responsibilities when faced with legal demands that conflict with their ethical responsibilities, including their ethical responsibilities about confidentiality and disclosure.

Learning Laws That Can Affect Therapists' Ability to Protect Confidentiality

Laws that affect confidentiality include both those that protect it and those that limit it. They vary from state to state, and therapists are responsible for learning the laws of their own state.[7] However, when told that they must learn a bunch of laws, therapists sometimes raise objections such as these:

OBJECTION #1: WHY BOTHER LEARNING LAWS IF I AM A THERAPIST, NOT AN ATTORNEY?

"If a clinician knows and understands the law, he or she can practice with legal concerns receding into the background of consciousness. Attention can focus on the patient and the clinical issues, which is where it belongs."[8] Therapists are not expected to be experts about all laws, but they do need to know about the laws that affect their ability to protect confidentiality and to understand them well enough to predict their implications for patients.

OBJECTION #2: WHY BOTHER LEARNING ABOUT LAWS THAT *PROTECT* CONFIDENTIALITY RIGHTS?

First, studying the protective laws can help therapists remember not to disclose inappropriately. Second, these laws often contain provisions that therapists can use for making legal arguments when contesting those laws that demand disclosure. Third, these laws sometimes contain provisions that can help therapists limit the scope of a disclosure, even if complete legal protection is impossible.

OBJECTION #3: WHY BOTHER LEARNING LAWS THAT *LIMIT* CONFIDENTIALITY?

Therapists must be prepared to explain to prospective patients the possible implications of laws that can require them to breach confidentiality. Therapists who understand these laws will be more prepared to provide honest answers to patients' questions about how they intend to respond if such laws should arise, will be more likely to predict the foreseeable legal complications and know how to avoid them when legally possible, and will be better prepared to respond to the "unavoidable" legal demands in ways least damaging to the patient and to the therapy relationship. Those who fail to learn about these laws are at risk for being taken by surprise by them, and this places their patients at risk.

One example of this potential problem is reflected in the fact that more than 75% of clinicians may be unfamiliar with their state's duty-to-protect law, "believing that they had a legal duty to warn when they did not, or assuming that warning was their only legal option, when actually other protective actions less harmful to client privacy were allowed."[9] Those therapists were doubly unprepared: unprepared to inform prospective patient accurately about what the law required, and unprepared to respond most protectively when the situation arose.

OBJECTION #4: WHY LEARN THE LAWS THAT DO BOTH—PROTECT CONFIDENTIALITY AND ALSO LIMIT IT?

Laws that both protect and limit confidentiality are often misunderstood. For example, the laws that grant "privileged" status to the patient–therapist relationship are designed to protect the confidentiality of that relationship by preventing the resulting information from being used as evidence in court proceedings. But these same laws also contain exceptions that place important limitations on those protections. The result is that therapists are sometimes required to provide patient records or to testify in a court case. Understanding both sides of that coin can help therapists prepare to make use of the protections and prepare for the limitations.

OBJECTION #5: WHY LEARN LAWS THAT MERELY *ALLOW* THERAPISTS TO DISCLOSE WITHOUT PATIENT CONSENT?

Laws that allow therapists to disclose not only reduce patients' legal protections about confidentiality, but they also create some of the confusion that leads therapists into less ethical positions about it. In pursuing the goal of providing patients with the best protection of their confidentiality rights, it is important to remember not to equate what is legally allowed with what is professionally most ethical. Therapists who find themselves raising this objection should review the definitions in Box 1.1, consult the Chapter 2 section entitled "Laws Allowing Therapists to Disclose Without Patient Consent," and see the Chapter 8 section warning against "Abusing 'Legally Allowed' Exceptions to Confidentiality."

OBJECTION #6: WHAT IF I DON'T KNOW HOW TO GET COPIES OF MY STATE'S LAWS?

In some states, the published laws and regulations are organized in ways that make it difficult to find all of those relevant to confidentiality, or difficult to clarify their implications. In searching for laws that might affect confidentiality in your own state, consult the examples in Appendix III, "Laws Affecting Confidentiality," as well as its linked version online.[10]

Some state professional associations provide a list of relevant laws for their members; and, in some states, an individual or agency maintains an up-to-date list for therapists in that state.[11] State licensing boards usually provide lists of laws and regulations to licensees of each mental health profession, but these lists rarely contain *all* of the laws relevant to confidentiality, so some homework may still be required.[12] However, even after obtaining such lists of laws, therapists may still have some detective work to do. To complete the search in some states, consultation may be needed, either with experienced colleagues, including those who specialize in forensics, or with attorneys who are familiar with mental health law.

Organizing Laws Based on Their Ethical Implications

Organizing laws into categories makes them easier to learn and also makes it easier to understand their ethical implications. Having a clear set of categories also makes it easier to add new laws to the list when they are discovered or enacted.

This is a good time to review the legal categories used in Chapter 2 (see "Laws Limiting Confidentiality") and to preview Chapter 7, where the discussion of Step 4 of the Ethical Practice Model uses the same categories:

1. Laws that require therapists to initiate disclosure of patient information
2. Laws allowing others to obtain access to patient information, and/or to redisclose it without patient consent
3. Exceptions in privilege laws that allow patient information or records to be used as evidence in a court proceeding

These are not formal legal categories, but they do organize laws based on what they require from therapists. Therapists are free to organize the laws into other categories if they prefer, but they should choose categories that are helpful in clarifying the ethical implications of the laws.

Once therapists are clear about the laws relevant to confidentiality, they can prepare to explain their implications to prospective patients in the intake interview. To be ready for that conversation, therapists must make some personal decisions in advance. Consultation can be helpful—and sometimes necessary—at this stage of the preparation process. For example, regarding the first category above, research suggests that not only are as many as 75% of psychologists misinformed about some of their legal duties and legal options, but that 90% of those are unaware of their error—confident that they are correct when they are not—which can lead to unnecessary disclosures and place patients at risk.[13]

Obtaining Consultation and Developing Resources

This preparation is difficult to implement alone. Therapists are responsible for developing policies that both protect patients' confidentiality rights and protect themselves from liability. These policies must take into account their ethics code, state and federal laws, and agency policies, but they must nevertheless be individualized to reflect the therapists' own personal intentions. This is a very complicated task.

Consultation at this stage is important because it is better to ask questions in advance than to wait until a confidentiality crisis occurs. Because this area of practice is complex and sometimes anxiety-provoking, it is important to establish, in advance, safe relationships for obtaining advice and support.

Consultation related to confidentiality can be about ethical issues, legal issues, or malpractice liability concerns. Initially, the consultation relationship can be created to help with such things as understanding ethical responsibilities, uncovering relevant laws, developing confidentiality policies, and creating of consent forms. The relationships developed through such consultations will then be in place in the event of a future crisis or dilemma. Later, when consulting about a specific case, it is important to remember the ethical mandates about confidentiality. For example, therapists must not disclose information that could reasonably lead to the identification of a patient during consultation, unless they have obtained the patient's prior consent to do so. Even then, they should disclose information only to the extent necessary to achieve the purposes of the consultation.[14]

The six-step Ethical Practice Model can be helpful during both ethics consultations and legal consultations. It is not only useful for personal planning, but also for helping others understand one's ethical responsibilities and for discussing how to place laws into ethical context.

CONSULTATION ABOUT ETHICAL ISSUES

Ethics consultation can be obtained from the state or national ethics offices of various professional associations,[15] and from respected colleagues. Ethics texts can also be a valuable resource about all aspects of decision making about confidentiality. They always contain a chapter on confidentiality, and they often provide a chapter on ethical decision making,[16] as well as helpful vignettes about confidentiality and related ethical dilemmas. However, ethics texts do not supply details about each state's legally imposed limits of confidentiality, so it is the therapist's responsibility to obtain those elsewhere.

CONSULTATION ABOUT LEGAL ISSUES

Legal advice can be sought from an attorney who is familiar with mental health law. Before seeking legal consultation, however, it can be important to be clear about the ethical issues. Attorneys are experts about laws, but therapists must take responsibility for being experts about the ethics of their own profession. They should be familiar with their ethical responsibilities, able to describe them clearly, and prepared to ask their legal questions from that perspective.

Many therapists become anxious when dealing with lawyers, and this can lead them to make mistakes that harm patients' interests and put themselves at risk. For example, it is never appropriate to obtain or follow only the legal advice offered by the attorney who issued a subpoena for patient records, especially if he or she is the attorney for someone who is in an adversarial relationship with the patient in a court case. When obtaining legal advice about what is required of therapists when they receive a legal demand for confidential information. it is also important to be cautious about accepting advice from uninformed colleagues or from attorneys not familiar with mental health law.[17]

CONSULTATION ABOUT RISK MANAGEMENT

Most malpractice insurers are available for case consultation. It is in their interest to help the therapist avoid a misstep that could lead to a malpractice suit. Sometimes this can include both ethical and legal advice, but it should not replace the ethical consultation described above. Similarly, risk management texts are available,[18] but they should not be treated as replacements for ethics texts.

PRACTICAL CONSIDERATIONS ABOUT CONSULTATION

With planning and consideration, mental health professionals can optimize their consultation experiences. These are only a few examples of the ways that can be accomplished.

Choose Consultants Carefully

Good consultants who match a therapist's own particular needs can sometimes be difficult to find. It can be useful to poll colleagues about the ethical and legal consultants that have been most helpful to them. When choosing legal consultants, it is important to try to find an attorney who is not only familiar with mental health laws in one's own state, but who will be respectful of one's own ethical position about confidentiality.

Prepare for the Consultation

It is important to arrive at the consultation with notes about the questions or issues or tasks that need clarification. Therapists can prepare by reviewing the Ethical Practice Model and clarifying their own ethical position about confidentiality. (See section below on "Clarifying Your Own Personal Position About Confidentiality.") For consultation with attorneys, it is important to remember that, whereas they should be experts about laws that can affect confidentiality, they should not be expected to be experts about the ethical standards of each mental health profession or aware of each clinician's personal position about it. The model can be useful for helping to place the legal information into ethical perspective, both before and during the consultation. (The legal annotations in Appendix V can be useful during this process.)

Consider Pooling Resources With Colleagues

During this planning stage, consider sharing group consultation hours with other therapists in your setting (or with colleagues who have similar practices in other settings). This can apply to both ethical consultation and legal consultation. It is often possible to learn as much from hearing answers to others' questions as from asking one's own.

Don't Be Afraid of Asking "Silly" Questions

The desire to avoid "looking bad" or "sounding stupid" with consultants (or in front of colleagues) probably contributes as much as anything else to therapists' frequent lack of accurate information about this subject. Therapists who don't have the answers they need must be willing to ask for more information.

Making Difficult Personal Decisions

"Clarifying one's ethical position about confidentiality involves more than knowing the words of one's Ethics Code."[19] After obtaining the basic ethical and legal information, therapists are left with the task of weighing the potentially conflicting demands. For example, there is disagreement about the extent to which confidentiality should be given priority over the social values represented by reporting laws or exceptions to privilege. In balancing the competing ethical, clinical, legal, and social values, therapists must also grapple with the potential consequences of following their own personal moral principles.[20] "The self-examination and critical thinking required to master confidentiality are daunting."[21]

Laws that demand disclosure of client information are explicitly giving priority to protection of the rights or safety of others in society, rather than to protection of the patient's right to confidentiality. Some argue that when weighing their ethical duties against such legal demands, therapists should balance the two in a way that gives priority to patient confidentiality as the primary ethical obligation.[22] Some go further to suggest that patient confidentiality should be absolute and that competing rights should be given no weight.[23] Others disagree, noting that, although confidentiality is *a* primary obligation, it is not always *the* primary obligation, and that therapists must consider competing obligations such as laws, institutional rules, and professional or scientific relationships. Still others, although agreeing that confidentiality is not always primary, suggest that therapists take a principle-based approach that combines meticulous protection of confidences and careful informing of patients and clients about the limits of that protection.[24]

CLARIFYING YOUR OWN BASIC POSITION ABOUT CONFIDENTIALITY

There are only two basic ethical positions about confidentiality to choose from—absolute (or "unconditional") confidentiality and conditional confidentiality. Almost all therapists choose to place some conditions or limits on confidentiality, either because they believe that certain other rights deserve more protection than the patient's right to confidentiality, or because they want to avoid the potential legal and financial consequences of breaking the law to provide absolute confidentiality.[25] However, once they decide to offer patients only conditional confidentiality, therapists are faced with an infinite number of possible variations on that theme, and this makes it impossible to adequately protect patients' rights about it on an ad hoc basis. Instead, therapists must spend time deciding exactly *what* conditions they intend to impose on patients' confidentiality protections.

> We strongly recommend that you do not adopt a policy or procedure simply because someone else uses it, it comes highly recommended, or most therapists in your community use it. Find out as many ways of doing things from as many sources … as possible, but use these examples only to inform—not replace—your own thinking. Try to create each policy and procedure so that it best fits your values, approaches, and goals.[26]

DECIDING WHAT THE REAL "LIMITS OF CONFIDENTIALITY" WILL BE

Therapists who plan to place some conditions on confidentiality must explain these conditions to the prospective patient at intake. This means they must already have decided when they might disclose information without further consent from the patient. Making these decisions in advance prepares therapists for the initial interview, in which they will (1) explain to prospective patients the legally imposed limits of confidentiality and any voluntary exceptions they intend to make to the confidentiality rule and (2) obtain the prospective patient's consent to accept those policies as a condition of receiving services. As reflected in Figure 1.2, this initial conversation will open an ethical door to disclosure by obtaining the informed patient's consent in advance for all of the therapist's general disclosure policies that might place conditions on confidentiality for all patients.

Patients' rights are best protected when therapists go beyond compliance with their ethics code's minimum standards of behavior about confidentiality and, instead of settling for that "ethical floor," decide to reach for the "ethical ceiling" about confidentiality.[27] "The ideals of professional psychology must include conscientious decision making, but they also must include virtuous deciders, who emphasize not so much what is permitted as what is preferred."[28] This requires therapists to integrate specific ethical and legal rules with the profession's aspirational ideals and with their own personal ethical values.[29] It does not require that they protect confidentiality absolutely in all circumstances. *What is advocated here, however, is that they reach for the ethical ceiling by protecting confidentiality to the extent legally possible.* This means not disclosing anything voluntarily without first obtaining the informed patient's consent, whether at intake or later. It means not disclosing without patient consent simply because HIPAA or the laws of one's state might legally allow that in a particular circumstance. Maintaining a high ethical posture, even when laws allow less, is one way to maintain a supererogatory position that goes beyond the minimum ethical requirements of many ethics codes.

Making Decisions About Legally Imposed "Conditions"

Therapists must take responsibility for engaging in personal decision making about each law that can require them to disclose information without patient consent. "This involves asking oneself such questions as, 'Am I willing to risk the consequences of disobeying this particular law in order to protect a patient's confidences?'"[30] Therapists who answer "Yes" to that question are advised to be clear about the potential legal, financial, and personal consequences of disobeying that particular law in their own state. Therapists who answer "No" must instead be prepared to explain to prospective patients what this law might require them to disclose, when, and to whom.

Either answer should be preceded by some serious personal soul-searching, which is probably the primary reason why therapists often fail to make clear decisions about this in advance. Yet, this may be the most important part of the preparation.

> Often, apparent conflicts between the law and ethics can be avoided if psychologists anticipate problems ahead of time or engage in integrative problem solving. At times, however, psychologists may need to choose between following the law and protecting the welfare of their patients or an ethical value. We suggest careful practical wisdom or deliberation when such decisions are made.[31]

To remind themselves why it is worth the trouble to make these difficult decisions *now*, therapists need only place themselves in the patient's position. "If I were the patient, would I want my therapist to disclose my deepest secrets in this circumstance without having warned me about that possibility in advance?" Box 4.1 illustrates some possible implications of working with an unprepared therapist.

To avoid the harm to patients that can arise from misunderstandings about how well their confidences will be protected, therapists must avoid misunderstandings of their *own*. For example, they must not only understand what the relevant laws say, but must decide how they will respond if faced with each of the circumstances in which they are legally required to disclose patient information.

It is important that therapists "not only decide what they *should* do in a variety of foreseeable circumstances—a difficult-enough task—but they must also be prepared to inform patients honestly about what they actually *will* do, which may be

BOX 4.1 Taking the Patient's Perspective at Step 1

Imagine that your therapist did not mention confidentiality at intake, so you asked about it at the next session. The therapist explored your concerns, helped you talk about early childhood invasions of your privacy that might make you more concerned about confidentiality, then assured you of his personal belief in the importance of confidentiality to the therapy process. Reassured by this discussion, you proceeded to disclose a great deal of personal information that could be very damaging to you if ever disclosed.

Six months into treatment, your therapist told you he had just *reported* something you told had him. His explanation was that he only recently learned that he could incur a large financial penalty—and perhaps even risk a malpractice suit—for failure to report such information, and he feared his nonreport might come to light. When asked why he did not discuss this with you before he made the report, he replied, "This report was not an optional disclosure; it was legally required, so it could not be avoided. It was not something we could decide together."

You later learned that, in fact, therapists of his profession are *not* actually legally required to make such reports. Nevertheless, following his report, he received a subpoena for your therapy records as part of a related investigation.

In such circumstances, would you consider your confidentiality rights protected?

This therapist entered the relationship unprepared, interacted with the patient in a misleading manner, and elicited confidences that were unprotected. By offering reassurance, rather than providing accurate information, he implied that he would ignore legal requirements. But, in fact, he had not made a carefully considered decision to disobey laws that limit confidentiality when faced with consequences to himself. Uninformed, he had been unable to accurately inform his patients about even the most "foreseeable" legal limits to the privacy he was promising. Uninformed, he misunderstood his own reporting obligations.

This was no way to begin a relationship. The ethical point, after all, is to make sure the patient knows what to expect about confidentiality when making the decision about whether or not to enter therapy, and then when making the decisions about what to confide to the therapist and when. Whether or not it was intentional on the therapist's part, you were misled at intake—and thus dealt with dishonestly. Having entered therapy uninformed about what the real limits of confidentiality would be for a therapist in his profession, he deprived you of your only opportunity to protect yourself from the risks that would arise when this therapist disclosed your confidences.

As therapy progressed, this therapist compounded the initial problems as he became increasingly confused about his ethical and legal obligations and failed to involve you in the discussion of possible alternatives. There is sometimes a legal means for avoiding making a report or for limiting the scope of the disclosure and reducing its implications for the patient–therapist relationship. But, because he was uninformed about the details of his state's reporting laws, the therapist was unable to adequately inform you. He thus deprived you of the opportunity to prevent information about you, as well as your status as a therapy patient, from being disclosed.

different."[32] Having done that, a therapist who is later faced with a legal requirement will be "free to disclose, not because that disclosure is legally allowed, but because the informed client already gave consent to accept that limit on confidentiality as a condition of receiving services."[33]

At this stage of preparation, it is helpful to review Step 4, as detailed in Chapter 7. Pausing now to learn about each law, and the legal options available for responding to it, will simplify the decision-making process and will result in policies that are clearer and more likely to be implemented. Note that therapists would have no ethical obligation to tell patients about a particular law if they planned to always disobey that law in order to protect their patients' confidences, but they *do* have an ethical obligation to be prepared to inform patients if they intend to obey that law and disclose patient information.

Making Decisions About Voluntarily Imposed "Conditions"

Most therapists impose some conditions on confidentiality quite voluntarily. These often include conditions related to emergencies and patient safety. But the limits therapists voluntarily place on confidentiality may also include circumstances imposed by the setting, such as access to patient information by other clinicians in the setting, or access by nonclinical staff who provide clerical or billing services. Group practices, agencies, and inpatient settings often use a team approach, in which cases are routinely discussed among clinicians; and in hospital settings, professionals of several other disciplines may have access to the therapist's records.

Other potential limits of confidentiality can arise from the contracts that therapists sign with managed care organizations and other third-party payers. Amazingly few therapists actually read these legally binding contracts, even though failure to do so leaves the therapist unprepared to inform prospective patients about their implications, including the numerous limits they can place on confidentiality (e.g., as part of compliance review, nonclinicians may read and audit treatment records, information provided for reimbursement may end up in a national data bank, etc.).[34] (To facilitate this preparation, see, in Chapter 7, the section "Third-Party Payer Access Provisions in Legally Binding Provider Contracts.")

Clinical considerations may also come into play when making decisions about voluntary disclosures. Even those therapists who take a supererogatory position about confidentiality will vary in their decisions about exactly what conditions they intend to impose for clinical reasons. After weighing the competing interests, many therapists decide that, in some circumstances, breaching confidentiality may be clinically necessary and professionally appropriate. For example, many therapists choose to breach confidentiality to prevent harm to self, even if such disclosure is not legally required in their state. However, the specifics of these decisions vary tremendously from therapist to therapist. For this reason, each therapist's initial informed consent conversation about confidentiality will vary, making each therapist (or practice group or agency) the only reliable "authority" about what voluntary limits will be imposed on confidentiality in their particular practice or setting.

For therapists who provide services to minors, policies about voluntary disclosures must include the therapist's own rules about what will be disclosed to parents. Therapists must clarify their policies about this in advance, in order to be prepared to present very clear rules at the outset and explain them to both the minor and the parents. Similarly, with couple and family cases, therapists must devise specific policies about what the rules will be about confidentiality and disclosure across participants. (See, in Chapter 11, the section, "Therapy Involving Multiple Related Parties.")

CLARIFYING RECORD KEEPING POLICIES

Inadequate policies about security of patient records are among the most important risks to patient confidentiality. Planning must include (1) establishing clear policies about storage and disclosure of records, (2) providing ethics-based staff training about confidentiality and security of records, and (3) providing for ongoing monitoring of staff compliance. In addition, therapists must make decisions about such things as electronic versus paper records and about keeping one set of records versus keeping both an official record and some separate "psychotherapy notes." (This topic is covered in detail in Chapter 10, "Record Keeping," and in Chapter 13, "Ethics-Based Staff Training About Confidentiality.")

EVALUATING THE DECISION-MAKING PROCESS AND LEVEL OF PREPARATION

Therapists might ask themselves questions such as the following: "Do I understand my ethical standards and state laws well enough to (a) formulate a clear ethical plan about each law that might limit confidentiality, so that I can (b) be honest with patients about how I intend to respond, should it arise in their case?" The only ethically responsible answer is "Yes." Obviously, it is impossible for therapists to do "b" until they have completed "a." But, although therapists will be on their own when they tell patients about their policies, they do not need to formulate and evaluate their policies alone.[35] Therapists who are still unsure at this stage of the preparation can consult further with colleagues and revisit previous consultants or develop new ones.

Devising Accurate Patient Handouts and Informed Consent Forms

"All that has been decided must be reduced to a simple understandable statement about confidentiality and its limits."[36] This is the end toward which all this preparation has been the means. At this point in the planning process, therapists know when they will disclose information voluntarily and how they intend to respond to disclosure laws. They have decided who, within their practice setting or elsewhere, will be allowed to have access to information about their patients. And (if necessary) they have obtained consultation about the ethical and legal implications of those policies and plans.

This is the time to put intentions about confidentiality into writing in the form of a very specific and personalized set of policies. The document can begin with the confidentiality rule and then list the exceptions to the rule, including both those that can be imposed by law and those the therapist will impose voluntarily. It should be written clearly and simply, using short sentences.[37] The handout must reflect the therapist's actual intentions about confidentiality and disclosure, so no "canned" information form will suffice. Therapists should exercise caution in relying on "universal" forms such as the sample "Notice of Privacy Practices" from a legal-based HIPAA workshop. Not only are these likely to be unintelligible to the average patient (and often to the therapist), but they are unlikely to describe the actual policies in the therapist's own setting. Therapists can review and adapt for their own use parts of the documents used by respected peers in the same state or setting, but they must personalize those to accurately describe their own policies. When describing potential voluntary disclosures or explaining legally compelled disclosures, "whatever the clinician writes or says related to informed consent needs to be accurate."[38]

Although most ethics codes do not require that this be provided to patients in writing,[39] the federal HIPAA regulations legally require that prospective patients receive a "Notice of Privacy Practices." Not only is a written document more protective of patients, but, as suggested in the risk management literature, it is also protective of the therapist.[40]

Promises about confidentiality have serious implications for patients. Once made, they should be kept, so therapists should write down exactly how they intend to behave, using very simple language. Creating a written document to describe confidentiality policies can be helpful in several respects. First, the process of writing serves as a self-test. Therapists who are unable to *write* their policies clearly probably won't be able to *say* them clearly either, whether at intake or when answering questions later, and they may not be able to live within them consistently or enforce others' compliance with them. Second, a written policy statement serves both as a reminder and as a documentation: It becomes permanent evidence of what the therapist said the rules would be about confidentiality, thereby avoiding later disputes about what was promised. Finally, it is important that the policy statement be tailored to reflect the therapist's actual intentions. Important decisions were made during this preparation process, and the written statement should reflect those decisions.

Practicing What You Will Say to Prospective Patients

The next chapter provides a detailed discussion of the initial informed consent conversation with prospective patients about confidentiality and its limits. After reading that chapter, it can be helpful to return here and complete the preparation by practicing exactly what will be said in that conversation. If the average patient would be unable to accurately predict how the therapist will behave, based on what was provided on the handout and discussed at intake, the therapist can keep practicing. *One's policies about confidentiality are not confidential, so the intake conversation can be practiced with anyone who will listen.*

It can be a major challenge to meet the ethical requirement to present the information in language that is reasonably understandable to patients.[41] If the general intake paperwork is extensive, it can be useful to create a separate single page that contains the confidentiality rule and a simple list of its foreseeable exceptions. This is this easier to follow than an oral narrative, so patients can choose to use it for reference during the initial conversation about confidentiality and its limits, then take it home to study further.

Practice Pointers

Therapists who practice in a "Don't worry about it until it happens" posture may tend to "finesse" conversations about confidentiality. When it comes to legal demands, they aren't sure exactly what their state laws really require or exactly how they might behave when faced with those laws. When it comes to voluntary disclosures, they may be using a form borrowed from a colleague or obtained from a legal workshop, and this may not accurately describe how they might actually behave about confidentiality. At the intake conversation, they may gloss over the written descriptions and make confidentiality promises they will later be unwilling or unable to keep.

This chapter is an invitation to study the ethical and legal documents in advance and to consider the issues at leisure: Reflect on the foreseeable complications, take a clear position, and develop policies that are as protective as possible of patients. Once therapists turn their attention toward the patients they might place at risk, and place themselves in the patient's shoes, it is impossible to justify an "insistently unprepared" posture.

On the other hand, for those who were already well prepared, this chapter becomes an invitation to share what they know. Some colleagues may be neglecting this ethical planning because they fail to understand its importance, others because they don't know how or where to begin. Both will benefit from seeing written copies of confidentiality policies and from having a peer consultant when developing their own policies and putting them into writing.

Once this preparation in Step 1 is complete, therapists will be able to comply with the next three steps of the Ethical Practice Model, which follow naturally from it:

Step 2: Informing prospective patients about what confidentiality's limits will be
Step 3: Obtaining the informed patient's consent for all voluntary disclosures
Step 4: Protecting confidentiality to the extent legally possible

5

Step 2: Telling Patients the Truth About Confidentiality's Limits

> Although psychiatrists and mental health professionals are well aware that absolute confidentiality is a fiction, patients are strikingly uninformed about the circumstances under which confidentiality can and cannot be compromised.
>
> Joseph & Onek (1999), *Confidentiality in Psychiatry*, p. 109

This chapter is about two conversations in which therapists must explain confidentiality and its limits. Therapists are ethically required to conduct informed consent conversations about confidentiality in two different contexts. First, at intake, prospective patients must be given enough information to allow them to make an informed decision about whether to confide in this therapist in the first place. Subsequently, that conversation must be reopened if the therapist believes the patient has forgotten the rules about confidentiality, or if the disclosure risks have increased because of changes in the patient's circumstances, changes in the law, or changes in the therapist's policies. This later conversation allows the prospective patient to pause and assess the risks of confiding further. This is why informed consent about confidentiality must be an ongoing process, not a static, one-time event.

Within the metaphor of Figure 1.2 describing ethical doors to disclosure, these two conversations both pertain to Door 1. The initial intake conversation opens that door; the subsequent followup conversations keep it open throughout the relationship.

Underlying Ethical and Legal Concept: Informing the Patient's Consent

The same ethical concept underlies both conversations: Patients have a right to be *informed* about the conditions and potential risks before giving or renewing their *consent* to receive services. This means that, unless therapists intend to protect confidentiality unconditionally, they have an ethical obligation to inform prospective patients about what the "conditions" will be. This ethical obligation is reflected in every therapist's ethical standards (see Appendix II).

In support of this ethical obligation, some laws also require therapists to inform prospective patients about the limits of confidentiality. Most state licensing boards and state agencies include this requirement in their regulations. At the federal level, the Health Insurance Portability and Accountability Act (HIPAA) regulations require that patients be informed about confidentiality and its limits in a written "Notice of Privacy Practices."

This combined ethical and legal duty prevents therapists from obtaining a patient's "uninformed consent" to receive therapy services. Once informed in advance about confidentiality's limits and conditions, prospective patients can then exercise their right to give—or to refuse to give—consent to receive therapy services under the described conditions. In other words, the initial informed consent conversation protects the patient's right to give "informed refusal" of services instead of informed consent, if they are unwilling to accept the described risks. The ongoing informed consent process protects a patient's right to reconsider the decision.

Practical Considerations About Informed Consent

Informed consent is a concept that can "trip up" therapists if they are not careful. Regrettably, "nothing blocks a patient's access to help with such cruel efficiency as a bungled attempt at informed consent,"[1] and nothing leaves patients' rights more unprotected than when the bungled topic is confidentiality. This topic is impossible for therapists to discuss clearly and honestly unless they have already informed themselves about its potential legal limits, decided about its voluntarily imposed limits, and prepared to describe those limits and conditions to patients. That is why Step 1—Preparing—may be the most important step in this Ethical Practice Model. Here, we expand further on the practical considerations involved in preparing for this initial conversation.

PROCESS

The informed consent process with a prospective therapy patient consists of three basic components: (1) the therapist provides information, (2) the informed patient voluntarily gives (or refuses to give) consent to receive therapy services under the described conditions, and (3) the therapist documents this process. These three facets of the informed consent process would apply regardless of the topic the patient is being informed about. Together, they are designed to achieve a simple result: An informed patient, understanding the information presented by the therapist, voluntarily consents (or refuses to consent) to accept the described risks of entering therapy (or, in a later conversation, to accept the risks of continuing therapy).

Informing Prospective Patients About Limits of Confidentiality

Confidentiality is only one of several topics that therapists are ethically required to cover in initial interviews.[2] It is permissible to include the information about confidentiality within a general handout that also covers the other required information. However, for ensuring that prospective patients are truly informed about confidentiality and its limits, it is better not to bury that information in the middle of a long form. A simple one-page handout can do triple duty: It is an information sheet that uses a simple, bulleted list to *inform* the prospective patient about the confidentiality rule and about what its exceptions will be in that setting; it can be a signature form for *obtaining the informed patient's consent* to accept those described limits of confidentiality as a condition of receiving services; and (when retained in the record) it can provide *documentation* of this mutual understanding.

Most ethics codes do not require that the information about confidentiality and its limits be presented to patients in writing.[3] The federal HIPAA regulations do legally require that patients receive this information in the form of a written "Notice of Privacy Practices." Note, however, that as mentioned in the Chapter 3 section, "Distinguishing Between Ethical Standards and Laws," this HIPAA notice is intended only as informational material, not as a consent document. The patient's signature at the bottom of a standard version of the HIPAA notice is only a verification that the patient received the information. Unless the form is modified, it does not reflect that the informed patient gave consent to accept the described limits of confidentiality as a condition of receiving services and therefore does not satisfy the ethical requirement for obtaining and documenting informed consent about confidentiality and its limits.

Regardless of whether the therapist practices in a setting that is required to conform to the HIPAA regulations, using a written informed consent contract has many advantages, and this is advocated by both ethics texts and malpractice insurers. "Many of the potential problems regarding confidentiality and privilege can be avoided through the appropriate use of written informed consent. By outlining the rules of treatment at the outset of the establishment of the professional relationship, psychotherapists can essentially form contracts with their clients about how the treatment information will be used."[4]

A written statement is a convenient way to organize the information, structure the conversation, invite questions, and ensure that the prospective patient understands what the rules will be about confidentiality and its limits. The patient can take the handout home, read the information carefully, and bring further questions to the next session. When signed by the patient, this informational form documents the mutual understanding about what confidentiality's limits will be. A former Chairman of the American Psychological Association (APA) Ethics Committee advises that absence of a written document leaves both patient and therapist vulnerable in the event of later disputes about what was discussed:

> One result of failing to provide written information is that psychologist and client alike become vulnerable in the course of an ethics investigation where remembered "facts" are suspect... And if a formal ethics complaint were initiated,... how would an Ethics Committee decide? Whose memory is to be trusted after a lapse of five years? And, what evidence could the psychologist provide that... indeed s/he *did* discuss the limits of confidentiality?[5]

For patients, a written handout would be a disadvantage only if it provided an incomplete list of the limits that the therapist intended to place on confidentiality. Patients who relied on that list would be betrayed if unexpected disclosures were made. For therapists, the only disadvantage of a written handout would arise from the fact that patients who receive confidentiality promises in writing are more likely to notice if a therapist fails to live up to them. Obviously, this would create problems only for therapists who were unsure about their own written policies or who were unprepared to follow them. (This becomes a lesson in preparing well and in not borrowing others' informed consent documents that do not reflect one's own actual intentions.)

Obtaining the Informed Patient's Consent to Accept Those Limits

To qualify as informed consent, the patient's consent must not only be given from an informed posture, but it must be given voluntarily. To proceed otherwise would have both ethical and legal implications. The purpose of the informed consent conversation is not to coerce patients into treatment, but to protect their right to give informed refusal of services, instead of informed consent, if they so choose.

> Truth telling and the process of reaching informed choice underlie the exercise of self-determination, which is basic to respect for persons; patients have the moral right... to be given accurate, complete, and understandable information in a manner that facilitates informed judgment; to be assisted with weighing the benefits and burdens and available options in their treatment, including the choice of no treatment; to accept, refuse, or terminate treatment without undue influence, duress, coercion, or penalty.[6]

Documenting the Informed Consent Process

Some ethics codes require that the informed patient's consent to receive services be documented in writing, with oral consent sufficing only in emergencies.[7] Toward this end, the patient handout that lists the foreseeable limits of confidentiality can include a signature line, above which can be an informed consent statement such as the following: "I have been informed about the limits of confidentiality described above; I have discussed them with this therapist; I accept them as a condition of receiving therapy services; and I am aware that I can raise questions about them at any time."

It is the therapist's responsibility to be sure that patients understand, because a signature on a consent form does not qualify as informed consent unless patients are truly informed about what they are signing. It is also the therapist's responsibility to personalize the confidentiality portion of the form so that it accurately describes when the therapist might actually disclose confidential information. "Personalizing written informed consent forms has been shown to foster rapport and more constructive patient expectations." However, "written forms should not be considered a substitute for ongoing verbal consent."[8]

The signed form that documents the patient's consent can be maintained in the patient's record. If the official records are electronic only, this signed document can be maintained on paper or can be scanned into the record. The important thing is to maintain a record of (1) what the patient was told and (2) the patient's written consent to accept the described limitations on confidentiality.

CONTENT OF THE INFORMATION PROVIDED TO PATIENTS

Exactly what should therapists tell their prospective patients about the limits of confidentiality? The answer to this question will be as simple or as complex as the therapist's own intentions, because that is what determines the content of the conversation. Honesty is important. Therapists who are reluctant to describe *all* of the foreseeable circumstances in which they might later disclose client information can benefit from taking the patient's perspective as they draft their informational statement about confidentiality's limits (see Box 5.1).

The patient has a right to be told about two things: (1) the confidentiality rule, as the therapist intends to apply it; and (2) the exceptions to the rule that the therapist reserves the right to make. For most therapists, the rule can be stated as simply as "I will disclose nothing without your consent." The ethical rule can still be accurately captured in that familiar old sentence. But this statement must be immediately followed by a description of the "conditions" the therapist might place on that

BOX 5.1 Taking the Patient's Perspective at Step 2

Imagine that you are entering therapy yourself, wishing for a safe place to discuss your deepest feelings, dreams, fears, and fantasies:

- Exactly *which* potential limitations on confidentiality do you want your therapist to "skip over" and not bother telling you about in advance?
- Exactly *which* risks to your privacy might you consider too "unimportant" to be mentioned?
- Exactly *which* of your therapist's voluntary "nonconfidentiality policies" do you prefer to remain *un*informed about?
- Exactly *which* legally required reports or disclosures do you want your therapist not to mention?

---

promise: "There are some important exceptions to that rule, some of them because of my voluntary policies, and some of them because of disclosures that are required by law."[9]

Many therapists stumble or fall short when trying to be specific about these exceptions. Therapists can use categories such as those in Box 5.2 for organizing the list of exceptions that will apply in their own setting, This can be presented in the form of an outline or as a simple bulleted list.

Regarding items I-A and IV, counselors have additional specific responsibilities if they use electronic technology or provide services in settings where this is used. The American Counseling Association (ACA) Ethics Code section, "Technology and Informed Consent" contains a list of 11 types of information that counselors must inform patients about, the first two of which explicitly involve confidentiality: "(1) Address issues related to the difficulty of maintaining the confidentiality of electronically transmitted communications" and "(2) Inform clients of all colleagues, supervisors, and employees, such as Informational Technology (IT) administrators, who might have authorized or unauthorized access to electronic transmissions."[10] It is good ethical practice to provide such explanations to prospective patients, whether or not required by one's ethics code.

Regarding item I-D, it is important to note that those therapists who voluntarily sign legally binding provider contracts with third-party payers thereby take on certain responsibilities for informing patients about some of the limitations that these impose, including foreseeable limitations on confidentiality.

> The managed care provider not only must review traditional aspects of confidentiality and privilege with a client, he or she must also address managed care access to confidential information. The consumer of mental health services has a right to understand how much information is being shared with the managed care company, how that information is transmitted, and what becomes of the information after it is transmitted. Consumers have a right to understand that, if they are going to consume services under a managed care policy, the details of their treatment are going to be shared with an organization and that organization does not necessarily have to keep that information confidential. In addition, if the managed care organization will have access to records, therapy notes, and related materials, this reality must be set out clearly at the outset of therapy. Finally, the consumer must understand the way utilization review (UR) is conducted and just how much information is shared with the managed care organization to obtain authorizations for continued treatment.[11]

Item III gives examples of some risks of redisclosure about which most patients may be unaware. In fact, of all the information therapists disclose to others with the patient's consent, the information they send to third-party payers can have

BOX 5.2 Organizing the Description of Foreseeable "Limits of Confidentiality"

I. Limits Imposed Voluntarily (i.e., Disclosures by Policy, Not Legally Required)

A. Access to Patient Information by Others in the Setting
1. Clinical colleagues in the setting (*include any with access to patient information*)
2. Nonclinical employees in the setting (*include any with access to patient information*)
3. Contracted agents (billing agents, answering service, computer guru, etc.)

B. Disclosures Which Therapist May Later Make Without Further Consent
1. Danger to self (*voluntary in states where not legally required*)
2. Danger to others (*voluntary in states where not legally required*)
3. Disclosures to parents about a minor therapy patient
4. Other

C. Dual Relationships or Conflicts of Interest That Might Compromise Confidentiality

D. Provider Contracts That Give Access by Third-Party Payers (e.g., *potential audits*)

II. Limits Imposed by Law (*These Vary By State*)

A. Laws Requiring Therapists to Initiate Disclosures Without Patient Consent
1. Mandated reporting laws
2. Duty-to-warn or duty-to-protect laws
3. Other

B. Laws Granting Access to Patient Information Without Patient Consent
1. Parent access to minor child's treatment records
2. Access following mandated reports or in court cases involving child abuse
3. Access to information/records for involuntary commitment proceedings
4. Laws allowing recipients of information to re-release without consent
5. Other

C. Exceptions to Therapist–Patient Privilege
1. Patient's mental health at issue in the case
2. Cases involving child abuse
3. Custody/visitation disputes
4. "Judicial discretion"
5. Other

III. Possible Redisclosure of the Information a Therapist Discloses

A. Patient application for health/life insurance, large mortgage or loan can trigger redisclosure of information held by third-party payer

B. Redisclosures legally required (e.g., court-ordered testimony by Court-Appointed Special Advocate [CASA] worker who obtained access to minor's records)

C. Redisclosures legally allowed (e.g., HIPAA-allowed sharing among providers)

IV. Possible Limitations on Confidentiality Created by Use of Technology

the longest-lasting consequences because of the risk of redisclosure. Therapists are sometimes reluctant to inform prospective patients about the potential risk of such redisclosure, even though, without that information, patients are unable to make an informed and autonomous decision about whether to seek third-party reimbursement.

For example, there are many circumstances in which people sign application forms that contain phrases authorizing the disclosure of "any and all" relevant information, including health care and mental health care information. Unless this is explained to patients in advance, most may be unlikely to know that if they later sign an application for life insurance or health insurance, or submit certain applications for a large mortgage, financial loan, or advance, they may be triggering a demand for redisclosure of their current or prior mental health records. (See further discussion of this in Chapter 6, in the section "Special Considerations with Disclosures to Third-Party Payers" and in Chapter 8, in the section, "Disclosures to Third-Party Payers Without Fully Informed Consent.")

TIMING

Obtaining informed consent is not a one-time thing. It is a process that should begin as early as possible and then be reopened as needed.

Initial Informed Consent Conversation

If confidentiality will have limits, patients should be informed about those limits as early as possible, hopefully before they confide sensitive personal material without knowing that their confidences might later be disclosed. The first thing a prospective patient says could be something that a therapist is legally required to report, or something that the therapist might later be required to disclose in response to a court order. The ethical rationale for entering into this conversation at the beginning of the first interview is a simple and compelling one: Patients have the right to be given enough information about confidentiality's limits to permit them to weigh the risks of confiding before they share secrets that might later be betrayed.

The intake conversation offers patients their first (and sometimes only) opportunity to accept or reject the "conditions" being offered by this particular therapist. This is not a novel idea and is not limited to confidentiality; therapists routinely initiate very early discussion of other practical matters. For example, fees, insurance coverage, and therapist availability are often discussed before personal information is elicited from a prospective patient (sometimes even in the initial telephone contact), because such "conditions" can affect whether the patient decides to begin a therapy relationship. Similarly, the fact that confidentiality has foreseeable limits is one of the several "conditions" that patients have a right to know about in advance, before deciding whether to enter therapy and confide in the therapist.

> All clients have a right to know the limits on confidentiality in a professional relationship from the outset. The initial interview with any client (individual or organizational) should include a direct and candid discussion of limits that may exist with respect to any confidences communicated in the relationship... Not only will failure to provide such information early on constitute unethical behavior, and possibly behavior illegal in health care settings, but such omissions may also lead to clinical problems later on.[12]

Ethics codes protect the right of the prospective patient to receive this information very early. The wording varies, but the intent seems clear: Psychologists are required to hold the initial conversation about limits of confidentiality "at the outset of the relationship" (Standards 4.02b, 10.02, 10.03) and "as early as is feasible" (Standard 10.01). Counselors must discuss the limits of confidentiality "at initiation" (Standard B.1.d.), social workers. "as soon as possible in the social worker–client relationship" (Standard 1.07e), and marriage and family therapists "as early as feasible in their professional contacts" (Standard 2.1).[13] State licensing boards often have legal regulations that parallel these ethical standards.

In some settings, nonclinical staff members are given the task of informing prospective patients about certain matters in advance. This may include obtaining the patient's signature on a "Notice of Privacy Practices." It is important to note that, although this fulfills the legal HIPAA requirement to document that the patient was given the form, it does not meet the ethical requirement to obtain an informed patient's consent to receive services under those conditions. Obtaining informed consent involves more than obtaining a signature on a form. The clinician must take responsibility for being sure that the patient understands the limits of confidentiality, for inviting questions, and for providing clear answers. Therefore, even if the required signature is obtained in advance, this conversation should be conducted by the clinician at the initial session because (1) the nonclinical staff member will not likely know the clinician's policies about all types of disclosures, and (2) this conversation may raise clinical issues that should not be fielded by nonclinical staff. (See further discussion of this issue in Chapter 13, "Ethics-Based Staff Training About Confidentiality.")

Reopening the Informed Consent Conversation

A therapist's responsibility to discuss confidentiality and its limits does not end at intake. "Although most practitioners might assume that informed consent generally pertains to the early stages of treatment, it is truly an ongoing process."[14] It has been suggested that the overriding danger of using a written consent form is that "it tempts the clinician to treat the transaction as a discrete task that is accomplished, and thus terminated, once the patient has signed the form"; this "defeats the very purpose of informed consent, which is to foster and sustain an ongoing dialogue... Ideally, informed consent is never over. At any point along the way, the patient should feel free to ask questions about the impact of the treatment."[15]

Ethics codes reflect the ethical importance of reopening the conversation if changes in circumstances signal a change in risk of disclosure. Psychologists must initiate a new conversation about confidentiality "as new circumstances may warrant" and social workers "as needed throughout the course of the relationship." Counselors must inform patients of the limits of confidentiality "throughout the counseling process" and must "seek to identify foreseeable situations in which confidentiality must be breached." Marriage and family therapists are reminded that "circumstances may necessitate repeated disclosures" about the potential limits of confidentiality.[16]

It would be difficult to make an ethical case against keeping the patient accurately informed of changes in the level of risk as the therapy relationship progresses. Sometimes the therapist becomes aware that the patient did not fully understand the conversation at intake, or has forgotten its details, and this would be a signal for reopening the conversation about confidentiality and its limits. Other events that might create the need to reopen the conversation could be changes in circumstances, such as changes in the voluntary confidentiality limitations imposed in the therapist's setting, changes in laws that limit confidentiality, or changes in the patient's circumstances that might affect privacy or confidentiality.

Another obvious circumstance that could create the need to reopen the conversation would be the presence of impending legal proceedings that might affect the therapist's ability to protect the patient's confidences. For example, in many states, confidentiality risks are greatly increased if the patient becomes involved in a court case. This is true whether the patient is being charged with a crime, brings a civil suit against someone (e.g., seeks compensation for alleged injuries that include emotional distress), or becomes involved in a custody proceeding. To be adequately prepared to conduct conversations about confidentiality in such circumstances, therapists must already be informed about some important legal facts regarding such circumstances (see Chapter 7, "Responding Ethically to Legal Demands").

Complications in Obtaining Informed Consent About Confidentiality

The possible complications that can arise in this informed consent process are too numerous to mention, but the three below are among those that are important to think about and plan for in advance.

QUESTIONS OF PATIENT'S CAPACITY TO GIVE CONSENT

In the present context, "capacity" is a word used to describe a person's competence to give consent to enter therapy. Therapists' ethical standards usually include recommendations about minors or other patients who do not have the capacity to give consent to receive services. These reflect the fact that even those who have been declared legally incompetent to give consent still have certain rights, and therapists should at least seek their "assent" (agreement) to participate.

No ethics code provides guidance about exactly how to evaluate or determine a prospective patient's capacity to consent to therapy if no legal determination has been made. However, much has been written elsewhere about this dilemma. Some recommend that an adult patient be presumed competent unless there is evidence to the contrary: "All adults are deemed competent to grant consent unless they are found to be incompetent in a court proceeding. (Children are presumed to be incompetent to grant consent under the law.)."[17]

> Legal standards for decision-making capacity for consent to treatment vary somewhat across jurisdictions, but generally they embody the abilities to communicate a choice, to understand the relevant information, to appreciate the...consequences of the situation, and to reason about treatment choices...The presumption intrinsic to a modern democracy is that the vast majority of persons are capable of making their own decisions. Hence, only patients with impairment that places them at the very bottom of the performance curve should be considered to be incompetent.[18]

The professional literature includes some criteria that might be used if a formal competence screening seems necessary. For example, it has been suggested that the therapist should assess whether the person has (1) "a factual understanding of the situation, which includes relevant needs and alternatives," (2) "an appreciation of the seriousness of the condition and the consequences of accepting or rejecting treatment," (3) the willingness to "express a preference. (This preference does not have to be consistent with the clinician's preference, or with what she thinks would be in the patient's best interests)," and is (4) "capable of working with the information presented by the clinician in a rational fashion."[19] Therapists are encouraged to consult ethics texts and other professional resources, and to seek consultation, when making these determinations. (Also see Chapter 11 sections about minor patients and elderly patients.)

Psychologists working with minors or with adult patients who have been determined to be legally incapable of giving informed consent are ethically required to take the following protective steps:

> (1) Provide an appropriate explanation, (2) seek the individual's assent, (3) consider such persons' preferences and best interests, and (4) obtain appropriate permission from a legally authorized person, if such substitute consent is permitted or required by law. When consent by a legally authorized person is not permitted or required by law, psychologists take reasonable steps to protect the individual's rights and welfare. (APA, 2005, Standard 3.10d.)

Counselors have an ethical standard requiring that the following safeguards be observed with patients who are unable to give consent:

> When counseling minors or persons unable to give voluntary consent, counselors seek the assent of clients to services and include them in decision making as appropriate. Counselors recognize the need to balance the ethical rights of clients to make choices, their capacity to give consent or assent to receive services, and parental or familial legal rights and responsibilities to protect these clients and make decisions on their behalf. (ACA, 2005, Standard A.2.d.)

For social workers, the ethics code contains the following provisions for informed consent discussions:

> In instances when clients lack the capacity to provide informed consent, social workers should protect clients' interests by seeking permission from an appropriate third party, informing clients consistent with the clients' level of understanding. In such instances, social workers should seek to ensure that the third party acts in a manner consistent with clients' wishes and interests. Social workers should take reasonable steps to enhance such clients' ability to give informed consent. (NASW, 2008, Standard 1.03c.)

COMPLICATIONS CREATED BY CULTURAL OR LANGUAGE DIFFERENCES

The cultural background of patients may need to be considered, both when formulating policies about confidentiality and when conducting the informed consent conversations.[20] "Although there are many practice settings in which psychologists' commitment to confidentiality may not be significantly and often altered by cultural influences, it is obvious that there are cultural issues bound up in confidentiality... Culture plays a role in how we understand the construct of confidentiality and how we carry out our commitments."[21]

> When working with clients from a different cultural or ethnic background, the ethical and multiculturally aware clinician must make a conscious effort to understand the client's understanding and perception of confidentiality. How does the client view confidentiality in the therapeutic process? For instance, does the client want family members or the spouse to be involved in the therapeutic process? If so, how and to what extent?[22]

If the patient is expecting to involve family members, the therapist should clarify policies about this at the outset and should obtain written consent for any communications that are mutually agreed upon. (See Chapter 6, "Obtaining Truly Informed Consent Before Disclosing Confidential Information Voluntarily.")

Language differences can create issues of confidentiality if interpreters are required. Therapists sometimes report dilemmas such as the following: "I have many indigenous clients whom I serve through the use of a language interpreter. I suspect that she spreads gossip about the clients in the community and has no concept of confidentiality."[23] A therapist in this circumstance would be ethically responsible for explaining to the interpreter the importance of not disclosing to others the information that is discussed in the therapy relationship.[24] The seriousness of this policy can be emphasized by having the interpreter sign a confidentiality contract.[25] Interpreters who have ongoing involvement with therapy patients in the setting might be required to attend a staff training about confidentiality. (See Chapter 13, "Ethics-Based Staff Training About Confidentiality.")

COMPLICATIONS CREATED BY CLINICAL ISSUES

With patients who present in clinical crisis, or who are actively psychotic, it is not always possible to begin the relationship with the informed consent conversation. Except in the most extreme circumstances, however, therapists should at least attempt to explain in very simple terms about confidentiality and its exceptions, and then reopen that conversation as soon as the patient is in a condition that allows a better weighing of the options. In other words, therapists should "attempt to obtain the best possible version of informed consent in all cases, even when treating distressed patients."[26]

Therapist Resistance to Informing Patients About Limits of Confidentiality

When the Federal HIPAA regulations went into effect, they legally required therapists to give prospective patients a written "Notice of Privacy Practices." Many therapists reacted with horror, as if this imposed an inappropriate new requirement. But, in fact, the duty to inform clients in advance about the foreseeable limits of confidentiality had long been present in therapists' ethics codes and in the professional literature;[27] HIPAA simply added the requirement that this information be presented to patients in *writing* in a particular form. In other words, the old ethical duty was now backed up by a new federal legal duty.

Many therapists nevertheless still remain reluctant to begin a therapy relationship by fully informing prospective patients about all the conditions that might actually limit confidentiality. Some complain that it feels too much like beginning the relationship with a Miranda Warning. In one national survey, although 80.2% of psychologists said they considered it very important to inform prospective patients about the limits of confidentiality, only 59.5% said they ordinarily did so before therapy began, 10.9% said they would discuss it "only when the issue arises," and 2.2% said they rarely or never talked about it.[28] This means that many therapy patients are at risk of confiding very personal information without knowing that the therapist might later disclose it to someone else without their consent.

Even those therapists who do bring up the topic of confidentiality may fall short of truly informing prospective patients. They may provide perfunctory information, such as "I don't promise to keep it a secret if you tell me you are going to kill yourself or someone else," but that brief statement does not begin to describe the potential realities. At the other extreme, some therapists provide an overly complex "Notice of Privacy Practices" (perhaps copied from a colleague or from a HIPAA workshop) that lists even more confidentiality limitations than they actually intend to impose and that uses language too complicated to be understandable to most patients.

Sometimes therapists who do provide patients with a realistic and understandable explanation of confidentiality's limits fail to do so early enough. During that delay, still-uninformed patients may confide something that the therapist is then legally required to report without their consent. The intended function of the informed consent process is to protect patients from just such betrayals, but this protection is available only if the conversation happens before patients begin to confide sensitive information. "Psychiatrists may be understandably reluctant to begin a consultation with a discussion of the limitations of confidentiality. On the other hand, if the psychiatrist delays such a discussion for only a brief time he may learn damaging information about the patient that he will be required to disclose in a custody case, or other proceeding."[29]

Some therapists dutifully obtain the patient's signature on a consent form that accurately describes the limits of confidentiality, and do so early enough, but neglect to determine whether the patient understands what is being signed. As noted earlier, obtaining an uninformed patient's signature on a consent form does not qualify as obtaining informed consent.

Therapists offer numerous rationales for short-cutting or omitting the ethically required informed consent conversation about confidentiality. Sometimes these involve rationalizations that reflect a blatant disregard for the client's informed consent rights. For example, one study indicated that of those who sometimes neglected to tell prospective patients that confidentiality might be breached, 46.7% either considered the conversation "not relevant or necessary" or were deliberately "avoiding the negative impact" of explaining confidentiality's limits. Of those therapists who completely skipped the informed consent conversation about confidentiality, 13.3% did so because they believed the patient "already has knowledge of the issue" and 7.5% because they believed patients were "unable to understand."[30]

Some of these rationales ignore the fact that the limits of confidentiality can vary from clinician to clinician, and from setting to setting, making it impossible for any prospective patient to already have knowledge of the limits that a particular therapist will impose on confidentiality. For that reason, the initial conversation about it is essential, never irrelevant. Regarding the other rationalizations, it is true that the subject matter can be complex, but that fact does not absolve therapists of the ethical responsibility for trying to help patients understand it, first by providing the information in writing using reasonably understandable language, and then by explicitly providing patients with sufficient opportunity to ask questions and receive honest answers.

However, one objection to this conversation arises from reasonable clinical concerns: What does it mean to patients for a therapist to begin the relationship—or to later interrupt the clinical process—with a discussion of the fact that confidentiality will have limits? Do such conversations inhibit patient self-disclosure[31] and limit the therapeutic outcome;[32] or do they enhance impressions of therapist trustworthiness and expertness[33] and strengthen the therapeutic alliance?[34] The research yields mixed results; the real answer may be "all of the above." Clinical opinions also vary on whether a prospective therapy patient is likely to be capable of wisely weighing the risk–benefit ratio of confiding in a therapist.

What is important for therapists to understand is that, regardless of how well based their clinical concerns may be, ethically speaking, these are completely irrelevant! Prospective patients have a right to know in advance what limits a therapist intends to place on confidentiality, and therefore such conversations are ethically required, regardless of their clinical impact.

> Clinically speaking, it may be preferable to begin a relationship by listening, not by explaining that what is about to be said may not remain confidential. Ethically speaking, however, psychologists who place conditions on confidentiality are not free to treat discussion of this risk as irrelevant or unnecessary, no matter how clinically inconvenient.[35]

In other words, the only ethical way to avoid these conversations about confidentiality's limits is to place no limits at all upon confidentiality. This chapter is therefore optional reading only for those therapists who are brave enough to offer unconditional confidentiality and are willing to keep that promise—willing to protect their patients' confidences regardless of the consequences to themselves. For those who offer anything less, the advice in this chapter must apply.

Practice Pointers

The initial informed consent discussion about limits of confidentiality will not go well if the therapist is reluctant to begin or resentful about the conversation. "Viewing consent as an obligation and burden makes it hard to meet the needs of patients... A first step in remedying the situation is to recognize that informed consent is not a static ritual but a *useful* process."[36] Once therapists remember that the whole purpose of this conversation about the limits of confidentiality is to protect the patient's best interest, they are more comfortable conducting it, more explicit in its content, and more likely to ensure that patients understand.

Practicing aloud, alone or with others, can help therapists reach this posture, allowing them to be relaxed, clear, and honest in this initial conversation, providing patients with adequate information for making truly informed decisions. One helpful way to step out of a resistant posture is to place oneself in the shoes of the prospective patient, as suggested in Box 5.1. It is easier to plan and practice the informed consent conversation about confidentiality when imagining what one would want to hear from one's own therapist, in order to avoid a later sense of betrayal.

6

Step 3: Obtaining Truly Informed Consent Before Disclosing Confidential Information Voluntarily

> To the extent possible, psychologists should treat clients as autonomous individuals who typically have given up none of their human rights by virtue of becoming clients, and they should participate as fully as possible in … making decisions about sharing their health care information.
>
> VandeCreek (2008), "Considering confidentiality within broader theoretical frameworks," pp. 372–373

This chapter emphasizes the three concepts that are visible in its title. First, the word *"confidential"* is a reminder that every disclosure of patient information constitutes an exception to the rule of confidentiality. Therapists are often tempted (or urged by others) to create their own "personal exceptions" to the rule without mentioning that to patients. This chapter is therefore a reminder that, ethically speaking, confidentiality is still the rule. As illustrated in Figure 1.2, in the absence of a legal requirement to disclose, information about a patient should ordinarily remain confidential, and therapists should not disclose it without first obtaining the patient's consent, either as part of the informed consent process at intake (as described in the previous chapter) or in preparation for a patient-specific disclosure (as described in this chapter).

Second, the term *"voluntarily"* emphasizes the distinction between the disclosures described here in Step 3 (which therapists are legally free *not* to make and which patients can therefore prevent by withholding consent) and the "involuntary" disclosures that will be discussed later in Step 4 (which the therapist can be legally required to make even if the patient objects). Although these terms are not used in ethics codes, they reflect a very important ethical distinction.[1] Note that voluntary and involuntary disclosures of confidential information are so different, ethically speaking, that the Ethical Practice Model places them in different steps, and they are discussed here in separate chapters, as illustrated in Box 6.1.[2]

BOX 6.1 Taking the Patient's Perspective at Step 3

What is the relationship between the patient of this chapter and the patient of the previous and next chapters?

1. This patient (from whom you are about to obtain consent to voluntarily disclose specific information to someone else) already agreed, when consenting to enter therapy, to accept the risks posed by the limits that you intend to place on confidentiality for *all* patients.

   Per Step 2, this patient was informed at intake about the potential for legally coerced disclosures and about other disclosures routinely required in the setting or that you want to be free to later make voluntarily by policy (including access to records by staff, etc.). This patient, having been informed about these foreseeable general limits of confidentiality that apply to all patients, consented at intake to accept the risks of such disclosures as a condition of receiving therapy services.
2. This patient, during therapy and forever thereafter, retains the right to give (or to withhold) consent for any voluntary disclosure to others of confidential information about him or her. The disclosure now pending is a *patient-specific* disclosure that requires explicit consent beyond the general consent obtained from all patients at intake.

   Per this Step 3, the patient has the right to give (or to withhold) consent for any patient-specific disclosures made voluntarily. This right does not end when therapy ends. The consent given by the patient (or former patient) must be informed (meaning that the patient has been told what will be disclosed, who will receive it, and the foreseeable risks of disclosing it) and must be freely given (meaning the patient was free to withhold consent, thus preventing a pending voluntary disclosure, or to retract a previously given consent, thus preventing further voluntary disclosures to that recipient).
3. This patient, however, has no legal right to prevent you from disclosing confidential information if ordered by a judge or required by law to disclose "involuntarily."

   Per the next Step 4, however, this patient does have the legal right to contest the legal necessity for such disclosures (e.g., to file a motion requesting that the judge quash a subpoena when someone attempts to "discover" the patient's therapy records as evidence in a court case). Patients should therefore be notified if you receive a subpoena, even if it is received after the therapy relationship has terminated. Similarly, unless clinically contraindicated, patients can be informed about a mandated report before it is made. Note that, although laws limiting patient confidentiality create ethical dilemmas for therapists, the real problems they create are for patients. It is *their* secrets, shared with a therapist in confidence, that can become very public if disclosed in certain legal contexts. That is why informing the patient of such risks at intake does not absolve you of further ethical responsibility to protect confidentiality to the extent legally possible when legal demands arise.

Third, the term *"truly informed"* is a reminder that obtaining informed consent involves much more than obtaining a signature on a form. It is a process that involves providing the patient with enough information for making an informed decision. Ethics codes use modifiers to punctuate that concept: "*valid* informed consent" (social workers), "*appropriate* informed consent" (psychologists), "*truly* informed consent, and "*fully* informed consent (psychiatrists).[3] "Just because clients sign consent forms does not mean they understand the consequences of doing so. Our obligation is to teach clients about the broader principles that frame their requests for release of information."[4] In other words, to be valid, consent must be given from an informed posture. A therapist who withholds from the patient relevant information about what will be disclosed, or about the foreseeable implications of disclosing it or not disclosing it, is abridging the patient's right to make an autonomous decision, and thus is obtaining not *truly informed consent* but "coerced consent" or "uninformed consent."[5]

As discussed in the previous chapter, when the patient does not have the capacity to understand the information or to give consent, mental health professionals may obtain consent from another legally designated person. However, ethical responsibilities also include attempting to obtain assent from such patients, as well as protecting their rights and welfare. (Also see, in Chapter 11, a discussion of obtaining consent from minors or elderly patients.)

Underlying Concepts: The Right to Confidentiality, Informed Consent, and Autonomy

This chapter is a reminder that it is the patient who holds the right to confidentiality. Therefore, unless a disclosure is legally required, it is the patient—not the therapist—who has the right to decide whether to waive that right to confidentiality. Because the patient holds the right to confidentiality, the therapist has an obligation to protect that right by making no voluntary exceptions to confidentiality without obtaining the patient's consent. Step 3 therefore protects the informed patient's right to autonomy, which includes the right to give "informed refusal" rather than give informed consent for information to be disclosed.

Informed consent is the common thread that connects all of therapists' ethical obligations about confidentiality. Within the Ethical Practice Model, it is the ethical concept that connects Steps 2, 3, and 4. The previous chapter (Step 2) covered the process of obtaining informed consent about confidentiality before therapy ever begins: Prospective patients give their consent to accept the confidentiality limits that therapists inform them about in advance—limits that would apply to all patients alike. In contrast, this chapter (Step 3) covers the therapist's subsequent ethical obligation to obtain a patient's consent before voluntarily releasing confidential information in patient-specific circumstances. Finally, the next chapter (Step 4) will consider how the initial informed consent process can help protect the autonomy of patients if therapists later face disclosure requirements that are imposed by law.

These ethical obligations related to informed consent are discussed here in separate chapters. However, the practices described in these three chapters are so interrelated that neglecting the patient's informed consent rights in any one of these respects can leave the patient unprotected in other respects as well.

Ethical Standards

In the context of the metaphorical graphic in Figure 1.2 ("Ethical doors to disclosure"), this chapter is about opening Door 2. Unless the therapist already obtained consent for the expected disclosure at intake (thereby opening Door 1), he or she must obtain consent now for specific disclosures to specific others.

Ethics codes vary in exactly how they describe this requirement, or in how much detail they provide about the process. However, even if the patient gives consent for information to be disclosed, therapists have an ethical responsibility to limit the disclosure to the minimum amount of information necessary for achieving the specific purpose of the disclosure.[6]

Legal Considerations

Most states have nondisclosure laws and licensing board regulations that require patient consent for voluntary disclosures. It confuses matters that most states also have laws and regulations that legally allow therapists to disclose information for certain purposes without the patient's consent, and that the federal Health Insurance Portability and Accountability Act (HIPAA) regulations allow broad disclosures without patient authorization.

As discussed earlier, the fact that a state or federal law allows a particular disclosure does not make it ethically appropriate for therapists to disclose without obtaining the patient's consent. (See discussion of this issue in Chapter 2, in the section, "Laws Allowing Therapists to Disclose Without Patient Consent" and in Chapter 8, in the section "Abusing Legally Allowed Exceptions to Confidentiality.") If the therapist plans to disclose confidential information in certain legally allowed situations, consent can be obtained in advance at intake. Otherwise, it must be obtained and documented as described in this chapter.. Whether or not one's state law requires that therapists obtain this consent in writing, it is required by some ethics codes and highly recommended in ethics texts and the professional literature.

Practical Considerations and Recommendations

Ethics codes contain no details about how to obtain the patient's consent for voluntary patient-specific disclosures. The following recommendations are therefore drawn from ethics texts and other professional literature. In general, the process includes (1) clarifying exactly what will be disclosed, (2) discussing the implications of disclosing (or not disclosing) it, (3) specifying the date when the consent will expire, and (4) documenting those understandings by obtaining the consent in writing on a "Consent for Release of Information" form.

Although the informed consent *process* in Step 3 parallels the process in Step 2, because the *context* differs, the *content* will also differ. At intake, the patient gave consent to accept the limits of confidentiality that would apply to all patients. Here, the consent involves potential disclosures that are specific to this individual patient (e.g., providing information to another professional or to a family member, agency, third-party payer, etc.).

CLARIFYING EXACTLY WHAT WILL BE DISCLOSED

Clients who give consent for a therapist to disclose information or records may not be aware of the contents of their records and may assume that only positive information will be shared. Therefore, principles of confidentiality and client autonomy suggest that providers need to fully inform their clients about the nature of the information that will be released. The most complete way to fully inform clients is to share the record (or the information to be disclosed) with the client before sending it on. Only then is the client fully informed.[7]

For example, when patients request that the therapist send copies of their records to another provider, they have a right to be informed about the content of those records before they give consent for them to be shared. "This need and this right are included in the meaning of *informed* in the term *informed consent,* and are based on respect for client autonomy and for people's rights and dignity."[8] Sometimes, after seeing the information contained in a clinical record, psychological report, or treatment plan, patients exercise their right to withhold consent for the therapist to disclose it. Through this process, patients can "gain an enhanced perspective on their rights to keep personal information confidential."[9]

DISCUSSING THE IMPLICATIONS OF DISCLOSING (OR NOT DISCLOSING) THE INFORMATION

Patients often sign a consent form without understanding the consequences of the potential disclosure. They can make autonomous, informed decisions about whether to disclose the information only if the therapist helps them consider both the advantages and disadvantages of disclosing it.

This discussion is especially important if the therapist believes that a particular disclosure may potentially have negative consequences (such as those described below and in Step 5), or if the therapist believes that failure to disclose may have negative consequences. Following this discussion, patients are free to decide not to give consent for the information to be disclosed if they recognize that disclosing it might not serve them in the way they had hoped.

CLARIFYING THE DURATION OF THE CONSENT

Placing an expiration date on the consent form limits the time during which the consent to release that particular information remains active. It is recommended that the date not extend more than 1 or 2 years beyond the date of signing. This means that the therapist does not have indefinite permission to disclose the information. If the patient so chooses, the consent can be renewed.

DOCUMENTING THE UNDERSTANDINGS ON A WRITTEN CONSENT FORM

The patient's informed consent for a specific disclosure should be documented in writing, with a signature on a consent form. This is highly recommended for all mental health professionals, whether or not it is ethically required by their profession.[10] "A common cause of needless problems is failing to obtain written informed consent to release confidential information... Obtaining written consent can help promote clarity of communication between therapist and patient in situations when misunderstandings can be disastrous."[11] In addition to such recommendations in the professional literature, written consent is also recommended by malpractice insurers to avoid unnecessary misunderstandings about what information will be released, thereby avoiding later complaints from patients.[12]

A standard "Release of Information" form usually contains, at the least, a description of the type of information to be disclosed, to whom it will be disclosed and for what purpose(s), and an indication of when the consent will expire. Finally, there is a signature line with a date, for documenting when and by whom the form was signed giving consent for the specific information to be disclosed to someone else.

Therapists vary in their preference about whether to use a one-way or two-way release form. With a *two-way form*, the patient gives consent for information to be exchanged between two entities (e.g., allowing the therapist and prescribing physician to have ongoing contact for the purpose of monitoring medication issues). In contrast, there are some circumstances in which it is more appropriate for the patient to sign a *one-way consent form* (e.g., allowing a former therapist to provide information about previous treatment, but without giving consent for the current therapist to share any information with the former therapist). To avoid confusion about the intent of the consent, some therapists choose to use only one-way consent forms, thereby ensuring that the patient is aware of exactly what will be disclosed by whom.

One potential source of misunderstanding arises if the therapist fails to be specific about exactly what will be disclosed. To ensure clarity, before obtaining the patient's consent, the therapist can determine whether there are certain things the patient does not want disclosed to this particular individual. For example, patients can collaborate with their therapists in deciding whether to disclose certain aspects of their history if it is not directly relevant to the purpose of the disclosure.

Patients have the right to revise or rescind a consent they have previously given. However, this would affect only future disclosures; it could not retroactively "undo" disclosures that were already made based on the previous consent.

RESPONDING TO SIGNED CONSENT FORMS OBTAINED BY OTHERS

The fact that someone else has obtained the patient's signature on a "Consent for Release of Information" form does not mean that the patient has been informed about exactly what information will be disclosed. In fact, if the consent is for the release of an entire treatment record, the therapist who created the record is the only person in a position to inform the patient about exactly what content is being disclosed. This means that a signature obtained by someone else likely represents not truly informed consent but "*un*informed consent." It is therefore important, when responding to consent forms obtained by others, to discuss with the patient (or former patient) exactly what information would be involved, as well foreseeable implications of disclosing or not disclosing it.

PREVENTING REDISCLOSURE

Once information leaves the therapist's possession, both therapist and patient lose control over its redisclosure. In some cases, information is released to someone who has the legal right to redisclose it (see discussion in Chapter 7), but ordinarily this is not the case. Therapists can try to reduce the likelihood that the recipient of patient information will disclose it further without the patient's specific consent. First, all information released to a third party can contain a notice that it is "Confidential—Not To Be Re-Released Without Patient Consent." Second, in states that have statutes legally prohibiting re-release, the notice can include the relevant statute number: "Re-release of this information without the patient's explicit consent is legally prohibited by state statute #_________."

Another redisclosure issue involves information the therapist has obtained from other sources. The therapist should respect the patient's right to give or refuse consent for the voluntary redisclosure of such information. Some therapists refuse to voluntarily redisclose information obtained from others, even if the patient gives consent, instead requiring the patient to request that information from the holder of the original document.

Special Considerations With Disclosures to Third-Party Payers

The fact that a third party will be paying for the therapy services does not give the therapist any ethical basis for shortcutting (much less omitting) the process of obtaining the patient's fully informed consent before releasing information to that payer. Although HIPAA allows therapists to treat disclosures to third-party payers as if they were exceptions to the rule of confidentiality, we take the position that these are voluntary disclosures, that patient consent is therefore required, and that all of the above considerations will apply.

There are many different variations on third-party payment. The third-party payer may be a formal payment entity (e.g., insurance company, managed care organization), an agency (e.g., social services agency, court), or a family member (e.g., parent of a young adult college student). Before reviewing some special considerations with each of these types of payers, note that the following guidelines would apply to all third-party payment situations.

At intake: Clarify who will pay. If all or part of the payment will be by a third party, inform the patient of any prior roles or contracts that might create conflicts of interest or otherwise raise concerns about this particular payer. Include discussion of the type of information that will be provided on billing forms, and whether the third party requires additional information or treatment reports as a condition of payment. (See Chapter 5 for discussion of this issue at intake, Chapter 7 about access to records, and Chapter 8 about preventing disclosures to third-party payers with inadequate informed consent.) As noted earlier, patients are often very naïve about the risks of sharing their information. Therapists can play a helpful role in teaching them about this before therapy begins, to help patients make an informed and autonomous decision about seeking third-party payment.[13]

At time of disclosure: If the "payer" requires information about the patient or about the treatment as a condition of providing reimbursement, then, before disclosing that information, the therapist should discuss with the patient (1) the nature, scope, and content of the planned disclosure, and (2) the implications of disclosing it to that particular third party.

DISCLOSURES TO INSURANCE COMPANIES AND MANAGED CARE ENTITIES

Confusion about whether disclosures to insurance companies and managed care entities are "voluntary" can arise from fact that, from the therapist's point of view, these disclosures can feel coerced—"financially coerced." But patients are free not to use their benefits, and the therapist is free not to sign provider contracts. From this point of view, therapists' disclosures of treatment plans and other information is voluntary.

Actually, managed care plans do create "special cases" about confidentiality, but in only one respect: *They place confidentiality at risk*. They require disclosure of more information and more frequently, providers must sign contracts that give the payer access to treatment records on demand for case review or for audit purposes, and some information may be re-released to employers or others as stipulated in their purchase contracts. Therapists routinely fax confidential patient information into open offices where they have no way of knowing who may eventually see it; and, once received, it is unclear how the security of these volumes of patient information will be maintained. During therapy and forever thereafter, information collected by third-party payers may be re-released to national data banks to join information from other health care providers, whence it may again be re-re-released based solely on the patient's signature on a new application for health or life insurance.

This does not absolve therapists from responsibility or potential liability. Quite the contrary. It increases the importance of informing managed care patients in advance about the possible risks and about exactly what information they are about to supply.

> Client confidentiality appears severely compromised under managed care. To receive mental health services covered by managed care insurance, the client must sign an agreement to release his or her mental health records. This gives the managed care company information about the legitimacy of what it is paying for, but this also means that the therapist's claim to client confidentiality is dissolved.[14]

Of all the disclosures that therapists ever make, including those in courtrooms, the information therapists provide for the purpose of obtaining third-party reimbursement may be the most likely to follow patients for the rest of their life. This makes it especially important not to short-change the informed consent process in this circumstance.

> When clients request that their information be shared with an insurance company for reimbursement, psychologists can inform clients that information on insurance forms usually does not stop at the desk of the claims manager. In fact, the information likely is further shared with national data banks where the information can be accessed by other insurance companies when the client elects to purchase another insurance product or a large home mortgage. Psychologists can play a helpful role in teaching clients about the risks of sharing their health information, and this information should be shared with them at the beginning of service.[15]

The Patients' Bill of Rights (1997), endorsed by 10 national professional associations, gives emphasis to the patient's right to be fully informed: "Individuals have the right to be informed by the treating professional of any arrangements, restrictions, and/or covenants established between third party payer and the treating professional that could interfere with or influence treatment recommendations. Individuals have the right to be informed of the nature of information that may be disclosed for the purposes of paying benefits."[16]

Those concerned with patient welfare, as well as those concerned about therapists' ethical and/or legal liability, express concern about the implications of shortcutting or omitting this informed consent process.

> Under the auspices of managed care, both the spirit and the letter of social work guidelines relating to confidentiality and informed consent are broken

> regularly. What the social worker may want to give the managed care company—a molehill of sufficient detail about the client—too often develops into a mountain of intimate detail on computer files, the access to which is outside of the worker's control... Informed consent is a time bomb ticking away for social workers and other mental health professionals."[17]

Finally, the patient has the right to revoke a consent; but, in reality, many of the usual guidelines break down within the managed care process. In part, this is because of frequent changes of entities, as when companies merge or the patient's employer changes third-party payer plans. But the problems are further exacerbated by the electronic storage and transmission of information.

> With managed care systems, the reality is often that the name of the individual or organization receiving the disclosure may change without notice, the information to be disclosed may consist of a verbatim account of the client's most sensitive information given to persuade a gatekeeper to continue to authorize services, and the statement about the client's being able to revoke consent at any time is an illusory proposition given the virtual irretrievability of electronic transmissions of data that are stored in various locations.[18]

DISCLOSURES TO FAMILY MEMBERS AS THIRD-PARTY PAYERS

It is not unusual for a family member to take responsibility for payment if the therapy patient is a minor, college student, or elderly parent. The fact that a family member is paying for someone's therapy does not, in itself, give them any right to receive any information from the therapist without the patient's explicit consent. If the therapist fails to clarify this with all parties in advance, there can be misunderstandings and complications that could later threaten to disrupt the clinical process. If the payer will receive billing statements, the therapist should inform the adult patient about exactly what information will be provided there (e.g., diagnoses, failed sessions, etc.) and obtain written consent to provide it. When the patient is a competent adult (e.g., college student), many complications can be avoided if the billing statement is sent only to the patient, who then has responsibility for obtaining reimbursement from the family member. When this arrangement is appropriate, the therapist need have no direct contact with the payer. When the patient is a minor, state laws vary as to the minor's right to give or refuse consent for disclosure. (See the Chapter 11 section on "Minors in Therapy.")

DISCLOSURES TO AGENCIES AS THIRD-PARTY PAYERS

Therapy services are sometimes paid for by agencies such as Social Services or some section of Court Services. It is recommended that, in such cases, the therapist obtain, in advance, a written contract with the agency that not only clarifies the services that will be provided but also stipulates the understandings about exchange of information. Unless such understandings are made clear to all parties in advance, the payer may later demand more information than the patient expected them to obtain, such as progress reports and diagnoses. (See, in Chapter 8, the section, "Disclosures to Third-Party Payers Without Fully Informed Consent.")

Informed Consent for Disclosures in Professional Presentations, Teaching, or Writing

The discussion above has been about obtaining informed consent before disclosing identifiable information about the patient. When therapists use clinical material in professional presentations, teaching, or clinical writing, they do not ordinarily identify the patient. However, the use of clinical information can nevertheless have important ethical, clinical, and practical implications that must be weighed when making decisions about using patient material in these contexts, even with the patient's consent.

Therapists of all professions are ethically free to use clinical material in writing or in didactic presentations if they have either obtained informed consent from the patient or have taken reasonable steps to disguise the information.[19] However, the fact that this is ethically allowed does not mean it would always be clinically appropriate.

When it comes to clinical and professional recommendations about using patient information in these contexts, there is no unanimity. Some advise that therapists always obtain informed consent from patients before presenting clinical information about them;[20] others suggest that clinicians should be cautious when deciding to obtain informed consent for presenting clinical material in their writing and should consider disguising the material instead.[21] Still others recommend that clinicians and researchers do both—obtain patient consent to use the material *and* carefully disguise it;[22] but others suggest that patients can have strong reactions to knowing that their clinical material was disguised.[23]

Some object to ever disguising clinical material and suggest instead that, if a detail about a patient might be identifiable, it should simply be left out, on the principle that "it is far better to omit a detail than to falsify a detail."[24] Others describe risks that can arise even if the information is disguised:

> First, how should one disguise a case? Moreover, how should one assess whether the disguise is sufficient to preserve confidentiality while not distorting the clinical material to the point that the material is no longer useful to the field? Second, how can we estimate the likelihood of clients reading clinical writing, particularly in the age of the Internet? ... Third, how does the presentation of clinical material influence public perceptions of psychotherapy and confidentiality? If these public perceptions, in turn, could influence the likelihood of seeking psychotherapy, might these attitudes be important to consider in ethical thinking about clinical writing?[25]

The potential for patient harm must always be considered when deciding whether to obtain consent to use patient material in written or oral clinical presentations:

> If the risk of asking a client for permission to use his or her clinical information in professional writing or presentation is assessed as too risky due to the client's vulnerability or dependence on the psychotherapist, if the psychotherapist is aware that the didactic use of client information may be harmful to the client over time even if the client freely consents to it, and if the psychotherapist is aware that seeking the client's consent to use his or her clinical information in this way could jeopardize the therapeutic alliance and relationship, it would be best to seek out alternatives to the use of client information in one's writing or presentations . . . . [I]t is always best to consider all available options and alternatives before making one's decision.[26]

Some professional journals impose specific requirements on authors who use clinical material in their articles. For example, one American Psychological Association (APA) journal now requires as follows: "When clinical case material is reported, Authors are required to state in writing which criteria they have used to comply with the ethics code (i.e., specific informed consent, de-identification, or disguise), and if de-identification or disguise is used, how and where it has been applied."[27]

When deciding whether to obtain the patient's informed consent for such uses of information, therapists might consider using the following checklist:[28]

1. Does the patient have sufficient ego strength to engage in a thorough informed consent process about information that might be included in clinical writing?
2. Might engaging in the clinical writing informed consent process reinforce dysfunctional patient behaviors?
3. Is there sufficient time and space in the course of therapy to devote to the clinical writing informed consent process?
4. Does engaging in an informed consent process about clinical writing run counter to your theoretical orientation?
5. Are you confident that you can use patient disguise or case composite in compliance with the policies of the journal in which you wish to publish, with relevant ethical standards, with HIPAA, and with state or federal laws?
6. Are you confident that you can effectively disguise the patient's identity while also maintaining the clinical validity of the case?

Informed Consent for Disclosures During Supervision or Consultation

Supervision and consultation are two quite different types of relationships. Although their activities do overlap, they raise different informed consent responsibilities. It is important to note, however, that both supervisors and consultants have an ethical obligation to maintain the confidentiality of the patient information they receive in those relationships.

The term "clinical supervision" is used here to mean a relationship between a trainee and an experienced clinician in a context in which the supervisee would not be qualified to provide services without that supervised relationship. The supervisor is ordinarily ethically and legally responsible for the trainee's work, and therefore needs to have access to all information about the patient, in order to be able to contact the patient or be available in clinical crises if necessary. Consent is obtained at intake, when the prospective patient is informed that the therapist is in supervision, and that the limits of confidentiality will include supervisor access to all information.[29]

The term "clinical consultation" is used to describe relationships with colleagues or other clinicians in which a therapist discusses clinical cases or raises clinical issues. Unlike supervision, consultation can be a peer relationship because (1) the consultee is qualified to practice without this relationship and has no obligation to follow the advice of the consultant, and (2) the consultant has no responsibility for the consultee's clinical work, so therefore has no need for obtaining identifiable information about the patient. Ordinarily, no identifiable patient information need be disclosed in a consultation relationship; however, in the initial informed consent conversation, many therapists inform prospective patients that they may obtain consultation in order to ensure quality of services, stipulating that they will provide consultant name(s) if requested. If the patient will be identified, or if hiding or disguising the patient's identity is not likely to be successful, the consultee should obtain the informed patient's consent.[30]

Practice Pointers

Whole chapters in ethics texts are devoted to discussion of the confidentiality rule and of the necessity of obtaining the patient's informed consent before disclosing confidential information voluntarily. Therapists can obtain there more details about some of the considerations described here.

But, reduced to its simplest description, the desired end is easy to understand. Here, we state it from the patient-protective supererogatory position that is advocated throughout this book:

> An *informed* patient voluntarily gives—or may exercise the right to withhold—*consent* for information about him or her to be voluntarily disclosed to someone else. Without that consent, a therapist ordinarily has no ethical basis for voluntarily disclosing any identifiable information about that patient unless legally compelled. *This consent can be obtained at intake or any time thereafter.*

7

Step 4: Responding Ethically to Legal Demands for "Involuntary" Disclosure of Patient Information

> It is crucial to realize that ethical behavior is more than simply avoiding violation of legal standards, and that one's ethical and legal duties may, in certain instances, be in conflict... Ethical awareness requires clearly distinguishing the two, and alertness to when they stand in conflict.
>
> Pope & Vasquez (2011), *Ethics in Psychotherapy and Counseling*, p. xiii

The previous chapter was about disclosures of confidential information that a therapist makes voluntarily. This chapter is about a very different matter: disclosures that are legally coerced. These two circumstances create very different ethical obligations for therapists, because the implications for patients can be very different indeed. Before making the voluntary disclosures discussed in the previous chapter, therapists are always ethically required to obtain the patient's explicit consent. In contrast, therapists may be legally required to make the disclosures discussed in this chapter even if the patient objects.

Definitions

It is very important to understand the ethical difference between voluntary disclosures and legally required or "involuntary "disclosures. Therapists who fail to recognize this distinction can place patients—and thereby also themselves—at risk.

Richard Redding, J.D., Ph.D., whose expertise combines mental health and law, served as the legal advisor for this chapter and reviewed the legal content for other sections of this book. He currently serves as Vice Chancellor for Graduate Education at Chapman University in Orange, California, where he is a Professor of Law and Psychology.

The differences between the two, discussed in detail in Chapter 3, are summarized briefly below.

For a disclosure of confidential information to be considered "voluntary," the patient must be free to withhold consent and the therapist must be legally free not to disclose. The patient's consent can be obtained in either of two ways: An informed patient can give consent at intake to accept the general limits on confidentiality that must be accepted by all patients as a condition of receiving services (see Chapter 5), or the patient can consent at any time to allow release of specific information to a specific person for a specific purpose (see Chapter 6). If the patient withholds consent in either or both of these contexts, and the disclosure is not legally required, the perspective represented in this book is that the therapist has no ethical basis for disclosing the information voluntarily.

In contrast, a disclosure can be considered "involuntary" if it is legally required and for that reason might sometimes need to be made even if the patient gives no consent and the therapist wishes not to disclose. Sometimes, a therapist might be willing to disclose confidential information in response to a particular legal demand (e.g., chooses to obey a reporting law), but it is nevertheless technically made "involuntarily" by the fact that the therapist is not legally free to do otherwise.

The ethical problems raised by these disclosures are compounded by the fact that they may be unlimited in scope (as when complying with court orders for release of a complete patient record), may publicly expose a patient's private history or current problems (as in legally coerced courtroom testimony), and may give sensitive information to someone who intends to use it to harm the patient (as when someone uses treatment information as evidence against a patient in a court case). To make such a disclosure against a patient's wishes would be deemed highly unethical if it were not legally required.

Sometimes, a patient, after being fully informed about the implications, chooses to give explicit consent for the legally demanded information to be disclosed, and, at that point, the disclosure would no longer be considered "involuntary." Ethically speaking, the patient's consent makes the disclosure "voluntary," so the ethical practices about voluntary disclosures (as described in Chapter 6) would then apply; and because the informed patient gave consent for the disclosure, the therapist would not be ethically obligated to contest the legal demand. However, the legal preparations in Chapter 1 and the legal details in this chapter would still be important since the therapist must be prepared to inform the patient about those details before obtaining consent to make the disclosure.

Limiting Disclosure to the Extent Legally Possible

This chapter, beneath its discussion of legal details, contains a recurring ethical refrain: *A therapist's ethical responsibilities do not end where the law begins.* That is because patients have certain rights about confidentiality that can be protected even when confidences are not legally protectable. As emphasized in Part I, one of the consequences of "conditional confidentiality" is that protecting the confidentiality rights of today's therapy patients requires the combined four-step approach described in these first four chapters of Part II.

This means that, within the Ethical Practice Model, Step 4 does not stand alone, but instead operates in conjunction with the previous three steps:

Step 1: Learn the relevant laws, obtain consultation as needed, anticipate and prepare for legal demands. This is the only way therapists can avoid being taken by surprise by legal demands and responding in an manner that is unethical or that fails to protect the patient's rights.

Step 2: Inform prospective patients about potential disclosure risks, including legally imposed limits of confidentiality. This gives informed patients their first (and sometimes their only) means of protecting themselves, which they can do either by giving "informed refusal" to receive services, or by limiting what they say to the therapist if they so choose.

Step 3: Obtain the informed patient's consent before disclosing information voluntarily. When it is legally possible for the therapist *not* to disclose, this allows patients to withhold consent for disclosure if they so choose.

Step 4: Respond ethically to legal demands for "involuntary" disclosure of information. When therapists are required by law to disclose, but the patient does not give consent, therapists can protect confidences at least to the extent allowed by law. This is a supererogatory ethical posture in the sense that it provides patients with more protection than most ethics codes require. An example of supererogatory actions in response to legal demands for disclosure would include contesting the demand by citing arguments that others have made successfully in behalf of maintaining confidentiality (such as those noted in Chapter 1, in the section on "Underlying Principles"), as well as citing laws and legal cases that underline the importance of protecting patient confidentiality.

ETHICAL CONTEXT

The ethical mandate to protect confidentiality does not require therapists to disobey the law in order to protect patient confidences. Instead, ethics codes contain an exception to the confidentiality rule that ethically allows therapists to breach confidentiality when legally required, even if the patient objects.[1] But this is not to be done lightly. Ethics codes do require therapists to take certain actions in response to laws that conflict with their profession's ethical standards. (See a detailed discussion in the Chapter 1 section on "Ethical Standards About Conflicts Between Ethical Duties and Other Duties.")

Therapists who wish to protect confidentiality as well as possible—beyond the "ethical floor" reflected in their ethics code—have the option of disobeying the law in order to protect patients' confidences:

> At times the laws under which psychologists function may appear to contradict generally recognized ethical values and/or good clinical care. When these circumstances arise, psychologists must determine if a conflict really exists and, if so, seek solutions that reconcile respect for the law with their ethical values. At times, psychologists may decide to follow the law despite their ethical concerns. At other times, they may determine that a conscientious objection is warranted.[2]

However, of all the actions that might qualify as "reaching for the ethical ceiling" about confidentiality, civil disobedience is the most radical.[3]

> When psychologists are considering disobeying a law, we recommend that they … (a) seek consultation to ensure that the law requires them to do what they believe it requires, (b) make certain that they understand their ethical obligations clearly, (c) consider alternatives that would allow them to follow the law while still upholding their values, and (d) contemplate violating a law only if no viable alternative is available… We suggest careful practical wisdom or deliberation when such decisions are made.[4]

Understandably, few therapists choose to incur the potential risks of engaging in unlawful behavior in order to protect a patient's confidentiality, but we applaud those who stand their ground in this way in spite of the potential consequences. When therapists hold fast to that position, it can sometimes lead to the creation of more protective confidentiality laws, as in the 1997 U. S. Supreme Court *Jaffee v. Redmond* case.[5] But civil disobedience can have severe consequences—personal, financial, and legal—so that such a step should be taken only with very careful consideration and consultation. For example, in 1992, a researcher spent 5 months in jail for contempt of court because he refused to obey a judge's order to disclose information about his research participants.[6]

Like therapists' ethics codes, the following discussion stops short of advocating civil disobedience. Instead, it leaves room for therapists to breach confidentiality when they have no legal alternative. Otherwise, therapists in many states would frequently be required to engage in civil disobedience. But therapists who are faced with a legal demand can take a supererogatory position by focusing not on obeying the law, but instead on maintaining an ethical position of protecting patients' confidentiality rights at least to the extent their laws allow. Although this does not require disobeying the law, it does require a willingness to take all the protective steps that are legally available.

LEGAL CONSIDERATIONS

Each type of law that requires disclosure may allow a different type of response. Before dealing with the specifics, however, it can be helpful to understand some general legal information and to clarify the types of laws that therapists might encounter.

First, this chapter deals only with laws that can legally require therapists to disclose. Laws that merely *allow* therapists to disclose confidential patient information will raise very different ethical implications, because they do not create a real ethical-legal conflict. Since these laws do not *require* therapists to do anything—do not legally coerce a disclosure—therapists who release information in response to these laws will be taking a *voluntary* action. This raises important informed consent issues, which is why such laws are discussed in Chapters 6 and 8, instead of here.[7]

Second, although the same federal laws and regulations apply nationwide, state laws vary widely. The legal categories used in this chapter would apply to the laws of any state, but the specific legal details—as well as the options for response—will differ from state to state. Therefore, although therapists can use these categories for clarifying the implications of their state laws, they might need legal advice when clarifying the specific legal options available in their own state when determining their options for responding ethically. For reference, Appendix III gives examples of each type of law described below.

Third, this chapter should be read in close connection with Chapter 4, "Preparation." Once faced with a legal demand, therapists often do not have sufficient time to consider the options, deliberate about the possibilities, and prepare to respond. Therapists who have learned in advance about the legal means available for protecting patients' confidences in their state, and who have obtained ethical and legal consultation in advance, will be much less likely to be taken by surprise by a legal demand and therefore less likely to respond in an unprotective manner.

The Role of Informed Consent in Responding to Legal Demands

Ethically speaking, a patient's right to give or to withhold consent for release of information is considered important enough that the mental health professions require therapists to go to great lengths to protect it. As long as the therapist remains legally free *not* to disclose information, it is relatively easy to protect the patient's right to withhold consent—easy to protect the patient's right to "have the last word" about whether or not secrets leave the therapy room. But how does the concept of informed consent apply to those situations in which therapists have no legal choice about whether to disclose?

In fact, informed consent is the ethical thread that connects all of the practices related to the protection of confidentiality rights. For the therapist, informed consent conversations can seem somewhat "inconvenient." It can be ethically challenging to be prepared to accurately and fully inform the patient at each of the steps along the way, and it can be clinically challenging to do this effectively within the context of the treatment relationship. For this reason, the informed consent conversation at intake is too often conducted in a perfunctory or otherwise inadequate manner. However, if the therapist has failed to conduct this conversation at the onset of the relationship, and has failed to obtain the informed patient's consent to accept the legal limits of confidentiality as a condition of receiving services, disclosures in response to any of the laws described below may understandably be experienced by the patient as a betrayal that could damage or end the clinical relationship.

From the patient's point of view, these informed consent conversations are the front-line safeguards of their confidentiality rights. When confidences are not legally protectable, it is only through the initial informed consent process that two of patients' confidentiality rights can be protected—their right to be informed about those limits in advance and their right to accept or reject services on that basis. This gives patients the opportunity to protect *themselves* from laws that require therapists to disclose information. Furthermore, a well-informed patient can be prepared to participate in the actions that might be required for responding protectively to legal demands if they do arise. In other words, unless the therapist intends to promise unconditional confidentiality—and intends to keep that promise by disobeying all disclosure laws—then these informed consent conversations form the cornerstone of the ethics of conditional confidentiality.

Responding Ethically to Specific Legal Demands

Prepared therapists develop a plan for responding to legal demands. This preparation is outlined in Chapter 4. Here, we describe some of the details that therapists must consider when making such plans and carrying them out. Ethically, therapists of each profession have slightly different formal obligations when faced with laws that demand disclosure of confidential information. The options described below would ordinarily be appropriate for any therapist, but therapists should also be very familiar with exactly what their own ethics code requires. (See, in Chapter 1, the section on "Ethical Standards About Conflicts Between Ethical Duties and Other Obligations.")

Legally, therapists must take responsibility for inserting into the six-step Ethical Practice Model the specifics of the laws in their own state.[8] The categories below are discussed in general terms, but these or other categories can be used by therapists to organize and study each of their own state's laws. Many laws that limit confidentiality will contain specific legal options that can be used when devising a realistic plan of ethical response. Every state also has laws that protect confidentiality rather than limiting it, and it can be important to cite them when trying to devise ethical responses to laws that do require disclosure. (See Chapter 2, "Laws Protecting Confidentiality.")

Each type of law described below requires different preparation in Step 1 and requires a different ethical response here, in Step 4. Below, we give examples of how therapists might prepare to respond ethically to these legal demands. The same five questions are asked about each type of law:

- What does this type of law require therapists to do?
- What is the potential impact of such laws on therapy patients?

- What ethical concerns do such laws raise for therapists?
- What legal options are available for responding in the most ethical manner?
- What are the possible risks or penalties for disobeying this type of law?

This sequence is important. The first task is to understand what each law requires a therapist to do, not in order to immediately *do* it, but in order to understand its potential impact on patients. If the therapist obeys this particular law without attempting to protect patient information, how might that affect the patient who wants the information protected? This focus on patient impact allows the therapist to clarify the *ethical* issues created by that law. With the ethical issues clear, the therapist can concentrate on how to carry out the legally possible actions in the most ethically appropriate manner. To reverse the sequence and focus first on the legal options might result in neglecting to focus on the ethical implications of choosing those particular legal options.

LAWS REQUIRING THERAPISTS TO INITIATE A BREACH OF CONFIDENTIALITY

This type of law includes mandated reporting laws, duty-to-warn laws, and sometimes duty-to-protect laws. They are discussed here separately because the legal requirements (and therefore the ethical implications) can be very different.

Mandated Reporting Laws

State laws can require therapists to initiate reports of such things as abuse of a child, abuse of an elderly or disabled adult, unprofessional conduct by another licensed mental health professional, or the fact that a health care professional is a mental health patient whose condition might impair his or her ability to practice safely. In some states, certain mental health professionals are legally required to report patients' conditions or diseases that might impair their driving or otherwise place the public at risk. Some states also require therapists to report certain types of domestic violence.

- *What does this type of law require therapists to do?* Requirements vary widely from state to state. In many states, reports of child abuse are required only if the victim is still a minor, but this is not true in all states. In many states, reports of misconduct or impairment on the part of another mental health professional are legally required only if the professional is licensed by the same licensing board as the reporting therapist, thus making therapists peer monitors only for their own professions. Many mandated reporting statutes contain provisions that can require therapists to provide complete patient records if so requested by the agency receiving such reports.
- *What is the potential impact of such laws on therapy patients?* If the therapist is reporting information that was learned from a patient, the reporting will involve a breach of confidentiality unless the patient has given consent

for the therapist to make the report. Reports can also put the patient at risk for having his or her confidences later sought as evidence in a court case or disciplinary hearing related to the report (e.g., a subpoena of treatment records and/or therapist testimony). Beyond this, the impact of reporting can vary greatly, depending on such things as the nature of the relationship between the patient and the person the report is about, the extent to which the patient must be identified in the report, and the extent to which confidences shared in therapy become public (as in high-profile abuse cases). Impact on the therapy relationship will be lessened if the therapist has clearly advised the patient in advance about this potential limit of confidentiality.

- *What ethical concerns do such laws raise for therapists?* The existence of such laws makes it ethically important for therapists to inform prospective patients about the risk of such disclosures before the patient begins to talk about things that might be reportable (see Chapter 5). In addition to this informed consent requirement, the ethical issues may depend partly on the nature of the disclosure required. For example, in the case of peer misconduct, most ethics codes recommend that the therapist first confront the colleague and try to resolve the problem informally; and, for some professions, therapists have no ethical duty to confront or report if this would require them to breach patient confidentiality.[9] However, some state laws require therapists to make a formal report even if this involves a breach of confidentiality, and, in those states, there is no easy way to avoid this ethical-legal dilemma.
- *What legal options are available for responding in the most ethical manner?* It is important to be clear about exactly what must be reported and to whom. One way to prevent ethically inappropriate disclosures is to begin by making a "hypothetical" report, protecting the patient's identity while determining whether a report is actually legally required in the situation. If no report is required, no confidential information has been disclosed. Ethically, unless the patient has given consent for broader disclosure, it is important to include in the report only what is legally required and only information germane to that purpose.

Some reporting laws absolve the therapist from reporting if they know that a report has already been made by someone else, so therapists should clarify whether this option is legally available for any of the reporting laws in their own state. When available, this offers the option of having the patient make the report instead of the therapist, thereby protecting the therapy relationship. The therapist can coach the patient through the reporting process, perhaps by having the patient make the report in the presence of the therapist. (This not only informs the therapist that the report was indeed made, but also gives the therapist immediate information about the client's reaction to having made the report.) Therapists can seek consultation in advance, while determining their own position about how to respond to this legal requirement, and they can seek support for carrying out their plan if the situation does arise.

- *What are the possible risks or penalties for disobeying this type of law?* Many reporting laws have a financial penalty for noncompliance that is stated within the statute or regulation. The amounts can vary from minimal to quite substantial. Some states have made failure to report child abuse a criminal offense. There is also the risk of a licensing board complaint or civil malpractice suit by someone who was harmed by a person about whom the therapist did not report when legally required to do so.

Duty-to-Warn and Duty-to-Protect Laws

The legal concepts of "duty to warn" and "duty to protect" have probably received more discussion in the clinical, ethical, and legal literature than any other legal requirement that affects therapists. Both involve the prediction of patient dangerousness,[10] but they can require different actions. A true duty-to-warn statute requires the therapist to directly warn a potential victim about possible harm from a patient. In contrast, a duty-to-protect statute requires that the therapist take *some* action to protect a potential victim, but it does not legally require that this action involve warning the victim, and it may not even legally require that confidentiality be breached. Instead, the statute may provide therapists with other legal options, such as those described below. These laws vary greatly from state to state. Recently, some "duty to protect" laws have been expanded to include the legal duty to protect patients from self-harm.[11]

- *What do such laws require therapists to do?* In states that have a true duty-to-warn law, therapists have an explicit legal requirement to warn potential victims in order to protect them from harm, and this will require a breach of confidentiality unless the patient has given consent for the disclosure. In contrast, duty-to-protect statutes usually give therapists several options for acting protectively, some of which can require breach of confidentiality (e.g., warn the potential victim, hospitalize the patient, call the police), but some of which do not (e.g., maintain the patient in the room until convinced that no harm will be done to others or to self).[12]
- *What is the potential impact of such laws on therapy patients?* The impact will depend on the specifics of the law and the therapist's decision about what action to take, but many of the options can include a breach of confidentiality that may affect the therapy relationship. Even if the crisis is resolved without a breach of confidentiality, the therapist's response can underscore the seriousness and possible consequences of making threats to harm others, and the clinical outcome can include helping the patient learn

to respond in a more constructive manner when experiencing homicidal or suicidal thoughts.

- *What ethical concerns do such laws raise for therapists?* Most ethics codes treat a breach of confidentiality in this circumstance not as an ethical requirement but as an ethically allowed exception to the confidentiality rule. However, as with every other law in this chapter, the prospective patient has a right to be informed about this possible disclosure in advance (see Chapter 5). Unlike some laws, this one is very easy to explain to patients. Therapists who place conditions on confidentiality usually put "harm to self or others" near the top of the list when informing prospective patients about confidentiality's limits. But for any therapist who promises to *protect confidentiality absolutely*, the homicidal patient may present the severest ethical test of all.[13]
- *What legal options are available for responding in the most ethical manner?* Most states do not have a duty-to-warn statute, and, in some states, the duty-to-protect statute contains options that require no breach of confidentiality (e.g., protecting a potential victim by retaining the patient in session until there seems no potential for imminent danger). It is therefore very important that therapists clarify their own state's statutes and not erroneously presume that they have a legal duty to warn a potential victim or otherwise breach confidentiality.[14]
- *What are the possible risks or penalties for disobeying this type of law?* State laws vary in whether there are penalties for failing to try to protect the patient or others from potential harm. Therapists are open to civil suit brought by an injured victim (or, as in *Tarasoff*, by the family of a deceased victim or a patient whom the therapist did not attempt to protect).

LAWS GRANTING ACCESS TO PATIENT INFORMATION WITHOUT PATIENT CONSENT

Laws of many different types fall into this category. In most states, parents have legal access to the treatment record of their minor child in certain circumstances. In some states, an agency to whom the therapist has reported suspicion of abuse may have legal access to any of the therapist's records that are relevant to the reported case. In court cases involving child abuse, many states use a Court-Appointed Special Advocate (CASA)—a lay volunteer who can be given legal access to a child therapist's records or other information related to the case in order to be a better advocate for the child. In cases involving involuntary commitment, some state laws allow access to treatment records or other information by the psychological evaluator, hearing officer, attorneys, law enforcement personnel, or others. Finally, some laws allow recipients of information provided to them voluntarily with the patient's consent to redisclose the information to others without the patient's further consent. (For example, some third-party payers who obtain information for reimbursement purposes may release certain information to employers who purchase health care insurance for their employees.)

Because these laws vary so much from state to state, the recommendations given here are very general. Therapists must adapt these to the legal circumstances in their own state.

Parent Access to Minor Child's Treatment Records

- *What does this type of law require therapists to do?* These laws require therapists to give parents access to their minor child's therapy records if requested. States differ in (1) the minor's age at which this parental right to access will end, (2) whether custody status might affect a parent's legal right to access, and (3) circumstances in which the therapist may legally deny parental access (e.g., if a court has found a parent guilty of abuse and/or has denied contact and access). These laws are often not specific about what level of "access" is legally required (e.g., the right to review the record vs. the right to obtain a copy of it, etc.).
- *What is the potential impact of such laws on therapy patients?* Potentially, anything a therapist writes in the minor's record may be later read by the parent(s), and knowing this may affect a minor's willingness to confide freely.
- *What ethical concerns do such laws raise for therapists?* Concerns include ethical implications of therapists' decisions about what to write in the record, as well as ethical obligations about informed consent conversations before services begin. In the initial contact with a minor client and with parents, when therapists inform all parties about exactly what the rules about confidentiality will be, there should be a discussion about such legal requirements, as well as about the therapist's voluntary policies about ongoing disclosures to parents of minor therapy patients. (See Chapter 11, "Minors in Therapy.") The minor may also want to speak privately with the therapist about exactly what will be written in the records. The therapist may wish to speak to the parents about the disadvantages of seeking records, instead offering ongoing parent consultation sessions to discuss the minor's progress. With older children and adolescents, the therapist's policies should be presented in writing, and both minors and parents should be asked to sign the informed consent document to indicate understanding of this potential limit on confidentiality.[15]
- *What legal options are available for responding in the most ethical manner?* Therapists should read their state laws carefully to determine whether any of the circumstances of the case create a legal exception to parental

access. Some states allow therapists to deny parental access to the records if, in their professional judgment, it would be detrimental to the child. The wording of such exceptions will vary, and often the therapist must have documented that opinion in the record in advance. Some states allow therapists to automatically deny access if the parent has been convicted of child abuse.

- *What are the possible risks or penalties for disobeying this type of law?* If a therapist refuses parent access to records or information, in spite of a state law that grants them access, the parents have the option of issuing a subpoena and attempting to obtain a court order to legally enforce their right to the records.

Access in Child Abuse Cases

- *What does this type of law ask therapists to do regarding patients' confidences?* Such laws require therapists to provide information or records to assist in investigating abuse allegations, prosecuting child abuse cases, or protecting the child during such proceedings.
- *What is the potential impact of such laws on therapy patients?* Like mandated reporting laws, these legal requirements are in direct conflict with maintaining the confidentiality of the information that patients provide to their therapists.
- *What ethical concerns do such laws raise for therapists?* Many therapists believe that it is important to protect children and others from abuse and to punish those who abuse them, and that this social need should take priority over a patient's right to confidentiality. Therapists who take this position might want to provide information to assist investigations and prosecutions even if it were not legally required. But patients do have the right to protect themselves by not talking about such matters, which is why therapists have an ethical obligation to inform them in advance about these or any other circumstances in which they intend to breach confidentiality even if not legally required to do so (see Chapter 5).
- *What legal options are available for responding in the most ethical manner?* Therapists can often limit the scope of the disclosure. For example, if the court orders that a CASA volunteer may have access to information about a child client, the therapist may be able to provide oral or written summaries rather than complete treatment records, which contain much information not pertinent to the proceedings. A parent's attorney, or a child patient's guardian *ad litem* can also request that the judge conduct an *in camera* review and issue an order protecting from disclosure any information that is not relevant to the case.
- *What are the possible risks or penalties for disobeying this type of law?* Such laws may or may not stipulate specific penalties for noncompliance.

Agencies that receive mandated reports (e.g., departments of social services) can always seek a subpoena or court order if the therapist refuses to disclose the requested information to which they legally may have access.

Access to Information/Records for Involuntary Commitment Proceedings

- *What does this type of law require therapists to do?* These laws vary widely from state to state. In some states, campus shootings or other tragedies have led to new procedures that involve extensive access to confidential information and/or complete records from therapists at various stages of the involuntary commitment process. Depending upon how the statutes are written, these laws can both require disclosures prior to and during the commitment proceeding, and can allow redisclosures afterward.[16]
- *What is the potential impact of such laws on therapy patients?* Disclosures in this context can greatly increase the number of people who have access to very personal information that may have no bearing on whether involuntary commitment is appropriate for the patient.
- *What ethical concerns do such laws raise for therapists?* In states that legally require therapists to disclose information or records in this context, it is important that prospective patients be informed in advance about this potential limit to confidentiality (see Chapter 5). Such laws make it ethically important to be cautious about what information is placed in the record. (See, in Chapter 8, the section "Writing Too Much: Unprotective Record Keeping and Report Writing." Also see Chapter 10, "Record Keeping.")
- *What legal options are available for responding in the most ethical manner?* In some circumstances, those involved in conducting involuntary commitment proceedings might welcome an oral or written summary, rather than a copy of a patient's complete record. However, time is often a factor, so the therapist would need to be willing to provide information in that form on short notice.
- *What are the possible risks or penalties for disobeying this type of law?* Such laws vary; most do not carry a statutory penalty. However, the therapist might be vulnerable to a licensing board complaint from the hearing officer or from family members of the patient.

Third-Party Payer Access Provisions in Legally Binding Provider Contracts

- *What do such contracts require therapists to do?* Therapists who sign third-party payer contracts are entering a legally binding arrangement to serve as a provider under contract to that company. (Note that therapists enter into provider contracts voluntarily, so disclosures to these payers are considered "voluntary." However, even though no law gives third-party payer access, these are legally binding contracts whose provisions allow access that can be legally imposed.) Every provider contract is different; third-party payers vary in the type and the amount of information they require before authorizing reimbursement and at what stage(s) of the therapy that information must be provided.

It is important for therapists to read their provider contracts carefully. Most managed care provider contracts grant access to the patient's complete record for audit or other purposes. Also, provider contracts sometimes stipulate that the on-call therapist who will see the patient if the therapist is unavailable must also be a contracted provider with their company. Finally, some provider contracts stipulate that the therapist must retain clinical records for a certain number of years after the provider contract ends (which might therefore require retaining old records for many years longer than would otherwise be ethically or legally required).

- *What is the potential impact of such contracts on therapy patients?* All of the above requirements have implications for the patient's confidentiality and privacy.
- *What ethical concerns do such contracts raise for therapists?* The presence of such clauses in a therapist's managed care contracts would create an ethical obligation to discuss these potential limitations of confidentiality in the initial informed consent conversation. This is the only way to protect the patient's right to make an autonomous decision about whether to seek third-party reimbursement[17] (see Chapter 5). If, during that conversation, the patient decides to protect his or her privacy by not seeking third-party reimbursement, therapists must know whether their provider contract allows them to provide services to this patient on a self-pay basis, or whether they will need to refer the patient to a noncontracted (i.e., "out-of-network") provider.
- *What legal options are available for responding in the most ethical manner?* Therapists sometimes have few alternatives about those disclosures that are required under these contracts. However, it is always appropriate to work with case managers to try to reduce the intrusions into the patient's privacy by limiting the amount of information that must be disclosed.
- *What are the possible risks or penalties for disobeying this type of contract?* Since this is a legally binding contract, therapists who try to operate outside the provisions of the contract could be at legal risk of being accused of breach of contract or of fraud.

Patriot Act Investigations and Security Clearances

- *What does this type of law require therapists to do?* Under the authority of the Patriot Act, Federal Bureau of Investigation (FBI) investigators can legally require a mental health professional to provide information and records about current or prior patients. For security clearances, however, no federal law requires the therapist to disclose information, so nothing should be disclosed in this context unless the patient has given consent. Technically, therefore, security clearance interviews do not belong in this chapter about "legal demands." We discuss it here only because some therapists mistakenly presume that they are legally required to answer a wide range of questions posed by the security officer who conducts the interview. In fact, the consent form (Form SF86, which must be signed by the patient who is to be the subject of the interview) authorizes the therapist to disclose information in response to only three questions: (1) Does the person have a condition that could impair his or her judgment, reliability, or ability to properly safeguard classified national security information? (2) If so, describe the nature of the condition and the extent and duration of the impairment or treatment. And (3), what is the prognosis?[18]
- *What is the potential impact of such laws on therapy patients?* Laws such as the Patriot Act potentially circumvent the patient's confidentiality protections. The full impact may depend upon the nature of the information that is recorded in the therapy record or otherwise provided by the therapist.
- *What ethical concerns does this law raise for therapists?* As with all legal demands for confidential information, the Patriot Act places therapists in the ethical position of trying to protect the information or of trying to limit the scope of the disclosure. Since it may be impossible to prevent or limit the disclosure in this instance, it is ethically important that the patient be told at intake about this potential limit of confidentiality.
- *What legal options are available for responding in the most ethical manner?* The Patriot Act, as amended in 2006, gives therapists the right to consult an attorney and to inform patients of the demand for their records before relinquishing them.[19] It would be ethically important to immediately notify patients of such a demand, in order to allow them the opportunity to contest it.

LAWS ALLOWING RECIPIENTS OF PATIENT INFORMATION TO REDISCLOSE WITHOUT PATIENT CONSENT

- *What does this type of law require therapists to do?* Unlike the preceding statutes, these legal provisions do not require therapists themselves to disclose information. Rather, they allow (or require) others to redisclose what the therapist or others have already disclosed to them. For example, in child abuse cases, the CASA statutes described above can allow the child advocates to be court ordered to testify about the information they earlier obtained from a therapist, without child or parental consent.

- *What is the potential impact of such laws on therapy patients?* As noted above, in some of the circumstances in which therapists are legally required to report or disclose information, the recipients are legally allowed to redisclose it. These statutes do not legally require therapists to do anything, but they place patients in a "double jeopardy" situation over which therapists have little or no control: These laws can give others a legal right to redisclose, without further patient consent, information that a therapist was initially legally forced to disclose without the patient's consent. This could include some of the statutes and regulations related to information received by third-party payers, as well as disclosure provisions in the legally binding provider contracts that the therapist has signed voluntarily.
- *What ethical concerns does this law raise for therapists?* Obviously, any legal or contractual provision that allows information to be redisclosed without the patient's further consent will potentially reduce that patient's privacy and confidentiality. As with many of the laws described in this chapter, the ethical considerations include the need for a careful informed consent procedure, informing patients about this possibility before they consent to release the information in the first place. This can be conducted at the onset of therapy (Chapter 5), or it can be discussed at the time of a specific voluntary disclosure (Chapter 6). (See specific suggestions in the Chapter 6 section, "Preventing Redisclosure.")
- *What legal options are available for responding in the most ethical manner?* Protective actions include care in record keeping and a willingness to limit all disclosures to the extent legally possible, so that less information is available for anyone to redisclose. Also, if the therapist practices in a state where redisclosure without the patient's further consent would be illegal, then any information disclosed to others can carry a notice quoting that state statute (including its penalties, if any). Finally, therapists can choose not to redisclose information received from others, even when that would be legally allowed.
- *What are the possible risks or penalties for disobeying this type of law?* These are not laws that therapists can obey or disobey—they are enabling laws that give therapists and others the legal right to redisclose what someone else has already disclosed to them. Since these laws do not command therapists to do anything, they contain no specific legal penalties against therapists who ignore them. But ignoring them completely would be ethically inappropriate, because therapists must understand these laws well enough to be prepared to inform patients about them.

Also, when therapists themselves have obtained information or records from other providers, it is ethically important that they do not respond to such enabling laws by automatically redisclosing that information voluntarily, without first obtaining the patient's consent to release it. Better still, the therapist can direct the patient to the original source of the information, if the patient wishes to obtain it or give consent for its release.

LEGAL EXCEPTIONS TO THERAPIST–PATIENT PRIVILEGE

- *What does this type of law require therapists to do?* Therapist–patient privilege statutes apply only in the context of a court case or other legal proceeding. The exceptions to privilege protection will vary from state to state, but all indicate circumstances when the judge might order that a therapist provide patient information as evidence in a court case. They thus open the door for attorneys to issue subpoenas for that evidence in the form of patient records, therapist testimony, or both.

  Exceptions can be written within the privilege statutes themselves or can appear in separate statutes or through case law. The most common circumstances that create exceptions to therapist–patient privilege are child abuse cases and cases in which the patient's mental health is at issue. The latter could include such circumstances as a civil commitment proceeding, a criminal insanity plea, a case in which the patient is suing someone for damages for emotional pain or suffering, or a child custody case.
- *What is the potential impact of such laws on therapy patients?* Depending upon the nature of the case, legal proceedings can be the most public settings in which therapists ever disclose information about a patient. Information provided by the therapist may be especially embarrassing or damaging to the patient in that context.
- *What ethical concerns do such laws raise for therapists?* Therapists have ethical responsibility for knowing in what circumstances their state's laws make exceptions to therapist–patient privilege (and, therefore, for being able to predict when a court might require a therapist to submit patient information as evidence). These exceptions to privilege create potential limits to confidentiality that must be explained to prospective patients before therapy begins, but that conversation should be reopened whenever the therapist foresees the likelihood of a court case that might fall within those exceptions (e.g., if the patient mentions a plan to sue someone for injuries that caused emotional distress, thereby bringing their mental condition into issue).

  Therapists must also be very clear about the difference between a discovery subpoena and a court order, in order to be prepared to exercise all the available legal options for protecting confidentiality if a subpoena arrives and the patient does not want the information to be disclosed (see the following sections). If the patient wishes to give written consent for the therapist to voluntarily provide records or testimony as evidence in a court case, then the ethical responsibilities in Chapter 6 would apply. For example, the therapist is responsible for obtaining *informed* consent (i.e., before obtaining consent, the therapist informs the patient about what was in the records or what the therapist might say in testimony and discusses the implications of this disclosure, including how this might affect the ongoing therapy relationship).

- *What legal options are available for responding in the most ethical manner?* This varies somewhat from state to state, but some of the general rules are described in the next sections. Upon receipt of a subpoena, there are legal means for contesting it; in the case of a court order, the only recourse would likely be an appeal to a higher court. In either case, legal consultation may be necessary. The therapist can consult with his or her own attorney or can obtain consent to consult with the patient's attorney, and can cooperate in devising the most protective legal plan.
- *What are the possible risks or penalties for disobeying this type of law?* Failure to make a timely response to a subpoena, or refusal to comply with a court's order, can result in a judge's citation for contempt of court, resulting in fines and/or incarceration.

Further Notes on Subpoenas and Court Orders

"A subpoena is a document issued by an attorney instructing the recipient to provide documents or to be present to give oral testimony."[20] Therapists who are unaccustomed to receiving subpoenas can easily become flustered and confused, especially if one arrives in the middle of a therapy session, delivered by a sheriff. In some states, a lawyer representing one party in a court case can initiate a subpoena simply by writing out the document and taking it to the clerk of the court, who sends it out under the court's name. At that stage, no judge has made a determination about whether the requested information is admissible as evidence and must be disclosed.

The most frequent mistakes in response to a subpoena occur when unprepared therapists respond too quickly, mistaking the subpoena for a court order and disclosing information without trying to protect it. The following advice is therefore important to remember:

> The first thing that a psychologist should do when a subpoena is served is *nothing*: that is, nothing should be surrendered to the party serving the subpoena no matter how aggressive the request. The document should be accepted, and the psychologist should then consult legal counsel regarding applicable law and resulting obligations.[21]

Following that advice prevents impulsive action, allows time to obtain sufficient information and advice, and leads to an informed decision about how to respond in the patient's best interest. However, to avoid legal sanctions from the court, the recipient of a subpoena must make *some* response prior to the deadline stated on the document.

DISTINGUISHING BETWEEN SUBPOENAS AND COURT ORDERS

Prior to a formal court case, attorneys may issue subpoenas in an attempt to "discover" potential evidence. At this stage, therapists might receive a *subpoena duces tecum* (which demands patient records or other physical evidence) or a witness subpoena (which compels the therapist to participate in giving a deposition). Once a trial or formal hearing is scheduled, there may be a further witness subpoena, demanding the therapist's appearance for courtroom testimony. Although the therapist who receives a subpoena is legally required to take some action in response, it is ethically important to remember that subpoenas issued without a judge's knowledge do not carry the legal weight of a court order and can be overturned by a judge.

A court order may look similar to a subpoena, but, legally, it is a very different document, and this legal difference has important ethical implications..The issuance of this court order indicates that the case has been reviewed by a judge. The judge can either order that the requested information be disclosed or can issue a protective order that prevents it from being "discovered" or admitted as evidence.

A court order can be distinguished from a subpoena by the fact that it is ordinarily identified as a court order on the first page, and it will be signed by the judge, not by a court clerk or an attorney. "If you are not sure whether the document is a court order, you may contact the court that issued the document and ask to speak to the judge's clerk."[22]

Understanding the difference between a subpoena and a court order becomes critically important, both ethically and legally. A subpoena simply compels a response, and, in some jurisdictions, an attorney can obtain one simply by asking the court clerk. A court order, on the other hand, typically flows from a hearing before a judge and compels a disclosure unless appealed in a higher court. In the end, the court must decide what qualifies as protected or not.[23]

RESPONDING ETHICALLY TO SUBPOENAS

"In general, a psychologist may only disclose information with the consent of the patient or in response to a court order. The receipt of a subpoena alone without the consent of the patient does not override this requirement."[24]

Preparations should be made in advance, based on the legal options available in one's state for responding to subpoenas in various circumstances.[25] As described above, if the therapist is not sure about the possible responses, the first thing to do in response to a subpoena is *nothing.*[26] This is not a posture the therapist can maintain for very long, because subpoenas offer limited response times. But, unless one already has an understanding of the options and has adopted a plan of action (such as the one described below), it is important to pause long enough to obtain consultation before acting. A recommended plan of action suggests that the therapist:

1. *Clarify who sent the subpoena and what it is demanding.* If the issuing attorney represents a party who is your patient's adversary in the court case, do *not* contact this attorney for clarification or legal advice. If the intent or origin of the subpoena is unclear, seek consultation from a neutral consultant (without disclosing the patient's identity).

> Turn over the information only if your subpoena qualifies as a court order. In most states, you can turn over the documents or show up to testify without obtaining your client's consent *only* if the subpoena you received qualifies as a court order from a judge, which is rare.[27]

2. *Notify the patient that the subpoena has been received.* In interacting with the patient, the American Psychological Association (APA) advises as follows:

> If the document is not a court order (the first subpoena you receive in a matter rarely is a court order), you will need to obtain your client's consent or authorization before turning over confidential information. This step is required because most state and federal jurisdictions recognize a psychotherapist–patient privilege that allows the client to prevent confidential material from being disclosed to others ... When obtaining this consent, you should tell your client exactly what you have been asked to turn over and explain that there is no guarantee that the information will be kept confidential ... The written consent that you obtain from your client should contain, at a minimum: Exactly what information will be disclosed; to whom the information will be disclosed (for example, to the requesting attorney); the purpose of the disclosure (to respond to a subpoena); the client's signature and date.[28]

3. *If the patient does not wish the information to be disclosed, obtain consent from the patient to consult with the patient's attorney about a planned response.* In some circumstances, this may include obtaining the patient's consent to advise the attorney about the nature of the record (or the potential content of the testimony) being requested, since this may affect the response decision. However, therapists who are unaccustomed to interacting with attorneys should exercise caution:

> Unfortunately, many attorneys do not understand that psychologists have limited discretion for releasing records. Attorneys representing patients (or sometimes attorneys representing parties adverse to the patient's interests) may misinform psychologists of their legal obligations and instruct them to release records in response to a subpoena alone. Do not be bullied by these tactics. It is best to seek [neutral] legal consultation in situations in which the requirements are unclear.[29]

If the patient has no attorney, the therapist can advise the patient that the subpoena can be legally contested and/or can proceed to contest the subpoena in the patient's behalf (if state law so allows).

> If a psychotherapist believes that a request for records violates confidentiality, he or she should assert the privilege on behalf of the client and let the respective court resolve it. Depending upon the laws of each state, a psychologist may be required to allow the presiding judge to review these materials *en camera*, which means in the confidentiality of his or her chambers. Again, one should never do this without legal advice.[30]

4. *Remember that, in the absence of the patient's explicit consent for the therapist to disclose the requested information, the most ethical position is to refuse to disclose anything unless a judge orders it to be disclosed.* For contesting a subpoena on the basis that the information should be deemed "privileged," someone (either the patient's attorney, the therapist, or the therapist's attorney) must file a motion to quash the subpoena, thereby bringing a judge into the picture.

COURT ORDERS

When someone files a "motion to quash" a subpoena, the judge will hold a hearing, following which a court order will be issued. The judge may decide to issue (1) a protective order (in which case the therapist will not be required to disclose the information requested in the subpoena) or (2) an order that the subpoenaed information (or testimony) be provided. If someone files a "motion to limit disclosure" in response to an overly broad subpoena, the judge's order may protect only portions of the information from being admitted as evidence. In either case, the issuance of this court order indicates that the case has been reviewed by a judge.

As described above, to protect confidentiality to the extent legally possible, therapists have an obligation to contest a subpoena if the patient objects to the disclosure. In contrast, a court order leaves therapists with few legal options.

> "In contrast to a subpoena, a court order, issued by a judge following a review of the request at hand, *does* override the need to obtain patient consent... In most instances, compliance with a court order is indicated. In the rare situation where the psychologist may wish to challenge the issuance of the court

> order, legal counsel will be necessary to avoid an indirect or direct appearance of contemptuous behavior."[31]

However, a therapist who is ordered to provide testimony "involuntarily" may have one further decision to make—whether to agree to be sworn in as an *"expert witness"* or whether to testify only as a *"fact witness."* (See the Chapter 12 discussion of this distinction in the section on "Involuntary Roles in Legal Contexts.")

Using Available Resources

Throughout this chapter, references have been made to consultation. Ideally, the consultation about ethical or legal issues can include face-to-face discussion with experts who are neutral, in the sense they have no involvement in the case.

> If confronted with a confusing question about confidentiality, psychotherapists should refrain from action until they have secured answers through consultation with peers with expertise in ethics and law, or with an attorney. Psychotherapists should not accept legal advice given to them by attorneys representing other individuals in a matter since they cannot represent the interest of the psychotherapist.[32]

For discussion of available resources, and for considerations in the consultation process, see, in Chapter 4, the section on "Obtaining Consultation and Developing Resources."

Practice Pointers

The legal details of this chapter can be difficult to absorb, even for therapists who are not intimidated by laws or courtrooms. Peer networks that provide consultation, collaboration, training, and support can be extremely helpful with this anxiety-producing aspect of practice. Mental health professionals can encourage their state professional associations to provide legal updates and ongoing training about state-related legal issues. If such larger groups are difficult to form or too far away to meet with on a regular basis, ongoing cooperation with even one other colleague can be much better than negotiating legal minefields alone. (See a further discussion of this in Chapter 9, "Talking About Confidentiality.")

Box 7.1 revisits the case introduced in Box 4.1, here using it to illustrate the importance of engaging in preparation about the legal details described in this chapter. As summarized in Box 7.1, this case also demonstrates the interrelationship among the first five steps of the Ethical Practice Model.

BOX 7.1 Taking the Patient's Perspective at Step 4

We return to the case example first described in Box 4.1. Revisiting that case allows us to reflect here on the interrelationships of the first five steps of the Ethical Practice Model:

Step 1 ("Preparing"): This therapist did not adequately inform himself about the laws which might later affect his ability to maintain confidentiality.

Step 2 ("Telling Prospective Patients the Truth About Confidentiality's Limits"): At intake, he failed to accurately describe the potential limits of confidentiality. Instead, he simply explored the patient's concerns and provided reassurance, implying a promise he later failed to keep.

Step 3 ("Obtaining Truly Informed Consent Before Disclosing Information Voluntarily"): He was actually making a "voluntary" disclosure, which requires the patient's' informed consent, but he neither informed the patient nor obtained consent before disclosing.

Step 4 ("Responding Ethically to Legal Demands"): There was no real "legal demand" to which he needed to respond. He behaved unethically because he believed he was legally required to disclose when, actually, he was not.

Step 5 ("Avoiding Preventable Breaches of Confidentiality"): This disclosure was very preventable, and it was made without the patient's knowledge or consent. Therefore, it was a breach of confidentiality, not an ethical disclosure. The therapist misunderstood his legal requirements, perhaps because he had received and followed bad advice rather than obtaining reliable consultation.

8

Step 5: Avoiding Preventable Breaches of Confidentiality

Respect for the obligation of confidentiality transcends the therapist's own judgment about whether or not the unauthorized release will be harmful to the patient. It is not the therapist's right to decide that an inappropriate disclosure is harmless just because he or she doesn't think the patient will suffer any adverse consequences. When patients discover that information has been released without authorization, they often feel as if a piece of themselves has been misappropriated. By maintaining a patient's confidence, a therapist transmits a defining behavioral message that is trust-enhancing and ego strengthening.

Epstein (1994), *Keeping Boundaries*, p. 182

As used here, the term "preventable" refers to voluntary disclosures, made without the patient's informed consent, in the absence of any legal requirement to disclose. This step in the Ethical Practice Model can therefore serve as a reminder to therapists that most behavior about confidentiality is entirely within their own control.[1] Although the legally coerced breaches of confidentiality can be more publicly exposing to the patient, the everyday garden-variety voluntary betrayals of patients' confidences may do more damage to patient–therapist relationships—and are also likely to do more damage to the credibility of the mental health professions.

Examples of preventable disclosures include conversations about patients in office elevators, within earshot of the waiting room, or with one's family or friends. They include appropriate conversations in inappropriate places (e.g., conducting peer consultations in hallways or public restaurants); potentially appropriate disclosures made without appropriate consent (e.g., disclosing sensitive personal history to a prescribing physician without first obtaining the patient's consent to do so); overdisclosures (e.g., disclosing beyond what the patient authorized, or beyond what is necessary in the circumstance); accidental disclosures; and "technology glitches" (including those caused by failing to train staff in security procedures, or permitting them to transport patient data on laptops or disks that are easily lost or stolen). Most of these would be considered unethical breaches of confidentiality. They place patients at risk, and they thereby also place the therapist at risk. With care and forethought, they are almost always preventable.

Finally, Step 5 is a reminder that role confusion and role multiplication can sometimes lead to confidentiality conflicts that are both clinically destructive and ethically impossible to resolve. It is also a reminder that the onset of managed care created no new ethically allowed exceptions to the rule of confidentiality; it simply made it harder to protect the information and more important to remember to obtain consent before disclosing it.

Ethical Responsibilities

When therapists voluntarily disclose identifiable information without the patient's consent, this constitutes a *breach of confidentiality* that is considered unethical by the ethics codes of all the mental health professions. The ethical standards listed in Appendix II as "Clarification, Amplification, and Application Standards" are designed to prevent such disclosures. Knowledge of these standards, along with forethought and professional caution, can greatly reduce the chances that therapists or their staff will make these inappropriate disclosures.

Avoidable Pitfalls

Disclosures that are potentially avoidable span a wide range of circumstances and situations. Since each profession emphasizes slightly different circumstances, the sections below illustrate how therapists can apply their combined ethical standards in six problematic situations. Therapists can add other categories that would apply in their own setting:

- Disclosing information with "inadequately informed" consent
- Talking too much
- Writing too much
- Failing to establish protective policies, procedures, and technology safeguards
- Wearing too many hats
- Failing to anticipate legal demands and avoid "legally preventable" disclosures

DISCLOSING INFORMATION WITH "INADEQUATELY INFORMED" CONSENT

As already described, a signature on a consent form does not qualify as informed consent; it merely documents that the patient signed the form. As discussed in Steps 2 and 3, unless the patient has been informed about what information will be disclosed to whom, and understands the potential implications of disclosing it, the signature on a consent form will represent "uninformed" or "inadequately informed" consent.

Disclosing to Third-Party Payers Without Fully Informed Consent

"The fact that a third party is reimbursing for services does not, in itself, entitle that party to any information about the patient without the patient's consent."[2] The American Counseling Association (ACA) Ethics Code requires that "counselors disclose information to third-party payers only when clients have authorized such disclosure."[3] The National Association of Social Workers (NASW) Ethics Code contains a similar ethical requirement.[4] Therapists place patients at risk if they treat disclosures to third-party payers as if they were special exceptions to the rule of confidentiality. As an ethical issue, this problem is not new,[5] but it received increased attention as managed care organizations began requiring practitioners to submit greater amounts of patient information.[6]

> The exceptions to confidentiality have multiplied, and the possible ways to deal with the exceptions have increased in number and complexity. The profession may be in danger of forgetting that these are exceptions... What occurs is a kind of *figure–ground reversal*. When there are too many exceptions, the exceptions become prominent, and the rule fades into the background.[7]

This figure–ground reversal has become especially visible in claims for third-party reimbursement, in which "extensive disclosure without adequately informed consent" is sometimes treated as if that were the rule. Although some therapists may experience their disclosures to third-party payers as involuntary (i.e., "financially coerced") disclosures, ethically speaking, they are voluntary; so, unlike the legally coerced disclosures of Step 4, disclosures to third-party payers always require the patient's truly informed consent. As described in Step 3, the Health Insurance Portability and Accountability Act (HIPAA) and some state laws do allow (but never legally require) providers to disclose for reimbursement purposes without informing patients about the content of each disclosure or obtaining consent for its release. Ethically, however, not only is patient consent required, but it must be *informed* consent.

Within the context of third-party reimbursement, what does this *informed* consent process actually require? The process of providing information should begin at intake, with a general discussion of the potential disclosures that may be required if the patient chooses to obtain third-party reimbursement for mental health services. One aspect of "inadequate informing" involves failure to discuss the potential risks of disclosing information to third-party payers (e.g., transfer of information into national databases if the patient files for future life or health insurance; implications on future insurability, depending on the diagnosis, etc.).[8]

Then, since it is impossible at intake to predict the actual content of future disclosures to third-party payers, it should be an ethical "rule of thumb" to reopen the informational conversation to discuss the content of treatment plans at the time they are transmitted.[9] Patients are best protected if they are asked to give consent for release of information to third-party payers only after being fully informed about exactly what will be disclosed and the implications of disclosing it. This level of protection would involve describing the content of treatment plans, including diagnosis and other specific information, and obtaining the patient's consent to disclose it before transmitting it. Obviously, it is not possible to accomplish this in advance at intake by asking patients to sign a form giving consent for all future disclosures.[10] This consent must therefore be obtained at Step 3.

> Principles of confidentiality and client autonomy suggest that providers need to fully inform their clients about the nature and content of the records that will be released... The most complete way to fully inform clients is to share the record (or the information to be disclosed) with the client before sending it on. Only then is the client fully informed.[11]

Regrettably, instead of providing this level of protection, clinicians and their support staff, assisted by advances in technology, have become dangerously accustomed to initiating routine electronic transmission of private and sensitive information, sometimes without adequately informing patients of the content or discussing the implications of the disclosure, and sometimes without even obtaining their consent at all. The risks are compounded if these transmissions contain overdisclosures in an attempt to guarantee reimbursement.

Disclosures to Patient-Related Third Parties Without Patient Consent

Therapists are not ethically free to acknowledge to family members someone's patient status, or to discuss a patient with a spouse, family member, or friend unless the patient has given explicit consent. Absent that consent, the confidentiality rule would apply, and, if contacted by others, therapists are free only to listen, not to disclose. Any foreseeable exceptions to this rule (including emergencies involving danger to self or others) need to be discussed with the patient at intake when describing the limits of confidentiality.

If the patient wishes to give consent for information to be disclosed to related others, the nature and content of each disclosure should be discussed and documented. Consent for contact with family members or others can be obtained either at intake (Step 2) or later (Step 3), as appropriate. "With minors or incapacitated adults, rules about contacts with family members or caretakers should be clearly established in advance, then carefully honored."[12] As noted earlier, if a parent is paying the bill for therapy services to their adult child patient (as with college students), the therapist should inform the patient about what information will be disclosed on the billing form. (In such cases, one way to avoid disclosure is to send the bill only to the patient, who then has responsibility for contacting other payers, if appropriate.)

Disclosures to Referral Sources and Other Professionals

It is natural for therapists to want to acknowledge referrals. Although this professional courtesy need not disclose any personal information that was confided by the new patient, it does disclose the fact that the patient sought and/or is receiving mental health services. This fact should not be disclosed without the client's explicit consent. Discussing the referral source with the patient at intake allows the therapist to either obtain consent to thank the referring party, or to uncover reasons why the patient wishes to refuse to give consent for that contact.

If the patient was referred by an agency that will be paying for the services, it is useful for therapists to obtain in advance a formal written contract with the referring agency, clarifying the expectations about disclosures. This can include understandings about what details the therapist will provide on the billing statements and whether the referring agent expects progress reports or other access to information. Such details can then be discussed with the patient, in advance, as part of the informed consent conversation about limits of confidentiality.[13]

Regarding the exchange of information with other professionals who are involved in the patient's care, it is helpful to distinguish between emergency and nonemergency situations. The expectation that confidential information may need to be released in emergency situations should be discussed in the initial informed consent conversation, so that the patient's consent to receive services can include advance consent for the therapist to make such disclosures. (This would include sharing information in such circumstances as emergency rooms and for civil commitment proceedings.) In nonemergency situations, HIPAA legally allows disclosures to other treating professionals. However, the fact that this is legally allowed does not absolve the therapist of the ethical responsibility for either (1) informing the patient about this plan at intake or (2) obtaining specific consent when the situation arises (as when requesting the patient's consent to have ongoing contact with a prescribing physician).

TALKING TOO MUCH

This category of disclosures spans a wide range of conversations and circumstances. Therapists should carefully review their own behaviors, as well as the practices of others in their clinical environment.

Informal Conversations

Informal conversations are the most easily preventable disclosures, and they are explicitly unethical.[14] The term "informal conversations" is used here to include any comments about the patient that were not explicitly authorized by the patient and not directly related to patient care.

Informal conversations include "sounding-off conversations about a patient with colleagues who are not involved with the case."[15] This overlaps with what is sometimes called "casual consultation" with colleagues and other professionals. These conversations range from unauthorized clinical chats over lunch to the audible-from-the waiting-room hallway exchanges with colleagues who have no need (and no right) to know, but who are willing to listen. Therapists sometimes rationalize such conversations by calling them "consultation," but these encounters do not deserve the name unless they are providing either crisis assistance or formal peer assistance (neither of which should take place in the hallway or other public place). True consultation deserves more time and requires much more privacy.

Some consultations are inappropriate only because they are conducted "informally" in the wrong setting. It is ethically important that consultations related to patients be conducted only in a space where privacy can be ensured.[16] Clinical consultations should therefore not take place in public restaurants or agency hallways where they can be overheard by others. Such practices place patients at risk, thereby placing the therapist at risk. When therapists fail to create sufficient opportunities for formal clinical consultation, conducted in a private setting, there may be greater risk of engaging in such inappropriate "informal" conversations about patients.

> We lead busy lives and want to make the most of our time. Often the most convenient way to catch a colleague for a quick consult is while we are walking through the halls of a clinic, or sitting together at a large table waiting for the last arrivals so that a meeting can begin, or at a restaurant during a lunch break, or in some other public place. The problem with such on-the-run consultations is that confidential information is often discussed within earshot of people who are not authorized to receive the information. Most of us have probably overheard such consultations in clinic hallways or elevators. Perhaps we heard the patient's name, someone we recognized as a friend, neighbor, or colleague. In one case a therapist consulted a colleague on a crowded elevator about a particularly "difficult" patient, unaware that the patient was standing only a few feet behind her, listening carefully.[17]

Informal disclosures also include inappropriate gossip about patients. Therapists have many reasons for talking about a patient in contexts that are beneficial to the patient, but gossip is not among them.[18] It is never ethical to disclose confidential information to others who have no involvement in the case, even if they are fellow clinicians. "Many of us know 'through the grapevine' who is in treatment with whom. To the extent that the information nourishing the grapevine is provided by counselors or therapists rather than by the patients, it is a clear ethical breach."[19]

> Professional gossip falls in a category by itself. It is perhaps one of the most serious threats to confidentiality for which one cannot suggest that there is any competing societal interest that would legitimately justify the disclosure. Instead, the compromise of confidentiality is motivated by psychological needs of the therapist to disclose for personal reasons. If one has a celebrity patient, there may be a strong urge to let others know to enhance one's

> own self-esteem and perhaps to enhance referrals ... Such capricious disclosure compromises not only the care that individual receives, but diminishes the reputation of the professional group as well ... At a personal level, one should always scrutinize one's motives for disclosure: Is it for genuine enhancement of knowledge or for personal aggrandizement?[20]

Therapists' patient-related conversations with their own family members or friends also fall into the category of "gossip," since these involve disclosures to others who have no involvement in the case. Such violations occur regardless of level of training or years of practice, often arising when the therapist's professional life is inadequately separated from personal relationships.[21] "Therapists can best avoid such disclosures by creating a firm boundary that avoids any discussion of patients with family or friends, instead establishing regular, frequent opportunities elsewhere to talk about cases on a professional basis."[22] This can include formal consultation, peer consultation groups, or individual therapy, in which the therapist's emotional reactions to the clinical material can safely be expressed and explored.

> Therapists are encouraged to examine their own practices concerning sharing of confidential information with their families. Therapists' families have their own rules, patterns, boundary issues, and power struggles which affect therapists' behaviors. Therapists can discuss this issue with their families and develop postures that insure clients' privacy ... It is our belief that the client's privacy is a commitment that should not be compromised, and the intimate context of the therapist's family should allow no exceptions.[23]

Overdisclosures

This category includes disclosures that are made in an appropriate context, but which are inappropriate because they reveal more than the patient authorized, or because they include private information beyond what is needed and appropriate in the circumstance. Whether disclosing information with the patient's consent or because required by law, therapists have an ethical responsibility to disclose no more than is necessary for the immediate purpose.

For counselors, the ACA Ethics Code requires that "when circumstances require the disclosure of confidential information, only essential information is revealed."[24] The American Psychological Association (APA) Ethics Code similarly requires that psychologists "include in written and oral reports and consultations only information germane to the purpose for which the communication is made."[25] For social workers, the NASW Ethics Code stipulates that "in all instances, social workers should disclose the least amount of confidential information necessary to achieve the desired purpose; only information that is directly relevant to the purpose for which the disclosure is made should be revealed," and that, in consultations, they should "disclose the least amount of information necessary to achieve the purposes of the consultation."[26]

WRITING TOO MUCH: UNPROTECTIVE RECORD KEEPING OR REPORT WRITING

The content of a patient's record can be governed by professional guidelines, state laws, and provider contracts. Therapists nevertheless have a great deal of control over how much information they place into the official record. The ethical standards and admonitions about "overdisclosure" in the previous section also apply to written information.

The topic of record keeping is covered in detail in Chapter 10. Here, we note only that, in creating a written record, therapists should keep in mind all of the ways it might eventually be seen by the patient or others, including those who might someday seek it as evidence against the patient.

When writing reports or informational letters about the patient, the ethical standards quoted above preclude disclosure of irrelevant private information (e.g., disclosing sexual information in a progress report to someone for whom that information is not relevant). "In assessment reports, overdisclosures would include information not necessary for the purposes of a particular evaluation, or not appropriate for explaining the results to a particular recipient (e.g., including medical information about family members who are not biologically related to the examinee when that is not directly relevant to the purpose of the evaluation or report)."[27]

FAILING TO ESTABLISH PROTECTIVE POLICIES, PROCEDURES, AND TECHNOLOGICAL SAFEGUARDS

Therapists have responsibilities about technological safety that extend beyond their own behavior. Staff carelessness in transmitting patient information electronically, including accidental misdials on the fax machine, can send confidential information to the wrong destination. Oversights, such as unattended computers or failure to institute password protections, can place all patient data at risk. Similarly, allowing staff members to remove patient data from the clinical setting can result in lost disks or stolen laptops that could undo the confidentiality of many patients at once.

Such risks, and their implications, should be discussed in formal confidentiality training that is attended by all staff, clinical and nonclinical. Formal policies should be established, and formal procedures should be in place to assure that all personnel in the setting conform to them. "The most effective way to prevent avoidable breaches of confidentiality is to ensure a 'culture of safety' in which confidentiality is viewed as everyone's responsibility."[28]

Poorly Trained Staff

Staff training is discussed in detail in Chapter 13, but here at Step 5 is the place for therapists to assess the level of staff training in their own setting, because it is "an essential component in the protection of patients' confidentiality rights."[29] Properly trained office staff can become very creative in preventing unnecessary access by those who have no reason to see or hear patient information. Staff training is important for avoiding "accidental breaches of confidentiality," which Knapp defines as "unintended lapses or unanticipated problems," in contrast to intentional gossip.[30] HIPAA legally requires "workforce training" for all personnel, but this does not replace ethics-based confidentiality training, which is recommended for both clinical and nonclinical staff in mental health settings.[31]

Confidentiality contracts can be required from all employees as a condition of employment.[32] In addition, therapists' business associates (such as billing agents, answering services, etc.), computer consultants with access to data, and even janitorial staff who might have accidental contact with patient data, can also be required to sign confidentiality contracts. Sample contracts are available from the Center for Ethical Practice.[33]

Technological "Glitches"

The obligation to protect the security of computer-based data during storage and transmission is reflected in ethical standards, professional record keeping guidelines, and legal regulations. These ethical and legal requirements are overlapping and are usually mutually consistent. Therapists who comply with all of them will be both protecting patient confidentiality and informing patients of the limitations of that protection when technology is used.

For counselors, the ACA Ethics Code contains extensive requirements related to technology. These cover not only safeguards in transmitting confidential information and in providing of services electronically, but also ethical responsibilities about informing patients about the potential risks of these uses of technology.[34]

Psychologists are ethically required to protect the confidentiality of patient information "obtained through or stored in any medium." Also, "Psychologists who offer services, products, or information via electronic transmission inform clients/patients of the risks to privacy and limits of confidentiality."[35] The APA Record Keeping Guidelines cover the topic of electronic records and other technology in detail.[36]

Social workers are ethically required to inform patients of risks and limitations if they plan to "provide services via electronic media";" must "take precautions to ensure and maintain the confidentiality of information transmitted to other parties through the use of computers, electronic mail, facsimile machines, telephones and telephone answering machines, and other electronic or computer technology";" and must "take reasonable steps to ensure that clients' records are stored in a secure location and that clients' records are not available to others who are not authorized to have access."[37]

Legal obligations about technology safeguards and the protection of computer-based patient data are described in extensive detail in the federal HIPAA Security Rule.[38] For a summary of those requirements and links to the regulations, see Appendix IV. (Also see the discussion of technology and electronic records in Chapter 10, "Clinical Record Keeping.")

Inadequate Environmental Safeguards

It is disconcerting to sit in the waiting room of a clinical setting and hear what is happening in nearby therapy sessions. The chance of this can be reduced with such safeguards as proper soundproofing, low music, and white-noise machines. Similarly, clerical offices and staff lounges can have doors that can be completely closed if there will be conversations about patients. Without such safeguards in place, patients have reason to be concerned about whether their privacy and confidentiality will be protected.

Similarly, just as computerized information is compromised unless therapists use passwords and encryption, the confidentiality of paper records will be compromised unless there is adequate file storage that can be securely locked when not in use. Otherwise, even the janitorial staff could obtain access to private patient information on paper records or forms.

WEARING TOO MANY HATS

Confidentiality issues often arise when mental health professionals engage in clinical roles with parties who are related to each other, take on multiple roles in the same clinical case, become confused about the role(s) they are playing, or fail to ask and answer the question, "What are my ethical obligations to *each* of the parties involved in this case, especially as they affect confidentiality?"[39] If we think of roles as the different "hats" that mental health professionals might wear, then to avoid this problem therapists must (1) be aware of exactly what hat(s) they are wearing at any given moment, (2) understand the ethical responsibilities of each hat they wear, (3) avoid multiplying hats unnecessarily, and (4) avoid wearing potentially conflicting hats. (In Chapter 11, see "Multiple-Party Cases.")

The problem about engaging in multiple roles with the same patient(s) is that each role might demand slightly different ethical responsibilities—not only different expectations about boundaries, but different rules about confidentiality and its exceptions. For this reason, multiplying roles will multiply the potential ethical dilemmas about both boundaries and confidentiality.

In forensic cases, therapists who engage in multiple roles with the same patient are creating not only ethical conflicts, but potentially also legal and ethical-legal conflicts. As reflected in Appendix VI, forensic evaluators do not have the same confidentiality duties and privilege protections as therapists, so wearing both hats with the same patient can create confidentiality conflicts, as well as conflicts of interest.[40] Therapists should therefore always say "no" when they receive a request to serve as forensic evaluator in a custody case in which they already have a clinical relationship with one of the parties. "It is easy to predict that the confidentiality risks to the patient (and therefore the risks to the mental health professional) are multiplied if a forensic hat is donned atop a therapist hat, especially if it is a multi-patient therapist hat, as in couple or family cases."[41] Similarly, complications can arise if a therapist hat is donned atop a forensic hat, even if the professional thinks the forensic aspect of the case has ended. The problem is that court cases can be reopened and forensic evaluators recalled to give testimony, so having begun a subsequent role as therapist can create conflicting confidentiality responsibilities as an expert witness.[42] (For further discussion, see, in Chapter 12, "Legal Settings and Forensic Roles.")

FAILING TO ANTICIPATE LEGAL DEMANDS AND AVOID LEGALLY PREVENTABLE DISCLOSURES

Therapists sometimes find themselves misunderstanding legal requirements or confused by legal issues. The examples below are only a few of the possible pitfalls that can ensnare therapists who fail to engage in the level of preparation recommended in Step 1 and the precautions discussed in Step 4.

Failure to Foresee and Prevent "Preventable" Subpoenas

In each state, there are certain circumstances in which therapist–patient privilege does not apply. Therapists familiar with their state's privilege laws can foresee circumstances in which an increased likelihood exists that a subpoena for records or testimony might be initiated, whether by adversarial parties or by patients themselves. In such circumstances, therapists can pause in the therapy process and reopen the informed consent conversation to be sure the patient understands the potential implications.

For example, if the patient describes a plan to sue someone for an injury that created emotional distress and insomnia, bringing their own mental health into issue will likely be considered a voluntary waiver of privilege and will usually open the door to a subpoena for information about the patient's mental health treatment.[43] The decision about whether to bring the lawsuit remains with the patient, but the therapist can inform the patient about the likely consequences (e.g., a subpoena for records or therapist testimony), so that the patient can make an informed decision about it. In such cases, the patient's attorney will have no knowledge of what is contained in the therapy records and may mistakenly believe that the therapist can be a "good character reference" for the patient. This advance conversation will allow patients to consult with their attorneys about potential implications before bringing their mental health into issue in such a lawsuit.

Therapists can reduce the likelihood of receiving a patient-initiated subpoena in a therapy case by including a "no-subpoena promise" in the initial contract.[44] This is especially helpful in couple and family cases, to discourage one party from later initiating a subpoena to use information from the therapy as evidence against another party in a court case. Since such a no-subpoena promise does not constitute a legally binding contract, it does not legally prevent the person from initiating a subpoena, but therapists who use this procedure report that it can reduce the likelihood that patients will do so.

In child and family cases, it is often useful to have the no-subpoena agreement include a statement that the welfare of the child patient requires a "zone of safety" in which concerns can be discussed outside of a custody conflict, and that entering these records into court in that context could be harmful to the child. Parents who sign such a statement may be more reluctant to enter the records into court, since it contains a tacit admission that this might harm the child. (See Chapter 7 for a discussion of subpoenas. Also see, in Chapter 11, "Multiple-Party Cases" and "Minors in Therapy.")

Misunderstanding Legal Requirements or Accepting Bad Advice

Therapists who misunderstand their state's laws are at risk for disclosing patient information because they believe that it is legally required, when actually it is not.[45] Earlier chapters stressed the importance of learning relevant laws and obtaining good legal advice. Therapists should not accept legal advice from the attorney of the patient's adversary in a court case, or from an attorney unfamiliar with mental health law.[46] Therapists who have no reliable ethics consultant may accept from uninformed colleagues some advice that turns out to be misguided or unethical. Knowing relevant laws and establishing trusted ethical and legal consultation relationships in advance can prevent such ethical and legal missteps.

Abusing "Legally Allowed" Exceptions to Confidentiality

"Confidentiality is the rule, and it is ethically inappropriate for therapists to seek legal rationalizations for making exceptions to the rule in order to disclose identifiable confidential information without the patient's consent."[47] There are many legally allowed exceptions to confidentiality, including those in the federal HIPAA regulations, that allow information to be disclosed without client authorization for purposes as broad as "treatment, payment, and health care operations."[48] Many state laws contain similarly broad exceptions to confidentiality. For example, Virginia's Health Record Privacy Statute,[49] although protective of confidentiality in some respects, legally allows patient information to be disclosed "in connection with the health care entity's own health care operations or the health care operations of another health care entity" or "in the normal course of business," according to standards of practice within that setting. It is hard to imagine broader legal exceptions to the rule. Note, however, that these legal exceptions to confidentiality do not *require* anything to be disclosed without consent; they merely *allow* it. The fact that a disclosure is legally allowed does not make it ethical. (See, in Chapter 2, "Laws Allowing Therapists to Disclose Without Patient Consent.")

These legally allowed disclosures have important implications for informed consent. "If one's personal policy is to disclose information in any of these routine circumstances, then this must be decided in advance and explained to the prospective patient at intake. The disclosure is then ethically appropriate, not because the therapist found a 'legal loophole' that allowed it, but because the patient either gave informed consent in advance at Step 2 to accept such disclosures as a condition of receiving services, or subsequently gave explicit consent at Step 3."[50]

Further Thoughts on "Reaching for the Ethical Ceiling" About Confidentiality

Ethics codes create the "ethical floor"—the minimum standards of behavior. But if therapists do no more than follow the minimum rules, they are missing the major point about confidentiality. Two of the things patients most seek and expect from therapy are "a feeling of safety and security" and "the chance to talk to someone in a safe environment and without fear of repercussion."[51]

> Positive ethics then asks, How can we facilitate that safe environment? Psychologists can help to create that environment by being meticulous about maintaining the confidentiality of the client's revelations. They can earn that trust by taking special care to inform clients about the limits to confidentiality at the outset of treatment and along the way as client disclosures raise questions about confidentiality.[52]

Rather than thinking about the ethics of confidentiality only in terms of obeying the minimum enforceable ethical standards and laws, therapists can think about it in terms of underlying moral principles and positive ethics, They can engage in planful practice and be prepared to take initiatives in behalf of patients' confidentiality rights. Thinking about confidentiality within these broader frameworks will make it "more likely to aim to be exemplary practitioners rather than to just avoid breaking rules."[53]

Practice Pointers

Step 5 is the place for stepping back to review workplace policies and behavior from the patient's point of view. Imagine yourself being a long-term patient who is notified that the confidentiality of all your records was compromised when a laptop was stolen, a flash drive was lost, or a shredding company failed to perform as promised. Imagine yourself being a prospective patient entering your clinical setting for the first time. Do you hear staff talking about other patients? Do you see identifiable information on the secretary's desk or computer screen? Do you hear therapy sessions from the waiting room?

Box 8.1 provides an opportunity to ask such questions using the topics covered in this chapter. This can be done on your own or as a cooperative exercise with others, as suggested in the next chapter.

BOX 8.1 Taking the Patient's Perspective at Step 5

Therapists can learn a great deal about gaps in their own protection of confidentiality by constructing a vignette for each of the sections and subsections of this chapter. Using the chapter outline below, consider engaging in that exercise by creating examples that are (1) written from the patient's point of view and (2) constructed from your own clinical setting. (This can also be a useful exercise when conducting conversations about confidentiality in a peer consultation group or clinical workshop, as described in the next chapter.)

The chapter outline below was created from the therapist's point of view. Reword each of the topics and subtopics to reflect the patient's point of view; then construct a brief vignette about each of these situations:

- Disclosing information with "inadequately informed" consent
- Disclosures to third-party payers without fully informed consent
- Disclosures to patient-related third parties without patient consent
- Disclosures to referral sources and other professionals
- Talking too much
- Informal conversations
- Overdisclosures
- Writing too much
    - Unprotective record keeping
    - Unprotective report writing
- Failing to establish protective policies, procedures, and technological safeguards
    - Poorly trained staff
    - Technological "glitches"
    - Inadequate environmental safeguards
- Wearing too many hats
- Failing to anticipate legal demands and avoid legally preventable disclosures
- Failing to foresee and prevent "preventable" subpoenas
- Misunderstanding legal requirements or accepting bad advice
- Abusing "legally allowed" exceptions to confidentiality

9

Step 6: Talking More About Confidentiality: Educating Each Other and the Public

First, therapists need to acknowledge that the issue exists. Is confidentiality important? If it is, then it's worth defending… Before anything, they can *talk* about the issue. The changes we describe in our book happened at least in part because the profession was asleep at the wheel. Now it needs to wake up and look the crisis in the face.

Christopher Bollas, from a 1995 interview about his book, *The New Informants*

With this epigraph, we return to where we began. Here, the author of the Chapter 1 epigraph advises therapists to wake up and start talking more about the problems if they hope to counteract the erosion of patient confidentiality. This final step in the Ethical Practice Model focuses on building relationships in which mental health professionals can educate and support each other about this aspect of practice and take actions toward providing better confidentiality protections.

This chapter is about the importance of creating conversations. Therapists' policies about confidentiality are not confidential. The dilemmas they face in upholding their policies can be talked about, with each other and with others, as long as patients are not identified. The Ethical Practice Model (in Box 3.1 and Appendix V) can provide a shared language that all mental health professionals can use for creating clearer conversations with each other about this difficult aspect of practice. But the conversations need not end there. The model can also be helpful for structuring student training and supervision about confidentiality, for teaching staff and employees in clinical settings, and for writing on the topic in academic and clinical journals. In even broader contexts, the model can be the basis for educating attorneys, judges, legislators, and the public.

In each of these conversational contexts, one of the topics of discussion can be the overlap and potential conflict between therapists' ethical obligations and the legal requirements that can limit their ability to protect patients' confidences. This has caused much confusion and many ethical-legal conflicts.

> If we, as a profession and as individual practitioners, are to address the possible conflicts between the law and the welfare of our clients, one of the initial steps is to engage in frequent, open, and honest discussion of the issue. The topic must be addressed in our graduate courses, internship programs, case conferences, professional conventions, and informal discussions with our colleagues.[1]

This chapter illustrates how the Ethical Practice Model can be useful in creating conversations toward such goals as (1) helping individual mental health professionals develop clearer personal positions and more ethical policies about confidentiality and disclosure, (2) planning joint projects for staff training, (3) creating consultation networks and ethics-based continuing education training about confidentiality, (4) providing better ethics training about confidentiality for clinical graduate students and supervisees, (5) helping attorneys and judges understand how differing roles affect the confidentiality rules, and (6) educating the public and lobbying for legislative reform toward better protections of confidentiality for mental health patients.

The complications about therapeutic confidentiality span all professions and settings. Conversations with a goal of self-understanding and mutual professional understanding can take place as dialogues with oneself, consultations among colleagues, or discussions among groups of mental health professionals. Through conversations such as these, therapists can cooperate in creating better resources for themselves and for others, can explore the possibilities for expanding collaborative consultation at the local level, and can advocate for multidisciplinary training and continuing education to be organized at the state level.

Finally, some conversational goals may require cooperation among state professional organizations and consumer groups. However, projects for public education and legislative reform ordinarily begin at the grass roots level, so they can be initiated by individual therapists, by peer groups such as those described below, or by local chapters of therapists' professional groups.

Regardless of the context of the conversation, it can be helpful to have available some of the basic resources related to the protection of patients' rights about confidentiality. These would include relevant ethics codes and professional recommendations, as well as up-to-date information about state and federal laws.[2]

Conversations Among Therapists

Therapists tend to become anxious when someone mentions confidentiality. This has created both self-imposed isolation and a great deal of secrecy about its complications. Yet, what therapists need is just the opposite—more open conversations in which they can discuss their problems in maintaining patients' confidences, more sense of mutual understanding of the complicated dilemmas and difficult legal and financial decisions that they face about this aspect of clinical practice, and more opportunities to learn from each others' successes and mistakes. Until therapists stop hiding their confidentiality problems, they can remain fearful of being "discovered," unwilling to ask for help in advance, unable to predict and avoid self-inflicted ethical dilemmas, and unlikely to learn enough from past mistakes, whether their own or those of others.

CONVERSATIONS TOWARD SELF-UNDERSTANDING, PLANNING, AND SUPPORT

Sometimes it is difficult for therapists to step back far enough to be clear about their own *real* position about the protection of patients' confidences. Regardless of the position they have chosen, they will need personal clarity and some extensive planning.

Those therapists who take an "absolute confidentiality" position will have the easiest task at the front end, because every situation has the very same solution: "Do not disclose." Down the road, however, these therapists may face some huge legal and financial consequences, because sometimes their absolute promises about confidentiality can be kept only by breaking the law. Regrettably, when faced with that ethical-legal conflict, therapists who begin by thinking they are absolutist about confidentiality usually end up deciding to break their confidentiality promise rather than break the law. This leaves the patient betrayed—unexpectedly holding all the risk. For this reason, it is ethically essential that therapists not take this position lightly—not promise absolute confidentiality in words or imply it by their silence—and then break that promise if the going gets tough.

Those therapists who do offer "absolute confidentiality" may not need help from each other in planning how they will behave—they will all behave exactly the same way, all the time. What they *will* need from each other, however, is support for maintaining their position and keeping their promise, and support for dealing with the consequences of how they intend to behave. They will need to band together to plan for the potential financial penalties and lawsuits that might result from disobeying reporting laws and other disclosure laws. They can also make plans to be available to attend to each others' clinical practices if they are incarcerated for contempt for disobeying court orders to disclose confidential information.[3]

For obvious reasons, most therapists take a "conditional confidentiality" position instead. This allows them to place some conditions on their promise of confidentiality, either to avoid risks to themselves or because they believe that some legally required disclosures serve social ends that are more important than a patient's right to confidentiality. For these therapists, the task is harder at the front end: They must decide in advance which circumstances they will treat as exceptions to the confidentiality rule and then must prepare to explain those limits of confidentiality to prospective patients. The therapists who make only conditional promises about confidentiality must therefore be very clear in advance about what "conditions" they will impose—must know exactly when they might make an exception to the rule of confidentiality—so that they can be clear with prospective patients about what the rules will really be and be ready to answer their questions honestly. Although the planning at Step 1 will take time, and the informed consent conversation at Step 2 may have some clinical consequences, it is the only honest and ethical choice available to therapists who want to avoid the personal consequences of engaging in civil disobedience.

For those therapists who offer this "conditional confidentiality," joint discussions can help prevent the isolation that arises when they single-handedly try to develop individualized policies that both protect patients' confidentiality rights and protect themselves from liability. Rather than becoming passive and helpless in the face of this seemingly impossible (but ethically required) task, therapists can engage in joint efforts like those described below.

Whether working alone or as a group, therapists must understand some very basic things about the ethics of "conditional confidentiality." How can one distinguish between (1) those who behave ethically, following predictable ethical rules about confidentiality, but who nevertheless differ in their behaviors about it in certain situations; (2) those who are well intentioned but are "winging it" (practicing ad hoc, with no consistent policies, sometimes behaving arbitrarily), thereby placing patients at more risk than they realize; and (3) those who (perhaps knowingly?) engage in blatantly unethical practices and completely ignore certain patients' rights about confidentiality? What can we learn from the first group? How can we teach the second group? What should we do about the third group?

When therapists use the Ethical Practice Model to structure conversations about confidentiality, most of the unsettling ambiguity about what constitutes "ethical behavior" will disappear. Therapists who follow the model are practicing within ethical limits, regardless of exactly *what* limits they place on confidentiality; therapists who do *not* may be placing patients at risk. By demonstrating where the risks can arise, the model opens the door for therapists to create better and more cooperative discussions about how to provide the best protections for therapy patients, and thereby for themselves, at each step along the way. The conversations can begin by asking some simple questions like those below.

How Can It Be Ethical for Each Therapist to Behave Differently About Confidentiality?

This is not easy to discuss. The confusion about the "ethics of conditional confidentiality" has become unsettling not only to the public but also among colleagues. Therapists are usually reasonably comfortable in talking about why their differences in *theoretical orientation* lead to differing interactions with patients about it. But their uncertainty level has increased to the point at which many are uncomfortable talking about how their differences in *ethical orientation* create differences in behavior about confidentiality.

The answer to the question is twofold: First, therapists have the ethical freedom to decide whether to promise absolute confidentiality (i.e., to make no exceptions to the confidentiality rule) or whether to place conditions on confidentiality. Second, among therapists who practice conditional confidentiality, differences in behavior are ethical because the legally imposed "conditions" will vary from state to state and from setting to setting within a state, and the voluntary "conditions" can even vary from therapist to therapist within the same setting since therapists maintain different personal positions about when to place limits on confidentiality.

How Can It Be Ethical for Therapists to Choose Their Own Exceptions to the Rule?

Using the Ethical Practice Model, it is easy to demonstrate that therapists' professions now give them the ethical freedom to decide what exceptions they will make to the confidentiality rule. Variations in state laws now require therapists to impose a wide range of limits on confidentiality, and circumstances in practice settings also require them to impose setting-specific limits; thus, the ethics codes of all mental health professions reflect the fact that such differences are ethically permissible. The Ethical Practice Model reflects the fact that therapists must make the most basic decision entirely on their own (at Step 1)—and that, at that basic level—therapists have only two choices: *Will I offer unconditional or conditional confidentiality?*

How therapists answer this question will have implications for their decision about the setting in which they will practice. Therapists who want to promise unconditional confidentiality must be either in independent practice or in some other setting that will support them if they must break the laws in order to keep that promise. The model demonstrates why it is unethical to make (or imply) that promise unless one actually intends to keep it. In contrast, therapists who promise only conditional confidentiality can practice in any setting. Sometimes, the setting will determine what conditions will apply; in some settings, the therapist may make that decision independently. The decisions about exactly what conditions will apply must be made in advance. The model makes it clear that it is unethical to limit confidentiality without explaining those limits in advance to prospective patients.

Therapists who choose to offer conditional confidentiality have a wide range of options about what those conditions will be. The options are not unlimited, because certain types of disclosures are always unethical, including gossip about patients or sharing identifiable information with others who have no involvement in the case. But, within each setting, there may be a unique set of possible limits of confidentiality, and prospective patients have no way of knowing what they will be until they hear it from their prospective therapist.

Do Therapists Still Have Any "Non-Negotiable" Ethical Rules About Confidentiality?

As reflected in the model, the answer is an unqualified "Yes." First, the model as a whole is non-negotiable, because it was constructed from ethical standards that govern the behavior of mental health professionals. Second, most of the specifics within each step of the model are also non-negotiable. For example, Step 2 applies to all who intend to place any conditions on confidentiality, regardless of the number or type of the exceptions they intend to make, and Step 3 applies to all therapists. Obviously, the content of some steps will vary from therapist to therapist. For example, the content of the conversations in Step 2 will differ depending on exactly when and how each therapist intends to limit confidentiality. Similarly, the content of Step 4 will vary, because each state has different laws, and within each state, each therapist may make slightly different decisions about how to respond to each of the legal demands. As for the content of Step 5, some of the "preventable" disclosures reflect "non-negotiable" rules (such as not gossiping about patients). Others (such as avoiding disclosures whenever legally possible unless the patient gives consent) reflect a supererogatory position that is recommended here, even though not always ethically required.

CONSULTATION FOR DEVELOPING POLICIES AND PATIENT HANDOUTS ABOUT CONFIDENTIALITY

Conversation among therapists can be useful for developing their policies, improving them, and creating patient handouts about confidentiality. This can be done either in consultation with an individual peer or in meetings with a consultation group. Each therapist may need to develop a slightly different set of policies and therefore will need to use a slightly different informed consent handout. However, within a peer consultation group, these can be discussed, reviewed, and edited. Such a group also provides the opportunity for role playing and practice. For example, therapists can each practice delivering their "intake speech" about confidentiality and its limits to become more comfortable at informing prospective patients about their policies, answering patients' questions honestly, and avoiding a defensive posture when describing the limits of confidentiality that will apply in their setting. The mutual trust that can be developed through this peer process can also make it more likely that these therapists will consult with each other in later crises about confidentiality, rather than trying to deal with them in isolation.

The Ethical Practice Model is useful in this process because it points to six separate ethically required actions, making it easier to recognize those areas where consultation and support might be needed. It also helps clarify the intimate interrelationship among these separate ethical requirements. Finally, the model can be helpful in conversations about legal issues with each other and with legal consultants.

Using Consultation Groups to Help Reduce the Confidentiality Risks

Therapists often join peer groups to discuss clinical cases and receive support in clinical crises. Clinical issues overlap with ethical issues, and the topic of confidentiality often arises in discussing clinical cases. In these situations, using the Ethical Practice Model can help clarify the ethical issues. However, for therapists who are still unclear about their ethical obligations about confidentiality, there can be advantages in creating a separate peer consultation group on that specific topic. The Ethical Practice Model can then be studied and discussed in a systematic way. Although clinical case examples can be useful in illustrating complications or dilemmas at each step in the model, the primary focus of such a group could be "the ethics of confidentiality" rather than the clinical issues. The desired outcome should be reduced risks to patients, and, thereby, also reduced risks to therapists. This systematic study of confidentiality ethics can also prepare therapists to teach others about confidentiality ethics, both in their training of nonclinical staff and in their clinical supervision relationships.

Sharing Legal Consultation About Confidentiality

For the purpose of making decisions about their voluntary disclosures, therapists can benefit from consultation and problem-solving sessions with colleagues from any jurisdiction. However, the *legal exceptions* that can be imposed on confidentiality will differ from state to state (and sometimes from agency to agency within each state), so for this discussion it is most helpful for therapists to join with colleagues who practice in similar settings within the same state. This makes it easier to obtain the relevant legal information and share ideas about how to integrate the legal requirements within one's own ethical practices.

Therapists often consult an attorney when faced with a patient crisis involving confidentiality (e.g., when they receive their first subpoena). However, it can be more protective to have some legal questions answered in advance, not in the midst of a crisis. Individual therapists are free to initiate this consultation, but there can also be benefits in contracting for this "preventive" consultation as a group. Not only will this reduce each therapist's cost, but it provides an opportunity to learn from the attorney's answers to others' questions. In this process, the model can help the therapists inform the consultant about their profession's ethical baseline, thereby increasing the likelihood that the consultant's recommendations will be consistent with clinical ethics as defined by their own professions. Appendix V uses italics to indicate how legal details fit into the ethical picture at each step of the model. The Center for Ethical Practice has also provided a color-coded version of the model that more clearly indicates how both state laws and federal Health

Insurance Portability and Accountability Act (HIPAA) regulations can be integrated into the six Steps.[4]

CONFRONTING PEERS

All therapists have ethical standards that require them to monitor their own professions by confronting colleagues who engage in ethical misconduct.[5] Most state licensing boards also legally require therapists to confront or report colleagues who fail to maintain their licensure standards. The Ethical Practice Model is a convenient description of therapists' collective ethical responsibilities about confidentiality. Therapists can use it for explaining ethical duties when confronting or educating peers who are not adequately protecting their clients' confidentiality rights.

PLANNING COLLABORATIVE STAFF TRAINING

Chapter 13 is about creating ethics-based confidentiality training for clinical and nonclinical staff in mental health settings. Here, we consider the possibility that such training might be planned and conducted as collaborative efforts by groups of therapists who practice in the same agency or who share similar private practice settings. In the process of such joint planning, each therapist can focus on one section of the training outline, with each then becoming "resident expert" about certain aspects of confidentiality, whether related to ethical standards or to legal issues. These individuals are then available as consultants to others who later have questions or face a crisis about that aspect of confidentiality policy or practice. As in the following section, this collaboration and training can be interdisciplinary in nature, as long as the ethical standards for each profession are considered and the ethics code of each profession is available for reference.

Conversations Creating Interdisciplinary Networks for Training and Continuing Education

Issues of confidentiality rarely raise turf battles across disciplines. This makes it easier to plan interdisciplinary support and education about confidentiality. Therapists can join together across disciplines to create local, regional, and state consultation resources (especially about issues of potential ethical-legal conflict); to present ethics-based continuing education opportunities (as opposed to legal-based attorney-led HIPAA-focused training); to provide regular updates about changes in ethical or legal requirements; and to be available to help train and mentor clinical graduate students and practicing therapists who are still in training or yet unlicensed.

IMPROVING CONFIDENTIALITY TRAINING FOR CLINICAL STUDENTS AND SUPERVISEES

In explaining how therapists got into the "confidentiality problem" in the first place, we may need to put "weakness in ethics training" first on the list:

> How did psychology reach a point where the confidentiality that animates the relationship is so besieged? The bases of this crisis are multidetermined ... 1. *Weakness in ethics training*: The self-examination and critical thinking required to master confidentiality are daunting. Psychologists in training have little hope of adequate preparation if faculty and supervisors have minimal direct experience in these challenges (a vulnerability in research-oriented programs) or if the program finds it unprofitable to devote adequate resources (a vulnerability in for-profit training programs). A remedy: Require accredited programs to demonstrate sophisticated ethics training.[6]

Research indicates that the ethical violations of clinical students and supervisees often involve breaches of confidentiality.[7] Their professional enculturation should therefore include clear training and high expectations about this aspect of practice.

> The very nature of many training clinics requires that trainees share more client information than ordinarily would be appropriate in clinical practice; but good training clinics carefully ensure that students understand the importance of respecting client confidentiality and do not misinterpret the sharing in training clinics as a license to treat patient confidences lightly.[8]

It does not help matters that those who teach, train, and supervise clinical graduate students may have received their own confidentiality training a generation before, under previous ethics codes and earlier laws, and perhaps before the onset of managed care. Often, they are not currently engaged in providing direct service to patients, and, in some cases, they have never practiced as therapists. In contrast, the practicing therapists who have educated themselves on this topic are prepared to provide confidentiality training to graduate students and other trainees. It is therefore important for therapists to include clinical trainees in the ethics-based confidentiality training provided for staff in any setting in which they supervise practicum or internship trainees. These students and interns can then carry their systematic knowledge to their future training sites and thus improve the confidentiality protections for patients in those settings.

For training and supervision purposes, the six steps of the Ethical Practice Model can be taught separately, but the model as a whole can be used to illustrate how the apparently unrelated ethical mandates fit together to form an integrated whole. For example, consider how the model might be used for teaching how confidentiality ethics applies to managed care: Step 1 requires careful reading of provider contracts, to clarify their disclosure provisions; Step 2 covers the initial discussion with clients about the kinds of disclosures that will be required if the patient chooses to obtain reimbursement, and the potential risks of that choice; Step 3 is a reminder that, when submitting treatment plans and claim forms, therapists should inform patients about the nature of the information being disclosed before it is sent to the third-party payer; Step 4 notes that provider contracts usually contain legally binding disclosure requirements; Step 5 helps punctuate the fact that the disclosures to third-party payers are *voluntary,* and that such disclosures should not be made without the patient's *informed* consent; and Step 6 is a reminder that state laws and regulations can greatly influence the confidentiality and security policies of insurance companies and managed plans.

CREATING MULTIDISCIPLINARY ETHICS-BASED CONTINUING EDUCATION ABOUT CONFIDENTIALITY

Confidentiality is a topic that lends itself well to interdisciplinary training. Therapists' ethics codes all protect confidentiality rights in similar ways, even though they may emphasize different aspects and issues.[9] Ethics-based continuing education training for multidisciplinary groups of therapists can therefore be provided as local training or can be sponsored by joint efforts of state professional associations.

Regrettably, much of the confidentiality training now available for practicing therapists is not based on their own ethical principles, but is instead based on legal requirements. Such training is often sponsored by law firms or conducted by attorneys. Although its topic may include the word "ethics," the content often focuses only on state laws and federal HIPAA regulations. More importantly, its emphasis is legal-focused (i.e., obeying laws) rather than built around the ethics of practice (i.e., protecting patients).

> Such legally based training creates several ethical problems for psychologists. First, it fosters the impression that attorneys—not clinicians—have become the only "real" experts about this aspect of practice. Second, it creates a legal language about confidentiality that threatens to usurp psychologists' own clinical or ethical language about it: Laws take center stage, when what is needed is a language for placing them into ethical context. Third, it exacerbates the figure–ground confusion (by substituting legal rules for ethical rules) and often takes a risk-management perspective that raises anxiety: It encourages psychologists to focus on obeying laws in order to avoid risks to *themselves*, when what they need is a clearer focus on their ethical obligations and the potential risks to *clients*. Finally, the legal emphasis obscures an important fact about risk management: Understanding and following the relevant ethical principles is an essential ingredient in avoiding a malpractice suit.[10]

In contrast, training that is grounded in professional ethics can place legal requirements into ethical context. The six steps of the Ethical Practice Model can help indicate how various legal issues fit into the ethical picture of "conditional confidentiality." This is even more apparent when trainers use the color-coded version of the model that indicates how state laws and HIPAA regulations fit into that ethical structure.[11]

Conversations Leading to Public Education and Legislative Reform

Therapists can help both their patients and themselves if they treat confidentiality less as a secret topic and more as a public issue. "The unchecked erosion of confidentiality is nothing less than an erosion of psychology, and of all health care, as professions and as independent entities."[12] If therapists want to help reverse this trend, they can create opportunities for conversations that educate court personnel, legislators, and the public about those confidentiality conflicts that are impossible to resolve within their individual practices, because they can be alleviated only through legislative monitoring and legal reform.

EDUCATING ATTORNEYS AND JUDGES

Legal professionals are easily confused by the fact that when mental health professionals change roles, they may need to change their confidentiality rules. As a result, they may behave very differently about confidentiality on two consecutive days, depending upon whether they are involved in the legal system voluntarily or involuntarily. One day, they will voluntarily serve as an expert evaluator for the court, willingly providing all available information from a recent evaluation in their report and in testimony; the next day, they will use all available legal means to avoid complying with a subpoena or testifying "involuntarily" about their therapy patient, whose confidentiality they have an ethical obligation to protect.

Individual therapists are rarely in a position to have personal conversations with judges about such matters, and it is not appropriate in the midst of a court case to initiate a formal training about their differing roles. However, if therapists themselves are very clear about which hat they are wearing whenever they appear in court, they can explain the limits of that role to the judge, and, through their behavior, they are educating the court about how their specific role in that case affects their ethical obligations about confidentiality.

Attorneys who are confused about therapists' roles can complicate matters for therapists and their patients. For example, attorneys sometimes suggest to clients that their therapist should be subpoenaed to testify "in their behalf" in a court case. The patient may agree to this plan, expecting that the therapist will serve as a good character reference for them. Sometimes, this decision is made without consultation with the therapist, even though both the patient and the attorney are completely uninformed about the content of the therapy record or about what the therapist might say on the stand. Chapters 7 and 8 (Step 4 and Step 5, respectively) contained recommendations about how therapists can anticipate (and hopefully avoid) the ethical, legal, and clinical complications that arise from such misunderstandings. But, when such incidents do arise, therapists can, with the patient's informed consent, use them as opportunities to initiate conversations that educate the attorney about the confidentiality implications of their specific roles. This can perhaps reduce some of the pressures (and some of the inappropriate subpoenas) that arise from those confusions.

Mental health professionals are occasionally offered the opportunity to provide formal or informal training for legal professionals. In such circumstances, the chart in Appendix VI can be useful in describing the differential ethical responsibilities in various court-related roles.[13]

EDUCATING THE PUBLIC AND LOBBYING FOR LEGISLATIVE REFORM

Public education can be important in the protection of the confidentiality rights of mental health patients. Public awareness and consumer support is necessary for monitoring and combating the confidentiality inroads created by managed care; for lobbying toward increased statutory protections of confidentiality, including better therapist–patient privilege laws; and for using court challenges to confront inadequate consumer protections, wherever they may exist. Conversations toward public education can be initiated by therapists as individuals or as groups. This can include letters to local or statewide newspapers, discussions with local consumer groups, conversations with parent groups, and more.

Conversations advocating legislative reform can include similar efforts. The lobbying of legislators is more powerful if undertaken by larger groups, such as coalitions of state or national mental health professional associations, but such efforts often begin through the initiation of individual therapists or through the combined pressures brought by local groups of therapists. Psychiatry is the only mental health profession whose ethics code currently includes an ethical mandate about such efforts: "A physician shall respect the law and also recognize a responsibility to seek changes in those requirements which are contrary to the best interests of the patient."[14] However, such efforts benefit all patients and are most effective when engaged in cooperatively by therapists of all professions.

In all such conversations, therapists can begin by making a case for the importance of confidentiality to the therapy process and to the patient's privacy. In Chapter 1, the section on "Underlying Ethical Principles" provides some resources that therapists can cite when educating legislators or lobbying for more protective legislation.

Practice Pointers

Why do therapists tend to be reluctant to discuss confidentiality? The issues therapists face about confidentiality are not confidential. The fact that patients run risks when confiding in a therapist is not confidential. As long as no identifiable patient information is disclosed, there are no impediments to educating each other, training young professionals, and informing the public in conversations using those formats described in this chapter.

For problem areas that are within the therapist's control, exercises such as those suggested in the previous chapters can provide ways to explore the topics, whether in peer consultation, supervision, or workshops. For other problem areas, including the need for legislative reforms, plans can be originated using the sections of this chapter.

For those therapists who are still reluctant to talk about confidentiality's complications, it might be important to try to identify the reasons:

- If your concern is about invading the privacy or breaching the confidentiality of a specific patient, this can easily be avoided by using hypothetical cases to illustrate the ethical and legal issues.
- If your concern is about the possibility of disclosing some mistake that would put you or another therapist at risk, this should not be a problem if examples are constructed as "hypotheticals" rather than presented as examples of the therapist's own behavior.
- If your concern is that you will sound uninformed about the *legal* issues, these conversations can help you become more informed. If, on the other hand, the concern is about sounding uninformed about the *ethical* issues, then once you become grounded in the Ethical Practice Model, you may find yourself prepared to teach others.

PART III

Practical Considerations

10

Clinical Record Keeping

Everything in the previous chapters would apply to all the information therapists know about a patient, whether or not they ever made a record of it. However, this chapter considers only ethical issues related to the confidentiality of patient information that has been recorded, whether on paper or electronically.

The past two decades have brought big changes in the professional discussions about record keeping.

> Until fairly recently, discussions of case recording and documentation focused almost entirely on clinical relevance. Discussions of ... documentation are no longer limited to clinicians who need to record their interactions with clients to facilitate the delivery of services. The profession has come to recognize the usefulness of documentation for risk management purposes.[1]

In other words, there has been a shift away from clinical (patient-centered) and ethical (patient-protective) considerations and toward a risk management (therapist-protective) focus. Documentation serves many functions, but we will address here only ethical and legal issues related to confidentiality, regardless of the function being served.

Ethical Standards and Professional Guidance

The ethical standards related to records apply to records in any form. In the American Psychological Association (APA) Ethics Code, the Privacy and Confidentiality section begins with the statement, "Psychologists have a primary obligation ... to protect confidential information obtained through or stored in any medium;"[2] and the Record Keeping section contains the mandate to "maintain confidentiality in creating, storing, accessing, transferring, and disposing of records ... whether these are written, automated, or in any other medium."[3] Similarly, the National Association of Social Workers (NASW) Ethics Code states that social workers must "protect the confidentiality of clients' written and electronic records."[4]

In addition to ethics codes, some professions provide further guidance about patient records, and these can be useful for all therapists, regardless of their profession. The APA Record Keeping Guidelines provide extensive and detailed recommendations.[5] The APA *Handbook of Ethics in Psychology* also contains a long chapter on confidentiality and record keeping.[6] The NASW provides a 100-page Law Note, "Social Workers and Clinical Notes."[7] The American Counseling Association (ACA) Legal Series includes a 128-page monograph, "Documentation in Counseling Records."[8] Most ethics texts also contain extensive chapters on record keeping and its impact on confidentiality.

Malpractice insurers also provide resources about record keeping; they consider well-documented clinical records a good defense for a therapist in the event of a patient lawsuit or licensing board complaint. The NASW Insurance Trust provides an online resource, "Client Records: Keep or Toss?"[9] The APA Insurance Trust provides recommendations about confidentiality of records throughout its risk management text.[10] The American Professional Agency offers articles entitled "Are Your Records Protected?"[11] and "Walking the Documentation Tightrope,"[12] the latter of which addresses the difficulty of balancing the potentially conflicting goals of creating accurate records, protecting client confidentiality, and reducing liability exposure.

The discussion here includes recommendations from all such sources and should be useful to therapists of all professions. In addition, as discussed in the chapters of Part II, each step of the Ethical Practice Model has implications for confidentiality of patient records. Mental health professionals would need to place within that model any state laws or organizational policies that have implications for record keeping.

> Using the Ethical Practice Model, therapists can place legal and organizational record keeping requirements into ethical context by learning them at Step 1, explaining their implications to clients at Step 2, obtaining consent at Step 3 before releasing records voluntarily, responding ethically to legal demands for records at Step 4, preventing security breaches and accidental disclosures at Step 5, and talking about confidentiality in Step 6.[13]

Legal Issues

At the state level, legal requirements about therapy records may appear as general statutes, state agency regulations, or state licensing board regulations, all of which vary from state to state. Sometimes, these legal requirements govern what must be documented in a therapy patient's record, but more often they involve requirements about such things as record storage and security.[14]

At the federal level, the Health Insurance Portability and Accountability Act (HIPAA) regulations contain very detailed requirements about storing, transmitting, and destroying patient records in a manner that protects their confidentiality. Some of those are described briefly in the sections below, but a detailed HIPAA summary is also included in Appendix IV. Websites of the national professional associations also contain HIPAA information for practitioners.[15] Because of the complexity of these regulations, most practice settings send one or more staff members to receive formal HIPAA training. This is readily available, usually sponsored and/or provided by law firms. As described in Chapter 13, this legal-based staff training can be integrated into broader ethics-based training about confidentiality of records.

Practical Issues

The sections below cover only a few of the many ethically relevant practical considerations about patient records. Recommendations that focus primarily on protecting the patient tend to come from ethics texts, although the professions now also focus on therapist liability and self-protection, as do the malpractice insurers.

RECORD CONTENT

Ethics codes do not impose detailed requirements about content of records. Instead, they contain general statements about what should be recorded and then defer to the detailed requirements that apply in the therapist's state or setting. For example, the ACA Ethics Code requires the following:

> Counselors maintain records necessary for rendering professional services to their clients and as required by laws, regulations, or agency or institution procedures. Counselors include sufficient and timely documentation in their client records to facilitate the delivery and continuity of needed services. Counselors take reasonable steps to ensure that documentation in records accurately reflects client progress and services provided. If errors are made in client records, counselors take steps to properly note the correction of such errors according to agency or institutional policies.[16]

Within the APA Record Keeping Guidelines, the "Content of Records" section contains the most extensive recommendations. It includes guidance about weighing and balancing the many considerations about what should be included in the records.[17]

Decisions about record content can involve a complex balancing act. If patient confidentiality were the only consideration, therapists' records might contain little or nothing! But decisions about what to document must take into account not only ethical issues about protecting confidentiality, but also clinical issues (such as need for enough detail to facilitate continuity of care in the event of therapist absence), as well as content requirements imposed by contractual agreements (with agencies or with managed care entities). When applicable, decisions about content must include considerations about documentation of supervision, as well as information necessary for obtaining reimbursement for services. Meanwhile, they also potentially involve considerations about legal liability issues (such as therapists' possible need to defend their decisions in the event of a later ethics complaint or lawsuit). In other words, documenting too much can put the patient's confidentiality at risk, but documenting too little can put patient care at risk and can be perilous for the therapist. It is not easy to strike a balance. "Admittedly, distinguishing between too much and too little detail can be difficult. It requires experience and reasoned decision-making."[18]

Further complicating therapists' documentation decisions are the legally binding contracts they sign as providers for managed care companies. These contracts usually contain detailed requirements about what must be written in the treatment record, as well as clauses that abridge patient confidentiality (such as requirements to make patient records available for audits by the third-party payer whenever requested).

Documenting Beginnings and Endings

Documentation about the beginning of a therapy relationship should include copies of the information forms that were provided to the patient at intake, because these describe what the patient was actually told about such things as confidentiality and its limits. Including signed HIPAA forms in the record will document the fact that the patient also received information about other rights related to privacy and confidentiality, such as the right to have access to the record, the right to request corrections to the record, and the right to request that the therapist's out-of-session contacts be made only in certain ways or at certain times (for example, not leaving messages on their home phone or calling at their workplace).

It is also recommended that therapists document the ending of the therapy relationship.[19] This makes it clear that the relationship has ended and that the therapist is no longer responsible for the patient's care. Documenting termination can be especially important if the patient ended the relationship prematurely or abruptly, or if the ending was initiated by the therapist. Malpractice insurers are also emphatic about the importance of documenting what the patient was told about the termination if it was caused by a non-reimbursement decision by a third-party payer:

> The fact of termination and the reason for termination should be noted. This is particularly crucial when treatment ends prematurely as a result of the insurer covering only a limited number of sessions. To me, this is the most important area a psychologist must document. The therapist must tell the patient, "I believe you are in need of further treatment. I want to be very clear with you on that. My recommendation is that you go to such and such mental

health center, or that you self-pay for continued treatment." Then record the fact that the patient was told. Also, if the patient turns down the recommendation for further treatment, that should be recorded as well."[20]

Documenting Telephone Contacts and Electronic Communications

All contacts should be documented, whether they are contacts with the patient or contacts with someone else regarding the patient. This would include not only in-person contacts, but also contacts via telephone, e-mail, texting, or any other electronic or internet-facilitated communications.

> Just as one would want to document all telephone contacts with a client, a client's family member, employer, other treating professional or anyone else one has contact with regarding the client, the same can be said for e-mail contacts. If no record of the interaction exists (either a copy of the email communication itself or an entry in the clinical record detailing the e-mail communication) we will not be able to refer back to it for clinical purposes in the future and we will not be able to use it as evidence of interactions with the client.[21]

Excluding Certain Content

When deciding what to record, therapists should imagine having over their shoulder all the people or agencies that might eventually obtain access to the patient's record. It is important to remember that the client may be among those who eventually see the treatment record, so documentation decisions should include that consideration.

Some things should *not* be included in a clinical record. "First, therapists should never discuss their own countertransference experiences—the feelings and fantasies that they have toward their patients—in the clinical record ... Second, don't record the innermost details of the patient's life. There is no need to record details about the patient's sex life, fantasy life, or potentially embarrassing information."[22] Therapists should "strive for objectivity ... show sensitivity in what they place in patient records, exclude any gratuitous remarks, and use behavioral descriptions whenever possible."[23]

RESPONDING TO CLIENTS' REQUESTS TO CREATE NO RECORDS

Most therapists have encountered at least one patient who requested that no record be made of their therapy sessions.

> A variety of rationales are proffered for this request, ranging from the wish not to weaken one's chances in a custody battle; the wish to avoid stigma for political or other reasons; the concern that a permanent record will be created containing embarrassing material that could be revealed; or overtly paranoid concerns ("The CIA might find out about me.")[24]

Therapists usually try to engage in clinical exploration of the reasons behind such requests, but this does not mean that the issue is negotiable. The APA Record Keeping Guidelines state that the therapist who receives such a request "then considers whether treatment can be provided under that condition."[25] The APA Insurance Trust recommends that therapists weigh the patient's request against ethical and legal standards, as well as relevant clinical considerations.[26] In short, therapists should not comply with a request that would require them to violate an ethical/professional standard of conduct about record keeping, a legal requirement about content of records, or a clinically important continuity-of-care consideration.[27]

Official Records Versus "Psychotherapy Notes"

The HIPAA regulations give special confidentiality protections to a therapist's private notes, but unfortunately it gives them the legal name of "psychotherapy notes." That term causes confusion because it is the phrase therapists traditionally used when referring to their official record of a patient's psychotherapy sessions. Under the HIPAA definition, however, "psychotherapy notes" contain only material that is *not* documented in the official record:

> We define "psychotherapy notes" to mean detailed notes recorded (in any medium) by a health care provider who is a mental health professional documenting or analyzing the contents of conversation during a private counseling session or a group, joint, or family counseling session. Such notes are used only by the therapist who wrote them, are maintained separately from the medical record, and are not involved in the documentation necessary for health care treatment, payment, or operations.[28]

In contrast, HIPAA defines the official records (sometimes termed a "system of records" or a "designated record set") to include "medication prescription and monitoring, counseling session start and stop times, modalities and frequencies of treatment furnished, results of clinical tests, and/or a brief summary of the following items: diagnosis, functional status, the treatment plan, symptoms, prognosis and progress to date."[29]

Should therapists keep two sets of records—an official record and a personal set of notes? There are recommendations in both directions.

Advantages of keeping separate "psychotherapy notes" include the fact that this allows the therapist to maintain both an official record and a "work product" that is less accessible to others. The "notes" are more protected, even from access by the patient. Whereas patients have a right to see the official record, they have no right to see the "psychotherapy notes" (unless a state law explicitly gives access, which most do not). Furthermore, the usual exceptions to confidentiality do not apply, so these notes may be voluntarily released only with explicit client consent.[30] However, for therapists to reap these legal advantages, they must place in their "psychotherapy notes" only the information described above, must maintain them separately, and must store them in such a manner that only the therapist who created the notes will have access to them.[31]

It has been suggested that the advantages of separating official records from private notes include ease in processing reimbursement claims, since it is appropriate to disclose only the information in the official record for that purpose:

> For reimbursement purposes, should both notes be combined as one, it is the clinical social worker's responsibility to extract the necessary information required to process a claim. The best practice is to keep the psychotherapy notes separated from the patient's record for heightened privacy protection under HIPAA. This also permits smooth processing of reimbursement through the use of proper progress notes.[32]

Long before HIPAA, psychotherapists or psychoanalysts who work from a psychodynamic or psychoanalytic perspective were sometimes advised to keep their "process notes" separate from the official record. "As a solid rule of thumb: there is no room for unconscious fantasies in a public record. (And—because of the possibility of subpoena—all records are potentially public). Process material, conscious and unconscious content, and the like belong in a private set of notes."[33] However, this advice presumes that such notes would be safe from subpoena, which, in fact, is not the case in many states.

Disadvantages of keeping separate "psychotherapy notes" would include the obvious added care and time burden involved in creating, coordinating, and providing secure storage for two separate sets of records. Therapists in most states should not go to the trouble of maintaining separate documents if their purpose is to prevent them from being used as evidence in a court case, because most state privilege laws do not legally distinguish between the two sets of records. This means that in most states, the "psychotherapy notes," although legally protected from voluntary disclosure without the patient's consent, are *not* protected from legally compelled disclosure. For example, if the therapist receives a subpoena or court order for disclosure of "any and all documents" about the patient to be used as evidence in a court case, this could capture both sets of records in most states.[34] If unclear about the legal status of "psychotherapy notes" in their own state, therapists "should obtain legal consultation when weighing the risks and advantages of keeping a private set of records."[35]

The American Mental Health Alliance has provided detailed information about "psychotherapy notes" in a question-and-answer format.[36] This summary is useful because the answers are quoted directly from the HIPAA regulations themselves. Often, however, it can be important to have help in interpreting those complex regulations. This is sometimes available from therapists' national professional organizations, or from attorneys familiar with mental health law.

Patient Access to Records

The ACA Ethics Code stipulates that patients should be able to obtain "clear information about their records."[37] However, most requirements about patient access to the clinical record arise from legal sources. For example, many state laws and regulations stipulate that patients have a right to access their own records. The federal HIPAA regulations also protect the patient's right to have access to the official clinical record, as well as the right to request changes if they believe the record contains errors. However, HIPAA does not give patients the legal right to obtain the therapist's private notes (or "psychotherapy notes").

Most states have laws or regulations protecting patients' rights to obtain access to their records. Although a few states may give patients access to their own records without exception, most state and federal laws do allow exceptions and contain instructions about therapists' responsibilities if they are refusing patient access to the official record on the basis that it would be harmful to the patient or to someone else. The federal HIPAA regulations, like some state laws, stipulate a maximum fee that may be charged for copies and include a requirement to inform patients that they have a legal right to obtain a second opinion about the therapist's decision to deny access.[38]

Confidentiality and Security of Records

Ethical standards require that therapists maintain the confidentiality of records and provide for their security. Although many of the ethical standards listed in Appendices I and II would apply to records, a few address records specifically. Counselors must "ensure that records are kept in a secure location and that only authorized persons have access to records."[39] Psychologists must "maintain confidentiality in creating, storing, accessing, transferring, and disposing of records under their control, whether these are written, automated, or in any other medium."[40] Social workers "should take reasonable steps to ensure that clients' records are stored in a secure location and that clients' records are not available to others who are not authorized to have access."[41] For psychiatrists, the ethics code confidentiality section begins with this statement: "Psychiatric records, including even the identification of a person as a patient, must be protected with extreme care."[42]

Legally, the federal regulations in the HIPAA Security Rule provide the most extensive requirements about maintaining the security of records. Staff training is an important component in this protection (see Chapter 13, "Ethics-Based Staff Training." In the HIPAA Summary in Appendix IV, see the section on "Staff Training Required by HIPAA Regulations").

SPECIAL CONSIDERATIONS WITH ELECTRONIC RECORD KEEPING

More and more clinical settings are now "paperless." Many private and government agencies, as well as clinics and hospitals, are requiring their therapists to maintain all patient data electronically.[43] Increasingly, third-party payers are requiring that reimbursement claims be submitted electronically.

Electronic records have both advantages and disadvantages when it comes to protecting patient confidentiality. Physically, they can be stored in a smaller space than would be required for paper records. They can be easily monitored, with clear policies and tightly enforced rules that forbid their physical removal from the setting on laptops, discs, or flash drives. Electronically, however, these records can be very vulnerable. Unless they are encrypted and password-protected, they can easily be accessed by unauthorized users, and they can be duplicated much more easily than paper records.[44] They can also be difficult to destroy (see below, "Confidentiality in Disposal of Records").

Psychologists whose electronic records of clinical services might be available to "persons whose access has not been consented to by the recipient" must "use coding or other techniques to avoid the inclusion of personal identifiers."[45] The "APA Record Keeping Guidelines" also contain extensive considerations about electronic technology.[46] For counselors, the ACA Ethics Code contains an entire section on "Technology and Informed Consent." Useful for mental health care providers of all professions, this includes mandates about such practices as the use of encryption in transmission of records and requires that patients be informed about the potential confidentiality risks of electronic storage and transmission of identifiable information.[47] For social workers, NASW provides *Standards for Technology and Social Work Practice.*[48]

Many millions of electronic patient records are lost or stolen every year, and there are increasing questions about the security of the electronic records maintained in national data banks.[49] "Creating protective policies and procedures is only the first step; clients are protected only if those policies are strictly enforced. Software safeguards such as encryption and passwords are useless if psychologists or their staff are careless with the hardware."[50]

Meanwhile, there are also increasing pressures on providers and patients to voluntarily maintain records in a national database or in internet-based "cloud" storage.[51]

It is recommended that providers who are considering the use of "cloud" technology proceed with caution:

> With the broad spectrum of electronic storage and management options available to practitioners, the abdication of control to a third-party, cloud-based company may represent unnecessary additional risk at this relatively early stage. In part, aggregation of documents from users worldwide may

create a much more appealing target for malicious hackers than a single office with only a few patient documents. Also, the question of liability has not yet been clearly defined. We are responsible for protecting patient information, but computing companies carry no such obligation beyond their own internal policies and contractual obligations.[52]

PROTECTING CONFIDENTIALITY IN THE EVENT OF A THERAPIST'S MOVE, RETIREMENT, INCAPACITATION, OR DEATH

Record confidentiality is easily compromised by the unexpected absence of a therapist. For this reason, the mental health professions advocate making advance provisions for protection of patient records in the event that the provider moves, terminates practice, becomes ill or incapacitated, or dies. The ACA has an ethical standard requiring counselors to have a plan for protecting the confidentiality of patient records in such circumstances.[53] Social workers have a similar ethical responsibility.[54] The APA Ethics Code requires psychologists to "make plans in advance to facilitate the appropriate transfer and to protect the confidentiality of records and data in the event of psychologists' withdrawal from positions or practice."[55]

Therapists who work in agencies or group practice settings usually have someone who can be available to patients in their absence and often have a contract that stipulates how the responsibility for records will be transferred in the event of the therapist's retirement, incapacitation, or death. Therapists in private practice are encouraged to provide patients with similar protections by attending to confidentiality issues when planning their retirement[56] or by drawing up a "professional will" containing enough detail to ensure that a colleague will take responsibility for maintaining the confidentiality of that therapist's records in the event of the therapists incapacitation or death. Sample published versions are available.[57]

CONFIDENTIALITY IN DISPOSAL OF RECORDS

On the subject of record retention times, professional recommendations vary, as do state laws and regulations.[58] Regardless of how long they are retained, however, ethics codes require that records be destroyed in a manner that preserves patient confidentiality. Psychologists are ethically required to "maintain confidentiality in disposing of records under their control, whether these are written, automated, or in any other medium."[59] Counselors similarly must "dispose of client records and other sensitive materials in a manner that protects client confidentiality."[60] Some professions have also provided further guidelines related to the disposal of records, including electronic records.[61]

Legal requirements are contained in the federal HIPAA regulations. The U.S. Department of Health and Human Services provides specific standards about how to "render unsecured protected health information unusable, unreadable, or indecipherable to unauthorized individuals." For "paper, film, or other hard copy media," these standards require shredding in a manner that renders them unreadable and unable to be reconstructed. "Redaction is specifically excluded as a means of data destruction."[62] Electronic media must be cleared, purged, or destroyed in a manner consistent with the "Guidelines for Media Sanitization" from the National Institute of Standards and Technology (NIST).[63]

Electronic records are more difficult to destroy than paper records. Whereas therapists can easily shred paper records, they may not have the technical expertise to adequately delete or erase computerized records. "Even though efforts to delete or erase records may be undertaken, the records may nevertheless remain accessible by those with specialized expertise."[64] Therapists who intend to donate or sell their used computers, who are unsophisticated about the destruction of electronic records, or who do not have the means for following the NIST guidelines, should hire experts.

> Practitioners who store records on computer should be aware that sophisticated hackers can often read data supposedly erased from hard drives—even after sophisticated data-erasure utility programs has [sic] been used. The only safe means of disposing of computer-based information requires first physically removing and then destroying the hard drive, preferably by smashing it and then burning the fragments. CD and DVD media should also be burned, as scratching them may not render them completely unreadable. In short, failure to properly safeguard confidentiality can result in a breach of confidentiality.[65]

Responding to Requests for Voluntary or "Involuntary" Disclosures

All of the ethical and legal information about disclosure that was provided in Parts I and II of this book would apply to disclosure of records, whether on paper or electronically stored. Within the Ethical Practice Model, Step 3 would apply when obtaining patient consent before voluntarily disclosing records, whether that disclosure is initiated by the therapist or requested by the patient or others. Step 4 would apply to legally demanded or "involuntary" disclosures of records. If the records include test reports that were created for clinical (rather than forensic) purposes, the best protection for the patient is to protect confidentiality—including the confidentiality of copyrighted test materials—to the extent legally possible. Step 5 addresses the ethical problems that are created by voluntarily releasing records with "uninformed consent" from the patient.

It is important to remember that, according to HIPAA and some state laws, therapists can refuse to *voluntarily* disclose their private notes ("psychotherapy notes") to the patient and are prohibited from disclosing them to others without the patient's explicit consent. As noted above, however, the privilege laws of many states do not protect "psychotherapy notes" from subpoena or court order, so therapists in those states can be legally required to disclose such notes "*involuntarily*", to be used as evidence in court proceedings.

Record Keeping Considerations With Specific Populations and in Specific Settings

The general record keeping recommendations in this chapter would ordinarily apply in all settings and with all patient populations. However, as discussed in the next two chapters, further record keeping considerations may apply when working with certain populations or in certain settings.

11

Confidentiality Considerations With Specific Populations

In most clinical cases, and with most types of patients, all of the previous chapters would apply. However certain types of cases require attention to some additional considerations about confidentiality and record keeping.

Multiple-Party Cases

Some clinical cases involve multiple patients, as in couple, family, or group therapy. Other cases may involve nonpatient parties who are collateral participants in someone else's therapy. Whenever therapists wear multiple hats in the same clinical case, it is important to clarify in advance exactly which hat they will be wearing with whom, because therapists sometimes play a different role with each party in the case. It is also essential that the therapist be clear about each party's confidentiality rights, since these can differ across roles, with the result that the therapist's ethical obligations about confidentiality may differ from one party to another.

The familiar question "Who is the client?" can be misleading in multiple-party cases, not only because the word "client" can be ambiguous, but because the question implies the need to give a singular answer.[1] It is sometimes necessary to ask "Who is the client?" as a *reimbursement* question, in order to obtain the singular answer required by a third-party payer. It is also sometimes necessary to ask this as a *legal* question, in order to clarify whether a particular party has the legal right to obtain access to the therapy record. But the more appropriate *ethical* question would be, "What are my ethical obligations to each of the parties in this case?"[2]

In any clinical case involving multiple parties, the initial informed consent conversation should include discussion of both (1) the level of confidentiality the therapist is promising to each party and, when applicable, (2) the understandings about the responsibility of all participants to protect each others' confidences. The therapist has the option of requiring that all participants sign a statement promising to respect the confidentiality of the other participants; in some circumstances (such as in group therapy), that statement can include an understanding that maintaining others' confidentiality is a condition of continuing to receive services.[3] However, as noted in the National Association of Social Workers (NASW) Ethics Code, participants in family, couples, or group counseling should be informed that the therapist cannot guarantee that all participants will honor such agreements.[4]

Multiple-party cases can also present complicated record keeping issues that have implications for confidentiality. This includes decisions about whether to keep a single record or whether to keep separate records for each participant. From the perspective of one of the participants, separate records can present confidentiality advantages, but from the perspective of the therapist, a single combined record can have clinical advantages for documenting participant interactions and system variables. Whatever record keeping policy is chosen, it must be explained to participants in advance. In other words, before giving consent to receive services and beginning to create a "record," patients have a right to know the expected nature of that record.

For making this record keeping decision, therapists can consult the guidelines of their own profession. On this issue, therapists can also learn from others' guidelines. For example, the following comments from the American Psychological Association (APA) Record Keeping Guidelines would apply to any mental health professional:

> In some situations, such as group therapy, it may make sense to create and maintain a complete and separate record for all identified clients. On the other hand, if a couple or a family system is the identified patient, then one might decide to keep a single record. This will vary depending upon practical concerns, ethical guidelines, and third-party reporting requirements. *Upon later requests for release of records, it will be necessary to release only the portions of a multi-client record that are relevant to the party covered by the release.* Given this complication, the psychologist may choose to keep separate records on each participant from the outset.[5]

If there is reason to believe that the records will later be sought in the context of a legal case, separate records might be more protective of each individual's confidentiality. Therapists should become familiar with any legal requirements that might affect their policies and decisions about release of a record containing information about multiple patients.

Finally, the multiple parties in the case may include the referring entity. For example, if patients are being seen on referral from an agency or from a court, the confidentiality rules must be clear to the referring party, as well as to all the prospective participants, before services are provided. This is especially important if the referring entity will be paying for the services and expects ongoing progress reports. In advance, the therapist can participate in formulating a formal written contract with the referral entity, stipulating the joint understandings about confidentiality.

This helps to ensure that confidentiality will be protected to the extent appropriate to the case, and also prepares the therapist to inform prospective patients about the confidentiality limitations contained in the contract. For example, what details will be provided on the therapist's billing statements? Will the referring party receive reports or treatment summaries, or have access to other information? Such disclosure implications in the contracted arrangement must be discussed with prospective patients in advance, as part of the informed consent conversation about limits of confidentiality.[6] (Also see Chapter 8, "Avoiding Preventable Disclosures.")

THERAPY INVOLVING MULTIPLE RELATED PARTIES

In therapy cases involving multiple parties who have prior relationships with each other, the therapist often has numerous roles. One of the first responsibilities will be the identification of who will be patients and who will be involved not as patients but as "collaterals" to someone else's therapy. For example, in family therapy cases, each family member is equally a patient, whereas in therapy cases involving an individual patient, others may be involved as collaterals—nonpatients who participate in the services being provided to the patient. Collateral participants can include spouses, partners, adult children, or friends who collaborate in someone's individual therapy; caretakers or adult children who attend an elderly parent's therapy sessions or serve as case managers; or parents whose minor child is in individual therapy and who attend some of the child's therapy sessions and/or receive separate parent consultation related to their child's therapy. It is important for everyone involved in the case to understand who is a therapy patient and who is a collateral participant. Additionally, from an informed consent perspective, "bringing any outside people into a session requires informed consent from *all* parties."[7]

Confidentiality must be clarified not only with therapy patients themselves but also with collateral participants, who must be informed that they do not have the same confidentiality rights as the therapy patient. For example, in the case of an adult therapy patient whose spouse attends the sessions, the therapist is not ethically free to disclose confidential information to that spouse outside the session without the patient's consent, but the collateral participant is not promised that same level of confidentiality. Therefore, before collateral participants give consent to participate, they must be informed that information obtained from them may be shared with the patient at the therapist's discretion, whether the collateral has provided the information by phone, by letter, or in person when the patient was not present. Collateral participants must also be informed about the nature of their role in the other person's therapy and about their own rights. Since collaterals may enter the relationship with erroneous notions about the confidentiality that is being promised (or with the mistaken impression that they are also "patients"), it is recommended that therapists provide the rules in writing and document this informed consent conversation carefully, in order to avoid later misunderstandings.

The APA Insurance Trust has provided a very helpful Collateral Consent Form for that purpose.[8]

Couple and Family Therapy Cases

When therapy patients are related to each other, confidentiality rights can become more difficult to protect, and record keeping decisions can become more complex than in single-patient cases. The therapist must enter the intake session well prepared, because the initial informed consent conversation is especially important for avoiding patient misunderstandings about the confidentiality rules in these cases.

Therapists' ethics codes describe informed consent responsibilities in similar ways, always including the necessity to clarify the therapist's role with each person.[9] Each party involved in the case should be informed about the confidentiality rules that will apply to his or her own particular role or circumstance. For example, in couple therapy cases, it is important for the therapist to explain that both parties are equally considered to be "patients," and the therapist's role is the same with both parties. In cases involving minors, the therapist must decide whether the case will be structured as a family therapy case (with each participant therefore being a "family therapy patient") or whether it will be structured as individual child therapy with collateral parent involvement. In the latter case, the clinician is both therapist to the minor patient and consultant to the parents, who may or may not be present in the child's therapy sessions. (See next section for discussion of this combination of roles.)

When discussing the limits of confidentiality, the therapist can distinguish between (1) potential involuntary (legally compelled) disclosures and (2) voluntary disclosures that the therapist might make by personal preference, by contracted understandings with a referring agency, or in compliance with policies in an organizational setting. (See a discussion of that distinction in the Chapter 3 section on "Making Ethically Important Distinctions." Also see Chapters 5 and 7.)

When making decisions about voluntary sharing of information among the participating parties, couple and family therapists are free to adopt whatever policy is most consistent with their own clinical perspective, as long as their policy is also consistent with their ethical standards and laws. For example, therapists' rules about disclosure can range from an extreme "no secrets" policy (in which the therapist does not promise to keep confidential from the other parties any information provided by one party when others are not present) to a "secret-keeper" policy (whereby the therapist promises to hold confidential all the information obtained from one party when others are not present), to many other possibilities in between, most of which involve leaving some decisions to the therapist's discretion.[10] Ethically speaking, however, regardless of the policy being adopted, it is important that, before providing services, the therapist inform all parties in a multipatient case about exactly what the confidentiality rules will be and how they will apply to each party.[11]

For family therapy, Gottlieb suggests that the confidentiality options might include (1) treating all information disclosed individually as confidential and not to be shared with the other parties, (2) setting a policy that no information disclosed individually is to be confidential, (3) agreeing that the therapist will hold certain information confidential as a matter of personal privacy, or (4) agreeing to keep certain information confidential temporarily, with the understanding that it may be disclosed to other parties later.[12] For couples, Kuo suggests a slightly different set of options: (1) treating no information as confidential within a couple, (2) disclosing individually revealed information only with that party's consent, (3) keeping certain individually revealed information confidential, or (4) allowing the degree of confidentiality to rely on the therapist's discretion.[13]

In deciding on a confidentiality policy in these cases, therapists should review the professional literature to understand the possible options, clarify their own policy in advance, and prepare to describe it clearly to prospective patients at intake. Failure to provide adequate explanations to all parties in advance is a common confidentiality pitfall in couple and family therapy.[14] From an informed consent perspective, the timing is important: All participants should give consent to accept the described limits of confidentiality before they begin to confide information that might later be shared with others in the family, or reported to outsiders, without their further consent.

It is important to remember that all patients in a given case do not necessarily have the same confidentiality rights. For example, in family therapy, minors may have more limited confidentiality rights if they are engaging in dangerous behavior that the therapist believes the parents need to know about. It is, therefore, important at the outset to inform both minors and their parents about what types of information disclosed privately to the therapist by a minor will be held confidential and what will be shared with the parents.[15]

For clinical purposes, a "relational diagnosis" can be useful in family therapy cases, since it describes the dysfunctional patterns within a dyad or system of individuals, rather than the disorder of a single individual within that system.[16] However, third-party payers usually require that there be one "identified patient," so, for reimbursement purposes, the therapist may need to name and provide a diagnosis for one individual. In that circumstance, the therapist should explain the confidentiality implications of being designated as the "identified patient" and of receiving a particular diagnosis (e.g., necessity to disclose symptoms to justify the diagnosis, requirements to submit treatment plans to clarify progress, possibility of redisclosure of this information into a national database, potential implications for future insurability, etc.).

Regardless of the purpose for which a person is being identified as "the" patient, it is important to clarify the ethical implications of that decision. From a clinical perspective, if a case is conceptualized as couple or marital therapy, then the therapist's answer to the question, "What are my ethical responsibilities about confidentiality?" should be the same for both parties, because both have the same rights about confidentiality. (This remains *ethically* true even if a third-party payer requires that one be named the "identified patient" for reimbursement purposes.) However, if the case is clinically conceptualized as individual therapy for one spouse, with the other spouse attending only as a collateral participant, then the therapist's answer to "What are my ethical responsibilities about confidentiality?" will be different for each spouse. (See discussion of collateral participants, above.)

Minors in Therapy

Therapy cases involving minor patients almost always involve others, even if the child is being seen in individual therapy. The clinical decision about how to structure the case can have important implications for how confidentiality will be handled. If the parent(s) will always be present in the room whenever the child is seen by the therapist, that could mean either that (1) the case is clinically structured as family therapy or (2) the case is clinically framed as individual child therapy with parent(s) present as collateral participants.

Often, a child or adolescent is seen in individual therapy sessions alone, with the therapist having separate meetings with the parent(s). In such a clinical case, it is important for therapists to clarify the two different roles: When with the child, they are wearing the professional hat of "individual therapist"; but when meeting with the parent(s), they are "the child's therapist serving as consultant to the parent(s)." In such cases, it is ethically important to clarify exactly what the confidentiality rules will be in both the therapy relationship and the parent consultation relationship, because they will usually not be the same. Therapists seeing a child patient under this clinical structure must also avoid further multiplying roles (e.g., agreeing to be the marital therapist to the parents or the individual therapist to one or both parents), since that could create conflicts of interest that would be difficult or impossible to resolve. Untangling such multiple roles would become even further complicated if the parents later separated or divorced.

Sometimes, adolescents request that a therapist provide services without parental knowledge or consent. In such a circumstance, therapists must clarify some legal issues in advance. When the therapy patient is a minor, state laws can affect the minors' legal rights about obtaining mental health services without parental consent, and about confidentiality and disclosure. Laws that define minors' rights are different in every state, and these state laws further affect minors' confidentiality rights under federal law. For example, some state laws give to minors the right to independently consent to mental health treatment and to control disclosure of records; and, when minors *do* exercise those rights at the state level, the federal Health Insurance Portability and Accountability Act (HIPAA) regulations generally permit them to exercise their own privacy rights.[17] In other words, under the HIPAA Privacy Rule, such a minor has essentially the same confidentiality rights as an adult. However, those federal rights can be limited if the state also has laws that give parents access to the record of that minor, or to control the decisions about disclosure of information about the minor.[18]

> Bringing together clinical, legal and ethical perspectives on confidentiality offers both challenges and opportunities in the treatment of adolescents... It

> may be helpful to think of law, ethics and clinical work in terms of a Venn diagram. The overlap is where law, ethics and good clinical care come together. We are always looking for ways to move the circles further together, toward an ideal state of complete consonance. Where the circles do not overlap represents some area of tension, for example between what is good clinical care and what the law demands.[19]

To clarify the legal issues, therapists should ask and answer in advance some legal questions, such as the following: Do minors in my state have the right to consent to services without a parent's knowledge or consent and, if so, under what circumstances? To what extent does the consenting minor have legal authority to control confidentiality and disclosure decisions in my state? Does my state give parents the legal right to have access to their minor child's records?

Clinically, therapists must also be prepared to assess the minor's capacity to give consent. Regardless of whether minors have the legal authority to give consent, the therapist remains responsible for assessing a minor's capacity to give "truly informed" consent to receive therapy services or to permit voluntary disclosure of confidential information.[20] Ethically, it is important to at least try to obtain assent from minors who do not have the capacity or the legal authority to give consent on their own. Regarding confidentiality, this "informed assent" would involve providing information using an age-appropriate explanation, seeking the minor's agreement to accept the described policies about limits of confidentiality, and considering the minor's preferences and best interests.[21] Meanwhile, it is appropriate to also obtain formal informed consent about confidentiality policies from a legally authorized person if this is permitted or required by law.

When obtaining parental consent, it is often advised that, except in very unusual circumstances, therapists seek consent from both parents, regardless of whether they are living together and regardless of the custody arrangements. "Obtaining consent to treatment from one parent may not be sufficient when psychologists treat a minor whose parents are divorced or separated … Both parents may be required to consent to the treatment if there is court-ordered joint custody. Even if it is not legally required, you may choose to request the consent of both parents—especially if you are initiating treatment of children in high-conflict families or in instances where parents are undergoing separation or divorce."[22]

Finally, preparation must also include making decisions about voluntary disclosures: Am I willing to work with minors without parental involvement, even if that is legally allowed in my state? What is my own policy about whose consent will be required? In other words, will I have a policy of requiring consent from both parents before beginning treatment, even if that is not legally required in my state? What are my policies about voluntary disclosures to parents and others without the minor's consent? If such questions are confusing, or if the personal preferences conflict with legal requirements, both ethical and legal consultation may be necessary.[23]

Clarifying these voluntary disclosure policies in advance is important, and there has been an increasing trend toward involving minors—especially adolescents—in this discussion.[24] Nevertheless, in their initial meetings with children and adolescents, some therapists are still tempted to promise an inappropriately high level of confidentiality out of concern that the minor will otherwise not confide at all. In spite of having made such promises in the initial interview, many child and adolescent therapists eventually decide that certain dangerous behaviors should be discussed with parents, even if they are not life-threatening. Such disclosures can create clinical complications, but they would create no ethical dilemma if the therapist already informed both minor and parents about this policy before providing services.[25] Initial confidentiality promises should therefore be clear, specific, and very carefully considered. If possible, therapists should include examples of when secrets will be kept and when they will not, in order not to make (or by silence to imply) confidentiality promises that they may later break. For documenting such understandings, it can be helpful to describe the policies on an informed consent form that can be signed by both minors and their parents. Sample forms are available online, but therapists must adapt them to their own use, to be sure that the content expresses what they actually intend to do in various circumstances[26]

This initial conversation about confidentiality is especially important if the parents are already involved in custody and visitation disputes.[27] However, since family disputes are difficult to predict, therapists can "clarify in advance that the purpose of child therapy is for treatment, not for generating information that will be used in custody proceedings."[28] Child and adolescent therapists who wish to avoid the clinical, ethical, and legal complications of participating in court proceedings may inform parents at intake that they "will not be discussing the case with any attorneys or any court," and/or that they will discuss the case with a court-appointed custody evaluator only "upon receipt of a court order or the appropriate releases from all the necessary parties."[29]

Clarifying this at intake can prevent many avoidable complications. Some therapists both document this conversation in the record and have parents sign a no-subpoena contract, in which they promise not to involve the child's therapist in any court proceedings.[30] Although this is not a legally binding document, it can reduce the likelihood that the parents will require the therapist to submit the child's records or to testify in court, both of which may be experienced by the child as a betrayal of confidences.

To be prepared to give examples of when secrets will be kept and when they will not, and in order to avoid making (or by silence implying) impossible promises about confidentiality, therapists must decide in advance what types of information they will voluntarily disclose to parents and when; they must learn about state laws that can require disclosure or otherwise limit their freedom about confidentiality policies; they must learn how HIPAA might apply; and then they must develop very clear policies that are consistent with all these constraints. "Only with such planning will the psychologist be prepared to fulfill the ethical obligation to describe in advance, to both the parent(s) and the minor(s), exactly when confidentiality will be protected and when information will be disclosed."[31] Finally, it is important for therapists to remember that they are clinicians first, and that, in describing potential future disclosures, they must leave room for breaching confidentiality if necessary when they uncover clinical issues or behaviors that raise safety concerns or legal issues.[32]

As in any clinical case, there are advantages to describing the confidentiality policy both verbally and in writing.[33] For minors who can read, providing them with their own copy of the written confidentiality agreement allows them to take it home and bring back any questions. Requiring both minor and parents to sign the informed consent document will prevent later disagreements about the agreed-upon policy by documenting that everyone was informed about the confidentiality rules in advance and agreed to accept them as a condition of receiving services.

This informed consent discussion should also include a description of the rules about parents' access to the records of their minor child, since most state laws allow such access for minors of certain ages. Even if the therapist's policy and the legal requirement indicate that parents may have access to information or records, in some cases, the therapist may believe it would be detrimental to the child to release that information to the parents.

> Discussing your concerns with the parent and/or offering to release limited information rather than the full record is often the best approach. If you are unable to come to a mutually agreeable solution, refusal to disclose treatment information that the parent is authorized to receive may be a legally supportable course of action. In such situations, it is advisable to consult with a knowledgeable health care attorney in your state.[34]

Difficult complications about parent access to the minor's records can arise when there are disputes between the parents. The APA Record Keeping Guidelines note potential complications:

> Psychologists may encounter situations in which it is not immediately apparent who should have access to records. For example, children in treatment following marital dissolution may be brought for services by one parent who wishes the record to be kept confidential from the other parent, or an adolescent who is near but has not quite reached the age of majority may request that records be kept confidential from the parent/guardian. A minor may have the legal prerogative to consent to treatment (e.g., for reproductive matters), but the parent may nevertheless press for access to the record. The psychologist is guided by the Ethics Code … as well as by state and federal regulations in these matters. Following marital dissolution, a psychologist may be unclear whether to release records to one of the parents, particularly when the release is not wanted by the other parent. In such a situation, the

> psychologist recognizes that the relevant court overseeing the marital dissolution may have already specified who has access to the child's treatment records.[35]

However, unless precluded by a court's order, agreed otherwise at intake, or deemed dangerous to the child, it is ordinarily appropriate to notify either parent if the other obtains access to the child's record and to offer to make it available to both parents equally.

Elderly Patients With Collateral Involvement

With older persons, ethical issues related to confidentiality can include lack of privacy; confusion about when to share information with family, caregivers, or advocates; and difficulty determining whether the patient is truly capable of giving informed consent for services. Privacy issues can become especially difficult if services are being provided in a hospital, nursing home, or other group living situation. When the patient is bedridden and shares a room, completely private conversations may not be possible. Regardless of the setting, however, the therapist must make decisions about how much information will be shared with caregivers. "Consistent with the APA's Ethical Principles, it is best to limit the transmission of information to the least number of people who need to know and whatever is in the best interest of the client."[36]

Even when an elderly patient seeks services independently, therapists often find it necessary to actively seek the involvement of family members, caretakers, or other collaterals, and may even need to work toward the appointment of an advocate or legal guardian in the evaluation or treatment of the elderly patient. This should be done with respect for the patient's right to confidentiality and autonomy. "It is important to note that unless declared incompetent, the older adult has a right to make decisions to initiate, withdraw, or terminate treatment" and that " to assure confidentiality, written permission should be obtained from older persons to communicate information regarding their status to relatives or to health care professionals."[37]

This should be discussed early, preferably in the initial informed consent conversation with the elderly patient. If others are not present at that time, the confidentiality rules can subsequently be clarified with all parties involved, to ensure that the collateral participants understand in advance exactly when, how, and with whom information will be shared.[38]

If the patient has been legally judged incompetent, then there will already be an appointed guardian with power of attorney, who can give consent in the patient's behalf. Sometimes, an elderly person will voluntarily sign a document giving another individual permission to manage his or her affairs, in which case that person can take responsibility for joining in giving consent for evaluation, treatment, or disclosure of information. If neither of these is in place, but the patient does not seem capable of giving truly informed consent, therapists have specific ethical standards that would apply. Psychologists are ethically required to "(1) provide an appropriate explanation, (2) seek the individual's assent, (3) consider such persons' preferences and best interests, and … take reasonable steps to protect the individual's rights and welfare."[39] Counselors have a similar ethical responsibility to seek the assent of patients to services and to "include them in decision making as appropriate." Counselors must also "recognize the need to balance the ethical rights of clients to make choices, their capacity to give consent or assent to receive services, and parental or familial legal rights and responsibilities to protect these clients and make decisions on their behalf."[40]

These decisions can be very complicated.

> "For older persons with dementia or other forms of significant cognitive impairment, confidentiality issues can become complex because questions may arise about the cognitively impaired older person's ability to give truly informed consent to release information… In some cases, the as yet legally competent older client may be willing to sign a consent form, yet the psychologist may have serious doubt about the client's ability to understand what is being requested. In this case, the psychologist must use best judgment guided by the principle that what is done is in the client's best interest.[41]

Finally, in most states, therapists are legally required to report suspicion of abuse or neglect of elderly or disabled adults. Since this must be explained to all parties in advance, the therapist must become familiar with his or her state laws related to such reports. Therapists who lead support groups for family or caretakers of the elderly must explicitly inform prospective participants about what their policies will be about breaching confidentiality to report suspected abuse.[42]

GROUPS

Sometimes, mental health professionals provide services to groups of people who have had no prior relationships with each other. This would include not only psychotherapy groups, but also support groups and educational groups of various sorts. The following recommendations about therapy groups would apply to those groups as well. The confidentiality rules among group members would be the same whether the group meets in an inpatient or outpatient setting.

Most of the ethical standards related to confidentiality would apply in group contexts. The few standards that explicitly mention groups ordinarily pertain to the initial informed consent conversation in group therapy (see Appendix II). With potential group therapy participants, psychologists have an ethical requirement to "describe at the outset the roles and responsibilities of all parties and the limits of confidentiality."[43] Counselors must "clearly explain the importance and parameters of confidentiality for the specific group being entered."[44] Social workers "should seek agreement among the parties involved concerning each individual's right to confidentiality and obligation to preserve the confidentiality of information shared by others."[45] Psychiatrists have no explicit ethics code provisions about groups, and some research suggests that, compared with other mental health professionals, they are less likely to begin with a discussion of confidentiality and less likely to reopen that conversation as group meetings continue.[46]

"Confidentiality in group therapy, once ignored in the literature on ethics, is gaining more attention as this modality becomes more widely practiced; so too is an acknowledgement that ethical dilemmas surrounding confidentiality in groups are commonplace"[47] Research has suggested that when group therapists discuss confidentiality with potential participants, they often provide too little information about the actual risks.[48] "Group therapy poses unique challenges in that there is no binding assurance of confidentiality between group members,"[49] and they tend to want to talk about their group experience with family and friends.[50] To avoid liability for others' breach of confidentiality, therapists should be sure that group members understand these risks in advance.[51] In addition to discussing confidentiality early, therapists "should make every effort to establish a group environment protective of confidentiality, take steps to ensure environmental privacy, and remain vigilant for 'confidentiality cracks.'"[52]

Another potential issue with groups involves privileged communications. In most states, privilege statutes are silent on the question of whether the therapist–patient privilege laws protect statements made in group therapy from being used as evidence in court.[53] For many years, therapists and patients assumed that confidences divulged in group therapy were as protected under the laws of privileged communication as were revelations made in individual therapy.[54] However, since the group therapy communications are made in the presence of third parties, a court might not deem them privileged. Therapists who conduct group therapy must be clear about the statutes and case precedents in their own state, and must inform group members of this potential exception to confidentiality if it applies in their jurisdiction.

Finally, record keeping decisions have an impact on the confidentiality of group members. "Although notes written about the entire group may capture important interactive themes, such notes can compromise the privacy and confidentiality of individual group members."[55] It is therefore recommended that group therapists create a separate record for each group member, rather than a joint record. Therapists who choose to maintain a separate set of personal notes (or "psychotherapy notes") can document broader group themes there.

Cases Involving Cultural Minorities

"Culture plays a role in how we understand the construct of confidentiality and how we carry out our commitments."[56] For therapists working with patients from cultures other than their own, cultural awareness and sensitivity can be important when clarifying patients' expectations about confidentiality. For example, when therapists are working with patients from cultures that frown on keeping secrets, they can take special care to ensure that the patient's decisions about disclosures to family members are actually voluntary.

Patients who are not proficient in English can be referred to speakers of their own language whenever possible; otherwise, the therapist can use interpreters to ensure that clients understand the confidentiality policies. If possible, interpreters themselves should receive training about confidentiality issues in mental health care, and, in order to avoid client intimidation or undue invasion of privacy, therapists should refrain from using family members or community authority figures as interpreters whenever possible.[57] (Also see, in Chapter 5, the section "Complications Created by Cultural or Language Differences.")

Cases Involving End-of-Life or After-Death Situations

"Confusion continues to exist with regard to the limitations on confidentiality in situations where clients are considering their options at the end of life, and after a client has died."[58] Some mental health ethics codes take a position about these circumstances, some do not.

CONFIDENTIALITY IN END-OF-LIFE CASES

Therapists face many complicated clinical and case management decisions in working with persons who are dying, but the greatest ethical dilemmas with this population arise around issues of confidentiality if a terminally ill patient confides a plan to hasten death.

For counselors, the American Counseling Association (ACA) Ethics Code directly addresses confidentiality in end-of-life circumstances: "Counselors who provide services to terminally ill individuals who are considering hastening their own deaths have the option of breaking or not breaking confidentiality, depending on applicable laws and the specific circumstances of the situation and after seeking consultation or supervision from appropriate professional and legal parties."[59]

For social workers, the NASW Ethics Code does not directly address this circumstance. However, it stipulates that "the general expectation that social workers will keep information confidential does not apply when disclosure is necessary to prevent serious, foreseeable, and imminent harm to a client."[60]

Similarly, for psychologists, the APA Ethics Code does not directly address end-of-life situations. However, it allows (but does not require) psychologists to breach confidentiality "to protect the client/patient ... from harm" where this is permitted by law.[61] It has been suggested that "a psychologist does not have an ethical obligation to break confidentiality if a client who is dying is considering taking action that may end his or her life"[62]:

> Our review indicates that the expectations for MHPs [mental health professionals] working with dying clients who are considering end-of-life options that may include hastening death are different from the expectations related to working with clients who are suicidal. Specifically, on the basis of ethics codes, associated organizational statements, *amicus* briefs, and state laws, we believe that therapists are fairly free to explore a variety of end-of-life decisions with clients who are dying, without needing to assume that there is a duty to protect in the traditional sense (e.g., hospitalizing, breaking confidentiality). Yet, we think that clinicians do have some responsibilities in these situations . . .[63]

Therapists of all professions should write their informed consent document in a way that reflects their own policy. Its wording might indicate that the therapist "can" or "may" or "reserves the right to" disclose in this circumstance, instead of promising that the therapist *will* breach confidentiality.

CONFIDENTIALITY AFTER A PATIENT'S DEATH

Do confidentiality rights survive after a patient has died? It can be important to decide in advance how to answer this question, in order to be prepared if a family member or legal representative requests that the therapist voluntarily disclose information or records after the patient's death, or if the therapist receives a subpoena or court order demanding "involuntary" disclosure of information in records or testimony about a deceased patient.

Ethically, the answer varies across professions. The clearest answer is available to social workers, because the NASW Ethics Code simply gives to deceased patients the same confidentiality protections as to living patients.[64] Counselors are ethically permitted to follow their setting's policies and their legal requirements.[65] Psychologists and psychiatrists have no specific mention of deceased patients in their ethics codes, but they do have general ethical provisions that allow disclosure of patient information to a legal representative.[66]

However, even when therapists are ethically and/or legally allowed to voluntarily disclose information about deceased patients, they should consider carefully whether it is "in the best interest of the client to do so."[67] Morally, it may also be important to remember that the deceased patient may not be the only one who will be affected by a disclosure. Clinical records "may hold sensitive information, not only about that patient but often also about other family members."[68] Finally, it may also be important to consider whether releasing the information is "in the best interest of the public trust or the reputation of the profession."[69]

> It is time for the psychology profession to clarify our beliefs about confidentiality "beyond the grave" when executors or relatives authorize release. I would like to see consensus built around the strongest possible commitment to confidentiality. Certainly there may be legal constraints, but, in my

> opinion, any breach except in a "most compelling circumstance" in the profession's commitment to confidentiality may have serious consequences both for the behaviors we accept and model in the profession as well as for the public trust we have worked so hard to create.[70]

Legally, the confidentiality rights of deceased patients will vary from state to state.[71] In the process of making these decisions, therapists must remember the ethical difference between legally allowed and legally required disclosures, in order not to treat those laws that legally *allow* them to disclose (and which therefore carry the ethical responsibilities of a voluntary disclosure) as if they were laws that legally *required* them to disclose information about a deceased patient. (In Chapter 1, see Figure 1.2; in Chapter 3, see the section on "Distinguishing Between Voluntary and "Involuntary" (Legally Required) Disclosures.")

At the federal level, the HIPAA regulations defer to state law on this issue. However, in a potentially relevant case, the U.S. Supreme Court held in *Swidler & Berlin v. United States* that the death of an attorney's client does not terminate attorney–client privilege with respect to records of confidential communications between the attorney and the client.[72] Although this case involved attorney–client privilege rather than therapist–patient privilege, it addressed the general question of whether testimonial privilege survives someone's death, and therefore it has implications for mental health professionals.[73]

Regrettably, discussion of this issue is often dominated by high-profile or highly publicized legal cases in which clinicians made very public and controversial disclosures about deceased clients.[74] In some cases, this led to professional or legal censure, and it is important that mental health professionals not treat these cases as models for ethical behavior.

12

Confidentiality in Specific Roles and Settings

Regardless of the professional hat they are wearing, or the setting in which they wear it, mental health professionals are required to uphold the ethical standards of their own profession. When it comes to the ethics of confidentiality, some roles and settings pose challenging dilemmas and require significant forethought and planning. This is especially true if the setting imposes severe limits on confidentiality, or if it imposes record keeping requirements that are inconsistent with the guidelines of one's own profession.

Educational Settings

"There may be no setting in which the informed consent interview is more important. This is true whether the educational setting is public or private, elementary, secondary, undergraduate or graduate."[1] As in any setting, the initial informed consent interview must cover many topics, but in educational settings, confidentiality and its limits will be among the most complicated topics that mental health professionals must be prepared to discuss.

What makes preparation so important is that the "informing" about confidentiality can be very lengthy and complex in educational settings. It requires being prepared to explain the nature and objectives of the services to be performed; the intended recipients of each type of service; the possible uses that will be made of the information obtained while providing services; the limits of confidentiality, including a description of who will be allowed access to which types of information under federal law and local policies; and the relationship one will have with each of the involved parties, including one's relationship and loyalties to the educational setting itself.[2]

Preparation for informing patients about such things includes asking and answering questions such as these in advance of the initial meeting:

- What will the *real* limits of confidentiality be here, including those voluntarily imposed by my own policies and the policies in this educational organization, as well as those imposed by law?
- Who might *really* obtain access to information or records in this setting, without the consent of the student and/or the parent?
- What are my roles (i.e., which professional "hat"—or combination of "hats"—will I be wearing when I interact with a student, a teacher, a parent, a principal, a dean, etc.), and how will each of those affect confidentiality?
- Who am I required to inform about my roles and about the confidentiality rules?

Note that the question, "Who is the client?" is not included in this list. In clarifying their roles in such circumstances, mental health professionals are often advised to ask that question. However, it is discouraged here because it elicits a singular answer, and, in this setting, there are ethical responsibilities to several different entities, not just one "client."[3] For example, there are ethical responsibilities to the person receiving therapy, counseling, or assessment services; to a minor's parents; to the educational institution by which one is employed or with whom one has contracted to provide services; and likely to others within the setting, including teachers, administrators, and other professionals.

Furthermore, most educational settings use a team approach that involves collaboration among multiple professionals (e.g., a teacher or professor who requests consultation about a student, a principal or dean who makes a referral and requests followup information, professionals with different specialties who provide services to the same student, etc.), all of whom might seek access to confidential information about a student. This must be explained in the initial informed consent interview. "When client treatment involves a continued review or participation by a treatment team, the client will be informed of the team's existence and composition, information being shared, and the purposes of sharing such information."[4]

In educational settings, "relationship confusions abound, and multiple relationships may be unavoidable."[5] It can sometimes be very difficult to remain clear about which professional "hat(s)" one is wearing from one moment to the next. If the primary role is as therapist or counselor to a minor student, that hat may seem clear when meeting with the student. But when one later meets with the student's parent(s), is one still in the role of therapist to the student, in the role of "parent consultant," or in both roles at once? If both, how do the confidentiality promises made in the former role affect what happens in the latter? Will the parents be promised confidentiality? If so, what will be its limits? Similarly, when meeting with the student's teacher, what hat(s) is one wearing (e.g., student's therapist or teacher's consultant or both), and how do the confidentiality promises earlier made to the student and to the parent(s) affect that conversation? Will one also make confidentiality promises to a teacher who uses this conference to confide about personal things, including some strong personal reactions to the student? In meetings with a principal, one may be wearing the underlying hat of an employee, but what other hats might one be wearing (e.g., consultant/adviser to the principal, agent of the principal, or both)? Must the confidentiality promises made in any of the other relationships now be broken, in order to disclose something to the principal? If so, how can one avoid making (or implying) promises that will be impossible to keep?

Those questions make obvious the fact that mental health professionals who work in educational settings, regardless of the hats they wear and the services they provide, are likely to experience conflicting loyalties. They will have certain responsibilities to the institution that hired them, to the individuals who are receiving services, and to all of those who are collaterals in the case—and these interests are sometimes in conflict. They "must be clear about exactly which professional hat(s) they are wearing from one moment to the next and about where their loyalties lie."[6] Otherwise, they might inadvertently disclose confidential information in an inappropriate context, or might make early confidentiality promises they will later have to break.

The confidentiality policies of an educational institution might sometimes seem to be in conflict with the ethical standards for psychologists, counselors, or social workers. When this occurs, mental health professionals in the setting have an ethical responsibility to confront the employer about such conflicts and to try to resolve them in a direction consistent with the ethics of their profession.[7] This is true not only for therapists of the major mental health professions (as listed in Appendices I and II), but also for those whose specialty or licensure is specific to school settings. For example, school psychologists and school counselors have separate ethics codes that impose ethical responsibilities in this situation,[8] and school social workers have position statements about confidentiality issues.[9]

Finally, decisions about confidentiality must take into account not only the professional's ethical standards and the institution's policies, but also the non-negotiable legal regulations that affect confidentiality policies in educational settings. These can be numerous and may include not only state-imposed regulations, but also federal regulations such as the Health Insurance Portability and Accountability Act (HIPAA),[10] the Family Educational Rights and Privacy Act (FERPA),[11] and the Individual Disabilities Education Act (IDEA),[12] among others.

COLLEGE COUNSELING CENTERS

College campuses, like small rural communities, increase the likelihood of chance encounters with patients and sometimes make it difficult to avoid dual relationships.[13] Both have potential implications for confidentiality and should be discussed with prospective patients.

Strains on confidentiality can also be imposed by administrators. These can range from challenges to the maintenance of confidentiality (including demands for disclosure of information that would ordinarily remain private) to negative consequences for therapists who do maintain confidentiality and refuse to disclose.[14] When deans or other administrators refer students for therapy or counseling, they often expect to receive progress reports or other information. This must be clarified in advance with all parties, and the patient's consent for such disclosures should be obtained at the initial informed consent interview.

Sometimes, the confidentiality dilemmas faced by therapists in these settings will arise in response to demands from deans or others who are both concerned about campus safety and fearful of litigation. The rising student suicide rate and the recent incidents of campus violence have led to an increase in such demands.

> Administrators see psychologists as central in the effort to prevent campus violence. Yet far from deferring to clinicians' expertise and judgment, these same administrators—who may have little or no mental health training—increasingly demand to know which students are receiving mental health services, and in some cases even push to become involved in aspects of clinical care. Responding to these pressures takes considerable clinical skill, political acumen, organizational understanding, and ethical reflection.[15]

Although most college students are not minors, many are still financially dependent on parents who are very much involved in their lives. In some states, counselors and therapists in public colleges and universities are now legally required to notify the parents of dependent students if they see risks of suicidal or homicidal behavior.[16]

Some states legally require public colleges and universities to form threat assessment teams to assist in identifying, evaluating, and monitoring any student who is at risk for dangerous behavior.[17] Many private colleges have voluntarily formed such teams. The therapist's initial informed consent interview must therefore include a description of any policies that require communication and disclosures in such circumstances, not only with college administrators and threat assessment teams, but also with family members. The described policies must then be followed; otherwise, the therapist may be pulled into either making inappropriate exceptions to the confidentiality rule or making promises that it will be impossible to keep. Ordinarily, someone from the college counseling center is assigned to be a member of the threat assessment team. For therapists assigned to such a team, this creates a dual role that involves potential conflicts of interest. Unless that team member is allowed to be absent when his or her own therapy patient is discussed, the therapist must explain the implications of this potential role to patients in advance.

OTHER SCHOOL SETTINGS

Mental health professionals in preschool, primary, or secondary school settings must be prepared to deal with the many complicated confidentiality dilemmas that arise when working with minors in an institutional setting. This includes the expectation on the part of teachers and principals who have referred students for therapy or counseling and who wish to obtain ongoing progress summaries.

> School counselors have the ethical obligation to respect the privacy of minor clients and maintain confidentiality. This obligation is often in conflict with laws related to minors because parents have the right to know about most treatments and to decide what is in the best interest of their children. Counselors must also take into consideration codes of ethics, applicable statutes, and policies of their local education agencies and their individual schools. Given this type of balancing act, it is not surprising that school counselors often face ethical dilemmas related to maintaining the confidentiality of client information.[18]

Legal requirements further complicate the confidentiality picture. If the school transmits student information to third-party payers electronically, HIPAA may apply.[19] However, the most prevalent legal requirements about confidentiality and record keeping in these settings will arise from the FERPA[20] and IDEA[21] regulations. Under these regulations, parents have the right to inspect and review the minor student's records and have the right to request that a school correct records that they believe to be inaccurate or misleading. Information may be shared among school personnel, but (with specific exceptions) schools must have written permission from the parent or eligible student in order to release any information from a student's education record to another party outside the school team. All this must be explained to both the minor and the parent(s) before mental health services are provided.

Academic and Training Settings

Each mental health profession has ethical standards that limit the use of identifiable patient information in classroom, public settings, or clinical writing.[22] Ethics texts also address this issue: "Any materials prepared for teaching that have sensitive or confidential material involve the full informed consent of the client."[23] This is especially important when the nature of the material might make it possible for others to identify the client, even if not named. "Public use of client information without consent may not only create potential harm to the client through a violation of confidentiality, but may also harm the profession by demonstrating a lack of trustworthiness that could deter others from seeking needed mental health services."[24] However, the decision to obtain a patient's informed consent can be a complicated one, because it may have important clinical implications. (See, in Chapter 6, the section on "Informed Consent for Disclosures in Professional Presentations, Teaching, or Writing"; for presentations involving information about deceased patients, also see, in Chapter 11, "Confidentiality After a Patient's Death.")

Most mental health ethics codes do not directly address other ethical obligations of classroom teachers, but ethical standards about dual relationships would apply. For example, it is ethically important that a teacher or professor who is also a therapist not serve in both roles with the same person (i.e., avoid serving as therapist to a current student whose performance will be evaluated) and that professor–student consultations not be mistaken as confidential therapeutic interventions. Confidentiality limitations imposed by the legal requirements of the FERPA regulations would also apply.

Research Settings

Sometimes, therapists work as researchers themselves or provide therapy services in settings where others are conducting research with the same patients. When the information collected for research purposes is identifiable, it should be treated as confidential. All of the confidentiality standards listed in Appendix II apply in this setting, unless otherwise specified. In addition, most ethics codes have special sections that describe ethical responsibilities about confidentiality in research settings.[25]

As in all settings, the initial informed consent conversation is an essential component of the protection of confidentiality rights. "Researchers bear a duty, ethically and legally, to protect participants from harm and to inform them in advance of any material risks resulting from research. Surely this duty subsumes protection from adverse legal and social consequences that may result from unintended disclosure of sensitive data to third parties."[26]

Psychologists are ethically required to inform prospective research subjects about "reasonably foreseeable factors that may be expected to influence their willingness to participate," including "limits of confidentiality."[27] For counselors, possible access by others, "together with the plans for protecting confidentiality," must be explained to participants as a part of the procedure for obtaining informed consent to participate in the research.[28]

Social workers have more detailed informed consent requirements about confidentiality and its protection: "Social workers engaged in evaluation or research should ensure the anonymity or confidentiality of participants and of the data obtained from them. Social workers should inform participants of any limits of confidentiality, the measures that will be taken to ensure confidentiality, and when any records containing research data will be destroyed."[29]

In some respects, protecting confidentiality is usually easier for researchers than for therapists, since researchers can use coding systems that separate the research data from the names of participants. Researchers are advised to obtain a federal confidentiality certificate that can provide some protection for both researchers and their participants, even though the extent and adequacy of its confidentiality protection is in dispute.[30] However, researchers can still be subject to legally imposed limits of confidentiality, including abuse reporting requirements. Other legal demands can come in the form of court orders for disclosure of confidential information about research participants, and failure to comply can lead to fines and incarceration. Unless they would be willing to follow in the footsteps of the researcher who recently chose an indefinite jail term rather than disclose confidential information about participants in his research project,[31] researchers must inform prospective participants about such potential legal limitations on confidentiality.

Medical Settings

Patients usually have less privacy and fewer confidentiality protections in hospitals and public clinics than in other settings. Records are unlikely to enjoy the same level of confidentiality generally afforded mental health records. "Often, multiple service providers access and contribute to the record. This potentially affects the degree to which the psychologist may exercise control of the record, its content, or its confidentiality."[32]

Therapists in this setting should therefore record only necessary information, and should inform patients of the possible risks of access by others. "The manner in which records are maintained may potentially affect the client in ways that may be unanticipated by the client. Psychologists are encouraged to inform the client about these situations. For example, in some medical settings, client records may become part of an electronic file that is accessible by a broad range of institutional staff."[33]

In medical settings, record keeping policies must not only comply with the requirements of HIPAA, but also with policies mandated by Medicare, Medicaid, and national accrediting organizations such as The Joint Commission (formerly JCAHO).[34] Legal requirements in relevant state statutes and regulations will also apply. All of these can include explicit requirements about record content, security, and retention time. Mental health professionals employed in hospitals and institutional settings may also encounter conflicts between the organization's policies about confidentiality and their own profession's ethical standards. This raises important ethical responsibilities, especially regarding informed consent. Mental health professionals can engage in a multidisciplinary dialogue in which providers of all professions share their concern and balance provider needs for access to mental health information against patient right to protection of confidentiality. (See, in Chapter 1, "Ethical Standards About Conflicts Between Ethical Duties and Other Obligations.")

Finally, therapists in private practice who consult with hospital staff or patients, or who provide therapy in hospital and institutional settings, may encounter special issues that necessitate the need to create their own forms in order to have appropriate documentation in their own records. For example, the institution's forms may not meet the standards required by one's own profession or one's licensing regulations:

> It should be assumed that all information and release forms maintained in a patient's institutional medical record cover only the institution and its

> defined entities. Therefore, private practitioners must obtain signed forms, such as notice of privacy practice receipts and all necessary release forms, to be maintained in their own office files. Transporting information between the medical institution and the private practitioner's office should be done with great discretion and in a manner that protects PHI [Protected Health Information]. [35]

Legal Settings and Forensic Roles

Mental health professionals serve in many different roles, several of which take them into legal settings. This book does not address the ethical responsibilities of those who take on specialized forensic roles in legal cases (e.g., conducting forensic evaluations, providing expert witness testimony when they have no prior clinical relationship with any of the parties involved, serving as court-appointed parenting coordinator). Specialized training is required for these roles, and guidelines are available elsewhere.[36] Here, the discussion applies only to those without specialized forensic training who serve in the primary role of therapist or clinical evaluator, but who sometimes become involved in legal proceedings, even though many of them would prefer not to. This is not ordinarily considered to be "forensic" practice.[37]

In legal settings, the ethical responsibilities about confidentiality will vary, depending on the role. This makes it important for mental health professionals to be very clear—for themselves and with others—about exactly which hat they are wearing and what its implications will be about confidentiality. The differential ethical obligations in various court-related roles are outlined in chart form in Appendix VI, "Ethical Responsibilities in Forensic Contexts: Which Hat Are You Wearing?"

Ethically speaking, the confidentiality duties and privilege protections for therapists are very different from those for forensic specialists. Combining the two roles can therefore create unresolvable ethical complications about confidentiality. For example, the informed consent interview for therapy patients will explain that confidentiality is the rule, that disclosure without patient consent is the exception, and that the information obtained in the therapist–patient relationship is privileged (i.e., protected to some degree from disclosure in court proceedings). In contrast, the informed consent interview for a court-ordered forensic evaluation will explain that information obtained during the evaluation will *not* be privileged and may be included in a report that will be provided to the court and/or to others. If a therapist agrees to conduct a forensic evaluation for a current or former patient, and then is required to testify on the stand, it can be impossible to separate the information obtained in those two separate roles. It may therefore be impossible to avoid revealing privileged information from the therapy relationship without the patient's consent in the midst of testifying about the nonprivileged forensic evaluation.

For such reasons, the American Counseling Association (ACA) Ethics Code explicitly prohibits the combining of therapeutic and forensic roles: "Counselors do not evaluate for forensic purposes individuals they currently counsel or individuals they have counseled in the past. Counselors do not accept as counseling clients individuals they are evaluating or individuals they have evaluated in the past for forensic purposes."[38] Although other ethics codes do not directly address this issue, this would be wise advice for all mental health professionals.

Legally speaking, taking on dual roles in a forensic context can create conflicts of interest that potentially jeopardize a client's civil rights in a court case. This concern, as well as potential problems of impaired objectivity, led to the following recommendation in the American Psychological Association (APA) Specialty Guidelines for Forensic Psychology:

> Providing forensic and therapeutic psychological services to the same individual or closely related individuals is considered a multiple relationship that may impair objectivity and/or cause exploitation or other harm. Therefore, when requested or ordered to provide either concurrent or sequential forensic and therapeutic services, forensic practitioners disclose the potential risk and make reasonable efforts to refer the request to another qualified provider.[39]

Judges do sometimes try to order a therapist to take on this dual role—to don a forensic evaluator hat atop an existing or prior therapist hat, for example. When this happens, it is the therapist's responsibility to decline, citing the ethical conflicts and potential legal complications.[40] (Also see Chapter 8, "Avoiding Preventable Disclosures.")

INVOLUNTARY ROLES IN LEGAL CONTEXTS

Involuntary roles are those that a mental health professional takes on not by choice, but because legally ordered to do so. Sometimes, services that were provided for purely clinical purposes become the subject of legal proceedings. For example, evaluators are always legally free to say "no" to requests that they conduct an assessment for forensic purposes, but the results of an evaluation previously conducted for another purpose could later become evidence in a court case, even though that evaluator has no training about providing testimony.

> Similarly, although a therapist can avoid *voluntarily* testifying about a patient if not fully prepared for being a courtroom witness, a court order may legally require providing records or testifying *involuntarily*. In such circumstances, it can be helpful to obtain consultation from a colleague who has served in that role, and perhaps to engage in role-playing before stepping into the minefield of courtroom cross-examination, where it is easy for the unprepared clinician to disclose more than is necessary or appropriate.[41]

Therapists sometimes receive a subpoena requiring that they provide the records of a current or former therapy patient who does not want the information released as evidence in a court case. If the patient has an attorney, the therapist can obtain the patient's consent to discuss the filing of a motion to contest or quash the subpoena. For patients who have no attorney, the therapist can advise them about that process or can (when permitted by their state's laws) file that motion in the patient's behalf. If the judge refuses to quash the subpoena and instead orders the therapist to provide the records in spite of the patient's objection, the therapist's writings will become part of the court record. Sometimes, this leads to a further subpoena for testimony regarding those records (see "Further Notes on Subpoenas and Court Orders" in Chapter 7).

If a judge orders the therapist to testify against the patient's wishes, the reluctant therapist may then have one further important decision to make. The attorney who issued the subpoena may request that the judge designate this person as an "*expert witness*." If the therapist is not a forensic expert, it may be important to refuse that designation and to testify instead only as a "*fact witness*."

> An expert witness is hired for the purpose of litigation—to give an opinion or do an assessment concerning "legal issues" such as competence to stand trial or causation of psychological damages. A therapist may be called as a fact witness when she or he has treated or is treating a client who also happens to be in litigation. This person would typically only testify to the "facts" of the therapy (i.e., what is in the records). A psychologist may want to examine whether there is potential for a dual relationship to develop if he or she combines these roles as a fact witness and as an expert witness.[42]

Even if a judge declares someone qualified to testify as an expert witness, no clinician can be forced to do so—and therapists who testify in that role without forensic training may be placing themselves at risk. Therapists who wish to provide the best confidentiality protection for their patients can simply refuse to be sworn in as expert witnesses. They can state that they are present involuntarily, against the patient's wishes; that they are a "treating expert," who is not trained as a forensic expert; that they are not being paid to provide expert witness testimony in this case; and that they will testify only as a fact witness.[43]

The process can be complicated, attorneys can be deliberately aggressive, and therapists who are naïve about the process are easily intimidated. Whether involved as involuntary provider of records or involuntary courtroom witness, a therapist who has no prior involvement with the legal process is advised to obtain legal consultation to be sure the legal requirements are followed. Equally importantly, the therapist who is unfamiliar with this process should establish a supportive consultation relationship with one or more colleagues familiar with courts and courtrooms. Sometimes, this takes more than one consultant, because it is helpful to have someone who can walk the therapist through the ethical/legal ropes, as well as someone who can provide clinical advice if this disclosure creates complications in the relationship with the patient.

Finally, there should be someone—whether consultant or personal therapist—who can provide support for the personal reactions that are often experienced when going through this legal process involuntarily, especially if for the first time. Therapists do not ordinarily work in contexts in which they will be cross-examined by someone whose role may include attempting to discredit them. And few therapists—even those already familiar with the court system—remain "unjolted" when going through the process of placing a patient's private information into a public setting against the patient's wishes.

VOLUNTARY ROLES IN LEGAL CONTEXTS

In response to a request from a current or former therapy patient, therapists sometimes voluntarily testify or provide records as evidence in court cases.[44] The therapist should obtain the patient's written consent to disclose information in that forum. But, first, the therapist must carefully explain to the patient exactly what this role might involve and what information might be disclosed. For example, for the patient to give *informed* consent for treatment records to be disclosed, the therapist must first inform the patient about the content of that record. Similarly, for the patient to give *informed* consent for the therapist to provide courtroom testimony, the therapist must have explained the types of questions that might be asked and the answers that might be given on the stand.[45] Since patients often mistakenly believe that their therapist will be a good character witness, it must be explained that any type of question may be asked on cross-examination, and that the therapist must answer honestly (see Appendix VI).

However, therapists who agree to take the stand should testify cautiously. Unlike the role of evaluator, the role of therapist is not an investigative or fact-finding role, so the data generated in treatment can include important limitations and biases. The testifying therapist should acknowledge the "limitation in his or her role, information base, and treatment methods used, and limit conclusions accordingly."[46]

Therapists who wish *never* to take on this role voluntarily can explain this to prospective patients at intake and state this position in the patient information forms. To prevent subpoenas to the extent possible, prospective patients can be asked to sign a "no-subpoena" contract, agreeing not to bring the therapist into that role.[47] Although such an agreement will not be legally binding, anecdotal evidence suggests that it can reduce the likelihood that patients will subpoena the therapist's records or request the therapist's testimony in a subsequent court case.

Another way therapists sometimes participate voluntarily in court cases involves providing court-ordered clinical intervention services. This can include court-ordered individual therapy, couple therapy, family therapy, or parenting consultation (see Appendix VI). In such roles, it is important that the mental health professional have a clear contract with the court that is not only specific about fees and services, but that also specifies the rules about confidentiality. For example, if the mental health professional who provides therapy to a court-ordered patient will be expected to provide progress reports, treatment summaries, or subsequent courtroom testimony, that must be clearly specified in the contract. Otherwise, the therapist will be unable to be clear with the prospective patient about what the actual limits of confidentiality will be.

Finally, therapists are now being encouraged to take on certain new court-related roles that should be undertaken only by those who have received the necessary specialized training.[48] These include the role of coach in collaborative divorce proceedings—a process involving several types of professionals and designed to prevent an adversarial court process. There is also a relatively new role of parenting coordinator. This quasi-legal role is created when judges, in attempting to prevent multiple return visits to court in high-conflict divorce and custody cases, sometimes give mental health professionals the legal authority to make determinations in such things as visitation agreements (see Appendix VI).

The APA Ethics Code requires that "when assuming forensic roles, psychologists are or become reasonably familiar with the judicial or administrative rules governing their roles."[49] In other words, whether or not they are trained as forensic specialists, psychologists who voluntarily assume a forensic role are expected to be prepared to wear that hat. Mental health professionals should never volunteer for a forensic role unless already trained and prepared to serve in that role, or willing to spend the time and money and obtain the supervision for becoming prepared.

Military and Intelligence Settings

The stresses of recent wars have created a demand for more mental health professionals to serve the needs of military personnel and their families.[50] Within military settings, all record keeping is now electronic, so the informed consent conversation about confidentiality needs to include information about exactly who might have access to the patient's electronic records, as well as the potential confidentiality or redisclosure implications of that access.

Mental health professionals who provide therapy or assessments in intelligence settings must sometimes adapt the informed consent process to the fact that they may be prohibited from revealing to prospective patients all the uses of the information that will be obtained in the course of an evaluation or therapy. Interestingly, one ethical standard in the APA Ethics Code seems to anticipate this problem: "If psychologists will be precluded by law or by organizational roles from providing such information to particular individuals or groups, they so inform those individuals or groups at the outset of the service."[51] In other words, these mental health professionals may need to begin their clinical relationships by explaining that they are not able to describe exactly how the information obtained from the patient might later be used.

Much has been written about the issue of detainee interrogations conducted by psychologists and psychiatrists.[52] As a result of the concern generated about this issue, the APA Ethics Code was amended in 2010 to clarify the ethical responsibilities of psychologists if ordered to act in ways that would be considered unethical by their profession.[53] So far, the literature on this topic has addressed confidentiality primarily in the context of other professionals failing to obtain patient consent before giving mental health interrogators access to medical records for planning their interrogations. However, even in this setting, mental health professionals would be expected to maintain the ethical standards related to informing patients about limits of confidentiality and obtaining consent for disclosure.

Business, Industrial, and Organizational Settings

Mental health professionals who provide consultation or therapy services in organizational settings often interact with several levels of personnel, not all of whom will be offered the same confidentiality protections. As a result, it creates ethical problems here, as elsewhere, if the psychologist relies on the question, "Who is *the* client?" because that question implies a singular answer. Instead, in such settings, it is important to *think plural.*

The APA Ethics Code requires that psychologists who deliver services to or through organizations explain in advance such things as "which of the individuals are clients, the relationship the psychologist will have with each person and the organization, the probable uses of services provided and information obtained, who will have access to the information, and the limits of confidentiality."[54] A mental health professional employed by a business or organization, or independently providing consultation or therapy services in such a setting, will often have interactions with a number of individuals who already have relationships with each other, usually hierarchical relationships: The recommendations below address psychologists, but they would apply to any mental health professional:

> [A] psychologist might have a contract with a corporation, specifying a plan for providing leadership consultation to the CEO, in addition to case consultation to several of his managers who have problematic relationships with their supervisees. The psychologist might meet with the CEO, with the managers, with their supervisees, and perhaps with other employees. Asking "Who is the client?" may lead to the simple answer: "The corporation is my client, because it issued the contract and pays my fee." But this answer provides the psychologist with no guidance about specific ethical responsibilities in the complex relationships that will be developed with individuals within this corporate system … It probably will not be appropriate for the psychologist to promise the same level of confidentiality in each of these relationships; so the limits of the confidentiality will need to be defined in advance, explained at the initial informed-consent interview with the CEO, and made clear to each individual at each level of the consultation process. None of this will be adequately clarified in the mind of the consulting psychologist who relies on the "Who is the client?" question and settles for its singular answer.[55]

Independent Clinical Practice

Therapists who work within an agency or institution face the ethical problem of dealing with its existing confidentiality policies and with the potential for conflicts between those policies and what their own profession considers to be ethical practices. Therapists in independent practice have the opposite problem: They are responsible for developing, on their own, clear confidentiality policies that reflect how they actually intend to behave, that conform to their ethics code, and that are also consistent with applicable state and federal laws. "This requires learning a great deal of complex ethical and legal information; weighing the competing interests, engaging in some personal soul searching; integrating all this into a clear policy about confidentiality and disclosure, and preparing to explain it to clients in a simple and undefensive manner."[56]

This is very difficult to do alone. Fortunately (as described in Chapters 4 and 9), therapists can collaborate with each other in this process, so they do not all need to rediscover the same wheel alone when it comes to developing policies or creating forms that will describe their policies to clients. They can obtain individual peer consultation or create peer consultation groups for sharing of resources. This can also have the effect of decreasing the isolation often experienced by psychologists in independent practice. "Creating ways to stay in connection with others seems to be one of the most basic, important, and helpful self-care strategies for many psychologists."[57] Collaborating with others in developing ethics-based confidentiality policies and coordinating ethics-based staff training can open up opportunities for creating and maintaining that connection with other therapists.

Therapists in independent practice who electronically transmit confidential patient information (e.g., through computerized submission of claims forms or other electronic transmission of patient records) must also determine how to comply with the HIPAA regulations about privacy and confidentiality. In a solo practice, the therapist can serve as both the HIPAA Privacy Officer and the HIPAA Security Officer, unless an employee is to be appointed to serve these functions.

Home Offices

Therapists who have their professional offices in their own homes face many confidentiality pitfalls. These can include "unsecured documents in the home, the telephone answering machine in the home, the family Internet account, the family computer, the shared fax machine, the shared mail box, the family dining table, the accidental revelation, the errant spouse, and exposure through litigation."[58] Nevertheless, the same ethical standards and HIPAA regulations apply as in a traditional office setting.[59]

Confidentiality and privacy issues arise when poor physical boundaries exist between the family living space and the professional space.[60] An informal survey found that psychotherapists who conducted groups in their home considered the biggest disadvantage to be the invasion of their privacy, whereas the group members themselves were most concerned about the impact on their own privacy and confidentiality in that setting. It is, of course, the latter that is of ethical concern.[61]

Pope and Vasquez have provided a list of questions that should be considered before a therapist decides to see patients in an office located in the therapist's home. All of these have implications for privacy and/or confidentiality:

- "Is it likely that patients—some of whom may not want anyone else to know that they are in psychotherapy—will encounter family members when arriving, waiting for the appointment, or leaving?
- Any chance that young children will interrupt therapy sessions?
- Will files, appointment books, message slips, and other documents be secure and out of sight when family members enter the office?
- Will family embers be able to overhear telephone calls or other discussions with patients?
- Is confidential information about patients stored on a computer that other family members use? If so, how is it secured against accidental discovery?
- Is the telephone answering machine that receives calls from or about patients shared with other family members? If so, how can those calls be protected against accidental playback for other family members?
- Are answering machine messages from or about clients ever played back in the presence of family members?"[62]

Rural and "Small-World" Settings

Many recommendations are available about confidentiality issues in rural settings.[63] When serving as therapist in rural settings or small communities, it can be very difficult to avoid dual relationships. If, for example, a therapist is the only nearby clinician who provides certain needed services, then the patients may all know each other, and many may also know the therapist and/or the therapist's family. Such dual or multiple relationships may not, in themselves, be unethical, as long as they do not impair clinical objectivity or cause harm to patients. But they do increase the likelihood that confidentiality will be breached. "Therapists must be constantly aware to keep original sources of information clear or run the risk of unintentional disclosure of confidential material."[64]

Psychologists living and practicing in small communities may experience chance encounters with patients at almost every turn, making it important for them to be prepared for interacting with clients outside the professional context. This can happen in almost any community, but it becomes part of the fabric of life in rural communities. "An important skill is for the psychologist to be present in an interaction as a good neighbor, but also as the individual's psychologist; to be engaged on both levels, but to be comfortable and flexible in engaging and disengaging from one or the other as is appropriate to the situation."[65] Outside the therapy room, continual self-monitoring may be necessary in order for the therapist to minimize unintentional disclosure of the fact that someone is a patient or disclosure of a patient's confidences. "Mastering the skill of communicating in social situations with appropriate professional vagueness is helpful."[66]

Although therapists in small-world settings may be unable to avoid all encounters with their patients outside the therapy room, they do have some control over behaviors that could create unnecessary dual relationships or confidentiality complications. For example, although these therapists may not be able to avoid crossing paths socially, they can have a policy of not socializing alone with patients or "chiming in during gossip sessions," and they can instruct their family members in how to interact in certain situations "while minimizing the details regarding why."[67] Some therapists explain to patients in advance that if they encounter each other in public, the therapist will acknowledge the patient only if the patient takes the lead and addresses the therapist first.

Isolated, self-contained communities exist not only in rural areas, but also in many other settings, including metropolitan areas. These present similar problems for a therapist:

> Small communities do not necessarily exist only in rural areas or geographical isolation. Close-knit military, religious, cultural, or ethnic communities existing within a much larger community can pose similar dilemmas. Therapists working in huge metropolitan settings can experience what amounts to small-world hazards, and the same need to view role conflicts in a sociocultural context pertains... Even when one cohesive population is embedded in a large city, complications similar to those faced by rural therapists can arise.[68]

College and university campuses are another example of "small-world" settings. Therapists in college counseling centers are likely to cross paths with their patients and must also be alert to avoid dual roles whenever possible. For example, a mental health professional who also teaches classes in which students are evaluated and graded should not also take on the potentially conflicting role of therapist to those students.

Finally, mental health professionals who work with military personnel are increasingly finding themselves in "small-world" settings. This can be true whether they work aboard ship or are embedded within military units in the field. Sometimes, this can have confidentiality implications even more complex than those described above, and this must be acknowledged when the relationship begins.

> How can a clinician deployed as an embedded member of a small team or military unit ethically manage pervasive and uncomfortable multiple-role relationships? Embedded practice often enhances the clinician's understanding of service members' needs and increases the likelihood of members to seek services. Yet, such proximity also ensures multiple roles with every member of

the community and diminishes the clinician's ability to employ usual ethical strategies for minimizing multiple-relationship hazards.[69]

Services Provided in the Patient's Home or Other Out-of-Office Setting

Home-based services are an established practice, especially if services are being provided to those who are elderly, ill, or homebound. However, confidentiality can easily be compromised when services are provided in the patient's home. Homes are not usually as private or as soundproofed as office spaces, and family members and other nonpatients may be present or within earshot.[70]

Confidentiality issues can also arise because of the potential boundary issues and role confusions that can arise in home settings. For example, the therapist may be treated more like a friend or guest than would likely be the case in a formal office setting, family members or others might be introduced or invited to join the conversation, food and beverages might be served or offered, and there may be requests for the therapist to assist the patient or others with household tasks. Therapists who provide in-home services should anticipate these social and environmental complications in advance and discuss them with the patient at the outset.

Services are sometimes provided in other out-of-office settings as part of the patient's treatment plan. This can be consistent with behavioral, systems, humanistic, cognitive-behavioral, multimodal, and other nonanalytic orientations,[71] but it can also raise ethical issues, including complications about confidentiality. This would be of special concern if the services are provided in a public setting. As with in-home services, therapists who provide any out-of-office services should foresee the possible confidential issues and address those with the patient from the beginning.

Consultation and Supervision Roles

Although the terms "consultation" and "supervision" are often used interchangeably, from a confidentiality perspective their differences are more important than their similarities. One thing that applies to both roles, however, is the ethical responsibility to explain to consultees and supervisees (1) exactly what the limits of confidentiality will be in *that* relationship (e.g., whether the supervisor or consultant will disclose information if it is legally reportable information such as suspicion of abuse, provider misconduct, etc.) and (2) whether or not the consultee or supervisee's patients must be informed about the existence of that relationship.

"Supervision" ordinarily refers to relationships in which one party is an accomplished professional who takes responsibility for monitoring and guiding the work of one or more less qualified professionals, whether clinical students, resident trainees, licensure candidates, or other unlicensed professionals. Ordinarily, without that supervision, the supervisee would not be considered qualified to provide the services that are being supervised. The supervisor is ethically and legally responsible for the supervisee's work. For that reason, the supervisee (1) must provide all identifiable client information that would allow the supervisor to contact the client in the absence of the supervisee, (2) is expected to follow the supervisor's recommendations, and (3) must inform prospective patients about the supervision relationship and about the limitations this relationship will necessarily impose on confidentiality. (See, in Chapter 6, "Informed Consent for Disclosures Made in Clinical Supervision or Consultation.")

Supervisors, as gatekeepers with a responsibility for the enculturation of their supervisees into the mental health professions, are expected to ensure that the supervisee understands the ethical and legal duties related to confidentiality.[72] It is recommended that supervisors keep some record of the supervision relationship, for the protection of the supervisor, the supervisee, and the patient.[73] In creating such a record, supervisors should use the same level of caution about content as with their own client records, because supervision records, if known to others, are sometimes vulnerable to subpoena or other legal demand for disclosure.

"Consultation," in contrast, ordinarily refers to a relationship in which someone seeks assistance from another professional, whether as an expert about a particular area of practice or as a professional who consults with peers individually or in a consultation group. The consultee is licensed or otherwise qualified to practice without the consultant's involvement and is therefore free to follow or to ignore any recommendations provided by the consultant. Documentation may be optional.

In this relationship, the consultee is not ethically free to provide any identifiable patient information to the consultant unless the patient has given explicit consent in advance for the information to be disclosed to the consultant. If no identifiable information will be shared, most mental health professionals do not believe they need to discuss that relationship with those patients whose cases will be discussed there. It is good practice, however, to inform prospective patients about the possibility of such consultation. ("In order to ensure that I am providing good clinical care, I sometimes consult with a colleague; but in doing so I will not provide any information that might identify you.") Many therapists also offer to provide the name(s) of their consultants if requested.

Absent patient consent, consultants should abstain from providing clinical consultation in a case if they discover that, because of personal knowledge or because of some past or present professional relationship, they are able to identify the patient. In that case, they can refer the therapist to another consultant.

In other words, whereas supervision relationships require that the supervisor be given all necessary contact information about the patient, a consultant should be given no identifiable information unless the patient has given explicit consent for that disclosure. Therapists' ethical standards reflect this distinction. For example, the APA Ethics Code requires as follows: "When consulting with colleagues, (1) psychologists do not disclose confidential information that reasonably could lead to the identification of a client/patient, research participant, or other person or organization with whom they have a confidential relationship unless they have obtained the prior consent of the person or organization or the disclosure cannot be avoided, and (2) they disclose information only to the extent necessary to achieve the purposes of the consultation."[74] The ACA Ethics Code contains an identically worded Standard.[75] The National Association of Social Workers (NASW) Ethics Code requires that "when consulting with colleagues about clients, social workers should disclose the least amount of information necessary to achieve the purposes of the consultation."[76]

13

Ethics-Based Staff Training About Confidentiality

It is important for all personnel in mental health settings to perform their assigned tasks competently, but for staff members who interact with mental health patients, or who have access to patient information, it is important that their competence include ethical awareness. In other words, whether their role is clinical or nonclinical, those who work in mental health settings must demonstrate more than technical competence. For the protection of patients and their rights, *ethical competence* is also important, especially as it applies to patient confidentiality and record security.[1]

In contrast to legal training about the Health Insurance Portability and Accountability Act (HIPAA) the confidentiality training described in this chapter is "ethics-based" in the sense that, instead of being based on laws, it is grounded in ethical mandates and professional recommendations from the mental health professions themselves. The Ethical Practice Model, which formed the outline for Part II of this book, reflects these ethical requirements and is useful in the training process. But the fact that the training is ethics-based does not mean that legal issues are ignored. The training recommended here incorporates the relevant legal requirements affecting confidentiality, including state laws and federal HIPAA regulations, in order to place those into ethical context.

Providing confidentiality training for all staff—clinical and nonclinical—can convey the message that everyone shares responsibility for protecting patients' rights about confidentiality and that all personnel in the setting must collaborate in creating a "culture of safety" that ensures that protection.[2] All who work in a mental health setting should attend such training, even if they were previously trained elsewhere: Legal requirements vary from state to state, and voluntary policies vary across settings within each state, so some confidentiality and disclosure policies that were acceptable in their previous setting may be inappropriate in the current one.

This training is especially important for nonclinical staff, because they do not usually have access to ethics training elsewhere; but it is also appropriate for clinical staff. Unlike "generic" ethics training, this training will be focused on setting-specific confidentiality policies that all personnel will be expected to follow.

Including clinical students, interns, and supervisees can also be important. Research suggests that the ethical violations of clinical trainees often involve breaches of confidentiality,[3] and participating in such training can be helpful in elevating the ethical awareness of the next generation of clinicians. This training can be part of a mentoring process that allows them to carry a clearer understanding of confidentiality ethics to their future settings.

If desired, confidentiality training can be conducted within a broader ethics training program, rather than presented as a stand-alone topic. Such broader ethics training might include topics such as creating an appropriate office environment, monitoring staff interactions with patients and their families, and respecting boundaries with patients.[4] (See the sample training outline in Appendix VIII.)

Ethical Standards and Professional Recommendations About Staff Training

The ethics codes of the mental health professions contain standards that reflect the importance of training staff and monitoring their performance. The American Psychological Association (APA) requires that psychologists who delegate tasks to others "take reasonable steps to ... see that such persons perform these services competently."[5] The National Association of Social Workers (NASW) ethically requires those with administrative responsibilities to "take reasonable steps to ensure that the working environment for which they are responsible is consistent with and encourages compliance with the NASW Code of Ethics;" to "eliminate any conditions in their organizations that violate, interfere with, or discourage compliance with the Code"; and to provide or arrange continuing education for all staff to "address current knowledge and emerging developments related to social work practice and ethics."[6] The American Counseling Association (ACA) requires counselors to "make every effort to ensure that privacy and confidentiality of clients are maintained by subordinates, including employees, supervisees, students, clerical assistants, and volunteers."[7]

Other professional guidelines also emphasize staff training. For example, the Record Keeping Guidelines of the APA stress the necessity for staff education about protecting the confidentiality of records:

> When the psychologist employs clerical or testing personnel, he or she is required by the Ethics Code (Standard 2.05) to take reasonable steps to ensure that the employee's work is done competently. Therefore, the psychologist strives to educate employees about confidentiality requirements and to

> implement processes that support the protection of records and the disclosure of confidential information only with proper consent or under other required circumstances (e.g., mandated report, court order).[8]

The APA Practice Organization and the APA Insurance Trust both recommend that clinical and nonclinical staff be required to sign a confidentiality contract as a condition of employment.[9] The website of the American Psychiatric Association (APsyA) provides a sample contract for that purpose.[10] If desired, such a confidentiality contract can be one component of a broader ethics contract.[11]

For the protection of both patients and themselves, mental health professionals must be free to discharge staff members who are unable or unwilling to follow the relevant ethical standards.[12] Toward that end, the APA Insurance Trust recommends that psychologists require all personnel to follow the APA Ethics Code, with failure to do so being grounds for termination.[13] In multidisciplinary settings, staff can be required to behave in a manner consistent with all the ethics codes that are represented in the setting. If such requirements are to be imposed as conditions of employment, however, this should be stipulated in the initial employment contract.

Legal Requirements About Staff Training

State laws and state agency regulations sometimes contain training requirements for those who assist clinicians in performing certain tasks. In addition, state law can forbid staff members from removing patient records or other identifiable patient data from the setting without the express consent of the owner. All such legal mandates can be included in the ethics-based training described below.

At the level of federal laws, the HIPAA regulations contain both explicit and implied training mandates about confidentiality.[14] The HIPAA Privacy Rule requires training for the entire workforce in health care settings.[15] This training must be provided within a reasonable time after someone joins the workforce, must apply to the person's specific job responsibilities, and must be tailored to the confidentiality policies that will apply in that setting. The provider must document that the training was provided.[16] The Privacy Rule also imposes a "minimum necessary" standard about disclosure of confidential information, requiring that staff members not be given access to levels of information beyond what is reasonably necessary for fulfilling their own specific duties.[17]

The HIPAA Security Rule requires Security Awareness Training, as well as contingency planning about staff responsibilities in disaster situations, and it requires that this training be documented.[18] Furthermore, HIPAA requires that sanctions be imposed on any staff member who fails to comply with the policies affecting privacy or record security.[19] For documenting that staff understood the information covered in the training, their performance on a post-test can be included in their personnel record.[20]

Integrating Ethical and Legal Training About Confidentiality

The relationship between ethics and laws can be very confusing. As described in earlier chapters, legal requirements about confidentiality sometimes overlap with ethical obligations, but they sometimes conflict with them.[21] An advantage of ethics-based training is that it can highlight both the ethical-legal overlaps and the potential ethical-legal conflicts.

DIFFERENTIATING BETWEEN LEGAL TRAINING AND ETHICS TRAINING

By definition, ethics-based training about confidentiality will focus on patient's rights and on therapists' responsibilities in protection of those rights, as defined by the mental health professions themselves. In contrast, legal-based training will focus on laws and regulations that are created by legislators, regulators, and courts. Training about the relevant laws will be necessary and important, but should not be treated as a substitute for ethics-based training.[22] Attorneys often provide some of the legal training about confidentiality. Although they are experts about the law, mental health professionals must be the experts about the ethical standards of their own professions and must retain responsibility for clarifying the ethical implications of the laws that are taught.

DISADVANTAGES OF LAW-BASED TRAINING

Confidentiality training that is based solely or largely on legal responsibilities can have several major disadvantages for therapists and their patients, as noted earlier:

> First, it fosters the impression that attorneys—not clinicians—have become the only "real" experts about this aspect of practice. Second, it creates a legal language about confidentiality that threatens to usurp psychologists' own clinical or ethical language about it: Laws take center stage, when what is needed is a language for placing them into ethical context. Third, it exacerbates the figure–ground confusion (by substituting legal rules for ethical rules) and often takes a risk-management perspective that raises anxiety: It encourages psychologists to focus on obeying laws in order to avoid risks to *themselves* when what they need is a clearer focus on their ethical obligations and the potential risks to *clients*.[23]

Some therapists report that legal-based risk management training can raise their anxiety to the point at which they cease to learn what is being taught. In fact, one thing obscured by the legal focus is the fact that the best risk management strategy begins with understanding and following the patient-protective ethical standards of one's profession.

ADVANTAGES OF ETHICS-BASED TRAINING ABOUT CONFIDENTIALITY

Laws can have ethical consequences, which is why it is not appropriate for staff training to focus only on the laws themselves. It is recommended that staff training be organized around the therapists' ethical standards; then, relevant laws can be integrated into that ethical structure. The Ethical Practice Model can be very useful for that purpose. The ethical topics of confidentiality and record keeping can be presented using that six-step model; then, the legal information can be placed into ethical context by incorporating it within that ethics-based outline, highlighting the ethical implications of both the legal protectors and the legal limiters of confidentiality[24] (see discussion in Chapter 3 and the annotated model in Appendix V).

Staff members who have been taught about therapists' ethical responsibilities will be aware that ethical requirements and legal demands might differ. In integrated training, staff will not simply learn the relevant laws but will learn to consider the ethical implications of those laws. Staff members who learn to notice when ethical and legal demands differ will learn to bring questions to the psychologist rather than responding to a legal demand without consultation.

The importance of providing training that places laws into ethical context is illustrated below using three training examples that contrast law-based HIPAA training with the ethics-based confidentiality training advocated here.[25]

Training Module 1: What If You Receive a Legal Demand for Patient Information?

HIPAA training might teach that a legal mandate is a sufficient basis for disclosing information without the patient's consent. Legally speaking, this is sometimes accurate. Ethically speaking, however, this circumstance is actually much more complicated, because therapists have ethical requirements when faced with ethical-legal conflicts (see, in Chapter 1, "Ethical Standards About Conflicts Between Ethical Duties and Other Obligations").

Ethically, the first step is to determine whether the patient wishes to give consent for the legally demanded information to be disclosed. If not, the therapist can seek ways to minimize disclosure and can sometimes protect the information completely.[26] Even if the information is not legally protectable, therapists should not delegate to nonclinical staff the responsibility for deciding whether to disclose it. In such circumstances, the therapist is advised to use a structured decision-making process for deciding whether to "follow the law despite their ethical concerns" or whether "a conscientious objection is warranted."[27] Although the ethics-based training can teach nonclinical staff how to behave ethically when a subpoena is initially delivered, therapists themselves have responsibility for weighing the competing values and deciding what to do next.

Training Module 2: Can You Disclose Without Patient Consent If Legally Allowed?

Some law-based training suggests that if a specific type of disclosure is allowed by law, then the patient's authorization is not needed. This has broad implications, because HIPAA legally allows disclosures for such vague and wide-ranging purposes as "treatment, payment and health care operations activities,"[28] and some states have laws allowing similarly broad disclosures without patient consent.

Ethically speaking, disclosing information without patient consent in the absence of a legal requirement to do so constitutes a *voluntary* breach of confidentiality. Whereas a legal requirement can create a true ethical-legal conflict (thereby invoking the ethical duties described in the module above), a voluntary disclosure involves no ethical-legal conflict at all. "There is thus a vital ethical difference between *legally mandated* disclosures (which can be legally compelled whether or not a patient gives consent) and those merely *legally allowed* (which psychologists remain free not to make, and for which a patient remains free not to give consent)."[29]

Throughout these chapters, we have advocated that therapists take the supererogatory ethical position that *voluntary disclosures without the patient's consent should be avoided whenever legally possible.* Consistent with this position, ethics-based training can teach that "legally allowed" is not synonymous with "ethically appropriate," and that only the mental health professional can decide whether and when to disclose in the absence of the patient's informed consent.

Training Module 3: What Must You Do to Protect Patients' Informed Consent Rights?

HIPAA trainers may teach that, in the name of efficiency, nonclinical staff can satisfy the legal requirement to inform prospective patients about limits of confidentiality by simply obtaining their signature on the HIPAA "Notice of Privacy Practices" when they first arrive. "This practice is not unethical in itself; but it is not a substitute for obtaining the client's truly informed consent to accept the potential risks that may be created by the limits that may be imposed on confidentiality."[30]

Legally speaking, the only purpose for obtaining a signature on the HIPAA notice is to document that the patient received it. Ethically speaking, however, obtaining a patient's informed consent involves more than this (see Chapter 5 about obtaining informed consent at intake and Chapter 6 about obtaining patient consent before disclosing patient-specific information). A further ethical problem is raised by the fact that most versions of the HIPAA notice are written in language that is unintelligible to average patients, and thus do not meet therapists' ethical requirement to inform patients in "developmentally and culturally appropriate" language that is "clear and understandable"[31]—or at least "reasonably understandable."[32]

In some clinical settings, nonclinical staff are given responsibility for informing prospective patients in advance about certain other things that may have implications for confidentiality, including information about third-party reimbursement, before they meet with a therapist for the first time. Although therapists are not always in control of such policies, they can meet their ethical and professional obligations by (1) providing ethics-based staff training about informed consent to the personnel who make that first contact, and then by (2) beginning their own initial sessions with a discussion that determines whether the patient has been adequately informed and understands the information. This includes inviting patients to ask questions about the limits of confidentiality and responding to those questions with clear answers about how the therapist actually intends to behave. It is important that the therapist be the one to conduct this conversation, not only because nonclinical staff may not know the accurate answers, but also because such conversations can raise clinical issues that nonclinical staff should not try to address.

Finally, since informed consent is an ongoing process, the limits of confidentiality must be discussed not only at the outset of the relationship, but also whenever thereafter that new circumstances might warrant. This renewed conversation cannot be delegated, because "such issues are best addressed when they arise, and that will likely be during a private session with the therapist."[33]

Separating Ethics-Based Training From Technical Training or Administrative Training

The ethics-based training advocated here is different from the technical training that is sometimes legally required for those who assist clinicians in certain types of tasks (e.g., psychological testing assistants). This training is also different from the task-specific ethics training that some employees may need if they perform specialized duties that have ethical implications (e.g., performing billing tasks or ensuring that proper authorizations are in place before disclosing information to others).

For conducting the ethics-based training described here, it can be useful to construct a training manual, and samples are available.[34] Such a manual should be separate from the broad policy manuals used in many settings. "It is recommended that the ethics-based training be presented separately, in its own self-contained manual. Otherwise, its importance may be diminished and its ethical intentions obscured by the large number of general administrative matters, business goals, and legally-required details in a general policy manual."[35]

Recommendations When Planning Integrated Staff Training

We will consider here only those recommendations related specifically to staff training on the topic of patient confidentiality, even though this training may be conducted within the context of a broader ethics-based curriculum.[36] Based on the ethical and legal considerations described above and throughout this volume, therapists or administrators who are planning or conducting staff training in their own mental health setting can consider the following:[37]

1. *Planning for the confidentiality training must begin by constructing a set of clear written policies that all staff will be expected to follow*. These must both conform to ethical standards and meet the legal requirements that apply in the setting. Constructing a training manual will help the clinician be more clear about the policies and more prepared to enforce them. If the policies are vague, unclear, or ineffective, so will be the training.

2. *There can be advantages in providing the same ethics-based confidentiality training to all personnel in the setting, including clinical staff and trainees, as well as nonclinical staff and volunteers.* Inappropriate or unethical behavior by anyone in the setting can harm a patient and/or reflect badly on the mental health profession. "Helping staff maintain ethical practices will not only create a culture of safety in which clients are protected in the current setting but also can help raise ethical standards in other settings where these employees might later work."[38]

Everyone in the setting can be given responsibility for monitoring performance and offering further recommendations about how to provide the best confidentiality protections for patients. It is important that trainers assure staff that there will be no retaliation if they call attention to gaps in the confidentiality safety in the workplace. It can be explained that the HIPAA Breach Notification Rule legally requires therapists to report any known breaches of confidentiality, and that staff can participate in that process.

3. *On subtopics that have both ethical and legal content, it is recommended that the training begin with the ethical standards and related professional recommendations.* Legal requirements can then be discussed within that context, to help staff understand their ethical implications. For example, training on the ethical subtopic of "Informing Prospective Patients About the Limits of Confidentiality" can begin by covering the relevant ethical standards listed in Appendix II and using the graphic in Figure 1.2. Within that context, there can also be discussion of the legally required HIPAA "Notice of Privacy Practices," explaining to staff that this legal form meets the "informing" requirement but not the "consent" requirement.

4. *Mental health professionals who are not sophisticated about legal issues may decide to invite some attorney-led training about certain aspects of confidentiality, such as responding to subpoenas.* However, such legal training should not be treated as a substitute for ethics training on that topic. If attorney-led training is presented within the practice setting, it should be placed into ethical context at the time (as described above) by a mental health co-leader. This plan should be explained to the invited attorney in advance. If staff will receive law-based training (e.g., HIPAA training) elsewhere, they will better understand its ethical implications if the related ethics-based training has been provided first.

5. *Confidentiality training should not be a one-time event.* Ethics codes and laws can change, making ethical and legal updates important. General refresher training

is also recommended, perhaps annually. Meanwhile, in the more frequent regular staff meetings, therapists can address ethical issues about confidentiality whenever they arise in the setting.

6. *Therapists, administrators, and trainers can evaluate staff's level of understanding through oral or written examinations.* These can be administered immediately after the training and repeated annually, or can be a required part of job-performance evaluations. Staff can be provided with certificates that document completion of the training.[39]

7. *All staff, both clinical and nonclinical, can be required to sign a confidentiality contract as a condition of employment,*[40] *and this signing can be renewed at annual refresher trainings, to emphasize its importance.* If a deliberate breach of that contract will be considered cause for dismissal, that should be explained in the hiring interview and in the initial employment contract.

APPENDIX I

Selected Ethical Standards Relevant to Confidentiality Listed Numerically

COUNSELORS

AMERICAN COUNSELING ASSOCIATION (ACA)

ACA Ethical Standard	Location in Ethical Practice Model (Box 3.1)
A. THE COUNSELING RELATIONSHIP	
A.2. *Informed Consent in the Counseling Relationship*	
A.2.a. Informed Consent	Step 2
A.2.b. Types of Information Needed	Steps 1, 2
A.2.d. Inability to Give Consent	Step 2
A.3. *Clients Served by Others*	Step 3
A.4. *Avoiding Harm*	(Entire Model)
A.5. *Roles and Relationships With Clients*	
A.5.e. Informing About Role Changes in Relationships	Step 2
A.6. *Roles and Relationships at Individual, Group, Institutional and Societal Levels*	Step 3
A.9. *End-of-Line Care for Terminally Ill Clients*	
A.9.c. Confidentiality With End-of-Life and Terminally Ill Clients	Steps 1, 2, 3
A.12. *Technology Applications*	
A.12.g. Technology and Informed Consent	Steps 1, 2, 3
A.12.h. Sites on the World Wide Web	Steps 1, 2, 3
B. CONFIDENTIALITY, PRIVILEGED COMMUNICATION, and PRIVACY	
B.1. *Respecting Client Rights*	Steps 1, 2, 3, 4
B.1.a. Multicultural/Diversity Considerations	Steps 1, 2, 3
B.1.b. Respect for Privacy	Steps 1, 3
B.1.c. Respect for Confidentiality	Steps 1, 2, 3, 4
B.1.d. Explanation of Limitations	Steps 1, 2

ACA Ethical Standard	Location in Ethical Practice Model (Box 3.1)
B.2. *Exceptions*	
B.2.a. Danger and Legal Requirements	Steps 1, 2, 3
B.2.b. Contagious, Life-Threatening Diseases	Steps 1, 2, 3
B.2.c. Court-Ordered Disclosure	Step 1, 4
B.2.d. Minimal Disclosure	Steps 2, 3, 4, 5
B.3. *Information Shared With Others*	
B.3.a. Subordinates	Steps 2, 3, 5
B.3.b. Treatment Teams	Steps 1, 2, 3
B.3.c. Confidential Settings	Step 5
B.3.d. Third-Party Payers	Steps 3, 5
B.3.e. Transmitting Confidential Information	Step 5
B.3.f. Deceased Clients	Steps 3, 5
B.4. *Groups and Families*	
B.4.a. Group Work	Step 1, 2
B.4.b. Couples and Family Counseling	Step 1, 2, 3
B.5. *Clients Lacking Capacity to Give Informed Consent*	
B.5.a. Responsibility to Clients	Steps 2, 3, 4, 5
B.5.b. Responsibility to Parents and Legal Guardians	Steps 1, 2, 3
B.5.c. Release of Confidential Information	Steps 2, 3
B.6. *Records*	
B.6.a. Confidentiality of Records	Steps 3, 5
B.6.b. Permission to Record	Steps 2, 3
B.6.c. Permission to Observe	Step 3
B.6.f. Disclosure or Transfer	Steps 3, 5
B.6.g. Storage and Disposition After Termination	Steps 3, 5
B.6.h. Reasonable Precautions (in event of clinician's death)	Step 5
B.7. *Research and Training*	
B.7.b. Adherence to Guidelines	Step 4
B.7.c. Confidentiality of Information Obtained in Research	Step 2
B.7.d. Disclosure of Research Information	Step 3
B.7.e. Agreement for Identification	Step 3
B.8. *Consultation*	
B.8.a. Agreements	Steps 2, 3
B.8.b. Respect for Privacy	Step 3
B.8.c. Disclosure of Confidential Information	Steps 1, 3
C. PROFESSIONAL RESPONSIBILITY	
C.2.e. Consultation on Ethical Obligations	Step 1
C.2.f. Continuing Education	Step 1
C.6.b. Reports to Third Parties	Steps 3, 5
D. RELATIONSHIPS WITH OTHER PROFESSIONALS	
D.2.d. Informed Consent in Consultation	Step 2
E. EVALUATION, ASSESSMENT and INTERPRETATION	
E.3.a. Explanation to Clients	Step 2

(*continued*)

ACA Ethical Standard	Location in Ethical Practice Model (Box 3.1)
E.4. Release of Data to Qualified Professionals	Step 5
E.13.a. Forensic Evaluation: Primary Obligations	Steps 4, 5
E.13.b. Forensic Evaluation: Consent for Evaluation	Steps 2, 3, 4, 5
F. SUPERVISION, TRAINING, and TEACHING	
F.1.c. Informed Consent and Client Rights	Steps 2, 5, 6
F.6.d. Teaching Ethics	Step 6
F.6.h. Professional Disclosure	Step 2
G. RESEARCH and PUBLICATION	
G.2.a. Informed Consent in Research	Step 2
G.2.e. Confidentiality of Information	Step 2, 3
G.2.f. Persons Not Capable of Giving Informed Consent (to Research)	Step 2
G.4.d. Disguise Identity of Research Participants, Unless Consent Obtained	Step 3
G.5.h. Professional Review	Steps 3, 5
H. RESOLVING ETHICAL ISSUES	
H.1.b. Conflicts Between Ethics and Laws	Steps 1, 4
H.2.b. Informal Resolution	Step 3
H.2.c. Reporting Ethical Violations	Steps 1, 2, 3, 4
H.2.d. Consultation	Steps 1, 5
H.2.e. Organizational Conflicts	Steps 1, 5

From American Counseling Association. (2005). *ACA Code of Ethics.*

MARRIAGE AND FAMILY THERAPISTS:

AMERICAN ASSOCIATION OF MARRIAGE AND FAMILY THERAPISTS (AAMFT)

AAMFT Ethical Standard	Location in Ethical Practice Model (Box 3.1)
1. RESPONSIBILITY TO CLIENTS	
1.2 Obtain Informed Consent	Step 2
1.2 Avoid Multiple Relationships	Step 5
1.6 Make Legally Required Reports of Unethical Conduct	Steps 1, 2, 4
1.8 Respect Clients' Decision-Making Autonomy	Steps 2, 3
1.12 Obtain Informed Consent before Recording/Observing	Step 3
2. CONFIDENTIALITY	
2.1 Inform About Limits of Confidentiality	Steps 1, 2
2.2 Disclose Only With Client Consent or Legal Requirement	Steps 1, 3
2.2 In Couple/Group Treatment, Obtain Consent from Each	Step 3
2.3 Present Identifiable Client Materials Only With Consent	Steps 3, 5
2.4 Store and Dispose of Client Records Appropriately	Step 5
2.5 Arrange for Safeguarding Records for Therapist Moving/Dying	Step 5
2.6 In Consultation, Share Identifiable Information Only w/Consent	Steps 1, 3, 5
3. PROFESSIONAL COMPETENCE AND INTEGRITY	
3.2 Maintain Adequate Knowledge of Laws and Ethics	Step 1
3.4 Avoid Conflicts of Interest that Impair Performance/Judgment	Step 5
3.6 Maintain Accurate and Adequate Clinical Records	Step 5
3.14 Avoid Conflicts of Interest in Custody Cases	Step 5
3.14 Do Not Both Provide Treatment and Conduct Custody Evaluation	Step 5
4. RESPONSIBILITY TO STUDENTS AND SUPERVISEES	
4.2 Do Not Provide Therapy to Current Students or Supervisees	Steps 5, 6
4.7 Disclosures Permitted Only to Colleague or Responsible Others in Setting	Step 5
4.7 Verbal Authorization Not Sufficient for Disclosure Except in Emergencies	Steps 3, 5
5. RESPONSIBILITY TO RESEARCH PARTICIPANTS	
5.2 Inform Prospective Participants of Risks	Step 2
5.2 Be Aware of Possibility of Diminished Consent If Also in Treatment	Steps 2, 5
5.3 Respect Autonomy, Especially If Researcher Also in Authority Relationship	Step 2
5.3 Avoid Multiple Relationships That Impair Judgment or Exploit	Step 5
5.4 Information Obtained in Research is Confidential; Written Waiver Required	Step 3
5.4 Inform Prospective Participant If Others Will Have Access to Info	Steps 1, 2

(*continued*)

AAMFT Ethical Standard	Location in Ethical Practice Model (Box 3.1)
6. RESPONSIBILITY TO THE PROFESSION	
6.1 If Organizational Policies Conflict, Make Known Commitment to Code	Steps 1, 4, 5
7. FINANCIAL ARRANGEMENTS	
7.2 Inform Prospective Clients of Potential Use of Collection Agency	Steps 1, 2
7.3 Give Reasonable Notice Before Using Collection Agency	Steps 2, 5
7.3 Disclose No Clinical Information to Collection Agency	Step 5

From American Association for Marriage and Family Therapy. (2001). *AAMFT Code of Ethics.*

PSYCHIATRISTS

AMERICAN PSYCHIATRIC ASSOCIATION (APSYA)

ApA Ethical Standard	Location in Ethical Practice Model (Box 3.1)
3 Seek Change in Legal Requirements That Are Not in Patients' Best Interest	Step 6
4 Safeguard Patient Confidences Within Constraints of the Law	Steps 1, 2, 3, 4, 5
4 (1) Protect Records with Extreme Care; Technology	Step 2, 5
4 (2) Disclose Only with Patient Authorization or Under Legal Compulsion	Steps 1, 3, 4, 5
4 (3) Disguise Patient Identity When Teaching or Writing	Step 5
4 (4) Maintain Duty of Confidentiality in Consultations	Steps 1, 3, 5
4 (5) Disclose No More Information Than Is Relevant	Step 5
4 (5) Usually Do Not Disclose Sensitive or Fantasy Material	Step 5
4 (6) Inform Patient in Advance About Lack of Confidentiality	Steps 1, 2
4 (7) Assure Minor Proper Confidentiality; Use Judgment in Parent Disclosures	Steps 1, 3, 5
4 (8) May Disclose Confidential Information If Risk of Danger Is Deemed Significant	Steps 1, 2, 3
4 (9) When Facing Legal Demands or Court Order, Give Priority to Confidentiality	Steps 1, 2, 4
4 (11) Present Patient to Media or Public Only with Fully Informed Consent	Steps 2, 3
4 (12) With Research, Retain Freedom to Reveal Data and Results	Steps 2, 3
5 Obtain Consultation and Continuing Education	Step 1, 6

From American Psychiatric Association. (2009, revised edition). Principles of medical ethics with annotations especially applicable to psychiatry.

PYCHOLOGISTS

AMERICAN PSYCHOLOGICAL ASSOCIATION (APA)

APA Ethical Standard	Location in Ethical Practice Model (Box 3.1)
1. RESOLVING ETHICAL ISSUES	
1.02 Conflicts Between Ethics and Law...	Step 1, 2, 4, 5, 6
1.03 Conflicts Between Ethics and Organizational Demands	Step 1, 2, 5, 6
1.04 Informal Resolution of Ethical Violations	Steps 4, 6
1.05 Reporting Ethical Violations	Steps 1, 2, 4, 6
1.06 Cooperating With Ethics Committees	Steps 2, 4, 6
2. COMPETENCE	
2.01 Boundaries of Competence (re: Undertaking Consultation)	Step 1, 6
2.05 Delegation of Work to Others	Step 5
3. HUMAN RELATIONS	
3.04 Avoiding Harm	(entire Model)
3.05 Multiple Relationships	Steps 2, 5
3.06 Conflict of Interest	Step 2
3.07 Third-Party Requests for Services	Step 2
3.09 Cooperation With Other Professionals	Steps 2, 4, 6
3.10 Informed Consent	Step 2
3.11 Psychological Services To/Through Organizations	Step 2
3.12 Interruption of Psychological Services	Step 5
4. PRIVACY and CONFIDENTIALITY	
4.01 Maintaining Confidentiality	Steps 1, 3
4.02 Discussing the Limits of Confidentiality	Steps 1, 2
4.03 Recording	Steps 2, 3, 5
4.04 Minimizing Intrusions on Privacy	Step 5
4.05 Disclosures	Steps 1, 2, 3, 4
4.06 Consultations	Steps 1, 3, 5, 6
4.07 Use of Confidential Information for Didactic/Other Purposes	Step 3, 5
6. RECORDKEEPING and FEES	
6.01 Documentation of Work and Maintenance of Records	Step 5
6.02 Maintenance, Dissemination, Disposal of Records	Steps 3, 5
6.04 Fees and Financial Arrangements	Steps 2, 5
6.06 Accuracy in Reports to Payers and Funding Sources	Steps 3, 5
7. EDUCATION and TRAINING	
7.04 Student Disclosure of Personal Information	Steps 2, 5
8. RESEARCH and PUBLICATION	
8.02 Informed Consent to Research	Steps 1, 2
8.03 Informed Consent for Recording in Research	Step 2
8.15 Reviewers	Step 5

(*continued*)

APA Ethical Standard	Location in Ethical Practice Model (Box 3.1)
9. ASSESSMENT	
9.03 Informed Consent in Assessments	Step 2, 5
9.04 Release of Test Data	Step 2, 4, 5
10. THERAPY	
10.01 Informed Consent to Therapy	Steps 1, 2
10.02 Therapy Involving Couples or Families	Steps 1, 2
10.03 Group Therapy	Steps 1, 2
10.09 Interruption of Therapy	Step 5

From American Psychological Association. (2002). *Ethical Principles of Psychologists and Code of Conduct.* Table adapted from: Fisher, M. A. (2008). Protecting confidentiality rights: The need for an ethical practice model. American Psychologist, 63, 1-13 DOI: 10.1037/0003-066X.63.1.1

SOCIAL WORKERS

NATIONAL ASSOCIATION OF SOCIAL WORKERS (NASW)

A. Ethical Standards Directly Addressing Confidentiality

NASW Ethical Standard	Location in Ethical Practice Model (Box 3.1)
1. SOCIAL WORKERS' ETHICAL RESPONSIBILITIES TO CLIENTS	
1.01 Commitment to Clients	(Entire Model)
1.03 Informed Consent	Step 2
1.06 Conflicts of Interest (esp. item (d) re multiple clients)	Steps 2, 5
1.07 *Privacy and Confidentiality*	
1.07a Respecting right to privacy	Steps 1, 3
1.07b Disclosure	Step 3
1.07c Confidentiality and exceptions	Steps 1, 2, 3, 5
1.07d Informed consent	Steps 1, 2, 4
1.07e Discussing limits of confidentiality	Steps 1, 2
1.07f Rules in families, couples, groups	Step 2
1.07g Sharing among parties in family, couple, marital, group	Steps 1, 2
1.07h Disclosures to third party	Step 3
1.07i Discussion in informal settings	Step 5
1.07j Protecting confidentiality in legal proceedings	Steps 1, 4, 5
1.07k Disclosures to media	Step 3
1.07l Security of records and electronic records	Step 5
1.07m Confidentiality of electronic transmissions	Step 5
1.07n Transfer or disposal of records	Step 5
1.07o Protections in event of termination, incapacitation, or death	Step 5
1.07p Disclosure only with consent for teaching or training purposes	Steps 3, 5
1.07q Disclosure of identifying information in consultation only w/consent	Steps 3, 5
1.07r Protecting confidentiality of deceased clients	Steps 3, 5
1.08 *Access to Records*	
1.08b Protecting confidentiality of other identified individuals	Step 3
1.14 Clients Who Lack Decision-Making Capacity	Step 2
2. SOCIAL WORKERS' ETHICAL RESPONSIBILITIES TO COLLEAGUES	
2.01 Incompetence of Colleagues	Steps 3, 4, 5
2.02 Maintain Confidentiality of Information Shared in Consultation	Steps 3, 5
2.05c In consultations, disclose least amount of information necessary	Steps 3, 5
2.11 Unethical Conduct of Colleagues	Steps 3, 4, 5

NASW Ethical Standard	Location in Ethical Practice Model (Box 3.1)
3. SOCIAL WORKERS' ETHICAL RESPONSIBILITIES IN PRACTICE SETTINGS	
3.08 Continuing Education and Staff Development	Step 1, 5
3.09 Commitments to Employers	Steps 1, 5
5. SOCIAL WORKERS' ETHICAL RESPONSIBILITIES TO THE SOCIAL WORK PROFESSION	
5.02 Evaluation and Research	
5.02l Confidentiality in evaluation and research	Steps w, 2, 3, 5
5.02m Anonymity or confidentiality in reporting research results	Steps 3, 5

From National Association of Social Workers. (1996). *NASW Code of Ethics.*

APPENDIX II

Selected Ethical Standards Relevant to Confidentiality Arranged in Categories Suggested by Knapp, S. and VandeCreek, L. D. (2006). *Practical ethics for psychologists: A positive approach.*

COUNSELORS

AMERICAN COUNSELING ASSOCIATION (ACA)

	Location in Ethical Practice Model (Box 3.1)
1. Key Standard:	
B.1.c Respect for Confidentiality	Steps 1, 2, 3, 4
2. Clarification, Amplification, and Application Standards	
A. Expanding on the Confidentiality Rule:	
B.1.a Multicultural/Diversity Considerations	Steps 1, 2, 3
B.2.a Obtain Consultation if Unsure About Validity of an Exception to Confidentiality	Steps 1, 2, 5
B.2.d Include Client in Decision Making Process About Disclosure	Steps 2, 3
B.2.d If Confidential Information Must Be Disclosed, Reveal Only Essential Information	Steps 2, 3, 4, 5
B.3.c Discuss Patient Information Only in Confidential Settings	Step 5
B. Applying the Confidentiality Rule in Specific Circumstances	
A3 Clients Served by Others	Step 3
B.1.b Respect for Privacy	Steps 1, 3
B.2.c Unless Client Consents, Contest Subpoena; Disclose Narrowly as Legally Possible	Steps 1, 4
B.3.d Disclose to Third-Party Payers Only If Client Authorizes the Disclosure	Steps 3, 5

(*continued*)

	Location in Ethical Practice Model (Box 3.1)
B.3.e Take Precautions When Electronically Transmitting Confidential Information	Step 5
B.3.f Protect Confidentiality of Deceased Clients to Extent Allowed by Law/Agency Policy	Steps 3, 5
B.4.b With Couples/Families, Document + Obtain Written Agreement re Each Party's Rights	Steps 1, 2
B.5.c With Minors and Incapacitated Adults, Obtain Consent From Legal Representative	Steps 2, 3
B.6.a. Confidentiality of Records	Steps 3, 5
B.6.b. Permission to Record	Steps 2, 3
B.6.c. Permission to Observe	Step 3
B.6.f. Disclosure or Transfer	Steps 3, 5
B.6.g. Storage and Disposition After Termination	Steps 3, 5
B.6.h. Reasonable Precautions (in event of clinician's death)	Step 5
B.7.b. Adherence to Guidelines in Conducting Research	Step 4
B.7.c. Confidentiality of Information Obtained in Research	Step 2
B.7.d Disguise Identity of Research Participants Unless Consent Has Been Obtained	Step 3
B.7.e Identification of Research Participants Ethical Only if Consent Was Obtained	Step 3
B.8.a. Agreements in Consultation Relationships	Steps 2, 3
B.8.b. Respect for Privacy in Consultations	Step 3
C.2.e. Obtaining Consultation on Ethical Obligations	Step 1
C.2.f. Obtaining Continuing Education	Step 1
C 6.b. Reports to Third Parties	Steps 3, 5
D.2.d Informed Consent in Consultation	Step 2
E 4 Release Assessment Data Only w/Client Consent and Only To Qualified Persons	Step 5
G.2.e Maintain Confidentiality of Information Obtained From Research Participants	Steps 2, 3
G.4.d Disguise the Identity of Research Participants Unless Consent Has Been Obtained	Step 3
H.2.b Confidentiality in Informal Resolution of Ethical Issues re Colleagues	Steps 1, 2, 3, 4
H.2.d Obtaining Consultation re Ethical Violations	Steps 1, 5
H.2.c Report Ethical Violations	Steps 1, 2, 3, 4
C. Informing Prospective Clients About Limits of Confidentiality	
A.2.b Client's Right to Receive Explanation of Limits of Confidentiality, Refuse Service	Steps 1, 2
A.2.a. Informed Consent	Step 2
A.2.d. Inability to Give Consent	Step 2
A.5.e. Informing About Role Changes in Professional Relationships	Step 2
A.12.g Inform Clients in Detail About Risks of Technology	Steps 1, 2, 3
A.12.h Informing About Limitations of Sites on the Web	Steps 1, 2, 3
B.1.d Explain Limits of Confidentiality At Initiation and Throughout Counseling	Steps 1, 2

(*continued*)

	Location in Ethical Practice Model (Box 3.1)
B.3.b Inform Client Who Is on Treatment Team and What Information Will Be Shared	Steps 1, 2, 3
B.4.a With Groups, Explain Importance/Parameters of Confidentiality to Group Members	Steps 1, 2
B.4.b With Couples/Families Explain Limits of Confidentiality and Each Party's Rights	Steps 1, 2, 3
B.5.b Inform Parents About Confidential Nature of Counseling Relationship With Child	Steps 1, 2, 3
B.5.c With Minors and Incapacitated Adults, Give Explanation Consistent With Ability	Steps 2, 3
B.8.c Disclosure of Confidential Information With Colleagues	Steps 1, 2, 3
E3.a Informed Consent for Assessment	Step 2
E.13a Primary Obligations in Forensic Evaluations	Step 2
E.13.b Informed Consent for Forensic Evaluation	Steps 2, 3, 4, 5
F 6.h Professional Disclosures in Supervision, Training, and Teaching	Steps 2, 3
G 2a Informed Consent to Research	Steps 2
D. Ensuring That Others Protect Patients' Confidentiality Rights	
B.3.a Ensure that Privacy/Confidentiality are Protected by Employees, Supervisees, Students	Steps 2, 3, 5
F.1.c Make Supervisees Aware of Clients' Confidentiality Rights	Steps 2, 5, 6
F.6.d Teach Ethical Responsibilities to Clinical Students and Supervisees	Step 6
E. Responding to Conflicts Between Ethical Duties and Other Duties	
H.1.b If Ethical Duties Conflict With Laws, Make Known Commitment to Code, Try to Resolve	Steps 1, 4
H.2.e If Ethical Duties Conflict With Agency Policy, Explain Duties, Attempt Policy Change	Steps 1, 5
3. Ethically Allowed Exceptions to the Key Standard	
A.9.c May Choose Whether to Disclose if Terminally Ill Patient Plans Suicide	Steps 1, 2, 3
B.1.c May Share Confidential Information With Client Consent	Step 3
B.1.c May Share Confidential Information With Sound Legal or Ethical Justification	Steps 1, 2, 4
B.2.a May Disclose for Protecting Client or Identified Other From Serious Harm	Steps 1, 2, 3
B.2.b May Disclose If Client Has Communicable Life-Threatening Disease and Identifiable Third Party Is at Demonstrable and High Risk	Steps 1, 2, 3

From American Counseling Association. (2005). *ACA Code of Ethics.*

MARRIAGE and FAMILY THERAPISTS

AMERICAN ASSOCIATION OF MARRIAGE AND FAMILY THERAPISTS (AAMFT)

	Location in Ethical Practice Model *(Box 3.1)*
1. Key Standard	
2.2 Disclose Only With Client's Written Authorization (see exceptions)	Steps 1, 3
2.2 In Couple/Group Treatment, Obtain Consent from Each	Steps 1, 3
2. Clarification, Amplification, and Application Standards	
A. Expanding on the Confidentiality Rule	
1.8 Respect Clients' Decision- Making Autonomy	Steps 2, 3
2.3 Present Identifiable Client Materials Only With Consent	Steps 3, 5
2.4 Store and Dispose of Client Records Appropriately	Step 5
2.5 Arrange for Safeguarding Records for Therapist Moving/Dying	Step 5
2.6 In Consultation, Share Identifiable Information Only w/Consent	Steps 1, 3, 5
3.4 Avoid Conflicts of Interest that Impair Performance or Judgment	Step 5
3.6 Maintain Accurate and Adequate Clinical Records	Step 5
4.7 Disclosures Permitted Only to Colleagues or Responsible Others in Setting	Step 5
4.7 Verbal Authorization is Not Sufficient for Disclosure Except in Emergencies	Steps 3, 5
B. Applying the Confidentiality Rule in Other Specific Circumstances	
1.2 Avoid Multiple Relationships	
3.2 Maintain Adequate Knowledge of Laws and Ethics	Step 1
3.14 Avoid Conflicts of Interest in Custody Cases	Step 5
3.14 Do Not Both Provide Treatment and Conduct Custody Evaluation	Step 5
4.2 Do Not Provide Therapy to Current Students or Supervisees	Steps 5, 6
5.2 Inform Prospective Research Participants of Risks	Step 2
5.3 Respect Autonomy, Especially if Researcher Also in Authority Relationship	Step 2
5.3 Avoid Multiple Relationships That Impair Judgment or Exploit	Step 5
5.4 Information Obtained in Research is Confidential; Written Waiver Required	Step 3
5.4 Inform Prospective Participant If Others Will Have Access to Info	Steps 1, 2
C. Informing Prospective Clients About Limits of Confidentiality	
1.2 Obtain Informed Consent before Recording/ Observing	Steps 2, 3

(continued)

	Location in Ethical Practice Model *(Box 3.1)*
1.6 Make Legally Required Reports of Unethical Conduct	Steps 1, 2, 4
2.1 Inform About Limits of Confidentiality	Steps 1, 2
5.2 Be Aware of Possibility of Diminished Consent If Research Participant Also in Treatment	Steps 2, 5
7.2 Inform Prospective Clients of Potential Use of Collection Agency	Steps 1, 2
7.3 Give Reasonable Notice Before Using Collection Agency	Step 2, 5
7.3 Disclose No Clinical Information to Collection Agency	Step 5
D. Ensuring that Others Protect Patients' Confidentiality Rights	
1.6 Make Legally Required Reports of Unethical Conduct	Steps 2, 6
E. Responding to Conflicts Between Ethical Duties and Other Duties	
6.1 Make known commitment to Ethics Code; attempt to resolve conflict	Steps 1, 4, 5
3. Exceptions to the Key Standard	
2.2 May Disclose With Client Consent	Step 3
2.2 May Disclose Where Mandated or Permitted by Law	Steps 1, 2, 3

From American Association for Marriage and Family Therapy. (2001). *AAMFT Code of Ethics.*

PSYCHIATRISTS

AMERICAN PSYCHIATRIC ASSOCIATION (APSYA)

	Location in Ethical Practice Model *(Box 3.1)*
1. Key Standard	
4 Safeguard Patient Confidences Within Constraints of the Law	Steps 1, 2, 3, 4, 5
4 (2) Disclose with Patient Authorization or Under Legal Compulsion	Steps 1, 3, 4, 5
2. Clarification, Amplification, and Application Standards	
A. Expanding on the Confidentiality Rule	
4(1) Protect Records with Extreme Care; Technology	Steps 2, 5
4 (5) Disclose No More Information Than Is Relevant	Step 5
4 (5) Usually Do Not Disclose Sensitive or Fantasy Material	Step 5
B. Applying the Confidentiality Rule in Specific Circumstances	
4 (3) Disguise Patient Identity When Teaching or Writing	Step 5
4 (4) Maintain Duty of Confidentiality in Consultations	Steps 1, 3, 5
4 (7) Assure Minor Proper Confidentiality; Use Judgment in Parent Disclosures	Steps 1, 3, 5
4 (11) Present Patient to Media or Public Only with Fully Informed Consent	Steps 2, 3
4 (12) With Research, Retain Freedom to Reveal Data and Results	Steps 2, 3
C. Informing Prospective Clients About Limits of Confidentiality	
4 (6) Inform Patient in Advance About Lack of Confidentiality	Steps 1, 2
D. Ensuring that Others Protect Clients' Confidentiality Rights	
E. Responding to Conflicts Between Ethical Duties and Other Duties	
4 (9) When Facing Legal Demands or Court Order, Give Priority to Confidentiality	Steps 1, 2, 4
3 Seek Change in legal Requirements That Are Not in Patients' Best Interest	Step 6
5 Obtain Consultation and Continuing Education	Steps 1, 6
3. Exceptions to the Key Standard	
4 (2) May Disclose With Patient Consent or Under Legal Compulsion	Steps 1, 3, 4, 5
4 (8) May Disclose Confidential Information If Risk of Danger Is Deemed Significant	Steps 1, 2, 3

From American Psychiatric Association. (2009, revised edition). Principles of medical ethics with annotations especially applicable to psychiatry.

PSYCHOLOGISTS

AMERICAN PSYCHOLOGICAL ASSOCIATION (APA)

	Location in Ethical Practice Model (Box 3.1)
1. Key Standard:	
4.01 Maintaining Confidentiality	Steps 1, 3
2. Clarification, Amplification, and Application Standards	
A. Expanding on the Confidentiality Rule:	
4.03 Recording	Steps 2, 3, 5
4.04 Minimizing Intrusions on Privacy	Step 5
4.06 Consultations	Steps 1, 3, 5, 6
4.07 Use of Confidential Information for Didactic or Other Purposes	Steps 3, 5
B. Applying the Confidentiality Rule in Specific Circumstances	
1.04 Informal Resolution of Ethical Violations	Steps 4, 6
1.05 Reporting Ethical Violations	Steps 1, 2, 4, 6
1.06 Cooperating with Ethics Committees	Steps 4, 6
2.01 Obtain Consultation as Needed	Steps 1, 6
3.09 Cooperation With Other Professionals	Steps 2, 4, 6
3.12 Interruption of Psychological Services	Step 5
6.01 Documentation of Work and Maintenance of Records;	Step 5
6.02 Maintenance, Dissemination, Disposal of Records	Steps 3, 5
6.04 Fees and Financial Arrangements	Steps 2, 5
6.06 Accuracy in Reports to Payers and Funding Sources	Steps 3, 5
8.15 Reviewers	Step 5
9.04 Release of Test Data	Steps 2, 4, 5
C. Informing Prospective Clients About Limits of Confidentiality	
3.05 Multiple Relationships	Steps 2, 5
3.06 Conflicts of Interest	Steps 2, 5
3.07 Third-Party Requests for Services	Step 2
3.10 Informed Consent	Step 2
3.11 Psychological Services To/Through Organizations	Step 2
4.02 Discussing the Limits of Confidentiality	Steps 1, 2
7.04 Informing Students	Steps 2, 5
8.02 Informed Consent to Research	Steps 1, 2
8.03 Informed Consent for Recording in Research	Step 2
9.03 Informed Consent in Assessments	Steps 2, 5
10.01 Informed Consent to Therapy	Steps 1, 2
10.02 Therapy Involving Couples or Families	Steps 1, 2
10.03 Group Therapy	Steps 1, 2

	Location in Ethical Practice Model (Box 3.1)
D. Ensuring that Others Protect Patients' Confidentiality Rights	
2.05 Delegating of Work to Others	Step 5
E. Responding to Conflicts Between Ethical Duties and Other Duties	
1.02 Conflicts Among Ethics and Law, Regulations, Governing Legal Authority	Steps 1, 2, 4, 5, 6
1.03 Conflicts Among Ethics and Organizational Demands	Steps 1, 2, 5, 6
3. Ethically Allowed Exceptions to the Key Standard	
4.05 May Disclose w/Client Consent or if Legally Required or Permitted	Steps 1, 2, 3, 4

From Fisher, M. A. (2012). Confidentiality and record keeping. In S. Knapp, M. Gottlieb, M. Handelsman, & L. VandeCreek (Eds.), *APA Handbook of Ethics in Psychology (p. 337).*

Ethical Standards from American Psychological Association. (2002). *Ethical Principles of Psychologists and Code of Conduct.*

SOCIAL WORKERS

NATIONAL ASSOCIATION OF SOCIAL WORKERS (NASW)

	Location in Ethical Practice Model (Box 3.1)
1. Key Standards:	
1.07a Respect Right to Privacy; Information Shared by Clients is Confidential	Steps 1, 3
1.07c Protect the Confidentiality of All Information (see exceptions)	Steps 1, 3, 5
2. Clarification, Amplification, and Application Standards	
A. Expanding on the Confidentiality Rule:	
1.07a Solicit Private Information Only If Essential for Services; Evaluation; Research	Step 3
1.07c Disclose Least Information Necessary; Must Be Relevant to Purpose of the Disclosure	Steps 3, 5
1.07d Before Disclosing, Inform Client About the Disclosure And Potential Consequences	Steps 1, 2, 4
1.07g Sharing Among Parties in Family, Couple, Marital, Group Therapy	Steps 1, 2, 3
1.07i Do Not Discuss Confidential Information in Public or Semi-Public Settings	Step 5
1.07l Protect Security of Written or Electronic Records	Step 5
1.07m Ensure Technological Security	Step 5
1.07n Protect Confidentiality in Transfer or Disposal of Client Records	Step 5
1.07o Protect Confidentiality in Closing Practice or Preparing for Absence or Death	Step 5
1.07r Protect Confidentiality of Deceased Clients	Steps 3, 5
B. Applying the Confidentiality Rule in Specific Circumstances	
1.06 Conflicts of Interest	Steps 2, 5
1.07h Disclose to Third-Party Payers Only With Client Consent	Step 3
1.07j During Legal Proceedings, Limit Disclosures to Extent Legally Possible	Steps 1, 4, 5
1.07k Respect Confidentiality When Talking to the Media	Steps 3, 5
1.07p Disclose No Identifying Information in Teaching or Training Unless Client Consents	Steps 3, 5
1.07q Disclose No Identifying Information in Obtaining Consultation Unless Client Consents	Steps 3, 5
1.08b When Giving Clients Access to Records, Protect Confidentiality of Others Named	Step 3
2.01 Respond to Incompetence of Colleagues	Step 2, 3, 4, 5
2.02 Protect the Confidentiality of Information Shared by Colleagues in Consultation	Steps 3, 5
2.05c Disclose Least Amount of Information Necessary in Consultations	Steps 3, 5
5.02 Protect Anonymity and/or Confidentiality of Research Participants	Steps 3, 5
5.02m Omit Identifying Information in Evaluation/Research Reports Unless Client Consents	Steps 3, 5

	Location in Ethical Practice Model (Box 3.1)
C. Informing Prospective Clients About Limits of Confidentiality	
1.03 Inform Prospective Clients of Risks of Receiving Services via Electronic Media	Step 2
1.07e Inform Clients About Potential Confidentiality Limits ASAP + Throughout	Steps 1, 2
1.07f With Families/Couples/Groups, Seek Agreement re: Each Party's Confidentiality Rights	Step 2
1.14 Responsibilities to Clients Who Lack Decision-Making Capacity	
5.02l Inform Prospective Research Participants of Limits of Confidentiality	Steps 1, 2, 3, 5
D. Ensuring that Others Protect Patients' Confidentiality Rights	
2.11 Unethical Conduct of Colleagues	Steps 2, 3, 4, 5
3.08 Educate Staff About Ethics	Steps 1, 5
E. Responding to Conflicts Between Ethical Duties and Other Duties	
1.07j If Court Orders Disclosure, Protect Confidentiality to Extent Legally Possible	Steps 1, 4, 5
3.09d If Organizational Policies Conflict With Ethics, Ethics Code Has Priority	Steps 1, 5
3. Ethically Allowed Exceptions to the Key Standard	
1.07b May Disclose With Client Consent	Step 3
1.07c May Disclose for Compelling Professional Reasons	Steps 1, 2, 3, 5
1.07c May Disclose to Prevent Serious, Foreseeable and Imminent Harm to Client or to Another Identifiable Person	Steps 1, 2, 3, 5

From National Association of Social Workers. (1996). *NASW Code of Ethics.*

APPENDIX III

Examples of Laws Affecting Confidentiality

I. Laws Protecting Confidentiality

A. LAWS PROHIBITING VOLUNTARY DISCLOSURE OF INFORMATION WITHOUT PATIENT CONSENT (CONFIDENTIALITY AND NONDISCLOSURE LAWS)

As defined here, these laws either (1) create a legal duty not to disclose patient information without the patient's consent or (2) impose a penalty for disclosing without the patient's consent. Sometimes these nondisclosure provisions are difficult to find, because they may consist of a single clause in a very long law or regulation. They may also be widely scattered within the state or federal legal codes, since they can appear in general statutes, in laws governing specific mental health professions, in licensing board regulations, and in state agency regulations. Some of the laws in this category protect confidentiality only in certain circumstances.

1. State

Statutes: State nondisclosure statutes are sometimes written broadly; their protections may apply not only to mental health professionals but to all health care providers. (For example, Virginia's brief statutory nondisclosure provision below is located within a very extensive 7,000-word Health Records Privacy Statute that applies to all health care providers in all settings.) In contrast, the provisions of some nondisclosure statutes are limited to a specific population or setting. (For example, the Florida statute below applies only in state agencies and institutions.)

NOTE: The content of this legal Appendix is also available online with links to each of the laws at http://www.CenterForEthicalPractice.org/LawsAffectingConfidentiality

Florida § **394.4615**: "A clinical record is confidential... Unless waived by express and informed consent,... the confidential status of the clinical record shall not be lost by either authorized or unauthorized disclosure to any person, organization, or agency."

Virginia: § **32.1-127.1:03** "A. There is hereby recognized an individual's right of privacy in the content of his health records... and, except when permitted or required by this section or by other provisions of state law, no health care entity, or other person working in a health care setting, may disclose an individual's health records."

Also in this category are confidentiality statutes that do not explicitly forbid disclosure, but which protect confidentiality by legally permitting therapists *not* to disclose information in certain circumstances. (For example, the Ohio statute below allows therapists to protect the confidentiality of minors over age 14, rather than informing parents about their treatment.)

Ohio: **§ 5122.04** "(A) Upon the request of a minor fourteen years of age or older, a mental health professional may provide outpatient mental health services, excluding the use of medication, without the consent or knowledge of the minor's parent or guardian."

This category would also include legal requirements about protecting patient confidentiality through ensuring the security of records during storage, retention, or destruction.

Virginia: § 32.1-127.1:01 Record Storage
"A. Medical records... may be stored by computerized or other electronic process or microfilm, or other photographic, mechanical, or chemical process; however, the stored record shall identify the location of any documents or information that could not be so technologically stored. If the technological storage process creates an unalterable record, the nursing facility, hospital, or other licensed health care provider shall not be required to maintain paper copies of medical records that have been stored by computerized or other electronic process, microfilm, or other photographic, mechanical, or chemical process. Upon completing such technological storage, paper copies of medical records may be destroyed in a manner that preserves the patient's confidentiality. However, any documents or information that could not be so technologically stored shall be preserved."

Wisconsin: § 134.97 Disposal of Records Containing Personal Information
"**(2)** A medical business holding medical or mental health records "may not dispose of a record containing personal information" unless it does one of the following: "134.97(2)(a) (a) Shreds the record before the disposal of the record.

134.97(2)(b) (b) Erases the personal information contained in the record before the disposal of the record. 134.97(2)(c) (c) Modifies the record to make the personal information unreadable before the disposal of the record. 134.97(2)(d) (d) Takes actions that it reasonably believes will ensure that no unauthorized person will have access to the personal information contained in the record for the period between the record's disposal and the record's destruction."

Finally, also in this category are laws that impose legal penalties for failing to protect confidentiality. These can be in the form of statutes (as in the Florida statutory examples below) or in regulations (as in the Florida Board regulations in the next section).

Florida
§ 490.009 Discipline—Psychologists; and **§ 491.009 Discipline—Counselors, Clinical Social Workers, and Other Therapists**
"(1) The following acts constitute grounds for denial of a license or disciplinary action . . . (u) Failing to maintain in confidence a communication made by a patient or client . . . "

Regulations: State nondisclosure regulations ordinarily apply only to specific providers, or in specific settings. For example, licensing board regulations apply only to licensees of a specific board (see first Ohio example, below), and state agency regulations apply only to providers in specific state agencies or institutions (see second Ohio example, below).

Ohio: Counselor, Therapist, and Marriage and Family Board—Standards of Ethical Practice and Professional Conduct OAC 4757-5-02 D "(1) Confidential information shall only be revealed to others when the clients or other persons legally authorized to give consent on behalf of the clients, have given their informed consent, except in those circumstances in which failure to do so would violate other laws or result in clear and present danger to the client or others. Unless specifically contraindicated by such situations, clients shall be informed and written consent shall be obtained before the confidential information is revealed."

Ohio: Requirements and Procedures for Mental Health Services Provided by Agencies OAC 5122-29-03 Behavioral Health Counseling and Therapy Service: "(4) It is the responsibility of the agency to assure contractually that any entity or individuals involved in the transmission of the information guarantee that the confidentiality of the information is protected."

State licensing board regulations can impose penalties for disclosures made in contradiction to the state's laws and regulations protecting confidentiality. (See Florida examples below.)

Florida—Licensing Board Regulations—Penalties for Breach of Confidentiality
64b19-17.002 (Board regulation for Psychologists): "(1) The Board shall impose one or more penalties if an applicant or a licensee for "failure to maintain confidence." [Penalty for first offense is a reprimand and a fine from $1,000 up to $5000, penalty for a second offence ranges from reprimand to revocation of license and a fine from $5,000 up to $10,000, and penalty for a third offence is revocation and $10,000 fine.]

64b4-5—5.001 (Board regulation for Counselors, Clinical Social Workers, and Other Therapists): "(1) The Board shall impose one or more penalties if 'an applicant, licensee, registered intern, provisional licensee, or certificate holder whom it regulates' fails to... (v) maintain in confidence any communication made by a patient or client in the context of services, except by written permission or in the face of clear and immediate probability of bodily harm to the patient or client or to others..." [Penalty for first offence is a $1,000 fine and reprimand or probation; penalty for second offence is a $,1000 fine and probation or revocation of license.]

Sometimes a state licensing board incorporates a profession's entire ethics code into the board's code of conduct, thereby giving to that profession's ethical standards about confidentiality the weight of legal regulations. (See Oregon Board of Psychology regulation, below.) In other cases, a licensing board may create its own code of ethics (See the Oregon regulation of the Board of Licensed Professional Counselors and Therapists and the Pennsylvania Board of Psychology statute, below.)

Oregon Board of Psychology Examiners:
858-010-0075: "The Board adopts for the code of professional conduct of psychologists in Oregon the American Psychological Association's "*Ethical Principles of Psychologists and Code of Conduct* effective June 1, 2002."

Oregon Board of Licensed Professional Counselors and Therapists
833-100-0011 through 833-100-0071: Code of Ethics
Pennsylvania Board of Psychology: § 41.61: Code of Ethics

Case Law: State Supreme Court decisions apply only in the state in which they were decided, although they sometimes have a broader impact elsewhere by being cited as examples in other states' cases. Examples of state cases that created or expanded confidentiality protections within a specific state include those such as the Virginia case summarized below.

Virginia Supreme Court (1997): *Fairfax Hospital v. Patricia Curtis*
This decision awarded $100,000 to a patient whose hospital records were voluntarily released without her consent in the context of a court case. The basis of that decision was that no judge had determined that these records were

admissible as evidence in the case. Some consider this a wake-up reminder to Virginia therapists that they have no legal basis (and therefore perhaps no ethical basis?) for disclosing information in response to a "discovery" subpoena without ensuring that someone files a "motion to quash" it. This brings a judge into the process and results in a determination—either a court order protecting the information from being used as evidence or a court order requiring it to be disclosed. (See discussion in this book regarding the importance of distinguishing between a subpoena and a court order in Chapter 7.)

2. Federal

Statutes: Most of the federal statutory protections of confidentiality apply only in substance abuse cases, providing extra confidentiality safeguards for patients receiving services in federally funded facilities. (For example, see **42 U.S.C. § 290dd-2**.)

Regulations: Some federal regulations elaborate upon those protections for patients in federally funded substance abuse facilities. (For example, see **42 C.F.R. Part 2**.)

By far the most prominent federal regulations affecting confidentiality and privacy are the Health Insurance Portability and Accountability Act (HIPAA) regulations, which are summarized in Appendix IV. These apply not only to mental health care providers, but to providers of all health care services who electronically transmit identifiable patient information. These regulations are discussed briefly in Chapter 2, their provisions are summarized in more detail in Appendix IV, and links to their text and interpretations are available on the website of the Center for Ethical Practice (2010). These regulations are extensive, which is why therapists and/or their staff often obtain specialized HIPAA training.

Other federal regulations affecting confidentiality include those that apply only in educational settings. These regulations include the **Family Educational Rights and Privacy Act (FERPA)** and the **Individual Disabilities Education Act (IDEA)**, both of which protect the confidentiality of student information, including mental health information.

B. LAWS CREATING THERAPIST–PATIENT PRIVILEGE IN COURT CASES

Therapist–patient privilege laws grant patients the right to protect the confidentiality of their communications to a therapist by preventing these from being used as evidence in a court proceeding. States vary in the extent of these protections. As noted in a later section, "Legal Exceptions to Therapist–Patient Privilege," states also vary a great deal in the exceptions to privilege (i.e., the circumstances in which these privilege protections do not apply).

1. State

Rules of Evidence: Some of the legal provisions granting therapist–patient privilege are found in a state's "Rules of Evidence" instead of within the general legal code. (For example, see evidence code provisions for therapist–patient privilege in California, Delaware, and Kentucky.) In some states, privilege and its exceptions are present in separate places. (For example, there is a Louisiana Privilege Statute, but the exceptions to therapist–patient privilege are then listed separately in the Louisiana Rules of Evidence.)

Statutes: Some privileged communications statutes are very protective of patient confidentiality. Thirteen states have privilege statutes that are explicitly modeled after attorney–client privilege, which is very protective unless there are extensive exceptions to that privilege within the statute or elsewhere. (See statutes for Alabama, Arizona, Arkansas, Georgia, Idaho, Kansas, Montana, New Hampshire, New Jersey, New York, Pennsylvania, Tennessee, Washington. Also see relevant sections of each of these privilege statutes listed by state on the Center for Ethical Practice website.) However, attorney–client privilege statutes do not address certain activities engaged in by mental health professionals but not by attorneys (e.g., services provided to court-ordered individuals, families, or groups).

Sometimes, the concepts of confidentiality (i.e., duty not to disclose) and privileged communications (i.e., protection from subpoenas or other legal disclosure demands in court cases) will be combined in the same statute, which can be conceptually confusing. (See Alabama and Florida statutes, below.)

> **Alabama § 34-26-2 Confidential Communications**: "The *confidential* relations and communications between licensed psychologists, licensed psychiatrists, or licensed psychological technicians and their clients are placed upon the same basis as those provided by law between attorney and client, and nothing in this chapter shall be construed to require any such *privileged* communication to be disclosed." [emphasis added]

> **Florida § 490.0137 Confidentiality and Privileged Communications**: "Communication between any person licensed under this chapter and her or his patient or client shall be *confidential.* This *privilege* may be waived under the following conditions: . . . " [emphasis added]

Sometimes, privileged communications statutes explicitly protect certain types of records. For example, one section of the Ohio privileged communications statute protects a therapist's "psychotherapy notes" from being used as evidence in a court case. (See below.)

> **Ohio § 2317.02** B)(1)(e)(iii). **Privileged communications**: "Division (B)(1)(e)(i) of this section does not require a mental health professional to disclose "psychotherapy notes" as defined by the HIPAA regulations."

Sometimes, a privilege statute explicitly gives a therapist the legal right to claim the privilege in the patient's behalf. (See Florida privileged communications statute below.) Although this right is not explicitly granted in most states, judges do often allow therapists to act in a patient's behalf to contest an attorney's subpoena or to file a motion asking the judge to quash it, especially if the patient does not want the information disclosed but has no attorney, or if the patient's attorney does not file a motion to quash.

Florida § 90.503 Psychotherapist-Patient Privilege—Therapist May Claim

"(2) A patient has a privilege to refuse to disclose, and to prevent any other person from disclosing, confidential communications or records made for the purpose of diagnosis or treatment of the patient's mental or emotional condition, including alcoholism and other drug addiction, between the patient and the psychotherapist, or persons who are participating in the diagnosis or treatment under the direction of the psychotherapist. This privilege includes any diagnosis made, and advice given, by the psychotherapist in the course of that relationship.

"(3) The privilege may be claimed by . . . (d) The psychotherapist, but only on behalf of the patient. The authority of a psychotherapist to claim the privilege is presumed in the absence of evidence to the contrary."

2. Federal

Statutes and Regulations: Patients who receive substance abuse treatment in federally funded facilities are given special protection from having their records routinely available as evidence in a court case. These additional protections arise both by federal statute (**42 U.S.C. § 290dd-2**) and by federal regulation (**42 C.F.R. Part 2**).

Case Law: Numerous U. S. Supreme Court cases have touched on issues of patient privacy and confidentiality, but one of the most prominent recent decisions affecting mental health patients was ***Jaffee v. Redmond*** in 1996. This decision, which strengthened and broadened the protections of therapist–patient privilege in federal court cases, reached the Supreme Court only because a social worker refused to disclose patient information (see Beyer [2000]).

II. Laws Limiting Confidentiality

These laws either *require* therapists to disclose confidential information without patient consent, allow others to obtain access to information without patient consent, or allow others to redisclose information received from therapists. *Prospective patients must be informed about these limits of confidentiality during the initial informed consent interview (see Chapter 5).*

A. LAWS REQUIRING THERAPISTS TO INITIATE DISCLOSURE

These laws arise at the state level and vary a great deal, not only state by state, but by profession and by setting within each state. Below are examples of these types of laws, but therapists are responsible for knowing the confidentiality limitations that apply in their own state and setting.

1. Mandated Reporting Requirements

All states have laws and/or regulations mandating the reporting of suspected child abuse or neglect, and most states also mandate the reporting of suspected abuse or neglect of elderly and/or vulnerable and/or incapacitated adults. These laws can be found in the state civil code or criminal code, or both (see Utah example, below). All such laws include mental health care providers in the list of mandated reporters and include definitions of the persons/conditions that must be reported. The wording of the reporting mandate varies; however, therapists are never required to investigate first, but instead are required to report if they have "reason to suspect" or "reasonable cause to believe" the abuse/neglect.

Reporting statutes often impose penalties for failure to report (see Kansas and Utah, below). Some indicate that reporting must be done "promptly" or "immediately" (see Kansas, below); others impose a specific time frame within which the report must be made; and some require both an oral report and a written report (see Massachusetts, below). In some states, reporting of child abuse is not legally required if the information on which the report is based is privileged (see Oregon, below).

Kansas: § 38–2223 Child Abuse/Neglect Reporting
Report Required: "When [any mental health professional] has reason to suspect that a child has been harmed as a result of physical, mental or emotional abuse or neglect or sexual abuse, the person shall report the matter promptly... Willful and knowing failure to make a report required by this section is a class B misdemeanor. It is not a defense that another mandatory reporter made a report... Intentionally preventing or interfering with the making of a report required by this section is a class B misdemeanor."

Massachusetts: XVII-119-51A Child Abuse/Neglect—Time Frame for Written Report, Section 51A: "(a) A mandated reporter who, in his professional capacity, has reasonable cause to believe that a child is suffering physical or emotional injury resulting from: (i) abuse inflicted upon him which causes harm or substantial risk of harm to the child's health or welfare, including sexual abuse; (ii) neglect, including malnutrition; or (iii) physical dependence upon an addictive drug at birth, shall immediately communicate with the department orally and, within 48 hours, shall file a written report with the department detailing the suspected abuse or neglect."

Oregon: § 419B.010 Child Abuse Report Not Required If Communication Is Privileged:

"(1) Any public or private official having reasonable cause to believe that any child with whom the official comes in contact has suffered abuse or that any person with whom the official comes in contact has abused a child shall immediately report or cause a report to be made... except that a psychiatrist, [or] psychologist... is not required to report such information communicated by a person if the communication is privileged."

Utah: **Adult Abuse/Neglect Reporting** [*same wording in both civil and criminal codes*]:

§ 62A-3-305 (Civil Code) and § **76-5-111.1** (Criminal Code): "Any person who has reason to believe that any vulnerable adult has been the subject of abuse, neglect, or exploitation shall immediately notify Adult Protective Services intake or the nearest law enforcement agency.... Any person who willfully fails to report suspected abuse, neglect, or exploitation of a vulnerable adult is guilty of a class B misdemeanor."

Many states also have laws requiring therapists to report misconduct by other providers. Sometimes, such reports are required about *any* health care provider (see Florida, below); sometimes, reports are legally required only about another mental health care provider; and, sometimes, reports are legally required only about someone licensed by the reporting therapist's own board (see Indiana and Louisiana, below). Some states provide penalties for failure to report (see Louisiana, below). Most states require reports even if this requires breaching confidentiality (this conflicts with the position of those professional Ethics Codes which do not require such a report if it would involve breaching confidentiality. For example, see APA Ethical Standard 1.05 and ACA Ethical Standard H.2.C); but others require a report only with the client's written permission (see Indiana, below).

Florida: **§ 456.063(3) Reporting of Allegations of Provider Sexual Misconduct**

"(1)... Sexual misconduct in the practice of a health care profession is prohibited. (3) Licensed health care practitioners shall report allegations of sexual misconduct to the department, regardless of the practice setting in which the alleged sexual misconduct occurred."

Indiana: 868 IAC 1.1-11-2—Reporting Provider Violations—Board of Psychology

"(e) When a psychologist has reason to believe there has been a violation by another psychologist of the statutes or rules of the board, the psychologist shall file a complaint with the consumer protection division of the office of the attorney general of Indiana. Information regarding such a violation obtained in the context of a professional relationship with a client is to be reported only with the written permission of the client."

Louisiana: § 2717 Board of Social Work Disciplinary Actions—Penalty for Failure to Report

"A. The board shall have the power to deny, revoke, or suspend any license, certificate, or registration issued by the board or applied for in accordance with this Chapter, or otherwise discipline a social worker for:...(8) Failure to report to the board knowledge of a violation or infraction of the social work practice act, rules and regulations promulgated by the board or ethical standards, or both."

Finally, as a result of recent violence on college campuses, some states have initiated mandated reporting requirements regarding at-risk students, requiring therapists in state college counseling centers to notify a college-based threat assessment team and/or the student's parents. (See Virginia statute, below and in Section 2,B, further below.)

Virginia: § 23-9.2:3 State College Counseling Centers Notify Parents of Student at Risk

"C. Notwithstanding any other provision of state law, the board of visitors or other governing body of every public institution of higher education in Virginia shall establish policies and procedures requiring the notification of the parent of a dependent student when such student receives mental health treatment at the institution's student health or counseling center...Such notification shall only be required if it is determined that there exists a substantial likelihood that, as a result of mental illness the student will, in the near future, (i) cause serious physical harm to himself or others as evidenced by recent behavior or any other relevant information or (ii) suffer serious harm due to his lack of capacity to protect himself from harm or to provide for his basic human needs...[exceptions]."

2. "DUTY TO PROTECT" LAWS

State case law ordinarily applies only in the state in which the case was decided; but the California *Tarasoff* case created major ripples across the country, and, subsequently, 36 states enacted laws requiring therapists to initiate action if their patients threaten direct harm to another person (see Werth, Welfel, & Benjamin (2009), *The Duty to Protect: Ethical, Legal And Professional Considerations for Mental Health Professionals*). Unlike a true "duty to warn" requirement, most states impose a duty to "protect"—which can often be accomplished in ways other than by issuing a warning to the victim or engaging in some other breach of confidentiality. As noted in Chapter 4, however, research indicates that up to 75% of psychologists are misinformed about what the laws of their state require about this, with 90% of those nevertheless being confident that they are right—which can create unnecessary disclosures, thus placing patients at risk.

Most states legally impose a "duty to protect" requirement only if the patient poses a threat to *others*, but a very few states legally impose on therapists a duty to protect a patient from harm to *self.* (See examples below quoted from statutes in Nebraska and New Jersey.) As described in a later section of this Appendix, however, many states explicitly *allow* disclosure in circumstances of danger to self, but do not legally *require* such disclosure.

> **Nebraska: § 38-2137**: "The duty to warn of or to take reasonable precautions to provide protection from violent behavior shall arise only under the limited circumstances specified in subsection (1) of this section" [i.e., "when the patient has communicated to the mental health practitioner a serious threat of physical violence against himself, herself, or a reasonably identifiable victim or victims... The duty shall be discharged by the mental health practitioner if reasonable efforts are made to communicate the threat to the victim or victims ***and*** to a law enforcement agency." [emphasis added]

> **New Jersey:** § **2A:62A-16—Duty to Warn and Protect**: "b. A duty to warn and protect is incurred when the following conditions exist: (1) The patient has communicated to that practitioner a threat of imminent, serious physical violence against a readily identifiable individual or against himself and the circumstances are such that a reasonable professional in the practitioner's area of expertise would believe the patient intended to carry out the threat; or (2) The circumstances are such that a reasonable professional in the practitioner's area of expertise would believe the patient intended to carry out an act of imminent, serious physical violence against a readily identifiable individual or against himself."

B. LAWS ALLOWING OTHERS ACCESS TO PATIENT INFORMATION AND/OR LAWS ALLOWING OTHERS TO REDISCLOSE INFORMATION

Laws of this type take many forms, and they can be difficult to discover within the state code. The first Virginia statute below reflects the existence of "threat assessment teams" at state colleges and university; these were created following recent episodes of campus violence in that state and elsewhere. This statute gives the threat assessment team legal access to certain mental health records, but it does not authorize redisclosure of that information.

The second Virginia examples below apply to the Child Abuse Special Advocate (CASA) program, which is present in several states. These statutes capture both of the confidentiality limitations above—one allows access to therapy information and records, the other provides for its redisclosure. Virginia is one of the states in which CASA lay volunteers can be given legal access to the child's therapy records in an abuse case, and can subsequently provide a written report and/or testimony in which they redisclose that information (see discussion in Chapter 7).

Virginia: State College Threat Assessment Team

§ 23-9.2:10—Access Allowed, but Not Redisclosure

"A. Each public college or university shall have in place policies and procedures for the prevention of violence on campus, including assessment and intervention with individuals whose behavior poses a threat to the safety of the campus community.... E.... Upon a preliminary determination that an individual poses a threat of violence to self or others, or exhibits significantly disruptive behavior or need for assistance, a threat assessment team may obtain... health records... No member of a threat assessment team shall redisclose any... health information obtained pursuant to this section or otherwise use any record of an individual beyond the purpose for which such disclosure was made to the threat assessment team."

Virginia: CASA Volunteers

§ 9.1-156—Access to Therapy Records: "A. Upon presentation by the advocate of the order of his appointment and upon specific court order, any state or local agency, department, authority, or institution, and any hospital, school, physician, or other health or mental health care provider shall permit the advocate to inspect and copy, without the consent of the child or his parents, any records relating to the child involved in the case. Upon the advocate presenting to the mental health provider the order of the advocate's appointment and, upon specific court order, in lieu of the advocate inspecting and copying any related records of the child involved, the mental health care provider shall be available within seventy-two hours to conduct for the advocate a review and an interpretation of the child's treatment records which are specifically related to the investigation."

§ 9.1-153—Redisclosure Allowed in Testimony: "A. Services in each local court-appointed special advocate program shall be provided by volunteer court-appointed special advocates, hereinafter referred to as advocates. The advocate's duties shall include: (1.) Investigating the case to which he is assigned to provide independent factual information to the court. (2.) Submitting to the court of a written report of his investigation... B.... The advocate may testify if called as a witness..."

C. LEGAL EXCEPTIONS TO THERAPIST–PATIENT PRIVILEGE

Sometimes, these exceptions to privilege are listed within the privilege statute itself; at other times, they appear as a separate free-standing statute

Certain exceptions to privilege exist in almost every state: Communications between therapist and patient are usually *not* privileged if (1) the patient brings his or her own mental health into issue in the court case (see Florida, below); (2) the case involves child (or sometimes elder adult) abuse or neglect (see Ohio, below);

(3) the court case involves an involuntary commitment proceeding (see Maryland, below); or (4) if the testimony is pursuant to a court-ordered psychological evaluation or examination of the patient (see California, below).

Many states, however, have additional exceptions to privilege. Examples of these can include cases in which the patient brings a complaint against the therapist or threatens to commit a crime or harmful act (see Oregon, below), or when the patient brings a personal injury claim (see Louisiana, below).

The broadest and least predictable exception to privilege is the "judicial discretion" exception, which applies in Virginia and North Carolina (see Virginia example, below). It is *broad* because any judge may determine that any communication between a patient and his or her therapist is admissible as evidence. It is *unpredictable* because there is no way for patient or therapist to know in advance what determination a judge will make in any particular case, so attorneys are more likely to issue subpoenas in attempts to obtain that evidence, leaving patients and their therapists to try to protect patient information, case by case.

California: Exception to Privilege if Therapist Conducted Court-Ordered Examination 1017 (Rules of Evidence): "(a) There is no privilege under this article if the psychotherapist is appointed by order of a court to examine the patient..."

Florida: Exception to Privilege if Patient's Mental State at Issue
§ 90.503: "(4) There is no privilege under this section:...(c) For communications relevant to an issue of the mental or emotional condition of the patient in any proceeding in which the patient relies upon the condition as an element of his or her claim or defense..."

Louisiana: Exception to Privilege in Personal Injury Claims
510 (Rules of Evidence): "(B)(2) Exceptions. There is no privilege under this Article in a noncriminal proceeding as to a communication: (a) When the communication relates to the health condition of a patient who brings or asserts a personal injury claim in a judicial or worker's compensation proceeding."

Maryland: Exception to Privilege in Involuntary Commitment Cases
§ 9.109: "(d) There is no privilege if (1) A disclosure is necessary for the purposes of placing the patient in a facility for mental illness."

Ohio: Exception to Privilege in Child Abuse Cases
§ 2317.02: Counselors, Clinical Social Workers, and Marriage and Family Therapists
§ 4732.19: Psychologists
§ 2317.02: Psychiatrists

Testimonial privilege does not apply, and mental health professionals may testify or may be compelled to testify about a patient if: "The communication or advice indicates clear and present danger to the client or other persons. For the purposes of this division, cases in which there are indications of present or past child abuse or neglect of the client constitute a clear and present danger."

Oregon: Exception to Privilege if Client Brings Complaint Against Therapist or Threatens to Commit a Crime or Harmful Act
§ **40.250—Rule 504-4** (Regulated Social Workers), and § **40.262—Rule 507** (Counselors):
"Client privilege does not apply if client initiates legal action or makes a complaint against the licensed professional; or if client communicates clear intent to commit a crime or harmful act."

Virginia: "Judicial Discretion" Exception to Therapist–Patient Privilege
§ **8.01-399** (Psychiatrists and Clinical Psychologists)
§ **8.01-400.2** (All Other Therapists)
Communications between patient and therapist are not privileged and may therefore be available as evidence in any court case *"when a court, in the exercise of sound discretion, deems it necessary to the proper administration of justice* [emphasis added]."

III. Laws Allowing Disclosure

Note: These laws allow (but do not require) therapists to disclose information without patient consent. These laws therefore do not create any real ethical-legal conflict, because *they do not legally require therapists to disclose anything*. However, therapists must inform prospective patients in advance if they do intend to disclose in these legally allowed circumstances (see Figure 1.2, Ethical doors to disclosure and Chapter 5, "Step 2: Telling Patients the Truth About Confidentiality's Limits").

These laws vary. Examples below are of laws that create legally permitted exceptions to confidentiality, thereby permitting disclosure. They may be found among the listed exceptions to confidentiality within a nondisclosure law (such as in the first Florida statute below), or they may be in the form of a stand-alone statute (as in the second Florida statute below).

Federal

The HIPAA regulations legally allow disclosures without patient authorization in a broad range of circumstances, as indicated by the Privacy Act regulation quoted below. The definition of the terms "treatment," "payment," and "health care operations" can be obtained at http://www.hipaa.com/2009/05/the-definition-of-treatment/

45 CFR 164.502(a)(1): "*Permitted uses and disclosures.* A covered entity is permitted to use or disclose protected health information as follows:... (ii) For treatment, payment, or health care operations..."

State

The Virginia statute below is an example of how broad the exceptions to confidentiality can be in some state statutes. This is also an example of how permission to disclose without patient consent can be hidden within a nondisclosure law, in this case, in a law called a "Health Records Privacy Act." Like the HIPAA regulations, its stated purpose is the protection of patient privacy, but it legally allows disclosure without patient consent for a very broad range of purposes. As with HIPAA, it is important for therapists to remember that, ethically speaking, there is a big difference between such "legally allowed" disclosures and a disclosure that is truly "legally required."

Florida: If Patient Presents Danger to Self, to Others, or to Society (Psychology)

§ 490-0147: Confidentiality and privileged communications: "Any communication between any person licensed under this chapter and her or his patient or client shall be confidential. This privilege may be waived under the following conditions:...(3) When there is a clear and immediate probability of physical harm to the patient or client, to other individuals, or to society and the person licensed under this chapter communicates the information only to the potential victim, appropriate family member, or law enforcement or other appropriate authorities."

Florida: Allowed Disclosure of HIV Status to Sexual Partner or Needle Sharer

§ **456.061**: "(1) A [health care] practitioner...shall not be civilly or criminally liable for the disclosure of otherwise confidential information to a sexual partner or a needle-sharing partner under the following circumstances:

(a) If a patient of the practitioner who has tested positive for human immunodeficiency virus discloses to the practitioner the identity of a sexual partner or a needle-sharing partner;

(b) The practitioner recommends the patient notify the sexual partner or the needle-sharing partner of the positive test and refrain from engaging in sexual or drug activity in a manner likely to transmit the virus and the patient refuses, and the practitioner informs the patient of his or her intent to inform the sexual partner or needle-sharing partner; and

(c) If pursuant to a perceived civil duty or the ethical guidelines of the profession, the practitioner reasonably and in good faith advises the sexual partner or the needle-sharing partner of the patient of the positive test and facts concerning the transmission of the virus."

[This must be done through protocols developed by the Department of Health.]

Virginia: Broad Disclosures Legally Allowed Without Patient Consent
§ 32.1-127.1:03: "D. Health care entities may... disclose health records:... 7. Where necessary in connection with the care of the individual;... 8. In connection with the health care entity's own health care operations or the health care operations of another health care entity... or in the normal course of business in accordance with accepted standards of practice within the health services setting;... 17. To third-party payors and their agents for purposes of reimbursement;... "

IV. Laws Requiring Therapists to Inform Prospective Clients About the Limits of Confidentiality

Just as most professional ethics codes require therapists to inform prospective patients about the limits of confidentiality, most states include this among the legal requirements for therapists. This usually appears within the state licensing board regulations, sometimes within the confidentiality section (See Maryland, below). Sometimes, they are combined with other informed consent requirements within the board's practice standards or code of conduct (see Virginia, below). Some states impose special requirements in particular cases or circumstances. For example, see below the Missouri informed consent regulations regarding third-party referrals, the Ohio informed consent regulations in cases involving multiple parties (e.g., couple or family therapy, nonpatient collateral participants), and the Montana regulation regarding the taping, recording, or observation of patients.

Maryland Regulations: Board of Psychology Examiners
10.36.05.08. 08: Confidentiality and Client Records: "A. A psychologist shall... 2) Discuss the requirements and limitations of confidentiality at the beginning of the professional relationship or at the intake interview."

Missouri Regulations: Committee of Psychologists
20 CSR 2235-5: "7(A)(2). When a psychologist agrees to provide services to a person or entity at the request of a third party, the psychologist shall explain and document the nature of the relationships with all individuals or organizations involved. This includes the role of the psychologist, who is the client, the probable uses of the services provided or the information obtained, and any known or probable limits to confidentiality."

Montana Board of Social Work Examiners
2419.801: "(vii) obtain informed written consent of the client or the client's legal guardian prior to taping, recording, or permitting third-party observation of the client's activities that might identify the client or place them at risk."

Ohio Regulations: Board of Counselors, Social Workers, Marriage and Family Therapists

OAC 4757-5-02: Standards of Ethical Practice and Professional Conduct – (B) Responsibility to clients/consumers of services as to informed consent:

"(6) When a counselor, social worker, or marriage and family therapist provides services to two or more clients who have a relationship with each other and who are aware of each other's participation in treatment (for example couples, family members), a counselor, social worker, or marriage and family therapist shall clarify with all parties the nature of the licensee's professional obligations to the various clients receiving services, including limits of confidentiality. A counselor, social worker, or marriage and family therapist who anticipates a conflict of interest among the clients receiving services or anticipates having to perform in potentially conflicting roles (for example a licensee who is asked or ordered to testify in a child custody dispute or divorce proceeding involving clients) shall clarify their role with the parties involved and take appropriate action to minimize any conflict of interest.

"(7) When a counselor, social worker, or marriage and family therapist sees clients for individual or group treatment, there may be reason for a third party to join the session for a limited purpose. The licensee shall ask the client or legal guardian to provide written authorization that describes the purpose and need for the third party to join the session and describes the circumstances and extent to which confidential information may be disclosed to the third party. The counselor, social worker, or marriage and family therapist shall make it clear that the third party is not a client and there is no confidentiality between the licensee and the third party. The counselor, social worker, and marriage and family therapist shall make it clear to the third party that he/she shall not have rights to access any part of the client's file including any session in which they participated unless the client signs a release. A counselor, social worker, or marriage or family therapist shall not make recommendations to courts, attorneys or other professional concerning non-clients."

Virginia: Board of Psychology

18 VAC 125-20-150: **Practice Standards:** "B (11). Inform clients of professional services, fees, billing arrangements and limits of confidentiality before rendering services. Inform the consumer prior to the use of collection agencies or legal measures to collect fees and provide opportunity for prompt payment."

V. Laws Relevant to Staff Training About Confidentiality

Laws and regulations can contain provisions about the responsibilities of mental health professionals in ensuring that their staff and employees understand how to protect patient confidentiality. Although this does not explicitly impose a legal requirement to train staff in a particular way, it does imply that each therapist must be sure that all staff members—clinical and nonclinical—understand the ethical and legal confidentiality requirements that apply to his/her profession.

1. State

Most of the relevant state requirements about staff training are in licensing board regulations rather than general statutes. (See examples below).

Florida: 64B19-19.006—Board of Psychology

"(5) The licensed psychologist shall also ensure that no person working for the psychologist, whether as an employee, an independent contractor, or a volunteer violates the confidentiality of the service user."

Indiana: 868 IAC 1.1-11-2 State Psychology Board

"(c) A psychologist shall ensure that all employees and psychology trainees are engaged only in activities consistent with their training and are aware of and adhere to the code of professional conduct as found in this rule."

Oregon: AR 833-100-0051(3)—Board of Licensed Professional Counselors and Therapists

"(3) A licensee, including employees and professional associates of the licensee, does not disclose any confidential information that the licensee, employee, or associate may have acquired in rendering services except as provided by rule or law. All other confidential information is disclosed only with the written informed consent of the client."

2. Federal

The federal regulations from HIPAA explicitly require confidentiality training for the entire "workforce" in medical and mental health settings. The term "workforce" is defined as paid employees plus trainees, supervisees and volunteers—anyone under direct control of the HIPAA-covered clinician. (For detailed summary of HIPAA workforce training requirements, see Appendix IV.)

HIPAA

Privacy Rule: (45 CFR 184 530 (b) (1)): "A covered entity must train all members of its workforce on the policies and procedures with respect to protected health information [PHI] required by this subpart, as necessary and appropriate for the members of the workforce to carry out their function within the covered entity."

Enforcement Rule: Explains the circumstances under which clinicians may be held accountable for HIPAA violations by a member of their *"workforce"* or by a contracted *"agent,"* unless the provider had required them to sign a confidentiality contract explaining the HIPAA policies, and they broke it. The Enforcement Rule allows the Department of Health and Human Services (HHS) to impose fines of up to $100 per violation, up to a maximum of $25,000 for violations of an identical requirement during one calendar year. (A continuing violation is deemed a separate violation for each day it occurs.)

APPENDIX IV

Health Insurance Portability and Accountability Act (HIPAA)

Summary of Selected Regulations

1. HIPAA PRIVACY RULE

A. Patients have certain RIGHTS about their health care information. These include:

   1. right to receive "Notice of Privacy Practices" before consenting to receive services

   2. right to review their records;

Note: Portions of this Appendix were summarized from the following documents:

APA Practice Organization (2005): *The HIPAA Security Rule Primer* http://www.apapracticecentral.org/business/hipaa/security-rule.pdf

USDHHS (2003a): *Health Insurance Reform: Security Standards,* http://www.cms.hhs.gov/SecurityStandard/Downloads/securityfinalrule.pdf

USDHHS (2003b): *Summary of the HIPAA Privacy Rule*, http://www.hhs.gov/ocr/privacy/hipaa/understanding/summary/privacysummary.pdf

USDHHS (2007): *Standards for Privacy of Individually Identifiable Health Information.* Retrieved from http://aspe.hhs.gov/admnsimp/nprm/pvc07.htm

HIPAA for Psychologists: Online CE Course, APA (2010c). Retrieved from http://apapracticecentral.org/ce/courses/1370022.aspx

APA Practice Organization, Office of Legal and Regulatory Affairs and Technology Policy and Projects Staffs (2005, June 7). *Contingency planning: Do you know what HIPAA requires?* http://www.apapractice.org/apo/insider/hipaa_reg/hipaa/hipaa_security_rule/contingency.html

3. right to request amendments to their records;
4. right to receive an accounting of all disclosures the provider has made.

B. Providers must train "workforce" about patients' privacy and confidentiality rights

2. HIPAA SECURITY RULE

Guidelines for assuring the security of confidential electronic patient health information (EPHI). This involves implementation of administrative, physical, and technical procedures which include:

Administrative:

- Appoint a HIPAA Security Officer
- Implement policies and procedures about employee access to EPHI
- Implement a security awareness and training program for all employees
- Implement policies and procedures to address breaches of security
- Establish policies and procedures for security in case of emergency
- Regularly evaluate technical and non-technical systems to ensure privacy
- Ensure that all business associates are in compliance with the Security Rule

Physical:

- Ensure that only authorized staff member have keys and access to office
- Describe appropriate function for each workstation used to access EPHI
- Ensure that computer workstations are secure and used appropriately
- Implement procedures to ensure security when equipment (or data) is moved

Technical:

- Implement technical means to allow only appropriate/authorized access to EPHI
- Implement mechanisms that monitor EPHI for security breaches
- Implement mechanisms to protect EPHI from improper alteration or destruction
- Insure that person seeking access is the one claimed (e.g., changing passwords)
- Guard against access to transmitted EPHI (e.g., encryption, secure transmission)

Each "covered entity" must maintain a "policies and procedures document," in written or electronic form. This must (1) document compliance with each step of

---

For extensive links to text of the HIPAA regulations and discussions of them, see the Center for Ethical Practice website at http://www.centerforethicalpractice.org/links-to-HIPAA-resources

Note: Portions of the section on staff training were provided by Samuel Knapp, Ph.D. (Director of Professional Affairs, Pennsylvania Psychological Association) and are used or adapted here with the authorization of the Pennsylvania Psychological Association's "What Should Your Employees Know About Confidentiality?" and "HIPAA Training Guide for Employees of Psychologists."

implementation and (2) outline an emergency contingency plan (i.e., Emergency Mode Operation Plan, Data Backup Plan, Data Recovery Plan, etc.). These plans must be tested periodically. The document must be maintained for 6 years and updated when relevant laws change.

3. HIPAA TRANSACTION RULE

This rule standardizes the electronic exchange of patient-identifiable health information related to administrative and financial procedures. This rule applies only to electronic submissions of patient information to health care plans when obtaining authorization, providing treatment plans, billing for reimbursement, etc. (Nonelectronic paper claims submissions are not covered under this rule.) Covered providers must obtain a National Provider Identifier (NPI) for this purpose.

4. HIPAA ENFORCEMENT RULE

The Privacy Rule is enforced by the U. S. Office of Civil Rights. The Security Rule is enforced by the Center for Medicaid and Medicare Services. For either rule, civil penalties can be up to $100 per violation, capped at $25,000 for each requirement or prohibition that is violated. A continuing violation is deemed a separate violation for each day it occurs. The Enforcement Rule is available online at ww.hhs.gov/ocr/hipaa/FinalEnforcementRule06.pdf

5. HIPAA BREACH NOTIFICATION RULE

According to this newest HIPAA rule (45 C.F.R. § 164, Subpart D), breaches of confidential client information must be reported to the affected individual(s). In addition, any confidentiality breach involving 500 or more clients must be promptly reported to the Secretary of Health and Human Services and to the media (USDHHS, 2009). Breaches involving fewer clients must be reported annually. Other 2009 changes broadened the Privacy and Security Rules to require a provider's business associates to document all electronic disclosures and to allow clients access to their own electronic records.

Legally Allowed Disclosures Without Patient Consent Under HIPAA

45 CFR 164.502

"(a) (1) *Permitted uses and disclosures.* A covered entity is permitted to use or disclose protected health information as follows: (i) To the individual; (ii) **For treatment, payment, or health care operations (see definitions below)**, as permitted by and in compliance with § 164.506; (iii) Incident to a use or disclosure otherwise permitted or required by this subpart, provided that the covered entity has complied with the applicable requirements of § 164.502(b), § 164.514(d), and § 164.530(c) with respect to such otherwise permitted or required use or disclosure;..." (emphasis added)

DEFINITIONS

Treatment: "The provision, coordination, or management of health care and related services by one or more health care providers, including the coordination or management of health care by a health care provider with a third party; consultation between health care providers relating to a patient; or the referral of a patient for health care from one health care provider to another." (Section 164.501)

Payment: "The activities undertaken by:... A covered health care provider or health plan to obtain or provide reimbursement for the provision of health care;" including but not limited to " billing, claims management, collection activities, obtaining payment under a contract for reinsurance (including stop-loss insurance and excess of loss insurance), and related health care data processing." (Section 164.501)

Health Care Operations: "The Privacy Rule permits certain incidental uses and disclosures that occur as a by-product of another permissible or required use or disclosure, as long as the covered entity has applied *reasonable safeguards* and implemented the *minimum necessary standard*, where applicable, with respect to the primary use or disclosure. See 45 CFR 164.502(a)(1)(iii). An incidental use or disclosure is a secondary use or disclosure that cannot reasonably be prevented, is limited in nature, and that occurs as a result of another use or disclosure that is permitted by the Rule. However, an incidental use or disclosure is not permitted if it is a by-product of an underlying use or disclosure which violates the Privacy Rule." (From Health and Human Services web page, "Incidental Uses and Disclosures," http://www.hhs.gov/ocr/privacy/hipaa/understanding/coveredentities/incidentaluandd.pdf

Note: It is important not to confuse "legally allowed" with "ethically appropriate." As discussed in detail in Part I, the fact that a disclosure without the patient's consent is "legally allowed" does not make it ethically appropriate, because that does not lessen the impact on the patient. Also see Chapter 8 for a discussion of the fact that because such disclosures are not legally required, they are made *voluntarily* and therefore have informed consent implications: Voluntary disclosures require the patient's consent, either (1) at intake, after being informed of the foreseeable limits of confidentiality and consenting to accept those as conditions of receiving services; or (2) by giving explicit written consent on a release of information form.

STAFF TRAINING REQUIRED BY HIPAA REGULATIONS

The HIPAA Privacy Rule requires that employees in health care settings receive training from their employers about confidentiality:

> "A covered entity must train all members of its workforce [see definition below] on the policies and procedures with respect to protected health information [PHI] required by this subpart, as necessary and appropriate for the members of the workforce to carry out their function within the covered entity" (45 CFR 184 530 (b) (1))

The HIPAA Security Rule and Transaction Rule also have implications for the confidentiality of information stored and transmitted by clinicians and/or members of their "workforce." (See definition below.) The Security Rule requires practitioners to safeguard electronic patient information from unauthorized alteration, destruction, or disclosure, both intentional and unintentional. That requires protecting electronic data, such as patient notes, e-mail with/about patients, insurance or financial records with identifying patient information, and the like from potential security risks. Under the Security Rule's "contingency planning standard," you must also develop an emergency plan to address how employees should respond to a loss of electronic information in the event of a disaster or emergency. This would include training employees about what to do if they are involved in an emergency situation and who they should contact to assess the seriousness of the situation. A disaster recovery plan should also encompass procedures such as developing an employee phone list to use in an emergency and procedures for patient contact in the event that appointments need to be verified or rescheduled.

The HIPAA Enforcement Rule describes the circumstances under which a clinician may be held accountable for the HIPAA violations of a member of the *"workforce"* or of an *"agent,"* unless the provider required a signed confidentiality contract explaining the HIPAA policies and it was broken. The Enforcement Rule allows HHS to impose fines of up to $100 per violation, up to a maximum of $25,000 for violations of an identical requirement during one calendar year. (A continuing violation is deemed a separate violation for each day it occurs.)

DEFINITIONS

"Workforce" is defined as paid employees PLUS trainees, supervisees, and volunteers who are under direct control of the HIPAA-covered clinician. It is not necessary for every employee, trainee, supervisee, or volunteer to know *everything* about HIPAA and patient privacy, but each should be trained about what is necessary for carrying out his or her own duties and trained not to handle patient information beyond his or her job description and training, unless specifically so authorized. The training must occur for all employees and others within a reasonable time after they join the workforce. The training must be tailored to the clinical setting, the employee's responsibilities, and the confidentiality policies/procedures within the setting.

This training must be documented, and the employee must demonstrate that the training has been understood. The employer may use a written test or an oral examination to ensure that the employee has understood the material. The employee must then sign a Confidentiality Contract. If an employee who violates patient confidentiality will be subject to disciplinary actions or will be removed from his or her position, this should be explicitly stated in the Confidentiality Contract.

An *"agent" or "business associate"* is defined as anyone acting on the clinician's behalf and at his or her discretion, including billing services, accountants, answering services, and the like. Contracted agents and business associates must sign a Business Associates Agreement, which includes confidentiality and security statements, as above, indicating that they understand and will abide by your HIPAA-compliant privacy and confidentiality policies.

Note: You are usually not considered liable for HIPAA violations of contracted agents or business associates if you have in place a HIPAA-compliant Business Associates Agreement that defines your expectations. However, you are not protected if you knew that they violated the privacy/security obligations of that agreement and you failed to take reasonable steps to remedy the problem.

HIPAA and Minimum Necessary Disclosures

HIPAA, 45 C.F.R. 164 514(d)(1): Subpart. (b) *Standard: Minimum necessary* (1) *Minimum necessary applies.* "When using or disclosing protected health information or when requesting protected health information from another covered entity, a covered entity must make reasonable efforts to limit protected health information to the minimum necessary to accomplish the intended purpose of the use, disclosure, or request.

"(d)(1) *Standard: Minimum necessary requirements.* In order to comply with §164.502(b) and this section, a covered entity must meet the requirements of paragraphs (d)(2) through (d)(5) of this section with respect to a request for, or the use and disclosure of, protected health information.

"(2) *Implementation specifications: Minimum necessary uses of protected health information.* (i) A covered entity must identify: (A) Those persons or classes of persons, as appropriate, in its workforce who need access to protected health information to carry out their duties; and (B) For each such person or class of persons, the category or categories of protected health information to which access is needed and any conditions appropriate to such access. (ii) A covered entity must make reasonable efforts to limit the access of such persons or classes identified in paragraph (d)(2)(i)(A) of this section to protected health information consistent with paragraph (d)(2)(i)(B) of this section. (3) *Implementation specification: Minimum necessary disclosures of protected health information.* (i) For any type of disclosure that it makes on a routine and recurring basis, a covered entity must implement policies and procedures (which may be standard protocols) that limit the protected health information disclosed to the amount reasonably necessary to achieve the purpose of the disclosure. (ii) For all other disclosures, a covered entity must:(A) Develop criteria designed to limit the protected health information disclosed to the information reasonably necessary to accomplish the purpose for which disclosure is sought; and (B) Review requests for disclosure on an individual basis in accordance with such criteria."

APPENDIX V

Using the Ethical Practice Model to Place Laws Into Ethical Context

Note: A color-coded version of the Ethical Practice Model, which integrates into this ethical framework relevant state laws and specific federal HIPAA regulations, is available online at http://www.CenterForEthicalPractice.org/EthicalPracticeModelAnnotated

Italics reflect where laws are placed into ethical context when integrated into this model.

Step 1. Prepare

A. Understand patients' rights and therapists' ethical responsibilities in behalf of those rights.

B. Decide what voluntary limits will be imposed on confidentiality in the practice setting.

C. *Learn the laws that can affect therapists' ability to protect confidential information.*

D. Clarify own personal ethical position about confidentiality and its *legal limits.*

E. *Develop plan for ethical response to each type of law that can require "involuntarily" disclosure.*

F. Choose reliable ethics consultants and *legal consultants* and use as needed.

G. Devise informed consent forms that reflect these actual policies and intentions.

H. Prepare to discuss confidentiality and its limits in understandable language.

Step 2. Tell Prospective Patients the Truth (Inform Their Consent)

A. Inform prospective patients about *potential limits that may be imposed on confidentiality.*
B. Explain any roles or potential conflicts of interest that might affect confidentiality.
C. Obtain informed patient's consent to accept limits as a condition of receiving services.
D. Reopen the conversation if/when patient's circumstances, *laws,* or therapist's intentions change.

Step 3. Obtain Informed Consent Before Disclosing Voluntarily

A. Disclose without patient consent only if *legally unavoidable.*
B. *Inform* patient adequately about the content and implications of potential disclosures.
C. Obtain and document the patient's *consent* before disclosing.

Step 4. Respond Ethically To Legal Demands For Disclosure

A. *Notify patient of pending legal requirement for a disclosure without patient's consent.*
B. *Respond ethically to legal obligations according to plan (from Step 1, E above):*
1. *Laws requiring therapists to initiate disclosures (e.g., reporting laws)*
2. *Laws granting others access to patient information without patient consent*
3. *Laws allowing recipients of information to redisclose without further patient consent*
4. *Exceptions to privilege in court cases*

C. *Limit disclosure to the extent legally possible, using protective laws when available.*

Step 5. Avoid Preventable Breaches Of Confidentiality

A. Establish and maintain protective policies and procedures.
B. Conduct ethics-based staff training about legal issues (*see HIPAA security and staff training requirements, Appendix IV and staff training outline, Appendix VIII).*
C. Monitor note taking and record keeping practices.
D. Avoid dual roles that might create conflicts of interest about confidentiality.
E. *Anticipate legal demands*; empower patients to act protectively in their own behalf.

F. Protect patient identity in presentations, research, consultations.
G. Prepare a professional will to protect patient confidentiality in event of illness or death.

Step 6. Talk About Confidentiality

A. Model ethical practices about confidentiality; confront others' unethical practices.
B. Provide peer consultation about confidentiality ethics.
C. Teach ethical practices to students, supervisees, employees.
D. Educate attorneys, judges, consumers, and the public.
E. *Lobby for legislative reform toward better legal protections of confidentiality.*

Adapted from Fisher, M. A. (2008). Protecting confidentiality rights: The need for an ethical practice model. *American Psychologist*, *63*, 1–13. DOI: 10.1037/0003–066X.63.1.1

(See color-coded integrated version: http://CenterForEthicalPractice.org/EthicalPracticeModelAnnotated)

APPENDIX VI

Ethical Obligations of Mental Health Professionals in Legal Contexts: Which Hat Are You Wearing?

ROLE: WHICH HAT ARE YOU WEARING?	POSSIBLE ACTIVITIES	ON WHOSE BEHALF DO YOU WEAR THIS HAT?	ETHICAL OBLIGATIONS
A. Involuntary Roles THERAPIST or EVALUATOR Receives subpoena to provide information about a current or former therapy patient or assessment client; judge refuses to quash subpoena; orders that information be produced as evidence. Participation is "involuntary" (i.e., is legally compelled, against patient's wishes and without patient's consent) [See Reference #4, below]	**A. Provider of Records or Documents About Current or Former Therapy Patient** (*Subpoena Duces Tecum*) **B. Provider of Records/Documents About Former Assessment Earlier Conducted for a Nonforensic Purpose** (*Subpoena Duces Tecum*) **C. Provider of Testimony** (*Witness Subpoena*)	? Certainly you are not here on behalf of your patient or assessment client, who objects to this disclosure. You obtained information for other purposes, but now you are about to disclose that confidential information as evidence in a court case, against his or her wishes and without his or her consent. Nor are you here on behalf of a party who is opposing your patient in this case, and who has subpoenaed your records or testimony. ?	**1.** At intake, inform each prospective therapy patient or assessment client about the foreseeable limits of confidentiality, including those imposed by law (such as court orders in court cases). **2.** Understand relevant laws: Legal exceptions to therapist–patient privilege vary from state to state and can include (a) child abuse or neglect cases or (b) patient places own mental condition at issue, and in some states (c) judge considers the information admissible as evidence because "necessary for the proper administration of justice." **3.** Patient does not consent to disclosure, so (a) file (or cooperate with patient's attorney in filing) a *motion to quash* the subpoena; (b) if court orders disclosure, limit disclosure to the materials specified, *remembering that your primary responsibility is to your patient.* **4.** Give no opinion about anyone other than the patient named in the subpoena unless (a) you evaluated or saw them in therapy ***and*** (b) they have given written consent for disclosure.

(*continued*)

ROLE: WHICH HAT ARE YOU WEARING?	POSSIBLE ACTIVITIES	ON WHOSE BEHALF DO YOU WEAR THIS HAT?	ETHICAL OBLIGATIONS
B. Voluntary Roles **1. THERAPIST** Participating voluntarily in legal process a. at patient's request and/or b. with patient's written, *informed* consent	**A. Provider of Records/Documents** **B. Provider of Testimony** **1. Fact Witness** (e.g., re: patient statements, behavior) **2. Opinion ("Expert") Witness** (e.g., re: diagnosis, prognosis, etc.) **C. Consultant to Patient's Attorney**	**Your Therapy Patient,** who has waived privilegeand has given *informed* consent for you to disclose in this context.	**1.** Before agreeing to disclose records or provide testimony voluntarily, *inform* patient of nature and content of records and/or potential testimony (e.g., explain that inviting your testimony opens the door to questioning and cross-examination about any aspect of his or her therapy, diagnosis, or mental condition; discuss how you might respond to such questions, etc.). Explain to patient (and his or her attorney) that you must answer questions truthfully and may not provide only positive information as a "good character" witness. **2.** In absence of a court order, you have no ethical basis for disclosing anything until you obtain patient's *written* consent to consult with his or her attorney or disclose records/information.
B. Voluntary Roles, cont. **2. PROVIDER of COURT-ORDERED CLINICAL INTERVENTION** a. Patient is court ordered to receive this service; and b. clinician voluntarily agrees to wear this hat and play this role.	**A. COURT-ORDERED THERAPY** (activities will vary case by case, depending upon clinical needs and details of court order) **(1) Providing court-ordered therapy services** **(2) Providing progress reports** **(3) Providing records** **(4) Testifying** **B. COURT-ORDERED CO-PARENTING CONSULTATION/ EDUCATION** This role involves providing court-ordered parent consultation and/or education in a custody case	**Court-Ordered Patient(s):** **(1)** informed in advance about the nature of this role; *and* **(2)** consented to accept the limits of confidentiality as specified in the court's order (e.g., if reports or testimony will be expected by court).	**NOTE:** Although a court can order the patient to obtain this service, a therapist is ethically obligated to *refuse* to take on this role in this particular case if (a) it creates dual relationship or conflict of interest, or (b) the nature of the case falls outside this therapist's area of competence. **1.** In advance, clarify court's expectations about services and about confidentiality; possibly participate in drafting or revising the court's order to ensure that it matches the services you are able/willing to provide and the information you are willing to disclose. **2.** Inform prospective patient(s) about scope and details of the court order, clarify your role, and discuss confidentiality *and its limits*.

	C. PARENT COORDINATION IN CUSTODY CASE This is a quasi-legal role, stipulated in the divorce agreement or in a judge's consent order, giving the mental health professional limited legal authority to impose certain conditions on the parents.	**The Court** The court is the primary client, so the parents who receive the services must be informed of the limits of confidentiality that will be imposed by that contracted relationship (e.g., sending reports to the court).	**This role requires specialized training.** For resources and training opportunities, see References below.
B. Voluntary Roles, cont. **3. PROVIDER of OTHER COURT-RELATED SERVICES IN WHICH CLIENTS PARTICIPATE VOLUNTARILY** a. Clinician voluntarily agrees to wear this hat and play this role. b. Client is *not* court ordered to receive this service.	**COLLABORATIVE DIVORCE COACH** Serves as member of a team of professionals (e.g., attorneys, accountants, child specialists, other mental health professionals) who are providing services to divorcing couples who are attempting to finalize divorce and custody arrangements without entering into an adversarial process.	**The Couple** who hires the collaborative team to facilitate their divorce/custody case	**This role requires specialized training.** For resources and training opportunities, see References below.
4. FORENSIC SPECIALIST **a.** ***Voluntarily*** participating in court case; and	1. ***Forensic Evaluator**** Specialized training required. **Assessing:** **A. Civil Case** Abuse, damages, mental distress, etc.	**The Court** or **One Party in the Case**	**1.** Obtain the training and experience required for practicing in these specialty roles. **2.** Refuse the referral if you have prior relationships with parties in the case. **3.** Refrain from offering opinions about any party not seen and/or evaluated. **4.** If a court-ordered evaluation, obtain copy of order to clarify court's referral question and expectations about your role; revise if needed.

(continued)

ROLE: WHICH HAT ARE YOU WEARING?	POSSIBLE ACTIVITIES	ON WHOSE BEHALF DO YOU WEAR THIS HAT?	ETHICAL OBLIGATIONS
b. Hired as **Independent Forensic Specialist,** with no prior relationship to any parties in the case. These roles require specialized training. For resources and training opportunities, see References below.	**B. Divorce/Custody Case** Parenting ability needs of child, etc. **C. Criminal Case** Competency to stand trial mental status at offense (*This can be either an initial evaluation or a "second-opinion evaluation.")		**5.** If for one party, obtain contract identifying them as client and clarifying scope of role. **6.** Before beginning, obtain consent from *each* person seen, *informing* them of: (a) nature of your role/loyalties; (b) limits of confidentiality (i.e., specify with whom you will share the information they give you; inform them that any information you obtain, and/or your opinions based on it, may be disclosed in your report and/or in testimony, and is ***not*** confidential).
	2. *Expert Witness* **A. Based on Evaluation** [above] **B. As "Independent" Expert (No contact with parties)** (e.g., testifying about relevant *issues* [such as developmental needs of 4-year-olds] or pursuant to role as reviewer of others' work [below])	**The Court** or **One Party in the Case** or **Guardian *ad Litem***	**1.** As above. **2.** Limit "expert" opinion testimony to those areas for which you have the necessary factual information, training, and/or professional expertise.
	3. ***Consultant*** **A. Advising Attorney** (with or without meeting his client) **B. Reviewing Another's Work** (reviewing and evaluating another's therapy notes or evaluation report; advising attorney; perhaps testifying [above])	**Attorney for One Party**	**1.** Obtain contract that identifies who your client is, and clarifies your role. If meeting with attorney's client or other parties, obtain informed consent. **2.** In role of "reviewer," conduct only an *internal* review of another's notes or report; base opinions/testimony only on the data provided there; do not re-interview or re-test another's client. [In contrast, see role of "second-opinion forensic evaluator," above.]
	4. ***Mediator*** Provide mediation services to help parties resolve a dispute.	**The Court** or **The Parties in the Case**	**1.** Obtain contract that identifies your role, explains confidentiality and its limits. **2.** To avoid dual relationship or conflict of interest, do not take the case if you have (or have previously had) a relationship with any party in the case.

References for Appendix VI

1. American Psychological Association. (2009). Guidelines for child custody evaluations in family law proceedings. Retrieved from http://www.apa.org/practice/guidelines/child-custody.pdf
2. American Psychological Association. (2012). Guidelines for the practice of parenting coordination. *American Psychologist, 67* (1), 63–71. DOI: 10.1037/a0024646
3. American Psychological Association and American Board of Forensic Psychology. (2011, August 20). *Specialty Guidelines for Forensic Psychology*. Retrieved from http://www.ap-ls.org/aboutpsychlaw/SGFP_Final_Approved_2011.pdf
4. American Psychological Association Committee on Legal Affairs. (2006). Strategies for private practitioners coping with subpoenas or compelled testimony for client records or test data. *Professional Psychology: Research and Practice* Vol. 37, No. 2, 215–222. DOI: 10.1037/0735–7028.37.2.215
5. American Psychological Association Practice Organization, Legal and Regulatory Affairs Staff. (2010, April). Tools and Training in Parenting Coordination. Retrieved from http://www.apapracticecentral.org/update/2010/04–29/parenting-coordination.aspx
6. Association of Family Conciliation Courts. (2005). Guidelines for Parenting Coordination. Retrieved from http://www.afccnet.org/Portals/0/AFCCGuidelinesforParentingcoordinationnew.pdf
7. Association of Family Conciliation Courts. (2011).Training for Parenting Coordination. Retrieved from http://www.afccnet.org/ConferencesTraining/AFCCTraining
8. International Academy of Collaborative Professionals. (2011). Collaborative Solutions for Divorce and More. Retrieved from http://collaborativepractice.com/

APPENDIX VII

Selected Ethical and Professional Resources Related to Confidentiality Ethics

A. Ethics Codes of National Mental Health Professional Associations

Counselors: *ACA Code of Ethics and Standards of Practice*, 2005
By mail: American Counseling Association (ACA)
5999 Stevenson Avenue
Alexandria, Virginia 22304
By phone: (800) 347-6647
Online: http://www.counseling.org/Resources/CodeOfEthics/TP/Home/CT2.aspx
Marriage and Family Therapists: *AAMFT Code of Ethics*, 2012
By mail: American Association of Marriage and Family Therapy (AAMFT)
112 South Alfred Street
Alexandria, VA 22314-3061
By phone: (703) 838-9805
Online: http://www.aamft.org/imis15/Documents/Final%202012%20AAMFT%20Code%20of%20Ethics.pdf
Psychiatrists: *Principles of Medical Ethics With Annotations Especially Applicable to Psychiatry*, 2008 (as amended)
By mail: American Psychiatric Association (APsyA)
1400 K Street, N.W.
Washington, DC 20005
By phone: (202) 682-6000
Online: http://www.psych.org/MainMenu/PsychiatricPractice/Ethics.aspx
Psychologists: *Ethical Principles of Psychologists and Code of Conduct*, 2010 (2002, amended)

By mail: American Psychological Association (APA)
750 First Street N.E.
Washington, DC 20002
By phone: (800) 374-2721
Online: http://www.apa.org/ethics/code.html
Psychologists (Canada): *Canadian Code of Ethics for Psychologists* (3rd edition, 2000)
By mail: Canadian Psychological Association (CPA)
151 Slater St., Suite 205
Ottawa, Ontario K1P 5H3
By phone: (613) 237-2144
Online: http://www.cpa.ca/aboutcpa/committees/ethics/codeofethics/
Social Workers: *Code of Ethics*, 2008 (as revised)
By mail: National Association of Social Workers (NASW)
750 First Street, NE, Suite 700
Washington, DC 20002-4241
By phone: (800) 638-8799
Online: http://www.naswdc.org/pubs/code/code.asp

B. Ethics Codes of School-Based Mental Health Professional Associations

School Counselors: *Ethical Standards for School Counselors* (2010)
By mail: American School Counselors Association (ASCA)
1101 King Street, Suite 625
Alexandria, VA 22314
By phone: (703) 683-ASCA
Online: http://www.schoolcounselor.org/files/EthicalStandards2010.pdf
School Psychologists: *Principles for Professional Ethics* (2010)
By mail: National Association of School Psychologists (NASP)
4340 East West Highway, Suite 402
Bethesda, MD 20814
By phone: (301) 657-0270; Toll Free (866) 331-NASP
Online: http://www.nasponline.org/standards/2010standards.aspx
School Social Workers: *NASW Standards for School Social Work Services* (2012)
By mail: National Association of Social Workers (NASW)
750 First Street, NE, Suite 700
Washington, DC 20002-4241
By phone: (800) 227-3390
Online: http://www.socialworkers.org/practice/standards/naswschoolsocialworkstandards.pdf
For ethics codes for other mental health subspecialties, see extensive links at http://kspope.com/ethcodes/index.php

C. Other Selected Documents Relevant to Ethics and Confidentiality from National Associations of Mental Health Professionals

AMERICAN COUNSELING ASSOCIATION

Forester-Miller, H., & Davis, T.E. (1996). A Practitioner's Guide to Ethical Decision Making. Online: http://www.ed.uab.edu/csi-zeta/docs/EthicalDecMakingTyson.pdf

THE AMERICAN COUNSELING ASSOCIATION LEGAL SERIES

Several of the monographs in this series have direct bearing on confidentiality:

Ahia, C. E., & Martin, D. (1993). The Danger-to-Self-or-Others Exception to Confidentiality.

Arthur, G. L., & Swanson, C. D. (1993). Confidentiality and Privileged Communication.

Mitchell, R. W. (2000). Documentation in Counseling Records.

Remley, T. P. (1991). Preparing for Court Appearances.

Salo, M. M., & Shumate, S. G. (1993). Counseling Minor Clients.

Stevens-Smith, P. S., & Hughes, M. M. (1993). Legal Issues in Marriage and Family Counseling.

Strosnider J. S., & Grad, J. D. (1993). Third-Party Payments.

AMERICAN PSYCHIATRIC ASSOCIATION

American Psychiatric Association. (1981). Position Statement: Confidentiality of Medical Records: Does the Physician Have a Right to Privacy Concerning His or Her Own Health Records? Retrieved from http://ajp.psychiatryonline.org/article.aspx?articleid=161362

American Psychiatric Association Committee on Confidentiality. (1987). Guidelines on confidentiality. *American Journal of Psychiatry, 144*, 11, 1522–1526.

American Psychiatric Association. (2009). Position Statement: HIV/AIDS and Confidentiality, Disclosure, and Protection of Others. Retrieved from http://www.psych.org

AMERICAN PSYCHIATRIC NURSES ASSOCIATION

American Nurses Association. (2012). *Scope and Standards of Practice for Psychiatric-Mental Health Nursing.* Order from http://www.apna.org/i4a/pages/index.cfm?pageid=3342

(Member download: http://rceoiaa.typepad.com/blog/2012/02/psychiatric-mental-health-nursing-scope-and-standards-of-practice-american-nurses-association-downloads.html)

AMERICAN PSYCHOLOGICAL ASSOCIATION

American Psychological Association Committee on Professional Practice and Standards. (2009). *Guidelines for Child Custody Evaluations in Family Law Proceedings.* Retrieved from http://www.apa.org/practice/guidelines/child-custody.pdf

American Psychological Association. (2007) Record Keeping Guidelines. *American Psychologist, 62,* 993–1004. Retrieved from http://www.apa.org/practice/record-keeping.pdf

American Psychological Association Committee on Legal Issues. (2006). Strategies for private practitioners coping with subpoenas or compelled testimony for client records or test data. *Professional Psychology: Research and Practice 27*, 215–222.

Note: Also see list at http://www.CenterForEthicalPractice.org/Links-Psychologists.htm and the reference list for this book.

NATIONAL ASSOCIATION OF SOCIAL WORKERS

(To access some of these files, you must be a member of NASW.)

NASW. (2001). Confidentiality and School Social Work. Retrieved from http://www.socialworkers.org/practice/school/default.asp

NASW. (2002). *Standards for School Social Work Services.* Retrieved from http://www.socialworkers.org/practice/school/default.asp

NASW. (2006). *HIPAA Security Rule Primer*. Retrieved from http://www.socialworkers.org/hipaa/primer0806.pdf

NASW. (2006). *NASW Standards for Social Work Practice With Family Caregivers of Older Adults.* Retrieved from http://www.socialworkers.org/practice/aging/standards/familyCaregivers-6–8-10.pdf

Reamer, F. G. (2009). *Social Work Ethics Casebook: Cases and Commentary.* Washington, DC: NASW Press. Retrieved from http://www.naswpress.org/publications/ethics/ethics-casebook.html

Robb, M. (2004). Client Records: Keep or Toss?. NASW Insurance Trust. Retrieved from http://www.naswassurance.org/pdf/PP_Record_Retention.pdf

D. Record Keeping Resources Online from National Professional Association Websites

COUNSELORS

Permission to Refrain From Making a Diagnosis (*Counseling Today Online*, July 1, 2006). http://ct.counseling.org/2006/08/ct-online-ethics-update-6/

Private Practice in Counseling: Maintaining Client Files (May 2005 Practice Update) http://ct.counseling.org/2007/11/private-practice-in-counseling-maintaining-client-files/

PSYCHOLOGISTS

(To access some of these files, you must be a member of the APA Practice Directorate.)
A Matter of Law: Patient Record Keeping
www.apapractice.org/apo/insider/practice/pracmanage/legal/record.html
Record Keeping Guidelines (2007)
www.apa.org/practice/recordkeeping.pdf
Record Keeping Under the New Ethics Code (2005)
http://www.apa.org/monitor/feb05/ethics.aspx
Are You Prepared for the Unexpected?
http://www.apapractice.org/content/apo/insider/practice/pracmanage/legal/will.html

SOCIAL WORKERS

Client Records: Keep or Toss?
http://www.naswassurance.org/pdf/PP_Record_Retention.pdf
Social Work and Clinical Notes (2001)
http://www.socialworkers.org/ldf/lawnotes/notes.asp
To access the documents below, you must be a member of the NASW Private Practice Specialty Practice Section)
Documenting Patient Care in the Private Practice Setting (2002)
linked from http://www.socialworkers.org/practice/clinical/default.asp
Psychotherapy Notes and Reimbursement Claims (2005)
linked from http://www.socialworkers.org/practice/clinical/default.asp
Social Workers and Post-Disaster Record Keeping Questions (2006)
linked from http://www.socialworkers.org/ldf/legal_issue/default.asp
Social Workers and Record Retention Requirements (2005)
linked from http://www.socialworkers.org/ldf/legal_issue/default.asp

APPENDIX VIII

Ethics-Based Staff Training: Sample Table of Contents

Sample Table of Contents for Ethics-Based Staff Training Manual in an Outpatient Mental Health Setting

I. GUIDING PRINCIPLES

II. OFFICE ENVIRONMENT

III. INFORMED CONSENT
- A. Ethical Standards Requiring Informed Consent
- B. Legal Requirements and Implications (state laws; Health Insurance Portability and Accountability Act [HIPAA])
- C. Our Policies Protecting Clients' Informed Consent Rights
  1. Obtaining Initial Informed Consent Before Providing Services
  2. Obtaining Informed Consent Before Disclosing Information
  3. Conducting Ongoing Informed Consent Conversations

IV. PRIVACY AND CONFIDENTIALITY
- A. Ethical Standards About Confidentiality
- B. Legal Requirements About Confidentiality (state laws; HIPAA)
- C. Ethical and Legal Consequences of Unethical/Unlawful Disclosures
- D. Our Policies Protecting Privacy and Confidentiality in This Setting
  1. Protecting Client's Right to Privacy While in Our Office
  2. Protecting Client's Right to Confidentiality (Nondisclosure)
     a. *Rule*: Disclose Information Only With Client Consent

  Policies: Handling Requests for Information; Telephone Interactions
     b. *Rule*: Protect Confidentiality in Storing, Transmitting, Disposal of Information

Policies: Using Computer, Copier, Fax, E-Mail; Transporting Data, etc.
3. Policies About Responding to Legal Demands (Subpoenas, Attorney Requests, etc.)

V. RELATIONSHIPS WITH CLIENTS (IN THERAPY, ASSESSMENT, AND CONSULTATION SETTINGS)
- A. Ethical Standards About Boundaries and Dual Relationships
- B. Legal Implications of Client Relationships
- C. Our Policies About Relationships With Clients

VI. BILLING AND THIRD-PARTY REIMBURSEMENT
- A. Ethical Standards Related to Billing and Reimbursement
- B. Legal Requirements and Limitations
- C. Our Policies Regarding Staff Responsibilities (Billing, Transmission of Claims, etc.)

VII. OTHER POLICIES WITH ETHICAL AND/OR LEGAL IMPLICATIONS
- A. Maintaining Competence and Remaining Within Job Description
- B. Understanding Procedures in Nonclinical Emergencies (e.g., computer failure, flood, etc.)
- C. Maintaining a "Culture of Safety"—Monitoring Ethical Compliance in the Workplace

VIII. DEMONSTRATING UNDERSTANDING AND SIGNING ETHICS CONTRACT

APPENDIX TO TRAINING MANUAL: (Optional)
Ethics Codes of the Mental Health Professionals in the Setting
Summaries of Relevant Legal Requirements (state laws; HIPAA)
Documents (e.g., Certificate Documenting Completion of Training; Confidentiality Contract)

Adapted from Fisher, M. A. (2009). Ethics-based training for non-clinical staff in mental health settings. *Professional Psychology: Research and Practice, 40,* 466. DOI: 10.1037/a0016642

NOTES

Introduction

1. The terms "ethical floor" and "ethical ceiling" were used by Bersoff in a 1994 article, "Explicit Ambiguity: The 1992 Ethics Code as an Oxymoron" (p. 385). This concept was more recently expanded by Knapp and VandeCreek in their 2006 ethics text, *Practical Ethics for Psychologists,* in their discussion of "positive ethics" or "active ethics" (pp. 9–14). It was applied specifically to confidentiality by Fisher (2008b) in the article, "Protecting Confidentiality Rights: The Need for an Ethical Practice Model."

2. Discussions of counselors' ethical responsibilities will use the Ethics Code of the American Counseling Association (ACA, 2005) unless a different ethics code is referenced.

Chapter 1: Ethical Responsibilities About Confidentiality

1. See Crowe, Grogan, Jacobs, Lindsay, & Mark (1985), "Delineation of the roles of clinical psychology"; Jagim, Wittman, & Noll (1978), "Mental health professionals' attitudes towards confidentiality, privilege, and third-party disclosure"; and Pope & Vetter (1992), "Ethical dilemmas encountered by members of the American Psychological Association."

2. The change in ethics codes happened so slowly that, for many years, therapists practiced under ethics codes that made no legal exceptions to the ethical requirement to maintain confidentiality, even though progressively more laws required them to breach it. This created a true ethical–legal conflict that began the confusion referenced in the epigram. For discussion of this history as it pertains to the ethics code for psychologists, see Fisher (2008b).

3. Bollas & Sundelson (1995), *The New Informants*; Donner (2008), "Unbalancing confidentiality."

4. Fisher (2008b); Younggren & Harris (2008), "Can you keep a secret?"

5. Behnke (2007b), "Disclosures of Information: Thoughts on a process."

6. Haas, Malouf, & Mayerson (1986), "Ethical dilemmas in psychological practice"; Pope & Vetter (1992).

7. Gonsiorek (2009), "Informed consent can solve some confidentiality dilemmas, but others remain," p. 374.

8. Bollas & Langs (1999), "It is time to take a stand," p. 1. Others, from a psychoanalytic perspective, question whether absolute confidentiality is even possible. For example, see Janes (2006), "'Quis custodiet': Who has ultimate responsibility for confidentiality in mental health services?": "I would argue that the clinical reality of working with patients continually dispels the myth that 'absolute' confidentiality can exist within the analytic relationship" (p. 316).

Also from a psychoanalytic perspective, see Grey (2006), "Confidentiality: A contribution to the debate": "We need to be able to hold firm in the face of demands for information that breach confidentiality when we believe it should be maintained. But perhaps we need, too, a space in our minds to come to our own decisions when we believe it right to speak of what usually remains private. The tensions that advocates of either position (absolute confidentiality or partial confidentiality) seek to dissolve are an essential part of the work" (p. 369).

9. Beck (1990), "The basic issues," p. 5 (emphasis added).

10. In the section that follows, the four concepts are only slightly revised from the list used in Fisher (2012), Confidentiality and Record Keeping, p. 334.

11. When reading this book, it will be helpful to have at hand the most recent edition of your profession's ethics code. For obtaining a copy online, the Reference section contains URLs for downloading; and for obtaining published copies, Appendix VII contains contact information. The Center for Ethical Practice provides links to mental health ethics codes, including some subspecialties, at http://www.centerforethicalpractice.org/ethical-legal-resources/ethical-information/ethics-codes; More extensive links for subspecialties are available at http://kspope.com/ethcodes/index.php

12. These rules of usage will apply throughout this book. However, there are instances when we quote others who use the terms slightly differently.

13. The text and Appendices focus on ethics codes from the larger national associations of mental health professionals: ACA (2005), APA (2010b), APsyA (2009), and NASW (2008). Appendices I and II also include ethical standards from the AAMFT (2001). Appendix VII includes links to ethical resources from the ASCA (2010) and the NASP (2010).

The Ethics Code of the Canadian Psychological Association (CPA, 2000) is not reflected in the Appendices, but the Reference section provides a URL for obtaining it online. For comparing and contrasting it with the APA Ethics Code see *Code Comparison: The Canadian Code of Ethics for Psychologists Compared with the APA and ASPPB Codes* (CPA, 2005), also available online.

14. Knapp & VandeCreek (2006), *Practical Ethics for Psychologists*, p. 112 (emphasis added).

15. APA (2007), "Record keeping guidelines," p. 997.

16. Koocher & Keith-Spiegel (2008), *Ethics in Psychology and the Mental Health Professions,* p. 190.

17. Nagy (2011), *Essential Ethics for Psychologists*, p. 105.

18. Knapp & VandeCreek (2006), p. 115.

19. For example, see Bollas & Sundelson (1995); and Caudill & Kaplan (2005), "Protecting privacy and confidentiality." Also see the amicus briefs from APA (1995) and NASW (2005a) cited below.

20. APA (1995), "Brief *amicus curiae* in *Jaffee v. Redmond*"; Clarborn, Berbaroglu, Nerison, & Somberg (1994), "The client's perspective"; Miller & Thelen (1986), "Knowledge and beliefs about confidentiality in psychotherapy"; Nowell & Spruill (1993), "If it's not absolutely confidential, will information be disclosed?"; Rubanowitz (1987), "Public attitudes toward psychotherapist–client confidentiality"; VandeCreek, Miars, & Herzog (1987), "Client anticipations and preferences for confidentiality of records."

21. United States Department of Health and Human Services (USDHHS) (1999), *Mental Health: A Report of the Surgeon General*, p. 440.

22. APA (1995), pp. 10–11.

23. American Psychiatric Association & American Academy of Psychiatry and the Law (1995), "Amicus brief in *Jaffee v. Redmond.*"

24. *Jaffee v. Redmond* (1996).

25. NASW (2005a), "Brief *amicus curiae* in *Bier v. Zahren,*" joined by the Colorado Psychological Association, Colorado Psychiatric Society, Colorado Society for Clinical Social Work, Colorado Organization for Victim Assistance, and Colorado Coalition Against Sexual Assault.

26. APA (2007); Haas & Malouf (2005), *Keeping Up the Good Work.*

27. Dingfelder (2009), "Stigma: Alive and well"; Kelly (2011), "Stigma proves hard to eradicate despite multiple advances"; USDHHS (1999).

28. See Knapp & VandeCreek (2003b), "Do psychologists have supererogatory obligations?" and Knapp & VandeCreek (2006).

29. The term "counselors" is used here to include licensed professional counselors, marriage and family counselors, substance abuse counselors, and any other group that describes its services as "counseling," even though the generic reference in these chapters is to "therapy."

30. As suggested in the ethics text by Knapp and VandeCreek (2006, p. 33), these categories would apply to all types of ethical standards, not exclusively to standards about confidentiality.

31. ACA Ethical Standard B.1.c ("Respect for Confidentiality").

32. AAMFT Ethical Standard II-2.2 ("Confidentiality").

33. APsyA Ethics Code Section 4.

34. APA Ethical Standard 4.01 ("Maintaining Confidentiality").

35. NASW Ethical Standards 1.07a, 1.07c, 1.07j ("Privacy and Confidentiality").

36. See in Appendix II section D: "Ensuring That Others Protect Patients' Confidentiality Rights."

37. Fisher (2009a), "Ethics-based training for nonclinical staff in mental health settings."

38. APA Ethical Standard 4.05 ("Disclosures").

39. NASW Ethical Standard 1.07 ("Privacy and Confidentiality").

40. APsyA Ethics Code, Section 4.

41. See ACA Ethics Code, Section B ("Confidentiality, Privileged Communication, & Privacy").

42. Barnett, Wise, Jonathan-Greene, & Bucky (2007), "Informed consent: Too much of a good thing or not enough?" p. 179.

43. Fisher (2008a), "Clarifying confidentiality with the ethical practice model." For a detailed discussion of informed consent, including the components required in the process of obtaining it, see Chapter 5. Most professional ethics texts also include discussions of informed consent.

44. See, for example, Pipes, Blevins, & Kluck (2008), "Confidentiality, ethics, and informed consent [a Letter in response to Fisher (2008b).]"

45. Fisher (2012), p. 336–337 (emphasis added).

46. Fisher (2008a), "Clarifying confidentiality with the ethical practice model."

47. Behnke (2004), "Disclosures of confidential information under the new APA Ethics Code: A process for deciding when and how," p. 78.

48. Although the terms "legally required" and "legally allowed" may sound similar, ethically speaking they are very different. The important differences are reflected in the definitions in Figure 1.1, and their differing ethical implications are discussed at length in later sections, including the section, "Abusing Legally Allowed Exceptions to Confidentiality," at the end of Chapter 8.

49. APA (2010b). For an article describing the 2010 amendments to the 2002 Ethics Code, see APA (2010a), "American Psychological Association amends ethics code to address potential conflicts among professional ethics, legal authority and organizational demands."

50. ACA Ethical Standards H.1.b ("Conflicts Between Ethics & Law") and H.2.e ("Organizational Conflicts").

51. NASW Ethical Standard 1.07j ("Privacy and Confidentiality") and "Statement of Purpose."

52. APsyA Ethics Code, Section 4 (9).

53. APA (2007).

54. For responding to subpoenas, see APA Committee on Legal Issues (2006), "Strategies for private practitioners coping with subpoenas"; APA Practice Organization (2008, Fall), *How to Deal with a Subpoena*; and APA Practice Organization Legal and Regulatory Affairs Staff (2008, December), *How to Deal with a Subpoena*. For specific populations, see, for example, APA Division 44, Committee on Lesbian, Gay, and Bisexual Concerns Joint Task Force (2000), "Guidelines for psychotherapy with lesbian, gay, and bisexual clients"; APA Working Group on Assisted Suicide and End-of-Life Decisions (2000), *Report to the Board of Directors*; and APA Working Group on the Older Adult (1998), "What practitioners should know about working with older adults." Also see Appendix VII, as well as the list of APA resources on the website of the Center for Ethical Practice at http://www.centerforethicalpractice.org/ethical-legal-resources/links/psychologists-links-apa-resources-online/.

55. Knapp, Gottlieb, Handelsman & VandeCreek (Eds.) (2012), *APA Handbook of Ethics in Psychology.* (See Volume 1, Chapter 13, "Confidentiality and Record Keeping.")

56. See Appendix VII for list of documents in *American Counseling Association Legal Series*. Although no longer in print, these helpful resources are available in libraries and through used bookstores.

57. See Appendix VII for listing of documents available online through NASW, including those available only to members.

58. Koocher & Keith Spiegel (2008), p. 21.

59. For obtaining a detailed ethical decision-making model, consider the following ethics texts or other resources: Fisher (2005), "Ethical decision-making model"; Forester-Miller & Davis (1996), "A practitioner's guide to ethical decision making"; Haas & Malouf (2005); Knapp & VandeCreek (2006); Koocher & Keith-Spiegel (2008); Mattison (2000), "Ethical decision making: The person in the process"; and Pope & Vasquez (2011), *Ethics in Psychotherapy and Counseling: A Practical Guide*. When a confidentiality dilemma involves both ethical and legal issues, using a structured decision-making process is especially important, because deciding how to respond to an ethical–legal conflict can require difficult personal soul-searching as well as careful decision making. See model for that purpose by Knapp, Gottlieb, Berman, & Handelsman (2007), "When laws and ethics collide: What should psychologists do?"

Chapter 2: Laws Affecting Confidentiality

1. These legal concepts are reflected in the definitions at the bottom of Box 1.1, which can be a helpful reference when reading this section.

2. Sources of information about the laws in one's own state include state licensing boards and state professional associations. In considering how the types of laws discussed in this chapter might apply in your own state, consult the examples in Appendix III and its online version at the Center for Ethical Practice (2011) on the webpage, "Laws Affecting Confidentiality."

3. Koocher & Keith-Spiegel (2008), *Ethics in Psychology and the Mental Health Professions*, p. 195.

4. See, for example, federal statute 42 U.S.C. § 290dd-2 and federal regulation 42 C.F.R. Part 2. See discussion of these legal protections in Lombardo (2000, Oct.), "Legal focus: Substance abuse treatment records: A special corner of medical privacy."

5. The HIPAA regulations (1996) are very extensive, and the summaries in this chapter and in Appendix IV provide very limited information. See the complete text of the HIPAA regulations at http://www.hhs.gov/ocr/hipaa. See links to other HIPAA information at http://www.CenterForEthicalPractice.org/HIPAA.htm.

6. Bradshaw (2011, Jan/Feb), "Techno breaches could cost practitioners big bucks," p. 1

7. USDHHS (2009), *Press Release: HHS Issues Rule Requiring Individuals Be Notified of Breaches of Their Health Information.*

8. Some states do recognize a secondary legal right on the part of a therapist to invoke privilege on behalf of and in the interest of the patient.

9. Koocher & Keith Spiegel (2008).

10. See Gottlieb, Lasser, & Simpson (2008), Legal and Ethical Issues in Couple Therapy, and Knapp & VandeCreek (1987), *Privileged Communications in the Mental Health Professions.* Also see examples of state privilege laws in Appendix III.

11. Federal Rules of Evidence, Rule 501. Retrieved from http://federalevidence.com/rules-of-evidence.

12. *Jaffee v. Redmond* (1996).

13. Beyer (2000), "First person: *Jaffee v. Redmond* therapist speaks," and Shuman & Foote (1999), "*Jaffee v. Redmond*'s impact: Life after the Supreme Court's recognition of a psychotherapist-patient privilege," p. 483.

14. Shuman & Foote (1999), p. 483.

15. Behnke (2007b), "Disclosures of information: Thoughts on a process," p. 62.

16. Younggren & Harris (2008), "Can you keep a secret? Confidentiality in psychotherapy," p. 589.

17. See Kalichman (1999), *Mandated Reporting of Suspected Child Abuse: Ethics, Law, & Policy*.

18. See Benjamin, Kent, & Sirikantraporn (2009), A Review of Duty-to-Protect Statutes; Welfel, Werth, & Benjamin (2009), Introduction to the Duty to Protect; Kagle & Kopels (1994), "Confidentiality after *Tarasoff*"; Werth, Welfel, Benjamin, & Salaka (2007, December), "Duty to warn"; and Werth, Welfel, Benjamin, & Sales (2009), Practice and Policy Responses to the Duty to Protect. Also see other chapters in Werth, Welfel, & Benjamin (Eds.) (2009), *The Duty to Protect: Ethical, Legal and Professional Considerations for Mental Health Professionals*.

19. Fisher (2012), p. 341.

20. APA Government Relations and Communications Staff (2006), "Patriot Act renewal tightens medical records safeguards"; Munsey (2006), "More protection for psychologists' records in renewed Patriot Act."

21. Fisher (2012), Confidentiality and Record Keeping, p. 342.

22. Fisher (2012), p. 341.

23. Knapp & VandeCreek (1987); Glosoff, Herlihy, Herlihy, & Spence (1997), "Privileged communication in the psychologist–client relationship."

24. Fisher (2012), p. 341.

25. See North Carolina Code, General Statutes § 8–53.3 (1998); Virginia Code, Statutes, § 8.01–399 (2009) and § 8.01–400.2 (2005).

26. APA & American Board of Forensic Psychology (2011, August 20), Standard 4.02.01, "Therapeutic-Forensic Role Conflicts," p. 7. Also see Fisher (2010b), "Which hat are you wearing?" (reproduced in Appendix VI); and Strasburger, Gutheil, & Brodsky (1997), "On wearing two hats: Role conflict in serving as both psychotherapist and expert witness."

27. These exceptions are in the HIPAA Privacy Act at 45 CFR 164.502(a)(1)—*"Permitted uses and disclosures."* Definitions of the terms "treatment," "payment," and "health care operations" can be obtained at http://www.hipaa.com/2009/05/the-definition-of-treatment/.

28. Steven Behnke, Director of the Ethics Office of the American Psychological Association, recommends that when the law says "Even though your client does not consent to your releasing this information, you may nevertheless do so," then the situation calls for both ethical and clinical consultation (Behnke & Kinscherff [2002, May], "Must a psychologist report past child abuse?," p. 90.

Chapter 3: Placing Laws Into Ethical Context

1. Pope & Vasquez (2011), *Ethics in Psychotherapy and Counseling*, p xiii. (See more extensive quotation in Chapter 1.)

2. Kipnis (2003, October), "In defense of absolute confidentiality," p. 1 (emphasis added).

3. Some ethics codes contain an explicit statement to this effect, but others evoke this responsibility only indirectly. Complying with this ethical requirement was easier 50 years ago, when most of the relevant *legal* requirements were located in the regulations governing the practice of each specific profession. Today, laws relevant to confidentiality are scattered throughout each state's legal code. (See Appendix III.)

4. The listing that follows was adapted from Fisher (2012), Confidentiality and Record Keeping, p. 342.

5. See, in Chapter 1, the section " Ethical Standards About Conflicts Between Ethical Duties and Other Obligations," and, in Appendix II, Sections 2e, "Responding to Conflicts Between Ethical Duties and Other Duties."

6. For example, see the decision-making model for responding to ethical-legal conflicts provided by Knapp, Gottlieb, Berman, & Handelsman (2007), "When laws and ethics collide: What should psychologists do?"

7. Knapp, Gottlieb, Berman, & Handelsman (2007), p. 54.

8. APA Committee on Professional Practice Standards (2003), "Legal issues in the professional practice of psychology," p. 596.

9. Fisher (2012), p. 343.

10. Fisher (2008b), "Protecting confidentiality rights: The need for an ethical practice model," p. 6.

11. Bennett, Bricklin, Harris, Knapp, VandeCreek, & Younggren (2006), *Assessing and Managing Risk in Psychological Practice*, p. 31.

12. Note, however, that the professions vary in how they describe therapists' ethical responsibilities when ethics and laws come into conflict. (See, in Chapter 1, the section "Ethical Standards About Conflicts Between Ethical Duties and Other Obligations," and, in Appendix II, Sections 2e, "Responding to Conflicts Between Ethical Duties and Other Duties." Also see Chapter 7, "Responding Ethically to Legal Demands.")

13. Behnke & Kinscherff (2002, May), "Must a psychologist report past child abuse?" Some ethics codes state that such disclosures require the patient's informed consent, others do not (see Appendix II). However, this position is adopted for the purposes of the discussions in this book, even though some therapists might consider this to be a supererogatory action (i.e., beyond what is required by their ethics code).

14. Acuff, Bennett, Bricklin, Canter, Knapp, Moldawsky, & Phelps (1999), "Considerations for ethical practice in managed care," p. 570.

15. Hansen & Goldberg (1999), "Navigating the nuances: A matrix of considerations for ethical-legal dilemmas," p. 496.

16. See final column of Appendix I and Appendix II to fit each profession's ethical standards into the steps of the Ethical Practice Model that is presented in Box 3.1.

Introduction to Part II: The Ethics of Conditional Confidentiality

1. The terms "ethical floor" and "ethical ceiling" were used by Bersoff (1994), "Explicit ambiguity: The 1992 ethics code as an oxymoron," p. 385. This concept was more recently expanded by Knapp & VandeCreek (2006), *Practical Ethics for Psychologists*, in their discussion of "positive ethics" or "active ethics" (pp. 9–14). It was applied specifically to confidentiality by Fisher (2008b) in "Protecting confidentiality rights: The need for an ethical practice model."

2. Fisher (2012), Confidentiality and Record Keeping, pp. 343–344.

3. The color-coded version of the model is provided by the Center for Ethical Practice (2010) at http://www.centerforethicalpractice.org/EthicalPracticeModelAnnotated

4. For an illustration of how this can be done, using research settings as an example, see Fisher, 2008b, p. 6.

5. Fisher (2012), p. 345. For citations to several ethical decision-making models, see endnote 59 for Chapter 1. For other examples of available models see the lists in Barnett, Behnke, Rosenthal, & Koocher (2007), "In case of ethical dilemma, break glass," and in Cottone & Claus (2000), "Ethical decision-making models: A review of the literature."

6. See, for example, the early steps in ethical decision-making models offered by Fisher (2005), "Ethical decision-making model"; Knapp & VandeCreek (2006); Koocher & Keith-Spiegel (2008), *Ethics in Psychology and the Mental Health Professions: Standards and Cases*; and Pope & Vasquez (2011), *Ethics in Psychology and Counseling: A Practical Guide*.

7. Fisher (2012), p. 345.

8. Hansen & Goldberg (1999), "Navigating the nuances: A matrix of considerations for ethical-legal dilemmas."

9. See decision-making model provided by Knapp, Gottlieb, Berman, & Handelsman (2007), in the article, "When laws and ethics collide: What should psychologists do?"

Chapter 4: Step 1: Preparing

1. Fisher (2012), Confidentiality and Record Keeping p. 345.

2. Fisher (2012), p. 345.

3. For an exception, see a discussion panel at the 2003 American Psychological Association (APA) Convention in which forethought was discussed from an ethical perspective, and in which the speakers addressed the fact that "anticipation of ethical pitfalls and consultation with colleagues are key to preventing practitioners' most common ethical dilemmas" (Bailey, 2003a, October, p. 68).

4. For example, the epigraph to this chapter originates from the APA Insurance Trust. Also see a more recent book from that same source, quoted at the end of this paragraph: Bennett, Bricklin, Harris, Knapp, VandeCreek, & Younggren (2006), *Assessing and Managing Risk in Psychological Practice: An Individualized Approach.*

5. Bennett et al. (2006), pp. 7, 28 (emphasis added).

6. These appendices are useful for reference, but therapists are responsible for being familiar with the entire ethics code of their profession. See Appendix VII for URLs for ethics codes of the national associations of the major mental health professions and some of their subspecialties. Links to many other ethics codes are available at http://kspope.com/ethcodes/index.php or at http://www.centerforethicalpractice.org/ethical-legal-resources/ethical-information/ethics-codes/

7. The importance of this is implied in most ethics codes, but it is an explicit requirement for marriage and family therapists. American Association of Marriage and Family Therapy (AAMFT), Ethical Standard 3.2 – Professional Competence and Integrity: " Marriage and family therapists maintain adequate knowledge of and adhere to applicable laws, ethics, and professional standards."

8. Beck (1990), The Basic Issues. In *Confidentiality Versus the Duty to Protect: Foreseeable Harm in the Practice of Psychiatry,* p. 6.

9. Pabian, Welfel, & Beebe (2009), "Psychologists' knowledge of their states' laws pertaining to Tarasoff-type situations," p. 8.

10. See http://www.CenterforEthicalPractice.org/LawsAffectingConfidentiality (Center for Ethical Practice, 2011).

11. For example, the Pennsylvania Psychological Association provides a partial listing of state laws affecting confidentiality at http://www.papsy.org/ces/Confidentiality. For Virginia psychologists, the Virginia Psychological Association (2009) provides the handbook, *Applying Virginia's Legal Standards in Your Own Practice*; and for all Virginia therapists, Fisher provides information about responding to subpoenas (2007a) as well as annual legal updates in a confidentiality manual, *Can You Keep A Secret?* (2010a). The Center for Ethical Practice provides links to laws relevant to confidentiality in Virginia (2011) as well as links to confidentiality laws in a few other states at http://www.centerforethicalpractice.org/ethical-legal-resources/legal-information-other-states/. The American Psychological Association provides partial listings of relevant laws in a series of state-specific books for psychologists. (See, for example, Porfiri & Resnick, 2000, *Law & Mental Health Professionals.*) Other advice about state-specific responses to subpoenas is sometimes

available in newsletters and online documents from state professional associations. For example, for Pennsylvania, see Baturin, Knapp, & Tepper (2003, August), "Practical considerations when responding to subpoenas and court orders," and for Ohio, see Moats & Johnson (2004, December), "Responding to a subpoena."

12. As part of the "legal homework," it can also be helpful to review Chapter 2, "Laws Affecting Confidentiality";" Chapter 7, "Responding Ethically to Legal Demands for Disclosure"; and legal examples in Appendix III, "Laws Affecting Confidentiality."

13. See Welfel, Werth, & Benjamin (2009), Introduction to the Duty to Protect, p. 4. Also see discussion of related issues at Step 4 and Step 5.

14. "Psychologists include in written and oral reports and consultations, only information germane to the purpose for which the communication is made" (APA Ethical Standard 4.04b, "Minimizing Intrusions on Privacy"). For counselors, "Written and oral reports present only data germane to the purposes of the consultation, and every effort is made to protect client identity and to avoid undue invasion of privacy" (American Counseling Association [ACA] Ethical Standard B.8.b, "Respect for Privacy"). Social workers "should disclose the least amount of information necessary to achieve the purposes of the consultation" (National Association of Social Workers [NASW] Ethical Standard 2.05c ("Consultation").

15. See Appendix VII for contact information for national professional associations.

16. See Chapter 1, endnote 59, for sources of ethical decision making models.

17. For example, see Harris & Younggren (2011, July-August), "But that's what the lawyer told me." Further discussion of misinformation is provided in Chapter 7, "Responding Ethically to Legal Demands" and in the Chapter 8 section on "Misunderstanding Legal Requirements or Accepting Bad Advice."

18. See, for example, Bennett, Bricklin, Harris, Knapp, VandeCreek, & Younggren (2006), *Assessing and Managing Risk in Psychological Practice: An Individualized Approach.* Rockville, MD: American Psychological Association Insurance Trust.

19. Fisher (2008b),, p. 8.

20. Behnke (2001, October), "Ethics matter: A question of values"; Behnke (2005b), "Letter from a reader regarding a minor client and confidentiality"; Behnke (2007b), "Disclosures of information: Thoughts on a process"; Donner (2008), "Unbalancing confidentiality"; Fisher (2008b); Knapp et al. (2007), "When laws and ethics collide"; Hansen & Goldberg (1999).

21. Gonsiorek (2009), "Informed consent can solve some confidentiality dilemmas, but others remain," p. 374.

22. Donner (2008).

23. See Bollas & Sundelson (1995), *The New Informants: The Betrayal of Confidentiality in Psychoanalysis and Psychotherapy*; Kipnis (2003, October), "In defense of absolute confidentiality"; and Siegel (1976, Fall), "Confidentiality." As of 1994, research suggested that one-quarter of therapists believed confidentiality should be absolute. (See Thelen, Rodriguez, & Sprengelmeier [1994], "Psychologists' beliefs concerning confidentiality.")

24. For several perspectives on this question, see the commentaries by C. B. Fisher and L. D. VandeCreek in Donner (2008).

25. As described in the Introduction, mental health professionals are still ethically free to offer patients *unconditional confidentiality* and make the promise that "Everything you tell me stays in this room," but only if they are prepared to disobey the law, eschew managed

care, and protect confidences in every circumstance, no matter how severe the legal, financial, and personal risks to themselves. Some who advocate absolute protection of confidentiality have acknowledged these potential consequences in great detail. (For example, see Bollas & Sundelson [1995].)

26. Pope, K. S., & Vasquez, M. J. T. (2005), *How to Survive & Thrive as a Therapist: Information, Ideas, and Resources for Psychologists in Practice*, p. 47.

27. Knapp & VandeCreek (2006), p. 9.

28. Jordan & Meara (1990), "Ethics & professional practice of psychologists: The role of virtues and principles," p. 112.

29. Handelsman, Knapp, & Gottlieb (2002), "Positive ethics."

30. Fisher (2012), p. 346.

31. Knapp et al. (2007), p. 58.

32. Fisher (2008b), p. 8 (citing Smith, McGuire, Abbott, & Blau [1991]).

33. Fisher (2012), p. 346.

34. For information about potentially problematic provisions in provider contracts and recommendations about amending them before signing, see Koman & Harris (2005), Contracting with Managed Care Organizations. For a glossary of terms used in managed care contracts, see Austrin (1999), *Managed Health Care Simplified: A Glossary of Terms*.

For general advice about managed care contracts, see APA Practice Organization, Legal and Regulatory Affairs Staff and Communications Staff (2005b, March), "A matter of law: Managing your managed care contracts." For advice about preparing for record audits see APA Practice Organization, Legal and Regulatory Affairs Staff (2005b, November), "A matter of law: Managed care record audits."For discussion of what therapists should be prepared to tell prospective managed care patients about these possible complications, see Acuff et al. (1999), "Considerations for ethical practice in managed care"; Appelbaum, Lidz, & Meisel (1987). *Informed Consent: Legal Theory and Clinical Practice*; Bilynsky & Vernaglia (1998), "The ethical practice of psychology in a managed-care framework"; Cooper & Gottlieb (2000), "Ethical issues with managed care"; Younggren (2000), "Is managed care really just another unethical Model T?"

35. Chapter 6 contains a discussion of the advantages of collaboration in establishing clear policies about confidentiality and in planning responses to legal demands.

36. Fisher (2012), p. 347.

37. The enactment of the federal HIPAA regulations created a flurry of unintelligible samples of the required "Notice of Privacy Practices." Long before HIPAA, however, there were already concerns that the ordinary informed consent forms used by therapists were written at a level beyond the reading ability of the average patient, often at the level of a professional journal article. See, for example, Handelsman et al. (1986), "Use, content, and readability of written informed consent forms." More recent research suggests that many informed consent documents are still written in language too complex for them to serve their intended purpose—namely, to protect patients by giving them sufficient information about the risks before obtaining their consent for treatment. See, for example, Hochhauser (1999), "Informed consent and patient's rights documents: A right, a rite, or a rewrite?" and Walfish & Ducey (2007), "Readability level of health insurance portability and accountability act [HIPAA] notices of privacy practices used by psychologists in clinical practice."

38. Werth, Welfel, Benjamin, & Sales (2009). Practice and Policy Responses to the Duty to Protect, p. 253.

39. For Counselors, Ethical Standard A.2a. (Informed Consent) states that: "Counselors have an obligation to review *in writing and verbally* with clients the rights and responsibilities of both the counselor and the client. Informed consent is an ongoing part of the counseling process, and counselors appropriately document discussions of informed consent throughout the counseling relationship" (emphasis added); and ACA Ethical Standard B.4.b (Couples and Family Counseling) explicitly requires counselors to document the confidentiality understandings in writing.

40. See, for example, Bennett et al. (2006) and Younggren & Harris (2008), "Can you keep a secret? Confidentiality in psychotherapy."

41. For example, ACA Ethical Standard A.2.c ("Developmental and Cultural Sensitivity") requires counselors to "use clear and understandable language when discussing issues related to informed consent." APA Ethical Standard 3.10 ("Informed Consent") requires psychologists to "obtain the informed consent of the individual or individuals using language that is reasonably understandable to that person or persons." NASW Ethical Standard 1.03 ("Informed Consent") specifies that social workers "should use clear and understandable language to inform clients."

Chapter 5: Step 2: Telling Prospective Patients the Truth About Confidentiality's Limits

1. Pope & Vasquez (2011), *Ethics in Psychotherapy and Counseling*, p. 171.

2. This initial conversation must cover many topics, not just confidentiality. For a chart listing the ethically required topics in informed consent conversations, as specified in the ethics codes for psychologists, counselors, and social workers, see Fisher (2006), "Selected ethical standards related to informed consent for therapy." For an extensive discussion of the issue of informed consent in the psychoanalytic literature, see Saks (2011), *Informed Consent to Psychoanalysis: The Law, the Theory and the Data,* especially the long list of references in its footnote 18.

3. See endnote 39 in Chapter 4.

4. Younggren & Harris (2008), "Can you keep a secret? Confidentiality in psychotherapy," p. 598. Also see the sample informed consent contract by Harris & Bennett (1998) on the website of the APA Insurance Trust at http://www.apait.org/download.asp?item=inf.doc

5. Nagy (1988), The Well-Educated Consumer: Informing Clients and Protecting Providers, pp. 1–2.

6. American Nurses Association (2001), *Code of Ethics for Nurses With Interpretive Statements.*

7. For example, counselors have the following ethical requirement when providing multiple-patient services: "In couples and family counseling, counselors … discuss expectations and limitations of confidentiality. Counselors seek agreement and document *in writing* such agreement among all involved parties having capacity to give consent concerning each individual's right to confidentiality and any obligation to preserve the confidentiality of information known" (ACA Ethical Standard B.4.b, "Couples and Family Counseling," emphasis added).

8. Beahrs & Gutheil (2001, Jan.), "Informed consent in psychotherapy," p. 8.

9. The ethics codes for the several mental health professions allow slightly different exceptions to the confidentiality rule, as illustrated in Appendix II, Section 3. These

exceptions must be listed among the "limits of confidentiality" that must be explained to prospective patients at intake if the therapist intends to disclose in these circumstances without obtaining further consent from the patient (see Figure 1.2).

10. American Counseling Association Ethical Standard A.12.g, "Technology and Informed Consent."

11. Younggren (2000), "Is managed care just another unethical Model T?," p. 256.

12. Koocher & Keith-Spiegel (2008), *Ethics in Psychology and the Mental Health Professions,* p. 194.

13. See APA Ethical Standards 4.02b, 10.02, 10.01, and 10.03; ACA Ethical Standard B.1.d; NASW Ethical Standard 1.07e; and AAMFT Ethical Standard 2.1.

The ethics code for psychiatrists mentions the initial informed consent conversation about confidentiality only in a specialized context: "Psychiatrists are often asked to examine individuals for security purposes, to determine suitability for various jobs, and to determine legal competence. The psychiatrist must fully describe the nature and purpose and lack of confidentiality of the examination to the examinee at the beginning of the examination" (APsyA, 2009, Section 4.6).

14. Nagy (2011), *Essential Ethics for Psychologists: A Primer for Understanding and Mastering Core Issues*, p. 92.

15. Gutheil, Bursztajn, Brodsky, & Alexandra (1991), Managing Uncertainty: The Therapeutic Alliance, Informed Consent, and Liability, p. 79.

16. See APA Ethical Standard 4.02b, NASW Ethical Standard 1.07d, ACA Ethical Standard B.1.d, and AAMFT Ethical Standard 2.1.

Psychiatrists have no mention of this in their ethics code, but ethics texts and articles in these disciplines do stress early timing. See, for example, Epstein (1994), *Keeping Boundaries: Maintaining Safety and Integrity in the Psychotherapeutic Process*; and Joseph & Onek (1999), Confidentiality in Psychiatry.

17. Koocher & Keith-Spiegel (2008), p. 252.

18. Appelbaum, P. S. (2007, November), "Assessment of patients' competence to consent to treatment," p. 1836.

19. Berner (1998), Informed Consent.

20. See, for example, APA Division 45/Society for the Study of Ethnic Minority Issues (2002), *Guidelines for Multicultural Proficiency for Psychologists.*

21. Pipes, Blevins, & Kluck (2008), "Confidentiality, ethics, and informed consent" p. 623 (referencing Meer & VandeCreek [2002], "Cultural considerations in release of information"; and Pettifor & Sawchuk [2006], "Psychologists' perceptions of ethically troubling incidents across international borders").

22. Meer & VandeCreek (2002), p. 155

23. Pettifor & Sawchuk (2006), p. 222.

24. This ethical responsibility arises from the ethical standards about delegating responsibility to others. For example, psychologists who use the service of interpreters must "take reasonable steps to (1) avoid delegating such work to persons who have a multiple relationship with those being served that would likely lead to exploitation or loss of objectivity; (2) authorize only those responsibilities that such persons can be expected to perform competently on the basis of their education, training, or experience, either independently or with the level of supervision being provided; and (3) see that such persons perform these services competently (APA Ethical Standard 2.05, "Delegation of Work to Others").

Counselors must "make every effort to ensure that privacy and confidentiality of clients are maintained by subordinates, including employees, supervisees, students, clerical assistants, and volunteers" (ACA Ethical Standard B.3.a, "Subordinates").

25. Fisher (2009a), "Ethics-based training for non-clinical staff in mental health settings." For sample confidentiality contracts to be signed by employees, or by contracted agents such as interpreters, see Center for Ethical Practice (2009), Staff Training: Sample Documents.

26. Stromberg et al. (1988), *The Psychologist's Legal Handbook*, p. 452.

27. Fisher (2008b) traced the presence of this requirement in the APA Ethics Code from its first drafting in the 1950s. In the professional literature during the 1970s, statements such as the following were found: "Limitations on confidentiality must be conveyed to prospective clients; guarantees of complete secrecy are tantamount to blatant misrepresentation of facts that should be known to all therapists" (From Hare-Mustin et al. (1979), "Rights of clients, responsibilities of therapists," p. 6, citing Bersoff (1975), "Professional ethics and legal responsibilities: On the horns of a dilemma." Also see Everstine et al. (1980), "Privacy and confidentiality in psychotherapy."

28. Somberg, Stone, & Claiborn (1993), "Informed consent: Therapists' beliefs and practices," p. 156.

29. Joseph & Onek (1999), p. 135.

30. Somberg et al. (1993), p. 157.

31. Nowell & Spruill (1993), "If it's not absolutely confidential, will information be disclosed?"

32. Bollas & Sundelson (1995), *The New Informants*.

33. Sullivan, Martin, & Handelsman (1993), "Practical benefits of an informed-consent procedure."

34. Joseph & Onek (1999).

35. Fisher (2008b), "Protecting confidentiality: The need for an ethical practice model," pp. 3–4.

36. Pope & Vasquez (2011), p. 171.

Chapter 6: Step 3: Obtaining Truly Informed Consent Before Disclosing Confidential Information Voluntarily

1. Later in this chapter, the discussion of disclosures to third-party payers illustrates the ethical importance of making this distinction. Therapists who treat voluntary disclosures as if they were "involuntary" may be more likely to short-change the informed consent process and obtain *uninformed* consent (by obtaining consent without informing patients about exactly what will be disclosed), or perhaps they may fail to obtain consent at all. The next chapter (Step 4), illustrates an *opposite problem*: Therapists who treat involuntary (i.e., legally required) disclosures as if they were "voluntary" may be more likely to disclose more than is legally required. Note that both of these ethical mistakes have similar outcomes: The therapist behaves *as if* a patient who actually gave *no* consent had consented to unlimited disclosure of confidential information about him or her. The subsequent chapter (Step 5) covers a broader problem that is reflected in both illustrations: Once therapists begin disclosing information, they sometimes tend to disclose too much, with or without the patient's consent.

2. Note that the second paragraph of Box 6.1 raises questions that will not be discussed here in detail. For example, how should a therapist respond if a patient (1) retracts

a consent given at intake or (2) refuses to consent to disclosures that are necessitated by a new policy in the setting? Such situations raise not only important clinical issues but also complex ethical and legal issues, and so should receive consideration in case consultation, case conferences, and confidentiality workshops.

3. See National Association of Social Workers (NASW) Ethical Standards 1.03a and 1.07b, and APA Ethical Standard 4.05. In the American Psychiatric Association (APsyA) Ethics Code, the terms "truly informed consent" and "fully informed consent" are used in reference to presentation of patient information to a scientific gathering, to the public, or to the media. (See APsyA, Ethical Standard 4 (10, 11).)

4. VandeCreek (2008), "Considering confidentiality within broader theoretical frameworks," p. 373.

5. Consent is valid only if given freely and voluntarily, and consent is considered voluntary only if the patient was first informed about the foreseeable implications of consenting. In the world of informed consent, therefore, the terms "voluntary" and "informed" are inextricably interrelated, making the term "voluntary informed consent" somewhat redundant.

6. Psychologists must "include in written and oral reports and consultations only information germane to the purpose for which the communication is made" (APA Ethical Standard 4.04, "Minimizing Intrusions on Privacy"). For counselors, "when circumstances require the disclosure of confidential information, only essential information is revealed" (American Counseling Association [ACA] Ethical Standard B.2.d, "Minimal Disclosure"). Social workers "should disclose the least amount of confidential information necessary to achieve the desired purpose; only information that is directly relevant to the purpose for which the disclosure is made should be revealed" (NASW Ethical Standard 1.07c, "Privacy and Confidentiality").

7. VandeCreek (2008), p. 373.

8. Ibid.

9. Ibid.

10. The American Association of Marriage and Family Therapy (AAMFT) does require that marriage and family therapists not disclose patient confidences "except by *written* authorization or waiver, or where mandated or permitted by law" (AAMFT Ethical Standard II-2.2 ("Confidentiality"), emphasis added.

11. Pope & Vasquez (2011), *Ethics in Psychotherapy and Counseling*, p. 282.

12. See, for example, Bennett, Bricklin, Harris, Knapp, VandeCreek, & Younggren (2006), *Assessing and Managing Risk in Psychological Practice*.

13. VandeCreek (2008).

14. Alleman (2001), "Personal, practical, and professional issues in providing managed mental health care," p. 418.

15. VandeCreek (2008), p. 373

16. Patients' Bill of Rights (1997), *Principles for the Provision Of Mental Health and Substance Abuse Treatment Services*, p. 1.

17. Davidson & Davidson (1996), "Confidentiality and managed care: Ethical and legal concerns," p. 212. This article presents a thorough treatment of some of the issues and concerns raised by these disclosures.

18. Davidson & Davidson (1996), p. 212.

19. The ACA Ethical Standard B.7.d requires as follows: "Counselors do not disclose confidential information that reasonably could lead to the identification of a research

participant unless they have obtained the prior consent of the person. Use of data derived from counseling relationships for purposes of training, research, or publication is confined to content that is disguised to ensure the anonymity of the individuals involved." ACA Ethical Standard B.7.e ("Agreement for Identification") similarly stipulates that "Identification of clients, students, or supervisees in a presentation or publication is permissible only when they have reviewed the material and agreed to its presentation or publication."

According to APA Ethical Standard 4.07 ("Use of Confidential Information for Didactic or Other Purposes"), "Psychologists do not disclose in their writings, lectures, or other public media, confidential, personally identifiable information concerning their clients/patients, students, research participants, organizational clients, or other recipients of their services that they obtained during the course of their work, unless (1) they take reasonable steps to disguise the person or organization, (2) the person or organization has consented in writing, or (3) there is legal authorization for doing so."

The NASW Ethics Code, in Ethical Standard 1.07 (p), stipulates that "Social workers should not disclose identifying information when discussing clients for teaching or training purposes unless the client has consented to disclosure of confidential information." Ethical Standard 1.07(k) requires that "Social workers should protect the confidentiality of clients when responding to requests from members of the media."

The APsyA Ethics Code similarly imposes differential requirements for professional presentations and public media presentations. Ethical Standard 4–10: "With regard for the person's dignity and privacy and with truly informed consent, it is ethical to present a patient to a scientific gathering if the confidentiality of the presentation is understood and accepted by the audience." Ethical Standard 4–11: "It is ethical to present a patient or former patient to a public gathering or to the news media only if the patient is fully informed of enduring loss of confidentiality, is competent, and consents in writing without coercion."

The AAMFT Ethics Code stipulates in Standard 2.3 that "Marriage and family therapists use client and/or clinical materials in teaching, writing, consulting, research, and public presentations only if a written waiver has been obtained … or when appropriate steps have been taken to protect client identity and confidentiality."

20. For example, see Blechner (2012, March), "Confidentiality: Against disguise; for consent."

21. For example, see Sieck (2012), "Obtaining clinical writing informed consent versus using client disguise and recommendations for practice."

22. For example, see Fischer (2012, March), "Comments on protecting clients about whom we write (and speak)."

23. Stephen Behnke, Director of the APA Ethics Office, notes some of the potential clinical complications: "Asking a client permission to disclose confidential information will likely have an effect on the client, whether done during a treatment or after the treatment has ended. Psychologists should be sensitive to how they ask for permission, and how the client experiences both the request and the knowledge that personal information is to be disclosed. If a psychologist uses disguise, the psychologist may want to consider whether the particular disguise interferes with the scientific or didactic value of presenting the information. Certain disguises, for example, may detract or mislead from the very point the psychologist wishes to make by virtue of how the disguises interact with the clinical material. In addition, psychologists may want to consider how a client who learns of a presentation

or publication would react to a disguise. As an example, clients have been known to react badly upon discovering that their gender, age or profession was altered, and have even concluded that the disguise reveals something about their psychologists' unspoken attitudes toward them" (Behnke [2005a], "Disclosing confidential information in consultations and for didactic purposes").

24. Blechner (2012, March), p. 16.

25. Woodhouse (2012, March), "Clinical writing: Additional ethical and practical issues," p. 22.

26. Barnett (2012, March), "Clinical writing about clients: Is informed consent sufficient?" p. 14.

27. This new guideline was recently added to the "Instruction to Authors" used by the journal *Psychotherapy.* See Samstag (2012, March), "Introduction to the special section on ethical issues in clinical writing," p. 2.

28. The list that follows was adapted from Sieck (2012), pp. 7–9. That article contains a detailed discussion of each item on the list, with considerations of how each should be weighed and considered in making a decision.

29. According to ACA Ethical Standard F.1.c ("Informed Consent and Client Rights"), "Supervisees provide clients with professional disclosure information and inform them of how the supervision process influences the limits of confidentiality. Supervisees make clients aware of who will have access to records of the counseling relationship and how these records will be used."

The APA Ethics Code, in Ethical Standard 10.01(c), requires that "When the therapist is a trainee and the legal responsibility for the treatment provided resides with the supervisor, the client/patient, as part of the informed consent procedure, is informed that the therapist is in training and is being supervised and is given the name of the supervisor."

30. The ACA Ethics Code, in Ethical Standard B.8.c, requires as follows: "When consulting with colleagues, counselors do not disclose confidential information that reasonably could lead to the identification of a client or other person or organization with whom they have a confidential relationship unless they have obtained the prior consent of the person or organization or the disclosure cannot be avoided. They disclose information only to the extent necessary to achieve the purposes of the consultation."

In almost identical language, the APA Ethics Code, in Ethical Standard 4.06 requires as follows: "When consulting with colleagues, (1) psychologists do not disclose confidential information that reasonably could lead to the identification of a client/patient, research participant, or other person or organization with whom they have a confidential relationship unless they have obtained the prior consent of the person or organization or the disclosure cannot be avoided, and (2) they disclose information only to the extent necessary to achieve the purposes of the consultation."

The NASW Ethics Code, in Ethical Standard 1.07(q) requires that "Social workers should not disclose identifying information when discussing clients with consultants unless the client has consented to disclosure of confidential information or there is a compelling need for such disclosure." Ethical Standard 2.02 further stipulates that "social workers should respect confidential information shared by colleagues in the course of their professional relationships and transactions. Social workers should ensure that such colleagues understand social workers' obligation to respect confidentiality and any exceptions related to it." Standard 2.05(c) provides that "when consulting with colleagues about clients, social workers should disclose the least amount of information necessary to achieve the purposes of the consultation."

Chapter 7: Step 4: Responding Ethically to Legal Demands for "Involuntary" Disclosure of Patient Information

1. The ethics code of every mental health profession contains an exception to the confidentiality rule that allows (but does not require) therapists to breach confidentiality in situations in which they are legally required to disclose confidential information. The wording of the exceptions will vary across profession. See a discussion of these differences in Part I, Chapter 1, in the subsection, "Exceptions to the Key Standard."

2. Knapp, Gottlieb, Berman, & Handelsman (2007), "When laws and ethics collide," p. 54.

3. "Civil disobedience," as used in this section, implies deliberate disobedience of a legal requirement and a willingness to accept the legal consequences of that action. This is in contrast to (1) ignorance of the law, (2) ignorance of the consequences of breaking the law, or (3) an attempt to disobey the law "under the table" in the hope of not suffering any consequences.

Although the mental health professions do not officially condone civil disobedience, therapists who break the law *in behalf of patient confidentiality* are not likely to incur ethical censure (see American Psychiatric Association Committee on Confidentiality [1987], "Guidelines on confidentiality").

In presenting their structured decision-making process for responding to ethical-legal conflicts, Knapp et al. (2007) include the option of civil disobedience: "If the conflict between the law and ethics is real and cannot be avoided, psychologists should either obey the law in a manner that minimizes harm to their ethical values or adhere to their ethical values in a manner that minimizes the violation of the law. In either situation, psychologists should anticipate and be prepared to live with the consequences of their decisions."

Bollas and Sundelson (1995), in their book, *The New Informants,* explicitly argue for civil disobedience. They do so not on ethical grounds but on the basis of the clinical necessity for unconditional confidentiality; but they are very clear about the potential legal penalties.

4. Knapp et al., 2007, pp. 57–58.

5. The U.S. Supreme Court strengthened federal privilege protections in their 1996 *Jaffee v. Redmond* decision. Ethically speaking, the important thing about the case is that it reached the Supreme Court only because Karen Beyer, a clinical social worker, refused to disclose information confided by her therapy client, even though this placed her at risk for being jailed for contempt of court. (See Beyer [2000], "First person: *Jaffe v. Redmond* therapist speaks.") Although the *Jaffee* decision applies only in federal court cases and allows some exceptions, it had broad national impact, and it is often quoted by those who are lobbying for better privilege protections at the state level.

6. See Monaghan, P. (2012, February 19), "Our storehouse of knowledge about social movements is going to be left bare."

7. For therapists who are unfamiliar with this distinction, this would be a good time to review the section of Chapter 1: "Making Ethical Distinctions Between Legally Required and Voluntary Disclosures." According to Stephen Behnke, director of the APA Ethics Office, hard ethical questions arise in response to a situation in which disclosure is legally allowed but the client does not consent to the disclosure. "In this instance, the law says to

the psychologist, 'Even though your client does not consent to your releasing this information, you may nevertheless do so.' This situation will call for both ethical and clinical consultation." (Behnke & Kincherff [2002, May], "Must a psychologist report past child abuse?" p. 91.

8. As an aid in deciding where to insert state laws into the model, consult the color-coded version provided by the Center for Ethical Practice (2010) at http://www.centerforethicalpractice.org/EthicalPracticeModelAnnotated.

9. The American Counseling Association (ACA) and APA Ethics Codes do not require therapists to confront or report colleague misconduct if doing so would involve violating patient confidentiality. It is also important to note that, unless they have the client's consent (obtained at intake or later), psychologists have no ethical basis for disclosing confidential information to report abuse or misconduct unless so required by law. See Behnke (2006, March), "Responding to a colleague's ethical transgressions," and Knapp & VandeCreek (2006), *Practical Ethics for Psychologists*.

10. For a seminal book on prediction of patient dangerousness, see Monahan (1981), *The Clinical Prediction of Violent Behavior.* "For his more recent discussion on the topic, see Monahan (1993), "Limiting therapist exposure to *Tarasoff* liability: Guidelines for risk containment."

11. For an excellent and extensive discussion of the ethical and legal issues related to the duty to protect, see Werth, Welfel, & Benjamin (Eds.) (2009), *The Duty to Protect: Ethical, Legal, and Professional Considerations for Mental Health Professionals*. Their chart of state requirements (pp. 12–15) reflects the wide range of forms that this mandate can take across states and disciplines:

"Thirty-two states currently mandate a duty to protect regarding professionals' responsibility with dangerous clients. Eighteen states or provinces do not mandate any particular action when clients disclose violent intent to their therapists. They permit a breach of confidentiality but do not require it. The law of 14 jurisdictions remains silent as to whether a duty to warn or protect exists. In some jurisdictions, a duty to protect (as opposed to a duty to warn") also exists with clients who are dangerous to themselves. A few jurisdictions specify different duties depending on the discipline of the professional." (p. 4)

12. As noted in Chapter 4, research indicates that up to 75% of therapists are misinformed about what is legally required in their own state regarding danger to self and/or others (see Welfel, Werth, & Benjamin [2009], Introduction to the Duty to Protect, p. 4.) It is important that in Step 1 therapists prepare by learning exactly what the legal options are in their own state.

13. See, for example, Beck (1990), The Basic Issues, and Bollas & Sundelson (1995).

14. Werth, Welfel, Benjamin, & Sales (2009), "Practice and policy responses to the duty to protect," and Welfel, Werth, & Benjamin (2009).

15. For adolescent therapy cases, Kraft (2005) provided an *Adolescent Consent Form* that can be used for planning and structuring this initial conversation. As with all informed consent forms, it must be revised and personalized to match each therapist's actual policies.

16. See, for example, the statutory changes in Virginia following the Virginia Tech campus tragedy, including "required disclosure of health information during the commitment process to facilitate informed decisions" (Bonnie et al. [2009], "Mental health system transformation after the Virginia Tech tragedy," p. 801).

17. Pomerantz and Handelsman, in a 2004 article, "Informed consent revisited: An updated written question format," revised their earlier informed consent questionnaire to emphasize the importance of providing sufficient information to help prospective clients make informed decisions about whether or not to seek third-party reimbursement. For other extensive discussions of the informed consent conversation with managed care patients, see Acuff et al. (1999), "Considerations for ethical practice in managed care"; Appelbaum (1993), "Legal liability and managed care"; Bilynsky & Vernaglia (1998), "The ethical practice of psychology in a managed-care framework"; Cooper & Gottlieb (2000), "Ethical issues with managed care: Challenges facing counseling psychology"; Younggren (2000), "Is managed care really just another, unethical Model T?"

For the possibility of amending the provisions in provider contracts, see Koman & Harris (2005), Contracting with Managed Care Organizations. For a discussion of preparing for managed care audits, see APA Practice Organization, Legal and Regulatory Affairs Staff (2005b, November), "A matter of law: Managed care record audits." For a glossary of terms used in managed care contracts, see Austrin (1999), *Managed Health Care Simplified: A Glossary of Terms.*

18. Henderson (2010, March 19), "Mental health and final security clearances." Also see Baker (2008, May 1), "DOD changes security clearance question on mental health."

19. See APA Government Relations and Communications Staff (2006), "Patriot Act renewal tightens medical records safeguards," and Munsey (2006), "More protection for psychologists' records in renewed Patriot Act."

The APA advises that it is important not to disclose too quickly: "Obtain legal advice or assistance in responding to an order" from the Foreign Intelligence Surveillance Act (FISA) court (APA, Government Relations and Communications Staff, 2006, p. 1). The Patriot Act now contains safeguards that psychologists should be prepared to invoke if someone demands client records under authority of that Act (Munsey, 2006). As amended in 2006, the Patriot Act stipulates that FBI agents must "show reasonable, factual grounds to believe that the records sought ... are relevant to a terrorism investigation and ... to the activities of a suspected terrorist or person in contact with a suspected terrorist"; they must provide a judge's' order specifying exactly what the court is ordering the psychologist to produce; and they must allow the person "to consult with an attorney and file a challenge to a records request with a FISA court judge" (Munsey, 2006, p. 15).

20. Bennett, Bricklin, Harris, Knapp, VandeCreek, & Younggren (2006), *Assessing and Managing Risk in Psychological Practice: An Individualized Approach*, p. 111.

21. This may be the single best piece of advice on the subject! It was emphasized by Koocher and Keith-Spiegel in early (1998) editions of their excellent ethics text. See Keith-Spiegel & Koocher (1985), *Ethics in Psychology: Professional Standards and Cases,* p. 74, and Koocher & Keith-Spiegel (1998), *Ethics in Psychology and the Mental Health Professions: Standards and Cases*, p. 130.

22. APA Practice Organization, Legal and Regulatory Affairs Staff (2008, December), *How to Deal with a Subpoena,* p. 3.

23. Koocher & Keith-Spiegel (2008), pp. 209–210.

24. Bennett et al. (2006), p. 111.

25. See Chapter 4 on "Preparing." Endnote 11 for that chapter cites examples of state-specific advice about responding to subpoenas. Also see Koocher (2005), Dealing with Subpoenas, as well as chapters in professional ethics texts on this subject.

26. See endnote 21, above.

27. APA Practice Organization, Legal and Regulatory Affairs Staff (2008, December), p. 3.

28. Ibid.

29. Bennett et al. (2006), p. 111.

30. Younggren & Harris (2008), "Can you keep a secret? Confidentiality in psychotherapy," p. 599.

31. Baturin, Knapp, & Tepper (2003, August), "Practical considerations when responding to subpoenas and court orders," pp. 1–2 (emphasis added).

32. Younggren & Harris (2008), p. 599.

Chapter 8: Step 5: Avoiding Preventable Breaches of Confidentiality

1. Fisher (2008b), "Protecting confidentiality rights: The need for an ethical practice model."

2. Fisher (2012), Confidentiality and Record Keeping, p. 355.

3. ACA Ethical Standard B.3.d ("Third Party Payers"), p. 8.

4. NASW Ethical Standard 1.07h ("Privacy and Confidentiality"), p. 11.

5. See, for example, Smith (1981), "Unfinished business with informed consent procedures."

6. See Acuff et al. (1999), "Considerations for ethical practice in managed care," and Nagy (1993), "Applying the new Ethics Code to practice."

7. Beck (1990), The Basic Issues. In *Confidentiality Versus The Duty to Protect: Foreseeable Harm in the Practice of Psychiatry*, p. 5 (emphasis added).

8. See NASW Ethical Standard 1.07d ("Privacy and Confidentiality"), p. 10: "Social workers should inform clients, to the extent possible, about the disclosure of confidential information and the potential consequences, when feasible before the disclosure is made."

9. Acuff et al. (1999), p. 570.

10. Koocher & Keith-Spiegel (2008), *Ethics in Psychology and the Mental Health Professions*.

11. VandeCreek (2008), "Considering confidentiality within broader theoretical frameworks," p. 373.

12. Fisher (2012), p. 354.

13. Fisher (2009b), "Replacing 'Who is the client?' with a different ethical question." Note that APA requires this informed consent discussion in Ethical Standards 3.07 ("Third Party Requests for Services") and 3.11 ("Psychological Services Delivered to or Through Organizations").

14. APA Ethical Standard 4.04 ("Minimizing Intrusions on Privacy") requires that psychologists discuss confidential information "only for appropriate scientific or professional purposes, and only with persons clearly concerned with such matters." The ACA, in Ethical Standard B.3.("Information Shared With Others"), requires that (a) "Counselors make every effort to ensure that privacy and confidentiality of clients are maintained by subordinates, including employees, supervisees, students, clerical assistants, and volunteers;" and that (c) "Counselors discuss confidential information only in settings in which they can reasonably ensure client privacy." The NASW stipulates in Ethical Standard 1.07(g) ("Privacy and Confidentiality") that "Social workers should not discuss confidential information in any setting unless privacy can be ensured. Social workers should not discuss confidential

information in public or semipublic areas such as hallways, waiting rooms, elevators, and restaurants."

15. Fisher (2012), p. 353.

16. From NASW: Ethical Standard 1.07i ("Privacy & Confidentiality"), p. 11: "Social workers should not discuss confidential information in any setting unless privacy can be ensured. Social workers should not discuss confidential information in public or semipublic areas such as hallways, waiting rooms, elevators, and restaurants." From ACA Ethical Standard B.3.c ("Confidential Settings"), "Counselors discuss confidential information only in settings in which they can reasonably ensure client privacy."

17. Pope & Vasquez (2011), *Ethics in Psychotherapy and Counseling,* pp. 278–279.

18. Behnke (2007c, May), "Gossiping about patients," p 70.

19. Pope & Vasquez (2011), p. 279.

20. Dyer (1988), *Ethics and Psychiatry,* p. 64.

21. Woody (1999), "Domestic violations of confidentiality," Baker & Patterson (1990), "The first to know: A systemic analysis of confidentiality and the therapist's family."

22. Fisher (2012).

23. Baker & Patterson (1990), pp. 295, 299.

24. ACA Ethical Standard B.2.d. ("Minimal Disclosure").

25. APA Ethical Standard 4.04 ("Minimizing Intrusions on Privacy").

26. NASW Ethical Standards 1.07c ("Privacy and Confidentiality") and 2.05c ("Consultation").

27. Fisher (2012), p. 353–354.

28. Knapp & VandeCreek (2006), *Practical Ethics for Psychologists: A Positive Approach,* p. 115.

29. Fisher (2012), p. 355.

30. Knapp (2002), "Accidental breaches of confidentiality," p. 6.

31. Fisher (2009a), "Ethics-based training for non-clinical staff in mental health settings." Also see Appendix IV for summary of HIPAA training requirements.

32. Fisher (2009a), Knapp (2002). Note that if maintaining confidentiality is a condition of employment, this should be explained at hiring and included in the written employment contract.

33. Center for Ethical Practice (2009), Staff Training: Sample Documents.

34. ACA Ethical Standard A.12 ("Technology Applications") and Ethical Standard B.3.e ("Transmitting Confidential Information").

35. APA Ethical Standards 3.10 ("Informed Consent"), 4.01 ("Maintaining Confidentiality"), and 4.02c ("Discussing the Limits of Confidentiality").

36. APA (2007), "Record keeping guidelines."

37. NASW Ethical Standards 1.03 ("Informed Consent"), and 1.07(l) and 1.07(m) ("Privacy and Confidentiality").

38. HIPAA (1996), 45 C. F. R. § 164.

39. Fisher (2009b).

40. See Fisher (2010b), "Which hat are you wearing? Roles and ethical responsibilities of mental health professionals in court cases." (The chart is reproduced in Appendix VI.)

41. Fisher (2012), p. 355. Also see APA and American Board of Forensic Psychology (2011, August 20), *Specialty Guidelines for Forensic Psychology*; Berson (2005), "Dual relationships for the psychologist when custody is an issue"; Strasburger, Gutheil, & Brodsky

(1997), "On wearing two hats: Role conflict in serving as both psychotherapist and expert witness."

42. For a review of the potentially conflicting confidentiality responsibilities, see Fisher (2010b).

43. This is easy to understand and explain to patients by using the analogy of suing someone for causing a car accident that results in a broken leg. Such a suit would likely result in a subpoena to the physician to obtain copies of the x-rays (to determine whether the leg was broken), as well as records of prior treatment (to determine whether the leg was broken prior to the accident).

44. See samples at Fisher (2004), "Sample non-subpoena contract."

45. For example, regarding misunderstandings about what is legally required in situations of potential harm to others, see Werth, Welfel, Benjamin, & Salacka (2007, December), "Duty to warn."

46. Bennett, Bricklin, Harris, Knapp, VandeCreek, & Younggren (2006), *Assessing and Managing Risk in Psychological Practice: An Individualized Approach*; Harris & Younggren (2011), "But that's what the lawyer told me."

47. Fisher (2012), p. 356.

48. HIPAA (1996), 45 C.F.R §164.502(a)(1).

49. Virginia Code, Statutes § 32.1–127.1:03 (2012).

50. Fisher (2012), p. 356.

51. Cullari (2001), The Client's Perspective of Psychotherapy, p. 104.

52. VandeCreek (2008), p. 373.

53. VandeCreek (2008), p. 372.

Chapter 9: Step 6: Talking About Confidentiality

1. Pope & Vasquez (2011), *Ethics in Psychotherapy and Counseling*, p. 89.

2. Regarding legal information, Appendix III gives examples of laws affecting confidentiality, and Appendix IV provides links to information about the federal HIPAA regulations. For professional resources, see Appendix VII. For discussion of how to obtain information about state laws, see Chapter 2, endnote 2.

3. As described in Part I, Bollas & Sundelson (1995) in their book, *The New Informants,* are very clear in their description of the potential legal and financial consequences of the "absolute confidentiality" position, and they offer detailed recommendations about how therapists and psychoanalysts can provide mutual financial, emotional, and clinical support in dealing with those consequences.

4. Center for Ethical Practice (2010), "Ethical Practice Model + state laws + HIPAA."

5. The ethical standards related to peer confrontation are extensive, but they are reproduced here in full because they are important for considering the conversations discussed in this section.

Psychologists have two relevant standards: Ethical Standard 1.04 ("Informal Resolution of Ethical Violations"): "When psychologists believe that there may have been an ethical violation by another psychologist, they attempt to resolve the issue by bringing it to the attention of that individual, if an informal resolution appears appropriate and the intervention does not violate any confidentiality rights that may be involved." Also Ethical Standard 1.05 ("Reporting Ethical Violations"): "If an apparent ethical violation has substantially harmed or is likely to substantially harm a person or organization and is not appropriate for informal resolution under Standard 1.04, Informal Resolution of Ethical Violations, or is not resolved properly in that fashion, psychologists take further action appropriate to the situation. Such action might include referral to state or national committees on professional ethics, to state licensing boards, or to the appropriate institutional authorities. This standard does not apply when an intervention would violate confidentiality rights or when psychologists have been retained to review the work of another psychologist whose professional conduct is in question."

Social workers have a four-paragraph Ethical Standard 2.11 ("Unethical Conduct of Colleagues"): "(a) Social workers should take adequate measures to discourage, prevent, expose, and correct the unethical conduct of colleagues. (b) Social workers should be knowledgeable about established policies and procedures for handling concerns about colleagues' unethical behavior. Social workers should be familiar with national, state, and local procedures for handling ethics complaints. These include policies and procedures created by NASW, licensing and regulatory bodies, employers, agencies, and other professional organizations. (c) Social workers who believe that a colleague has acted unethically should seek resolution by discussing their concerns with the colleague when feasible and when such discussion is likely to be productive. (d) When necessary, social workers who believe that a colleague has acted unethically should take action through appropriate formal channels (such as contacting a state licensing board or regulatory body, an NASW committee on inquiry, or other professional ethics committees)."

Counselors have the most extensive standards on this issue under Ethics Code Section H.2, "Suspected Violations." Ethical Standard H.2.a ("Ethical Behavior Expected"): "Counselors expect colleagues to adhere to the *ACA Code of Ethics*. When counselors possess knowledge that raises doubts as to whether another counselor is acting in an ethical manner, they take appropriate action." Ethical Standard H.2.b ("Informal Resolution"): "When counselors have reason to believe that another counselor is violating or has violated an ethical standard, they attempt first to resolve the issue informally with the other counselor if feasible, provided such action does not violate confidentiality rights that may be involved." Ethical Standard H.2.c ("Reporting Ethical Violations"): "If an apparent violation has substantially harmed, or is likely to substantially harm, a person or organization and is not appropriate for informal resolution or is not resolved properly, counselors take further action appropriate to the situation. Such action might include referral to state or national committees on professional ethics, voluntary national certification bodies, state licensing boards, or to the appropriate institutional authorities. This standard does not apply when an intervention would violate confidentiality rights or when counselors have been retained to review the work of another counselor whose professional conduct is in question." Ethical Standard H.2.d ("Consultation"): "When uncertain as to whether a particular situation or course of action may be in violation of the *ACA Code of Ethics*, counselors consult with other counselors who are knowledgeable about ethics and the *ACA Code of Ethics*, with colleagues, or with appropriate authorities."

6. Gonsiorek (2009), "Informed consent can solve some confidentiality dilemmas, but others remain," p. 374. In this article, Gonsiorek lists inadequate training as the first of four sources of the confidentiality problems now faced by the mental health professions.

7. Fry, vanBark, Weinman, Kitchener, & Lang (1997), "Ethical transgressions of psychology graduate students: Critical incidents with implications for training."

8. Fisher (2012), Confidentiality and Record Keeping, p. 357.

9. Appendix II reflects the similarity. Note that all mental health professions have ethical standards that include a confidentiality rule, safeguards that apply or elaborate upon that rule, informed consent requirements, peer monitoring requirements, guidelines for responding to ethical/legal conflicts, and specific exceptions to the confidentiality rule.

10. Fisher (2008b), "Protecting confidentiality rights," p. 6.

11. Center for Ethical Practice (2010).

12. Gonsiorek (2009), p. 375.

13. The chart in Appendix VI is reproduced online at Fisher (2010b) as "Which hat are you wearing? Roles and ethical responsibilities of mental health professionals in court cases," at http://www.centerforethicalpractice.org/CourtroomRoles.htm

14. American Psychiatric Association (APsyA) Ethics Code, Section 3. The NASW Ethics Code addresses this possibility less directly in Ethical Standard 5.01c: "Social workers should contribute time and professional expertise to activities that promote respect for the value, integrity, and competence of the social work profession. These activities may include … legislative testimony, presentations in the community, and participation in their professional organizations." Although the current (2002) version of the American Psychological Association (APA) Ethics Code does not address the issue, earlier versions did so. See, for example, the aspirational statement in the 1992 Ethics Code's Principle on Social Responsibility: "Psychologists comply with the law and encourage the development of law and social policy that serve the interests of their patients and clients and the public."

Chapter 10: Clinical Record Keeping

1. Reamer (2001, October), "Documentation in social work: Evolving ethical and risk-management standards."

2. APA Ethical Standard 4.01 ("Maintaining Confidentiality").

3. APA Ethical Standard 6.02 ("Maintenance, Dissemination, and Disposal of Confidential Records of Professional and Scientific Work.")

4. NASW Ethical Standard 1.07(l) ("Privacy and Confidentiality").

5. APA (2007), "Record keeping guidelines."

6. Fisher (2012), Confidentiality and Record Keeping.

7. Morgan & Polowy (2001), *Social Workers and Clinical Notes*. (See link to ordering info at http://www.socialworkers.org/ldf/lawnotes/notes.asp. Also available from NASW is a practice update, "Documenting Patient Care in the Private Practice Setting," but this is available online only to members of the NASW Private Practice Section.)

8. Mitchell (2007), *Documentation in Counseling Records: An Ethical, Legal, and Clinical Overview.*

9. Robb (2004), *Client Records: Keep or Toss?*

10. Bennett et al. (2006), *Assessing and Managing Risk in Psychological Practice.*

11. Marine (undated), *Are Your Records Protected?*

12. Welch (1998), "Walking the documentation tightrope."

13. Fisher (2012), pp. 357–358.

14. See, for example, Virginia Code, Statutes § 32.1–127.1:01 (2012), "Record Storage."

15. For links to the complete text of the HIPAA regulations, as well as interpretations of them, see http://www.centerforethicalpractice.org/links-to-HIPAA-resources. Extensive

information about implementation of the HIPAA regulations is available on websites of the national professional associations.

16. ACA Ethical Standard A.1.b. ("Records").

17. APA (2007).

18. Reamer (2001), p. 7.

19. Davis & Younggren (2009), "Ethical competence in psychotherapy termination."

20. Welch (1998), p. 2.

21. Barnett (2009), "Ethics for psychologists: Documentation and the use of the internet," p. 12.

22. Welch (1998), p. 1.

23. Knapp & VandeCreek (2006), *Practical Ethics for Psychologists: A Positive Approach,* p. 126.

24. Gutheil & Hilliard (2001), "'Don't write me down':" Legal, clinical, and risk-management aspects of patients' requests that therapists not keep notes or records," p. 157.

25. APA (2007), p. 996.

26. Bennett et al. (2006).

27. For more discussion of this issue, see Miller (2000), "Protecting privacy with the absence of records."

28. United States Department of Health and Human Services (USDHHS) (2007), *Standards for Privacy of Individually Identifiable Health Information. B. Definitions,* p. 20.

29. USDHHS (2007), p. 23.

30. See HIPAA, 45 C.F.R. § 164.508(a)(2).

31. In APA (2007), see p. 1000, footnote 10.

32. Coleman (2005, May), "Practice update: Psychotherapy notes and reimbursement claims," p. 1.

33. Gutheil (1980), "Paranoia and progress notes: A guide to forensically informed psychiatric recordkeeping."

34. Bennett et al. (2006), p. 119.

35. Fisher (2012), p. 359.

36. Dunlap (2000), "The contentious matter of 'psychotherapy notes' under HIPAA."

37. ACA Ethical Standard A.2 ("Informed Consent: Types of Information Needed").

38. For example, see the HIPAA regulations, as well as allowed fees for providing copies at 45 CFR 164.524.

39. ACA Ethical Standard B.6 ("Confidentiality of Records").

40. APA Ethical Standard 6.02 ("Maintenance, Dissemination, and Disposal of Confidential Records of Professional and Scientific Work").

41. NASW Ethical Standard 1.07(l) ("Privacy and Confidentiality").

42. APsyA Ethics Code, Section 4, Statement 1.

43. For an example of federal government encouragement to establish a national electronic patient records system by 2014, see APA Practice Organization, Government Relations Staff (2007), *The Health Information Technology for Economic and Clinical Health Act (HITECH).* For indications of how this might affect therapists' HIPAA contracts with business associates, see APA Practice Organization (2010), "Instructions for HITECH amendments to business associates contracts."

44. Sanbar (2007), "Medical records: Paper and electronic." Also see Tracey (1998), "Be aware of malpractice risks when using electronic office devices."

45. APA Ethical Standard 6.02b.

46. APA (2007).

47. ACA Ethical Standard A.12.g ("Technology Applications).

48. NASW (2005b), *Standards for Technology and Social Work Practice.*

49. For example, see Nicastro (2011, May 3), "Large patient information breach list climbs"; and Spragins & Hager (1997, June 30), "Naked before the world: Will your medical secrets be safe in a new national databank?"

50. Fisher (2012), p. 360.

51. Little has been written so far about the confidentiality issues involved in using the "cloud" for mental health records, as opposed to general medical records. Those considering this technology might consider reviewing resources such as the following: American Psychological Association Practice Organization, Legal & Regulatory Affairs Staff (2011, October 14). *Basics of Cloud Computing*; Klein, C.A. (2011), "Cloudy confidentiality: Clinical and legal implications of cloud computing in health care"; Kuo, A. M-H. (2011), "Opportunities and challenges of cloud computing to improve health care services."

52. Devereaux & Gottlieb (2012, In Press), "Record keeping in the cloud: Ethical considerations," pp. 5–6.

53. ACA Ethical Standard C.2.b ("Counselor Incapacitation or Termination of Practice") states that "When counselors leave a practice, they follow a prepared plan for transfer of clients and files. Counselors prepare and disseminate to an identified colleague or 'records custodian' a plan for the transfer of clients and files in the case of their incapacitation, death or termination of practice." ACA Ethical Standard A.2.b ("Informed Consent: Types of Information Needed") requires that "Counselors explicitly explain to clients ... continuation of services upon the incapacitation or death of a counselor." See discussion of this new ethical requirement for counselors at http://www.counseling.org/Publications/CounselingTodayArticles.aspx?AGuid=5533c9ab-318f-480b-abfb-4454622b9309.

54. NASW Ethical Standard 1.07(o) ("Privacy and Confidentiality"): "Social workers should take reasonable precautions to protect client confidentiality in the event of the social worker's termination of practice, incapacitation, or death."

55. APA Ethical Standard 6.02(c) ("Maintenance, Dissemination, and Disposal of Confidential Records of Professional and Scientific Work").

56. See Koocher (2003), "Ethical and legal issues in professional practice transitions," and McGee (2003), "Observations on the retirement of professional psychologists."

57. For discussion of what information professional wills should contain, see Holloway (2003, February), "Professional will: A responsible thing to do," and Pope & Vasquez (2011), chapter 8, "*Creating a Professional Will.*" For a sample professional will, see Ragusea (2002), "A professional living will for psychologists."

58. For example, the APA Record Keeping Guidelines (2007) recommend that "in the absence of a superseding requirement, psychologists may consider retaining full records until 7 years after the last date of service delivery for adults or until 3 years after a minor reaches the age of majority, whichever is later" (p. 999); and the APA Insurance Trust recommends retaining "the originals of all patient records" according to those guidelines or in a manner consistent with state laws (Bennett et al., 2006, p. 216). In contrast, "the NASW

Insurance Trust strongly recommends retaining records *indefinitely*" (Robb, 2004, *Client Records: Keep or Toss?,* p. 1).

Legal requirements about record retention can be imposed by licensing boards or state statutes, and these will vary state by state. Finally, legally binding provider contracts often stipulate retention times, sometimes requiring that records be retained for the duration of the contract or beyond.

59. APA Ethical Standard 6.02a ("Maintenance, Dissemination, and Disposal of Confidential Records").

60. ACA Ethical Standard B.6.g ("Storage and Disposal After Termination").

61. See, for example, APA (2007), "Record keeping guidelines."

62. United States Department of Health and Human Services (USDHHS) (2008), *Guidance to Render Unsecured Protected Health Information Unusable, Unreadable, or Indecipherable to Unauthorized Individuals,* p. 1.

63. National Institute of Standards and Technology (NIST) (2006), Guidelines for Media Sanitization, p. 1.

64. APA (2007), p. 1002.

65. Robb (2004), p. 2.

Chapter 11: Confidentiality With Specific Patient Populations

1. To avoid that ambiguity in this book, except when quoting someone else, we have used the term "patient" to refer to a person receiving therapy, counseling, or other direct clinical service. We use the term "client" to refer to others with whom therapists interact professionally, but who are not themselves receiving therapy (e.g., individual or organizational consultation client; contracted client, such as an attorney or agency with whom a mental health professional has a contract to provide assessments, therapy, or other clinical services to another party; collateral personnel who attend sessions with therapy clients but are not themselves receiving therapy services; etc.). As so defined, not all "clients" have the same confidentiality rights as therapy patients, and the ethical obligations owed to these clients are often different from the ethical duties owed to therapy patients.

Note that this differs from the usage in ethics codes. The NASW Ethics Code uses the term "client" to refer to "individuals, families, groups, organizations, and communities" and does not use the term "patient" at all. The ACA Ethics Code similarly uses the term "client" throughout. The APA Ethics Code uses the term "client/patient." The APsyA Code uses only the term "patient."

2. Fisher (2009b), "Replacing 'Who is the client?' with a different ethical question," p. 5.

3. Knapp & VandeCreek (2006), *Practical Ethics for Psychologists: A Positive Approach.*

4. NASW Ethical Standard 1.07 ("Privacy and Confidentiality"), paragraph f.

5. APA (2007), "Record keeping guidelines," p. 1001, "Multiple Client Records" [emphasis added].

6. Fisher (2012), Confidentiality and Record Keeping.

7. APA Public Interest Initiatives (2011), "Potential problems for psychologists working with the area of interpersonal violence," paragraph 5.

8. APA Insurance Trust (2006), *Sample Outpatient Services Agreement for Collaterals.*

9. For example, "Psychologists working with couples or families are required to clarify, at the outset, "(1) which of the individuals are clients/patients and (2) the relationship the

psychologist will have with each person. This clarification includes the psychologist's role and the probable uses of the services provided or the information obtained" (APA Ethical Standard 10.02, "Therapy Involving Couples or Families").

Similarly, counselors must clarify, at the outset, "which person or persons are clients and the nature of the relationships the counselor will have with each involved person... Counselors clearly define who is considered 'the client' and discuss expectations and limitations of confidentiality" (ACA Ethical Standards A.7, "Multiple Clients," and B.4.b, "Couples and Family Counseling").

Social workers providing services to families or couples must "clarify with all parties which individuals will be considered clients and the nature of social workers' professional obligations to the various individuals who are receiving services... Social workers should seek agreement among the parties involved concerning each individual's right to confidentiality" (NASW Ethical Standard 1.06, "Conflicts of Interest," and 1.07, "Privacy and Confidentiality").

Marriage and family therapists have an ethics code that presumes the therapist will have interactions with multiple parties who are related to each other. Their ethics code stipulates that "when providing couple, family or group treatment, the therapist does not disclose information outside the treatment context without a written authorization from each individual competent to execute a waiver. In the context of couple, family or group treatment, the therapist may not reveal any individual's confidences to others in the client unit without the prior written permission of that individual" (AAMFT, Principle 2, "Confidentiality," Section 2.2). *Note*: If the therapist has a policy of revealing one participant's confidences to others, consent to accept the limits of confidentiality imposed by this policy should be obtained in writing at intake, before the therapy begins.

10. For a detailed discussion of ethical and clinical implications of some of these options, see Chapter 2, "Confidentiality Traps" in Weeks, Odell, & Methven (2005), *If Only I Had Known ... Avoiding Common Mistakes in Couple Therapy.* Also see Gottlieb (1996), Some Ethical Implications of Relational Diagnoses; Kuo (2009), "Secrets or no secrets: Confidentiality in couple therapy"; and Patten, Barnett, & Houlihan (1991), "Ethics in marital and family therapy: a review of the literature."

11. Knapp and VandeCreek (2006) include a discussion about private conversation initiated by one party when others are not present, suggesting that therapists must weigh the clinical importance of the private communication to the therapy when making decisions about its confidentiality:

Some of the information obtained from private conversations deals with other family members; other information deals only with the individual... Sometimes family members reveal information privately because they fear engendering anger or embarrassment with other family members but believe that the psychologist needs to know this information. At other times they want to develop a special alliance with the psychologist to increase their influence within therapy. Psychologists disagree on how to handle these kinds of situations. Some receive and use information from private conversations; others do not. (p. 117)

Ethically speaking, however, the important thing is for the therapist to inform all parties in advance about exactly what the rules will be in such circumstances. If the policy is that the therapist will disclose to other parties at his or her discretion, then that is part of what all parties must understand when giving consent to receive services.

12. Gottlieb (1996).

13. Kuo (2009).

14. Weeks et al. (2005).

15. Fisher (2012); Knapp & VandeCreek (2006).

16. Gottlieb (1996).

17. APA (2005), *A Matter of Law: Privacy Rights of Minor Patients,* p. 2.

18. Under HIPAA, the parent or guardian ordinarily exercises the minor's rights (e.g., receives the "Notice of Privacy Practices," gives consent for releasing records, has the right to access or amend records, etc.). But the minors' legal status under state law can change that: "[I]n the area of minors' rights to confidentiality, the [HIPAA] Privacy Rule determines who controls the child's privacy rights by looking to certain issues under state law. One of these issues is whether the law allows a minor to consent to treatment. *If a minor has consented to treatment under a state law that allows for it, the Privacy Rule generally lets the minor exercise his or her own privacy rights"* (APA, 2005, p. 2, emphasis added.) In other words, under HIPAA, that minor has essentially the same confidentiality rights as an adult.

19. Behnke (2007a, February), "Adolescents and confidentiality: Letter from a reader."

20. Knapp & VandeCreek (2006), p. 102. Giving "truly informed" consent would mean that the minor had the capacity to understand the explanatory information that was provided before giving consent.

21. Fisher (2008b) described this process as obtaining "informed assent" (p. 9). The process ethically required in this circumstance is described in APA Ethical Standard 3.10b ("Informed Consent"), in ACA Ethical Standard A.2.d ("Inability to Give Consent"), and in NASW Ethical Standards 1.03c ("Informed Consent") and 5.02f ("Evaluation and Research").

22. APA Practice Organization (2011), "Good practice: Working with children and adolescents," p. 4.

23. APA Practice Organization, Legal and Regulatory Affairs Staff (2005a, June), "A matter of law: Privacy rights of minors."

24. See, for example, Beeman & Scott (1991), "Therapists' attitudes toward psychotherapy informed consent with adolescents."

25. Fisher (2002), "Ethical issues."

26. For example, see sample form by Kraft (2005), *Sample Adolescent Informed Consent Form.*

27. See Licht & Younggren (2006), "Guidelines for treating children in high-conflict divorce."

28. Fisher (2012), p. 363.

29. Bennett et al. (2006), *Assessing and Managing Risk in Psychological Practice*, p. 95.

30. Fisher (2004), "Sample non-subpoena contract."

31. Fisher (2009b), p. 3, citing Fisher (2002).

32. Behnke (2005b), "Letter from a reader regarding a minor client and confidentiality"; Behnke & Warner (2002, March), "Confidentiality in the treatment of adolescents."

33. The ACA Ethics Code states that "counselors have an obligation to review in writing and verbally with clients the rights and responsibilities of both the counselor and the client" (ACA [2005] Section A.2, "Informed Consent in the Counseling Relationship"). Although

other professions do not require that a written informed consent document be part of this initial conversation, it is highly recommended (see Chapters 4 and 5).

34. APA Practice Organization (2011, Winter).

35. APA (2007), p. 997. The APA has also provided guidelines for evaluations in legal matters of child protection and child custody. See APA Committee on Professional Practice & Standards (1998), *Guidelines for Psychological Evaluations in Child Protection Matters* and (2009), *Guidelines for Child Custody Evaluations in Family Law Proceedings*. Both have recommendations about confidentiality decisions with minors.

36. Zarit & Zarit (1996), "Ethical considerations in the treatment of older adults," p. 275.

37. APA Working Group on the Older Adult (1998), "What practitioners should know about working with older adults," p. 425.

38. APA Insurance Trust (2006); Fisher (2009b); Zarit & Zarit (1996).

39. APA Ethical Standard 3.10 ("Informed Consent").

40. ACA Ethical Standard A.2.d. ("Inability to Give Consent").

41. APA Working Group on the Older Adult (1998), p. 425.

42. Bergeron & Grey (2003), "Ethical dilemmas of reporting suspected elder abuse."

43. APA Ethical Standard 10.03 ("Group Therapy").

44. ACA Ethical Standard B.4.a ("Group Work").

45. NASW Ethical Standard 1.07(f) ("Privacy and Confidentiality").

46. See Roback, Purdonn, Ochoa, & Bloch (1993), "Effect of professional affiliation on group therapists' confidentiality attitudes and behaviors."

47. Lasky & Riva (2006), "Confidentiality and privileged communication in group psychotherapy," p. 455.

48. Roback, Moore, Bloch, & Shelton (1996), "Confidentiality in group psychotherapy: Empirical findings and the law."

49. Gross (2006), "Group concerns," p. 37.

50. Davis & Meara (1982), "So you think it is a secret."

51. Paradise & Kirby (1990), "Some perspectives on the legal liability of group counseling in private practice."

52. Gross (2006), p. 38.

53. Knapp & VandeCreek (1987), *Privileged Communications in the Mental Health Professions*.

54. Meyer & Smith (1977), "A crisis in group therapy."

55. Knauss (2006), "Ethical issues in recordkeeping in group psychotherapy," p. 415.

56. Pipes, Blevins, & Kluck (2008), "Confidentiality, ethics, and informed consent," p. 623.

57. APA Division 45 (2002), *Guidelines for Multicultural Proficiency for Psychologists*. Also see Salter & Salter (2012), "Competence with Diverse Populations" in Knapp et al. (2012), *APA Handbook of Ethics for Psychologists*, Volume 1; Chapter 8.

58. Werth, Burke, & Burdash (2002), "Confidentiality in end-of-life and after-death situations," p. 205.

59. ACA Ethical Standard A.9c ("End-of-Life Care for Terminally Ill Clients").

60. NASW Ethical Standard 1.07c, "Privacy and Confidentiality."

61. APA Ethical Standard 4.05 ("Disclosures").

62. Werth, Burke, & Burdash (2002), p. 210.

63. Werth & Richmond (2009), "End-of-life decisions and the duty to protect," p. 202, citing the report of the APA Working Group on Assisted Suicide and End-of-Life Decisions (2000), *Report to the Board of Directors*.

64. NASW, Ethical Standard 1.07.r ("Protecting Confidentiality of Deceased Clients"): "Social workers should protect the confidentiality of deceased clients consistent with the preceding standards" (i.e., the confidentiality protections provided to all clients).

65. ACA Ethical Standard B.3.f. ("Confidentiality of Deceased Clients"): "Counselors protect the confidentiality of deceased clients, consistent with legal requirements and agency or setting policies."

66. Although the APA Ethics Code does not directly answer the question, it does allow (but does not require) disclosure of confidential information in the following circumstances: "Psychologists may disclose confidential information with the appropriate consent of ... the individual client/patient, or another legally authorized person on behalf of the client/patient unless prohibited by law" (APA Ethical Standard 4.05 ["Disclosures"]). This would seem to permit disclosure of information about a deceased patient (1) if the patient, while living, gave consent for such postmortem disclosure, or (2) if consent is obtained from an executor or other legally authorized representative.

67. Vasquez (1994), "Implications of the 1992 Ethics Code for the practice of individual psychotherapy," p. 324.

68. Robinson & O'Neill (2007), "Access to health care records after death: Balancing confidentiality with appropriate disclosure," p. 634.

69. Werth, Burke, & Burdash (2002), p. 216.

70. Burke (1995), "Until death do us part: An exploration into confidentiality following the death of a client," p. 280.

71. Some state associations provide this state-specific information. For example, for Pennsylvania, see Baturin, Knapp, & Tupper (2005), "Confidentiality and the release of treatment records following the death of a client."

72. *Swidler & Berlin v. United States* (1998).

73. Behnke (1998), "Testimonial privilege and the problem of death: The Vincent Foster case and beyond."

74. For example, see Burke (1995).

Chapter 12: Confidentiality in Specific Roles and Settings

1. Fisher (2012), Confidentiality and Record Keeping, p. 365.

2. This list paraphrases the informed consent requirements for psychologists who provide services within an organization. (See APA Ethical Standard 3.11, "Services Provided To or Through Organizations").

3. Fisher (2009b), "Replacing '"Who is the client?'" with a different ethical question."

4. ACA Ethical Standard B.3.b. ("Treatment Teams").

5. Fisher (2012), p. 365.

6. Fisher (2012), p. 365 (citing Behnke (2008a, May), "Multiple relationships in campus counseling centers"; Behnke (2008b, June), "The unique challenges of campus counseling"; and Sharkin (1995), "Strains on confidentiality in college-student psychotherapy: Entangled therapeutic relationships, incidental encounters, and third-party inquiries."

7. These ethical responsibilities are described in ethics codes as follows:

Psychologists: "If the demands of an organization with which psychologists are affiliated or for whom they are working are in conflict with this Ethics Code, psychologists clarify the nature of the conflict, make known their commitment to the Ethics Code, and take reasonable steps to resolve the conflict consistent with the General Principles and Ethical Standards of the Ethics Code. Under no circumstances may this standard be used to justify or defend violating human rights" (APA Ethical Standard 1. 03, "Conflicts Between Ethics and Organizational Demands").

Counselors: "Counselors alert their employers of inappropriate policies and practices. They attempt to effect changes in such policies or procedures through constructive action within the organization. When such policies are potentially disruptive or damaging to clients or may limit the effectiveness of services provided and change cannot be effected, counselors take appropriate further action. Such action may include referral to appropriate certification, accreditation, or state licensure organizations, or voluntary termination of employment" (ACA Ethical Standard D.1.h, "Negative Conditions").

Social workers: "(c) Social workers should take reasonable steps to ensure that employers are aware of social workers' ethical obligations as set forth in the *NASW Code of Ethics* and of the implications of those obligations for social work practice. (d) Social workers should not allow an employing organization's policies, procedures, regulations, or administrative orders to interfere with their ethical practice of social work. Social workers should take reasonable steps to ensure that their employing organizations' practices are consistent with the *NASW Code of Ethics* (NASW Ethical Standard 3.09, "Commitments to Employers").

Psychiatrists: "Psychiatrists have a long and valued tradition of being essential participants in organizations that deliver health care. Such organizations can enhance medical effectiveness and protect the standards and values of the psychiatric profession by fostering competent, compassionate medical care in a setting in which informed consent and confidentiality are rigorously preserved, conditions essential for the successful treatment of mental illness. However, some organizations may place the psychiatrist in a position where the clinical needs of the patient, the demands of the community and larger society, and even the professional role of the psychiatrist are in conflict with the interests of the organization. The psychiatrist must consider the consequences of such role conflicts with respect to patients in his/her care, and strive to resolve these conflicts in a manner that is likely to be of greatest benefit to the patient. Whether during treatment or a review process, a psychiatrist shall respect the autonomy, privacy, and dignity of the patient and his/her family" (APsyA, p.23, "Addendum to Principles of Medical Ethics With Annotations Especially Applicable to Psychiatry").

8. School psychologists: "Psychologists employed by the schools may have less control over aspects of service delivery than practitioners in private practice. However, within this framework, it is expected that school psychologists will make careful, reasoned, and principled ethical choices based on knowledge of this code, recognizing that responsibility for ethical conduct rests with the individual practitioner" (National Association of School Psychologists [NASP] *Principles for Professional Ethics,* Introduction, p. 2).School counselors: "Adhere to ethical standards of the profession, other official policy statements, such as [American School Counselors Association] ASCA's position statements, role statement

and the ASCA National Model and relevant statutes established by federal, state and local governments, and when these are in conflict, work responsibly for change" (ASCA "Ethical Standards for School Counselors" Standard F.1.e ("Professionalism").

9. School Social Work Association of America (2001), *School Social Workers and Confidentiality.*

10. Health Insurance Portability and Accountability Act of 1996 (HIPAA), Pub. L. No. 104–191, 104th Congress.

11. See Family Educational Rights and Privacy Act (FERPA) (2009).

12. Individual Disability Education Act (IDEA) (2009).

13. Behnke (2008a), Behnke (2008b).

14. Sharkin (1995).

15. Behnke (2008b), p. 88

16. For example, see Virginia Code, Statutes § 23–9.2:3 (2008), Paragraph C. Also see Appendix III for partial text of this statute as an example of legal complications about confidentiality in campus settings.

17. For example, see the practices now recommended under Virginia Code, Statutes § 23–9.2:10 as described at http://youthviolence.edschool.virginia.edu/threat-assessment/pdf/college-threat-recommended-practices.pdf.

18. Glosoff & Pate (2002), "Privacy and confidentiality in school counseling," p. 26

19. HIPAA (1996).

20. FERPA (2009).

21. IDEA (2009).

22. For a list of these, see endnote 19 for Chapter 6.

23. Koocher & Keith-Spiegel (2008), *Ethics in Psychology and the Mental Health Professions*, p. 215.

24. Fisher (2012), p. 366

25. For psychologists, see ethical standards in Section 8 ("Research and Publication"). For social workers see ethical standards in Section 5.02 ("Evaluation and Research"). For counselors, see ethical standards in Section G ("Research and Publication"), as well as Sections B.7.c ("Confidentiality of Information Obtained in Research") and B.7.d ("Disclosure of Research Information").

26. Melton (1990), "Certificates of confidentiality under the Public Health Service Act: Strong protection but not enough," p. 67.

27. APA Ethical Standard 8.02 ("Informed Consent to Research").

28. ACA Ethical Standard G.2.e ("Confidentiality of Research Information").

29. NASW Ethical Standard 5.02 ("Evaluation and Research").

30. Haggerty & Hawkins (2000), "Informed consent and the limits of confidentiality"; Melton (1990); Traynor (1997), "Countering the excessive subpoena for scholarly research."

31. See Monaghan (2012), "Our storehouse of knowledge about social movements is going to be left bare."

32. APA (2007), "Record keeping guidelines," p. 1000.

33. APA (2007), p. 997.

34. Joint Commission (2009), 2010 Pre-publication Standards.

35. Benefield, Ashkenazi, & Rozenski (2006), "Communication and records: HIPAA issues when working in health care settings," p. 276.

36. See, for example, APA & American Board of Forensic Psychology (2011), *Specialty Guidelines for Forensic Psychology.*

37. "Psychological practice is not considered forensic solely because the conduct takes place in, or the product is presented in, a tribunal or other judicial forum....[P]sychological testimony that is solely based on the provision of psychotherapy and does not include psychological opinions is not ordinarily considered forensic practice" (APA & American Board of Forensic Psychology [2011], "Introduction," p. 1).

38. ACA Ethical Standard E.13 ("Forensic Evaluation: Evaluation for Legal Proceedings"), Section C, "Client Evaluation Prohibited."

39. APA & American Board of Forensic Psychology (2011), Standard 4.02.01, "Therapeutic-Forensic Role Conflicts," p. 7.

40. In contesting a request from an attorney or court to engage in dual roles, therapists can consult (and can cite for attorneys and the court) such professional sources as the following: APA & American Board of Forensic Psychology (2011); Bailey (2003b, October), "Should you testify for your client? Mixing forensic and clinical roles creates an ethically sticky situation"; Gold (1998, Fall), "Why use a forensic psychiatrist? Role conflict between the treating psychiatrist and the forensic psychiatrist"; Greenberg & Gould (2001), "The treating expert"; Greenberg & Shuman (1997), "Irreconcilable conflict between therapeutic and forensic roles"; Shuman, Greenberg, Heilbrun, & Foote (1998), "An immodest proposal: Should treating mental health professionals be barred from testifying about their patients?"; Strasburger, Gutheil, & Brodsky (1997), "On wearing two hats: Role conflict in serving as both psychotherapist and expert witness"; Weithorn (1987), *Psychology and Child Custody Determinations: Knowledge, Roles, and Expertise.*

41. Fisher (2012), p. 366.

42. APA, Committee on Professional Practice and Standards. (2003), "Legal issues in the professional practice of psychology," p. 598. Also see endnote 37, above.

43. Although attorneys may argue against this posture on the therapist's part, judges will usually respect this position, since the therapist is there involuntarily and is often unpaid, in contrast to forensic expert witnesses who are often highly paid for being in that role.

For further discussion of voluntary and involuntary therapist testimony and the issue of "fact witness" versus "expert witness "versus "treating expert," therapists can consult (and can cite for attorneys or the court) professional sources such as the following:

APA, Practice Organization, Legal and Regulatory Affairs Staff and Communications Staff (2005a, February 15), "A matter of law: Q&As for practitioners: What is the difference between serving as an "expert witness" and a "fact witness" in a legal proceeding?"; Baturin, Knapp, & Tepper (2003), "Practical considerations when responding to subpoenas and court orders"; Bennett, Bricklin, Harris, Knapp, VandeCreek, & Younggren (2006), *Assessing and Managing Risk in Psychological Practice: An Individualized Approach* (see section 3, chapter 5, "Court Testimony," pp. 129–142).

44. The ethical responsibilities of this role are described in Appendix VI, which also lists several specialized forensic roles that mental health professionals can voluntarily pursue. The discussion here, however, is limited to forensic activities undertaken by mental health professionals who are acting first in the role of therapist and who would therefore be donning (voluntarily or involuntarily) a forensic hat when they also wear the therapist hat.

45. Greenberg & Gould (2001).

46. Greenberg & Gould (2001), p. 477.

47. See, for example, the sample no-subpoena contract by Fisher (2004), Sample Non-Subpoena Contract

48. See, for example, DeAngelis (2011), "Portnoy's complainants [re: Collaborative Divorce Coaching]"; Grossman et al. (2003, Winter), "Forensic roles of family psychologists"; Holloway (2005, May), "Spreading the word about a new practice opportunity: Parenting coordinators help divorcing families."

49. APA Ethical Standard 2.01(f) ("Boundaries of Competence").

50. Munsey (2008, February), "New options for military psychologists," and Munsey (2009, April), "Needed: More military psychologists."

51. APA Ethical Standard 3.11 ("Psychological Services Delivered to or Through Organizations").

52. See, for example, a listing of over 300 articles, books, and chapters addressing this controversy at http://kspope.com/interrogation/index.php.

53. APA (2010a), "American Psychological Association amends ethics code to address potential conflicts among professional ethics, legal authority and organizational demands (February 24, 2010)."

54. APA Ethical Standard 3.11 ("Psychological Services Delivered to or Through Organizations").

55. Fisher (2009b), p. 4. Also see Knapp, Gottlieb, Berman, & Handelsman (2007), "When laws and ethics collide: What should psychologists do?"

56. Fisher (2012), p. 367, citing Knapp et al. (2007), "A question of values." Also see Behnke (2007b), "Disclosures of information: Thoughts on a process."

57. Pope & Vasquez (2005), *How To Survive & Thrive As a Therapist: Information, Ideas, & Resources for Psychologists in Practice*, p. 16.

58. Woody (1999), "Domestic violations of confidentiality," p. 607.

59. Nordmarken & Zur (2010), "Home office: When the office is located at the home."

60. Morgan & Polowy (2009), *The Social Sorker and the Home Office*.

61. Pepper (2003, March), "Be it ever so humble … the controversial issue of psychotherapy groups in the home office setting."

62. Pope & Vasquez (2011), *Ethics in Psychotherapy and Counseling*, p. 281.

63. See, for example, Behnke (2008c, December), "Exploring ethics in rural settings"; Campbell & Gordon (2003), "Acknowledging the inevitable: Understanding multiple relationships in rural practice"; Catalano (1997), "The challenges of clinical practice in small or rural communities"; Schank & Skovholt (1997), "Dual-relationship dilemmas of rural and small-community psychologists"; Schank & Skovholt (2005), *Ethical Practice in Small Communities: Challenges and Rewards for Psychologists*.

64. Catalano (1997), p. 25.

65. Behnke (2008c), p. 44.

66. Campbell & Gordon (2003), p. 434.

67. Koocher & Keith-Spiegel (2008), p. 291.

68. Koocher & Keith-Spiegel (2008), p. 292.

69. Koocher & Keith-Spiegel (2008), p. 291.

70. Zur (2012), *In-Home Therapy and Home Visits: Home-Based Mental Health*.

71. Zur (2001), "Out-of-office experience: When crossing office boundaries and engaging in dual relationships are clinically beneficial and ethically sound"; Zur (2010), *Beyond*

the Office Walls: Home Visits, Celebrations, Adventure Therapy, Incidental Encounters and Other Encounters Outside the Office Walls.

72. See, for example, Vasquez (1992), "The psychologist as clinical supervisor: Promoting ethical practice."

73. Falvey & Cohen (2003), "The buck stops here: documenting clinical supervision."

74. APA Ethical Standard 4.06 ("Consultations").

75. ACA Ethical Standard B.8.c. ("Consultation—Disclosure of Confidential Information").

76. NASW Ethical Standard 2.05c ("Consultation").

Chapter 13: Ethics-Based Staff Training About Confidentiality

1. Bennett, Bricklin, Harris, Knapp, VandeCreek, & Younggren (2006), *Assessing and Managing Risk in Psychological Practice*; Fisher (2009a), "Ethics-based training for non-clinical staff in mental health settings"; Fisher (2012), Confidentiality and Record Keeping; Koocher & Keith-Spiegel (2008), *Ethics in Psychology and the Mental Health Professions.*

2. Knapp & VandeCreek (2006), *Practical Ethics for Psychologists: A Positive Approach,* p. 115.

3. Fry, vanBark, Weinman, Kitchener, & Lang (1997), "Ethical transgressions of psychology graduate students: Critical incidents with implications for training."

4. See Fisher (2009a). This article, which contains a sample outline for broad-based ethics training, is also available online at http://www.centerforethicalpractice.org/articles/articles-mary-alice-fisher/ethics-based-training-for-non-clinical-staff/. A sample training manual is also available for purchase at www.CenterForEthicalPractice.org/Manuals-EmployeeContents-Natl.htm.

5. APA Ethical Standard 2.05 ("Delegation of Work to Others").

6. NASW Ethical Standards 3.07 and 3.08 ("Continuing Education" and "Staff Development").

7. ACA Ethical Standard B.3.a ("Subordinates").

8. APA (2007), "Record keeping guidelines," p. 997.

9. APA Practice Organization, Office of Legal and Regulatory Affairs (2006), *Final HIPAA Enforcement Rule Takes Effect*; Bennett et al. (2006).

10. See APsyA (2011), *Confidentiality Policy and Form for Staff to Sign.*

11. See sample staff contracts at Center for Ethical Practice (2009), Staff Training: Sample Documents.

12. Regarding malpractice risks that can arise with staff or employee use of electronics, see Tracey (1998), "Be aware of malpractice risks when using electronic office devices."

13. Bennett et al. (2006).

14. HIPAA (1996).

15. "Workforce" is defined in HIPAA to include paid employees plus trainees, supervisees, and volunteers under direct control of the HIPAA-covered clinician. It is not necessary for every employee, trainee, supervisee, or volunteer to know *everything* about HIPAA and patient privacy, but each should be trained about what is necessary for carrying out his or her own duties and trained not to handle patient information

beyond their job description and training unless specifically so authorized. See HIPAA, 45 C.F.R. 164.530(b) (1); see summary, "Staff Training Required by HIPAA Regulations" in Appendix IV.

16. HIPAA, 45 C.F.R. 164.530(b) (1): "A covered entity must train all members of its workforce on policies and procedures with respect to protected health information."

17. In Appendix IV, see HIPAA re: "minimum necessary disclosures."

18. HIPAA, 45 C.F.R. 164.308. Also see APA Practice Organization, Office of Legal and Regulatory Affairs and Technology Policy and Projects Staffs (2005, June), *Contingency Planning: Do You Know What HIPAA Requires*?

19. HIPAA, 45 C.F.R. 164.308(a)(1)(ii)(C);164.530(e)(1). Training requirements are summarized in Appendix IV and at www.CenterForEthicalPractice.org/StaffTraining-HIPAA.htm. Also see links to HIPAA-Compliance resources at www.CenterForEthicalPractice.org/HIPAA.htm.

20. For a HIPAA training guide and a sample HIPAA test for demonstrating staff understanding of that material, see Knapp (2005), "What should your employees know about confidentiality? A HIPAA training guide." Ideally, a post-test would include not only this legal material but also the voluntary privacy and confidentiality policies that apply in the setting.

21. Donner (2008), "Unbalancing confidentiality"; Knapp, Gottlieb, Berman, & Handelsman (2007), "When laws and ethics collide: What should psychologists do?"; Pope & Bajt (1988), "When laws and values conflict: A dilemma for psychologists."

22. Fisher (2009a).

23. Fisher (2008b), "Protecting confidentiality rights: The need for an ethical practice model," p. 6.

24. For making this process clear, and for showing how laws fit into the Ethical Practice Model, trainers can use the color-coded version of the model provided by the Center for Ethical Practice (2010) at http://www.centerforethicalpractice.org/EthicalPracticeModelAnnotated.

25. The following three examples were adapted from Fisher (2009a), pp. 460–461.

26. See, for example, APA Committee on Legal Issues (2006), "Strategies for private practitioners coping with subpoenas or compelled testimony for client records or test data," and APA Practice Organization, Legal & Regulatory Affairs Staff (2008, December), *How to Deal With a Subpoena*.

27. Knapp et al. (2007), p. 54.

28. HIPAA, CFR § 164.506.

29. Fisher (2009a), p. 461.

30. Ibid.

31. ACA Ethical Standard A.2 ("Informed Consent in the Counseling Relationship") paragraph c.

32. APA Ethical Standard 3.10 ("Informed Consent").

33. Fisher (2009a), p. 461.

34. See, for example, Fisher (2009a) and Appendix VIII.

35. Fisher (2009a), p. 462.

36. The sample outline provided by Fisher (2009a) and reproduced in Appendix VIII is an example of a broader ethics curriculum that includes the topic of confidentiality, among other topics such as privacy, boundaries, informed consent, relationships with patients, and the like.

37. The following paragraphs are loosely adapted from the sections "Integrating Ethical and Legal Training Requirements" and "Advantages of Ethics-Based Training" in Fisher (2009a), pp. 461–462.

38. Fisher (2009a), p. 465.

39. See sample certificate at Center for Ethical Practice (2009).

40. See sample contracts at Center for Ethical Practice (2009).

REFERENCES

Acuff, C., Bennett, B. E., Bricklin, P. M., Canter, M. B., Knapp, S. J., Moldawsky, S., & Phelps, R. (1999). Considerations for ethical practice in managed care. *Professional Psychology: Research and Practice*, 30, 563–575.

Alleman, J. R. (2001). Personal, practical, and professional issues in providing managed mental health care: A discussion for new psychotherapists. *Ethics & Behavior*, 11, 413–429.

American Association of Marriage and Family Therapy (AAMFT). (2012). *Code of Ethics.* Alexandria VA: Author. Retrieved from http://www.aamft.org/imis15/Documents/Final%202012%20AAMFT%20Code%20of%20Ethics.pdf

American Counseling Association (ACA). (2005). *ACA Code of Ethics and Standards of Practice.* Retrieved from http://www.counseling.org/Resources/CodeOfEthics/TP/Home/CT2.aspx

American Nurses Association (ANA). (2001). *Code of Ethics for Nurses with Interpretive Statements.* Washington DC: Author. Retrieved from http://nursingworld.org/MainMenuCategories/EthicsStandards/CodeofEthicsforNurses/Code-of-Ethics.pdf

American Psychiatric Association (APsyA). (2009). *The Principles of Medical Ethics with Annotations Especially Applicable to Psychiatry.* Washington DC: Author. Retrieved from http://www.psych.org/MainMenu/PsychiatricPractice/Ethics/ResourcesStandards/PrinciplesofMedicalEthics.aspx

American Psychiatric Association (APsyA). (2011). *Confidentiality Policy and Form for Staff to Sign.* Retrieved from http://jeremymartinezmd.com/userfiles/1410818/file/Practice%20Management.pdf

American Psychiatric Association (APsyA) & American Academy of Psychiatry and the Law. (1995). Brief *amicus curiae* in *Jaffee v. Redmond.* (No. 95–266) WL 767892.

American Psychiatric Association (APsyA) Committee on Confidentiality. (1987). Guidelines on confidentiality. *American Journal of Psychiatry*, *144*(11), 1522–1526.

American Psychological Association (APA). (1992). Ethical principles of psychologists and code of conduct. *American Psychologist*, 47, 1597–1611.

American Psychological Association (APA). (1995). Brief *amicus curiae* in *Jaffe v. Redmond.* Retrieved from http://www.apa.org/about/offices/ogc/amicus/jaffee.pdf

American Psychological Association (APA). (2005). *A Matter of Law: Privacy Rights of Minor Patients.* Retrieved from http://www.apapracticecentral.org

American Psychological Association (APA). (2007). Record keeping guidelines. *American Psychologist*, 62, 993–1004. DOI: 10.1037/0003–066X.62.9.993 (Also online at http://www.apa.org/practice/recordkeeping.pdf)

American Psychological Association (APA). (2010a). American Psychological Association amends ethics code to address potential conflicts among professional ethics, legal authority and organizational demands (February 24, 2010). Retrieved from http://www.apa.org/news/press/releases/2010/02/ethics-code.aspx

American Psychological Association (APA). (2010b). *Ethical Principles of Psychologists and Code of Conduct (2002, amended 2010)*. Retrieved from http://www.apa.org/ethics/code/index.aspx

American Psychological Association (APA). (2010c). *HIPAA for Psychologists: Online CE Course*. Retrieved from http://apapracticecentral.org/ce/courses/1370022.aspx

American Psychological Association (APA). (2012). Guidelines for the practice of parenting coordination. *American Psychologist*, 67(1), 63–71. DOI: 10.1037/a0024646

American Psychological Association (APA) and American Board of Forensic Psychology. (2011, August 20). *Specialty Guidelines for Forensic Psychology*. Retrieved from http://www.ap-ls.org/aboutpsychlaw/SGFP_Final_Approved_2011.pdf

American Psychological Association (APA) Committee on Legal Issues. (2006). Strategies for private practitioners coping with subpoenas or compelled testimony for client records or test data. *Professional Psychology: Research and Practice*, 27, 215–222. DOI: 10.1037/0735-7028.37.2.215 (Also available at http://content.apa.org/journals/pro/37/2/215.pdf)

American Psychological Association (APA) Committee on Professional Practice & Standards. (1998). *Guidelines for Psychological Evaluations in Child Protection Matters*. Washington, DC: Author. (Available at http://www.apa.org/practice/guidelines/child-protection.pdf)

American Psychological Association (APA) Committee on Professional Practice and Standards. (2003). Legal issues in the professional practice of psychology. *Professional Psychology: Research and Practice*, 34, 595–600. DOI: 10.1037/0735-7028.34.6.595

American Psychological Association (APA) Committee on Professional Practice & Standards. (2009). *Guidelines for Child Custody Evaluations in Family Law Proceedings*. Retrieved from http://www.apa.org/practice/guidelines/child-custody.pdf

American Psychological Association (APA) Division 44, Committee on Lesbian, Gay, and Bisexual Concerns Joint Task Force. (2000). Guidelines for psychotherapy with lesbian, gay, and bisexual clients. *American Psychologist*, 55(12), 1440–1451. DOI: 10.1037//0003-066X.55.12.1440

American Psychological Association (APA) Division 45/Society for the Study of Ethnic Minority Issues. (2002). *Guidelines for Multicultural Proficiency for Psychologists*. Retrieved from http://www.apa.org/pi/oema/resources/policy/multicultural-guidelines.aspx

American Psychological Association (APA) Government Relations and Communications Staff. (2006). Patriot Act renewal tightens medical records safeguards. Retrieved from http://www.apapractice.org

American Psychological Association (APA) Insurance Trust. (2006). *Sample Outpatient Services Agreement for Collaterals*. Retrieved from http://www.apait.org/apait/resources/riskmanagement/cinf.aspx

American Psychological Association (APA) Practice Organization. (2008, Fall). *How to Deal With a Subpoena*, pp. 2–5, 20. Retrieved from http://search.apa.org/practice?query=Good+practice+fall+2008

American Psychological Association (APA) Practice Organization. (2010). Instructions for HITECH amendments to business associates contracts. Retrieved from http://www.apapracticecentral.org/business/hipaa/primer/secure/hitech-instructions.aspx

American Psychological Association (APA) Practice Organization (2011, Winter). *Good Practice: Working With Children and Adolescents*, pp. 2–5. Retrieved from http://search.apa.org/practice?query=Good+practice+winter+2011

American Psychological Association (APA) Practice Organization, Government Relations Staff. (2007). *The Health Information Technology for Economic and Clinical Health Act (HITECH).* Retrieved from http://www.apapracticecentral.org/advocacy/technology/hitech-act.aspx

American Psychological Association (APA) Practice Organization, Legal and Regulatory Affairs Staff. (2005a, June). A matter of law: Privacy rights of minor patients. Retrieved from http://www.apapractice.org/apo/insider/practice/pracmanage/legal/minor.html#

American Psychological Association (APA) Practice Organization, Legal and Regulatory Affairs Staff. (2005b, November). A matter of law: Managed care record audits. Retrieved from http://www.apapracticecentral.org/business/legal/professional/secure/record-audits.aspx

American Psychological Association (APA) Practice Organization, Legal and Regulatory Affairs Staff. (2008, December). *How to deal with a subpoena.* Washington, DC: Author. Retrieved from http://search.apa.org/practice?query=%22how+to+deal+with+a+subpoena%22

American Psychological Association (APA) Practice Organization, Legal and Regulatory Affairs Staff. (2010, April). Tools and Training in Parenting Coordination. Retrieved from http://www.apapracticecentral.org/update/2010/04–29/parenting-coordination.aspx

American Psychological Association (APA) Practice Organization, Legal & Regulatory Affairs Staff. (2011, October 14). *Basics of Cloud Computing.* Retrieved from http://www.apapracticecentral.org/update/2011/10–14/cloud-computing.aspx

American Psychological Association (APA) Practice Organization, Legal and Regulatory Affairs Staff and Communications Staff (2005a, February 15). A matter of law: Q&As for practitioners: What is the difference between serving as an "expert witness" and a "fact witness" in a legal proceeding? Retrieved from http://search.apa.org/practice?query=+%22what++is+the+difference%22

American Psychological Association (APA) Practice Organization, Legal and Regulatory Affairs Staff and Communications Staff. (2005b, March). A matter of law: Managing your managed care contracts. Retrieved from http://www.apapracticecentral.org/business/legal/professional/secure/managed-care-contract.aspx

American Psychological Association (APA) Practice Organization, Office of Legal and Regulatory Affairs. (2006). *Final HIPAA Enforcement Rule Takes Effect.* Washington, DC: Author. Retrieved from http://www.apapracticecentral.org/good-practice/secure/Winter07-Enforcement.pdf

American Psychological Association (APA) Practice Organization, Office of Legal and Regulatory Affairs and Technology Policy and Projects Staffs. (2005, June 7). *Contingency Planning: Do You Know What HIPAA Requires?* Washington, DC: Author. Retrieved from http://search.apa.org/practice?query=%22Contingency+Planning22

American Psychological Association (APA) Public Interest Initiatives, Ad Hoc Committee on Legal and Ethical Issues in the Treatment of Interpersonal Violence. (2011). Potential problems for psychologists working with the area of interpersonal violence. Retrieved from http://www.batteredmotherscustodyconference.org/APA_public_interest_initiatives.htm

American Psychological Association (APA) Working Group on Assisted Suicide and End-Of-Life Decisions. (2000). *Report to the Board of Directors.* Retrieved from http://www.apa.org/pubs/info/reports/aseol.aspx

American Psychological Association (APA) Working Group on the Older Adult. (1998). What practitioners should know about working with older adults. *Professional Psychology: Research and Practice*, 29(5), 413–427.

American School Counselors Association (ASCA). (2010). *Ethical Standards for School Counselors*. Alexandria VA: Author. Retrieved from http://www.schoolcounselor.org/files/EthicalStandards2010.pdf

Appelbaum, P. S. (1993). Legal liability and managed care. *American Psychologist*, 48, 251–257.

Appelbaum, P. S. (2007, November). Assessment of patients' competence to consent to treatment. *New England Journal of Medicine*, 357(18), 1834–1840.

Appelbaum, P. S., Lidz, C. W., & Meisel, A. (1987). *Informed Consent: Legal Theory and Clinical Practice*. New York: Oxford University Press.

Association of Family and Conciliation Courts. (2005). *Guidelines for Parenting Coordination*. Retrieved from http://www.afccnet.org/Portals/0/PublicDocuments/Guidelines/AFCCGuidelinesforParentingcoordinationnew.pdf

Association of Family and Conciliation Courts. (2011). *Training for Parenting Coordination*. Retrieved from http://www.afccnet.org/conferencesTraining/AFCCTraining

Austrin, M. S. (1999). *Managed Health Care Simplified: A Glossary of Terms*. Albany, NY: Delmar.

Bailey, D. S. (2003a, October). Ethics as prevention. *Monitor on Psychology*, 34(9), 68.

Bailey, D. S. (2003b, October). Should you testify for your client? Mixing forensic and clinical roles creates an ethically sticky situation. *Monitor on Psychology*, 34(9), 72.

Baker, F. W. (2008, May 1). DOD changes security clearance question on mental health. Retrieved from http://www.defense.gov/news/newsarticle.aspx?id=49735

Baker, L. C., & Patterson, J. E. (1990). The first to know: A systemic analysis of confidentiality and the therapist's family. *American Journal of Family Therapy*, 18, 295–300.

Barnett, J. E. (2009). Ethics for psychologists: Documentation and the use of the internet. *The National Psychologist*, 18(2), 12.

Barnett, J. E. (2012, March). Clinical writing about clients: Is informed consent sufficient? *Psychotherapy*, 49(1), 12–15. DOI: 10.1037/a0025249

Barnett, J. E., Behnke S. H., Rosenthal, S. L., & Koocher, G. P. (2007). In case of ethical dilemma, break glass: Commentary on ethical decision making in practice. *Professional Psychology Research and Practice*, 38, 7–12.

Barnett, J. E., Wise, E. H., Jonathan-Greene, D., & Bucky, S. F. (2007). Informed consent: Too much of a good thing or not enough? *Professional Psychology: Research and Practice*, 38, 179–186. DOI: 10.1037/0735-7028.38.2.179

Baturin, R. L., Knapp, S. J., & Tepper, A. M. (2003, August). Practical considerations when responding to subpoenas and court orders. *Pennsylvania Psychologist*, 63(8), 16–17.

Baturin, R. L., Knapp, S. J., & Tepper, A. M. (2005). Confidentiality and the release of treatment records following the death of a client. Retrieved from http://www.papsy.org/ces/Confidentiality/

Beahrs, J. O., & Gutheil, T. G. (2001, Jan.). Informed consent in psychotherapy. *American Journal of Psychiatry*, 158(1), 4–10.

Beck, J. C. (1990). The Basic Issues. In J. C. Beck (Ed.), *Confidentiality Versus the Duty to Protect: Foreseeable Harm in The Practice of Psychiatry* (pp. 1–8). Washington, DC: American Psychiatric Press.

Beeman, D. G., & Scott, N. A. (1991). Therapists' attitudes toward psychotherapy informed consent with adolescents. *Professional Psychology: Research and Practice*, 22, 230–234.

Behnke, S. (1998). Testimonial privilege and the problem of death: The Vincent Foster case and beyond. *Journal of the American Academy of Psychiatry and the Law*, 26(4), 639–648.

Behnke, S. (2001, October). Ethics matter: A question of values. *Monitor on Psychology*, 32(9), 86. Retrieved from http://www.apa.org/monitor/oct01/ethics.html

Behnke, S. (2004, September). Disclosures of confidential information under the new APA Ethics Code: A process for deciding when and how. *Monitor on Psychology*, 35(8), 78–79. Retrieved from http://www.apa.org/monitor/sep04/ethics.html

Behnke, S. (2005a, April). Disclosing confidential information in consultations and for didactic purposes. *Monitor on Psychology*, 36, 76–77. Retrieved from http://www.apa.org/monitor/apr05/ethics.aspx

Behnke, S. (2005b, December). Letter from a reader regarding a minor client and confidentiality. *Monitor on Psychology*, 36, 78–79. Retrieved from http://www.apa.org/monitor/dec05/ethics.aspx

Behnke, S. (2006, March). Responding to a colleague's ethical transgressions. *Monitor on Psychology*, 37(3), 72. Retrieved from http://www.apa.org/monitor/mar06/ethics.html

Behnke, S. (2007a, February). Adolescents and confidentiality: letter from a reader. *Monitor on Psychology*, 38, 46–47. Retrieved from http://www.apa.org/monitor/feb07/adolescents.aspx

Behnke, S. (2007b, April). Disclosures of Information: Thoughts on a process. *Monitor on Psychology*, 38(4), 62. Retrieved from http://www.apa.org/monitor/apr07/ethics.aspx

Behnke, S. (2007c, May). Gossiping about patients. *Monitor on Psychology*, 38(5), 70. Retrieved from http://www.apa.org/monitor/may07/ethics.aspx

Behnke, S. (2008a, May). Multiple relationships in campus counseling centers: A vignette. *Monitor on Psychology*, 39(5), 76. Retrieved from http://www.apa.org/monitor/2008/05/ethics.html

Behnke, S. (2008b, June). The unique challenges of campus counseling. *Monitor on Psychology*, 39(6), 88. Retrieved from http://www.apa.org/monitor/2008/06/ethics.html

Behnke, S. (2008c, December). Exploring ethics in rural settings: Through the lens of culture. *Monitor on Psychology*, 39(11), 44. Retrieved from http://www.apa.org/monitor/2008/12/ethics.html

Behnke, S., & Kinscherff, R. (2002). Must a psychologist report past child abuse? *Monitor on Psychology*, 33. Part 1 (May, pp. 90–91), retrieved from http://www.apa.org/monitor/may02/ethics.aspx ; and Part 2 (July/August, p. 90) retrieved from http://www.apa.org/monitor/julaug02/ethics.aspx

Behnke, S. H., & Warner, E. (2002, March). Confidentiality in the treatment of adolescents. *Monitor in Psychology*, 33, 44–45. Retrieved from http://www.apa.org/monitor/mar02/confidentiality.aspx

Benefield, H., Ashkanazi, G., & Rozensky, R. H. (2006). Communication and records: HIPAA issues when working in health care settings. *Professional Psychology: Research and Practice*, 37, 273–277. DOI: 10.1037/0735–7028.37.3.273

Benjamin, G. A. H., Kent, L., & Sirikantraporn, S. (2009). A Review of Duty-to-Protect Statutes, Cases, and Procedures for Positive Practice. In J. L. Werth, E. R. Welfel, &

G. A. H. Benjamin, *The Duty to Protect: Ethical, Legal, and Professional Considerations for Mental Health Professionals* (pp. 9–28), Washington DC: American Psychological Association.

Bennett, B. E., Bricklin, P. M., Harris, E., Knapp, S. VandeCreek, L., & Younggren, J. N. (2006). *Assessing and Managing Risk in Psychological Practice: An Individualized Approach*. Rockville, MD: American Psychological Association Insurance Trust.

Bennett, B. E., Bryant, B. K., VandenBos, G. R., & Greenwood, A. (1990). *Professional Liability and Risk Management*. Washington, DC: American Psychological Association.

Bergeron, L. R., & Grey, B. (2003). Ethical dilemmas of reporting suspected elder abuse. *Social Work*, 48, 96–105.

Berner, M. (1998). Informed Consent. In L. E. Lifson & R. I. Simon (Eds.), *The Mental Health Practitioner and the Law*. Cambridge, MA: Harvard University Press.

Bersoff, D. N. (1975). Professional ethics and legal responsibilities: On the horns of a dilemma. *Journal of School Psychology*, 13, 359–376.

Bersoff, D. N. (1994). Explicit ambiguity: The 1992 ethics code as an oxymoron. *Professional Psychology: Research and Practice*, 25, 382–387.

Berson, J. (2005). Dual relationships for the psychologist when custody is an issue. Retrieved from http://www.apadivisions.org/division-31/publications/articles/new-jersey/berson.pdf

Beyer, K. (2000, September). First person: *Jaffe v. Redmond* therapist speaks. *American Psychoanalyst*, 34. Retrieved from http://jaffee-redmond.org/articles/beyer.htm

Bilynsky, N. S., & Vernaglia, E. R. (1998). The ethical practice of psychology in a managed-care framework. *Psychotherapy*, 35(1), 54–68.

Blechner, M. J. (2012, March). Confidentiality: Against disguise; for consent. *Psychotherapy*, 49(1), 16–18. DOI: 10.1037/a0027145

Bollas, C., & Langs, R. (1999). It is time to take a stand. *Newsletter of the International Psychoanalytical Association (IPA)*, 8(2), pp. 1, 7–8. Retrieved from http://www.academyprojects.org/roundtable.htm

Bollas C., & Sundelson, D. (1995). *The new informants: The Betrayal of Confidentiality in Psychoanalysis and Psychotherapy*. Northvale, NJ: Jason Aronson, Inc.

Bonnie, R. J., Reinhard, J. S., Hamilton, P., & McGarvey, E. L. (2009). Mental health system transformation after the Virginia Tech tragedy. *Health Affairs*, 28(3), 793–804. DOI: 10.1377/hlthaff.28.3.793 Retrieved from http://content.healthaffairs.org/content/28/3/793.full.pdf+html

Bradshaw, J. (2011, Jan/Feb). Techno breaches could cost practitioners big bucks. *National Psychologist*, 20, 1, 3.

Burke, C. A. (1995). Until death do us part: An exploration into confidentiality following the death of a client. *Professional Psychology: Research and Practice*, 26, 278–280.

Campbell, C., & Gordon, M. (2003). Acknowledging the inevitable: Understanding multiple relationships in rural practice. *Professional Psychology: Research and Practice*, 34, 430–434.

Canadian Psychological Association (CPA). (2000). *Canadian Code of Ethics for Psychologists* (3rd Ed.). Ottawa, Ontario: Author. Retrieved from http://www.cpa.ca/cpasite/userfiles/Documents/Canadian%20Code%20of%20Ethics%20for%20Psycho.pdf

Canadian Psychological Association (CPA). (2005). *Code Comparison: The Canadian Code of Ethics for Psychologists Compared With the APA and ASPPB Codes.* Retrieved from http://www.cpa.ca/cpasite/userfiles/Documents/publications/operationsmanual.pdf

Catalano, S. (1997). The challenges of clinical practice in small or rural communities: Case studies in managing dual relationships in and outside of therapy. *Journal of Contemporary Psychotherapy*, 27, 23–35.

Caudill, O. B., & Kaplan, A. I. (2005). Protecting privacy and confidentiality. *Journal of Aggression, Maltreatment & Trauma*, 11(1), 117–134. DOI: 10.1300/J146v11n01_10

Center for Ethical Practice. (2009). Staff Training: Sample Documents. Retrieved from http://www.centerforethicalpractice.org/staff-training

Center for Ethical Practice. (2010). Ethical Practice Model + state laws + HIPAA. Retrieved from http://www.centerforethicalpractice.org/EthicalPracticeModelAnnotated

Center for Ethical Practice. (2011). Laws Affecting Confidentiality. Retrieved from http://www.centerforethicalpractice.org/lawsaffectingconfidentiality

Clarborn, C. D., Berbaroglu, L. S., Nerison, R. M., & Somberg, D. R. (1994). The client's perspective: Ethical judgments and perceptions of therapist practices. *Professional Psychology: Research and Practice* 25, 268–274.

Coleman, M. (2005, May). Practice update: Psychotherapy notes and reimbursement claims. *Clinical Social Work.* Retrieved from http://www.socialworkers.org/practice/clinical/csw0805.pdf

Cooper, C. C., & Gottlieb, M. C. (2000). Ethical issues with managed care: Challenges facing counseling psychology. *The Counseling Psychologist*, 28, 179–236. DOI: 10.1177/0011000000282001 Retrieved from http://tcp.sagepub.com/cgi/content/abstract/28/2/179

Cottone, R. R., & Claus, R. E. (2000). Ethical decision-making models: A review of the literature. *Journal of Counseling & Development*, 78, 275–283.

Crowe, M. B., Grogan, J. M., Jacobs, R. R., Lindsay, C. A., & Mark, M. M. (1985). Delineation of the roles of clinical psychology: A survey of practice in Pennsylvania. *Professional Psychology: Research and Practice*, 16, 124–137.

Cullari, S. (2001). The Client's Perspective of Psychotherapy. In S. Cullari (Ed.), *Counseling and Psychotherapy* (pp. 92–116). Boston: Allyn & Bacon.

Davidson, J. R., & Davidson, T. (1996). Confidentiality and managed care: Ethical and legal concerns. *Health and Social Work* 21, 208–215.

Davis, D. D., & Younggren, J. N. (2009). Ethical competence in psychotherapy termination. *Professional Psychology: Research and Practice*, 40, 572-578. DOI: 10.1037/a0017699

Davis , K. L. , & Meara, N. M. (1982). So you think it is a secret. The Journal for Specialists in Group Work , 7 , 149–153 .

DeAngelis, T. (2011, July). Portnoy's complainants: Massachusetts psychologist teams up with lawyers to ease the turmoil of divorce. *Monitor on Psychology*, 42(7), p. 54. Retrieved from http://www.apa.org/monitor/2011/07–08/portnoy.aspx

Devereaux, R. L., & Gottlieb, M. C. (2012, In Press). Record keeping in the cloud: Ethical considerations. *Professional Psychology: Research and Practice*. DOI: 10.1037/a0028268

Dingfelder, S. F. (2009). Stigma: Alive and well. *Monitor on Psychology* 40(6), 56. Retrieved from http://www.apa.org/monitor/2009/06/stigma.html

Donner, M. B. (2008). Unbalancing confidentiality. *Professional Psychology: Research and Practice*, 39, 369–372. DOI: 10.1037/0735–7028.39.3.369

Dunlap, M. P. (2000). The contentious matter of "psychotherapy notes" under HIPAA. Retrieved from http://membership.americanmentalhealth.com/hipaa-notes.trust

Dyer, A. R. (1988). *Ethics and Psychiatry: Toward Professional Definition*. Washington, DC: American Psychiatric Press.

Epstein, R. S. (1944). *Keeping Boundaries: Maintaining Safety and Integrity in the Psychotherapeutic Process*. Washington, DC: American Psychiatric Press.

Everstine, L., Everstine, D. S., Heymann, G. M., True, R. H., Frey, D. H., Johnson, H. G., et al. (1980). Privacy and confidentiality in psychotherapy. *American Psychologist*, 35, 828–840.

Falvey, J. E., & Cohen, C. R. (2003). The buck stops here: Documenting clinical supervision. *Clinical Supervisor*, 22, 63–80. DOI: 10.1300/J001v22n02_05

Family Educational Rights and Privacy Act (FERPA). (2009). Retrieved from http://www.ed.gov/policy/gen/guid/fpco/ferpa/index.html

Fischer, C. T. (2012, March). Comments on protecting clients about whom we write (and speak). *Psychotherapy*, 49(1), 19–21. DOI: 10.1037/a0026486

Fisher, M. A. (2002). Ethical issues (a letter responding to Behnke & Kinscherff, 2002). *Monitor on Psychology*, 33(Oct), 4.

Fisher, M. A. (2004). Sample non-subpoena contract. Retrieved from http://centerforethicalpractice.org/sample_handouts/

Fisher, M. A. (2005). Ethical decision-making model. Retrieved from http://www.centerforethicalpractice.org/decision_making_model

Fisher, M. A. (2006). Selected ethical standards related to informed consent for therapy. Retrieved from http://www.centerforethicalpractice.org/informedconsentchart

Fisher, M. A. (2007a). Ethical and legal responsibilities of Virginia mental health professionals in response to a subpoena. Retrieved from http://www.centerforethicalpractice.org/Virginia-RespondingToSubpoenas.htm

Fisher, M. A. (2008a). Clarifying confidentiality with the ethical practice model. (Response to letter by Pipes, R. B., Blevens, T., & Kluck, A.). *American Psychologist*, 63, 624. DOI: 10.1037/0003-066X.63.7.624

Fisher, M. A. (2008b). Protecting confidentiality rights: The need for an ethical practice model. *American Psychologist*, 63, 1–13. DOI: 10.1037/0003–066X.63.1.1 (Online in html at http://www.centerforethicalpractice.org/articles/articles-mary-alice-fisher/protecting-confidentiality-rights/)

Fisher, M. A. (2009a). Ethics-based training for non-clinical staff in mental health settings. *Professional Psychology: Research and Practice*, 40, 459–466. DOI: 10.1037/a0016642 (Online in html at http://www.centerforethicalpractice.org/ethics-based-training-for-non-clinical-staff/)

Fisher, M. A. (2009b). Replacing "Who is the client?" with a different ethical question. *Professional Psychology: Research and Practice*, 40, 1–7. DOI: 10.1037/a0014011 (Online in html at http://www.centerforethicalpractice.org/articles/articles-mary-alice-fisher/replacing-who-is-the-client-with-a-different-ethical-question/)

Fisher, M. A. (2010a). *Can You Keep A Secret? Confidentiality and Its Limits in Virginia*, 6th edition. Charlottesville, VA: The Center for Ethical Practice, Inc.

Fisher, M. A. (2010b). Which hat are you wearing? Roles and ethical responsibilities of mental health professionals in court cases. Retrieved from http://www.centerforethical-practice.org/Which-Hat

Fisher, M. A. (2012). Confidentiality and Record Keeping. In S. Knapp, M. Gottlieb, M. Handelsman, & L. VandeCreek (Eds.), *APA Handbook of Ethics in Psychology* (pp. 333–375). Washington DC: American Psychological Association. DOI: 10.1037/13271-013

Forester-Miller, H., & Davis, T. (1996). A practitioner's guide to ethical decision making. American Counseling Association. Free ACA publication retrieved from http://www.ed.uab.edu/csi-zeta/docs/EthicalDecMakingTyson.pdf

Fry, B. J., vanBark, W. P., Weinman, L., Kitchener, K. S., & Lang, P. R. (1997). Ethical transgressions of psychology graduate students: Critical incidents with implications for training. *Professional Psychology: Research and Practice*, 28, 492–495.

Glosoff, H. L., Herlihy, S. B., Herlihy, B., & Spence, E. B. (1997). Privileged communication in the psychologist-client relationship. *Professional Psychology: Research and Practice*, 28, 573–581.

Glosoff, H. L., & Pate, R. H. Jr., (2002). Privacy and confidentiality in school counseling. *Professional School Counseling*, 6, 20–27. Retrieved from http://studentwellbeingmackillopcollege.wikispaces.com/file/view/privconf+counselling.pdf

Gonsiorek, J. C. (2009). Informed consent can solve some confidentiality dilemmas, but others remain. *Professional Psychology: Research and Practice*, 39, 372–375. DOI: 10.1037/0735-7028.39.3.369

Gottlieb, M. C. (1996). Some Ethical Implications of Relational Diagnoses. In Kaslow, F. W. (Ed.), *Handbook of Relational Diagnosis and Dysfunctional Family Patterns* (pp. 19–34). New York: John Wiley & Sons.

Gottlieb, M. C., Lasser, J., & Simpson, G. (2008). Legal and Ethical Issues in Couple Therapy. In A. Gurman, *Clinical Handbook of Couple Therapy* (4th ed., pp. 698–717). New York: Guilford.

Grey, A. (2006). Confidentiality: A contribution to the debate. *British Journal of Psychotherapy*, 22, 363–372.

Greenberg, L. R., & Gould, J. W. (2001). The treating expert: A hybrid role with firm boundaries. *Professional Psychology: Research and Practice*, 32, 469–478

Greenberg, S. A., & Shurman, D. W. (1997). Irreconcilable conflict between therapeutic and forensic roles. *Professional Psychology: Research and Practice*, 28, 50–57.

Gross, B. (2006, Spring). Group concerns. *Annals of the American Psychotherapy Association*, 9, 36–38. Retrieved from http://www.accessmylibrary.com/article-1G1-152760490/group-concerns-issues-group.html

Grossman, N. S., Brice-Baker, J., Gottlieb, M., Kaslow, F., Nurse, R., Okun, B., & Schwartz, L. (2003, Winter). Forensic roles of family psychologists as applied to issues of custody and divorce. *The Family Psychologist*, 19(1), 12. Retrieved from http://www.apa.org/divisions/div43/news/NewsArchives/SpringNews03.pdf

Gutheil, T. G. (1980). Paranoia and progress notes: A guide to forensically informed psychiatric recordkeeping. *Hospital and Community Psychiatry* 31, 479–482.

Gutheil, T. G., Bursztajn, H. J., Brodsky, A., & Alexandra, V. (Eds.). (1991). Managing uncertainty: The therapeutic alliance, informed consent, and liability. In *Decision-Making in Psychiatry and the Law* (pp. 69–86). Baltimore, MD: Williams & Wilkins.

Gutheil, T. G., & Hilliard, J. T. (2001). "Don't write me down": Legal, clinical, and risk-management aspects of patients' requests that therapists not keep notes or records. *American Journal of Psychotherapy*, 55(2), 157–165.

Haas L. J., & Malouf, J. L. (2005). *Keeping Up the Good Work: A Practitioners Guide To Mental Health Ethics* (4th ed.). Sarasota FL: Professional Resource Press.

Haas, L. J., Malouf, J. L., & Mayerson, N. H. (1986). Ethical dilemmas in psychological practice: results of a national survey. *Professional Psychology: Research and Practice*, 7, 316–321.

Haggerty, L. A., & Hawkins, J. (2000). Informed consent and the limits of confidentiality. *Western Journal of Nursing Research*, 22, 508–514. DOI: 10.1177/01939450022044557

Handelsman, M. M., Kemper, M. B., Kesson-Craig, J. McC., & Johnsrud, C. (1986). Use, content, and readability of written informed consent forms for treatment. *Professional Psychology: Research and Practice*, 17, 514–518.

Handelsman, M. M., Knapp, S. J., & Gottlieb, M.C. (2002). Positive Ethics. In C.R. Snyder & S. J. Lopez (Eds.), *Handbook of Positive Psychology* (pp.731–744). New York: Oxford University Press.

Hansen, N. D., & Goldberg, S. G. (1999). Navigating the nuances: A matrix of considerations for ethical-legal dilemmas. *Professional Psychology: Research and Practice*, 30, 495–503.

Hare-Mustin, R. T., Marecek, J., Kaplan, A. G., & Liss-Levinson, N. (1979). Rights of clients, responsibilities of therapists. *American Psychologist*, 34, 3–16.

Harris, E., & Bennett, B. (1998). Sample Psychotherapist-Patient Contract. In Koocher, J., Norcross, J., & Hill, S. (Eds.), *Psychologists Desk Reference* (p. 191). New York: Oxford University Press. (Also available on APA Trust website at http://www.apait.org/apait/download.aspx)

Harris, E., & Younggren, J. (2011, July-August). But that's what the lawyer told me. *National Psychologist*, 20(4) 13, 17.

Health Insurance Portability and Accountability Act of 1996 (HIPAA). Pub. L. No. 104–191, 104th Cong. (1996). [See as USDHHS regulations at http://www.hhs.gov/ocr/privacy]

Henderson, W. (2010, March 19). Mental health and final security clearances. Retrieved from http://www.clearancejobs.com/cleared-news/126/mental-health-and-final-security-clearances

Hochhauser, M. (1999). Informed consent and patient's rights documents: A right, a rite, or a rewrite? *Ethics & Behavior* 9, 1–20.

Holloway, J. D. (2003, February). Professional will: A responsible thing to do. *Monitor on Psychology*, 34(2), 34–35. Retrieved from http://www.apa.org/monitor/feb03/will.html

Holloway, J. D. (2005, May). Spreading the word about a new practice opportunity: Parenting coordinators help divorcing families, and the new niche helps expand psychology's reach. *Monitor on Psychology*, 36(5), 52.

Individual Disability Education Act (IDEA). (2009). Retrieved from http://idea.ed.gov/

International Academy of Collaborative Professionals (2011). *Collaborative Solutions for Divorce and More.* Retrieved from http://collaborativepractice.com/

Jaffee v. Redmond, 116 Supreme Court. 95–266, 641. W. 4490 (June 13, 1996).

Jagim, R., Wittman, W., & Noll, J. (1978). Mental health professionals' attitudes towards confidentiality, privilege, and third-party disclosure. *Professional Psychology*, 9, 458–466.

Janes, E. (2006). 'Quis custodiet': Who has ultimate responsibility for confidentiality in mental health services? *Psychoanalytic Psychotherapy*, 20, 316–325.

Joint Commission. (2009). 2010 Pre-publication Standards. Retrieved from http://www.jointcommission.org/Standards/

Jordan, A. E., & Meara, N. M. (1990). Ethics & professional practice of psychologists: The role of virtues and principles. *Professional Psychology: Research and Practice*, 21, 107–114.

Joseph, D., & Onek, J. (1999). Confidentiality in Psychiatry. In Bloch, P. Chodoff, & S. A. Green (Eds.), *Psychiatric Ethics* (3rd ed., pp. 105–140). New York: Oxford University Press.

Kagle, J. D., & Kopels, S. (1994). Confidentiality after Tarasoff. *Health and Social Work* 19(3), 217–222.

Kalichman, S. C. (1999). *Mandated Reporting of Suspected Child Abuse: Ethics, Law, & Policy* (2nd ed.) Washington DC: American Psychological Association. DOI: 10.1037/10337-001

Keith-Spiegel, P., & Koocher, G. P. (1985). *Ethics in Psychology: Professional Standards and Cases*. New York, Random House.

Kelly, J. (2011), Stigma proves hard to eradicate despite multiple advances. *Psychiatric News*, 46(1), 10–15.

Kipnis, K. (2003, October). In defense of absolute confidentiality. *Virtual Mentor*, 5(10). Retrieved from http://virtualmentor.ama-assn.org/2003/10/hlaw2-0310.html

Klein, C. A. (2011). Cloudy confidentiality: Clinical and legal implications of cloud computing in health care. *Journal of the American Academy of Psychiatry and the Law*, 39(4), 571–578.

Knapp, S. (2002). Accidental breaches of confidentiality. *Pennsylvania Psychologist*, 62, 6–7.

Knapp, S. (2005). What Should Your Employees Know About Confidentiality? A HIPAA Training Guide. In L. VandeCreek (Ed.), *Innovations in clinical practice: Focus on adults* (pp. 125–134). Sarasota FL: Professional Resource Press. Retrieved from http://www.apadivisions.org/division-31/publications/articles/pennsylvania/confidentiality.pdf

Knapp, S., Gottlieb, M., Berman, J., & Handelsman, M. M. (2007). When laws and ethics collide: What should psychologists do? *Professional Psychology: Research and Practice*, 38, 54–59. DOI: 10.1037/0735-7028.38.1.54

Knapp, S., Gottlieb, M., Handelsman, M. M., & VandeCreek, L. B. (Eds.). (2012). *APA Handbook of Ethics in Psychology*. Washington DC: American Psychological Association.

Knapp, S., & VandeCreek, L. (1987). *Privileged Communications in the Mental Health Professions.* New York: Van Nostrand Reinhold Co.

Knapp, S., & VandeCreek, L. (2003b, Fall). Do psychologists have supererogatory obligations? *Psychotherapy Bulletin*, 38(3), 29–31.

Knapp, S. J., & VandeCreek, L. (2006). *Practical Ethics for Psychologists: A Positive Approach.* Washington DC: American Psychological Association.

Knauss, L. K. (2006). Ethical issues in recordkeeping in group psychotherapy. *International Journal of Group Psychotherapy*, 56, 415–430. DOI: 10.1521/ijgp.2006.56.4.415

Koman, S. L., & Harris, E. A. (2005). Contracting with Managed Care Organizations. In Koocher, G. P., Norcross, John C., & Hill, Sam S. III (Eds.), *Psychologists' Desk Reference, Second Edition*. New York, Oxford University Press, pp. 653–657.

Koocher, G. P. (2003). Ethical and legal issues in professional practice transitions. *Professional Psychology: Research and Practice*, 34, 383–387.

Koocher, G. P. (2005). Dealing with Subpoenas. In G. P. Koocher, J. C. Norecrodd, & S. S. Hill III (Eds.), *Psychologists' Desk Reference, Second Edition*. New York: Oxford University Press.

Koocher, G. P., & Keith-Spiegel, P. (1998). *Ethics in Psychology: Professional Standards and Cases* (2nd edition). New York: Oxford University Press.

Koocher, G. P., & Keith-Spiegel, P. (2008). *Ethics in Psychology and the Mental Health Professions: Standards and Cases* (3rd edition). New York: Oxford University Press.

Koocher, G. P., & Spiegel, P. K. (2009). "What Should I Do? – 38 Ethical Dilemmas Involving Confidentiality." A Continuing Education module retrieved from http://www.continuingedcourses.net/active/courses/course049.php

Kraft, S. (2005). *Sample Adolescent Informed Consent Form.* Retrieved from http://CenterForEthicalPractice.org/Form-AdolescentConsent

Kuo, A. M-H. (2011). Opportunities and challenges of cloud computing to improve health care services. *Journal of Medical Internet Research*, 13(3). DOI:10.2196/jmir.1867. Retrieved from http://www.jmir.org/2011/3/e67/

Kuo, F.-C. (2009). Secrets or no secrets: Confidentiality in couple therapy. *The Journal of Family Therapy*, 37, 351–354. DOI: 10.1080/01926180701862970

Lasky, G. B., & Riva, M. T. (2006). Confidentiality and privileged communication in group psychotherapy. *International Journal of Group Psychotherapy*, 56, 455–476.

Licht, M., & Younggren, J. N. (2006, September-October). Guidelines for treating children in high-conflict divorce. *The California Psychologist*, 39(5), 31–34.

Lombardo, P. A., (2000, Oct.). Legal focus: Substance abuse treatment records: A special corner of medical privacy. *Virginia Bar Association VBA News Journal*, 26. http://216.230.13.18/oct00.htm

Marine, E. C. (undated). *Are Your Records Protected?* American Professional Agency, Inc. Retrieved from http://www.americanprofessional.com/risk2.html

Mattison, M. (2000). Ethical decision making: The person in the process. *Social Work*, 45, 201.

McGee, T. F. (2003). Observations on the retirement of professional psychologists. *Professional Psychology: Research and Practice*, 34, 388–395.

Meer, D., & VandeCreek, L. (2002). Cultural considerations in release of information. *Ethics & Behavior*, 12, 143–156.

Melton, G. B. (1990). Certificates of confidentiality under the Public Health Service Act: Strong protection but not enough. *Violence and Victims*, 5, 67–71.

Meyer, R. G., & Smith, S. R. (1977). A crisis in group therapy. *American Psychologist*, 32, 638–643.

Miller, D. J., & Thelen, M. H. (1986). Knowledge and beliefs about confidentiality in psychotherapy. *Professional Psychology: Research and Practice*, 17, 15–19.

Miller, I. (2000, Spring). Protecting privacy with the absence of records. The Independent Practitioner, Division of Independent Practice (42) of the American Psychological Association. Retrieved from http://www.academyprojects.org/miller1.htm

Mitchell, R. W. (2007). *Documentation in Counseling Records: An Overview of Ethical, Legal, and Clinical Issues* (3rd edition). Alexandria, VA: American Counseling Association.

Moats, J. R., & Johnson, B. T. (2004, December). Responding to a subpoena. *Ohio Psychologist Update*, 51(4), 1.

Monaghan, P. (2012, February 19). Our storehouse of knowledge about social movements is going to be left bare. *Chronicle of Higher Education.* Retrieved from http://chronicle.com/article/5-Minutes-With-a-Sociologist/130849/

Monahan, J. (1981). *The Clinical Prediction of Violent Behavior*. Washington, DC: Government Printing Office.

Monahan, J. (1993). Limiting therapist exposure to Tarasoff liability: Guidelines for risk containment. *American Psychologist*, 48(3), 242–250. DOI: 10.1037/0003–066X.48.3.242

Morgan, S., & Polowy, C. (2001). *Social Workers and Clinical Notes.* National Association of Social Workers, Law Note Series. Summary retrieved from http://www.socialworkers.org/ldf/lawnotes/notes.asp?print=1&

Morgan, S., & Polowy, C. I. (2009). *The Social Worker and the Home Office.* National Association of Social Workers. Retrieved from www.rinasw.info/socialworkerhomeoffice.doc

Munsey, C. (2006, April). More protection for psychologists' records in renewed Patriot Act. *Monitor on Psychology*, 37(4), 15.

Munsey, C. (2008, February). New options for military psychologists. *Monitor on Psychology* 39(2), 13.

Munsey, C. (2009, April). Needed: More military psychologists. *Monitor on Psychology*, 40(4), 12.

Nagy, T. F. (1988). The Well-Educated Consumer: Informing Clients and Protecting Providers. Paper presented at the California State Psychological Association Annual Convention, San Diego.

Nagy, T. F. (1993, Sept/Oct). Applying the new Ethics Code to practice. *National Psychologist*, 2(5), 6A–7A.

Nagy, T. F. (2011). *Essential Ethics for Psychologists: A Primer for Understanding and Mastering Core Issues*. Washington DC: American Psychological Association.

National Association of School Psychologists (NASP). (2010). *Principles for Professional Ethics*. Bethesda, MD: Author. Retrieved from http://www.nasponline.org/standards/2010standards/1_%20Ethical%20Principles.pdf

National Association of Social Workers (NASW). (2002). *Standards for School Social Work Services.* Retrieved from http://www.naswpress.org/publications/standards/school-services.html

National Association of Social Workers (NASW). (2008). *NASW Code of Ethics.* Retrieved from http://www.socialworkers.org/pubs/code/code.asp

National Association of Social Workers (NASW). (2005a). Brief *amicus curiae* in *Bier vs. Zahren.* Retrieved from http://www.socialworkers.org/ldf/brief_bank/briefDocuments/BierAmicusBrief_(DN_85795_1).PDF

National Association of Social Workers (NASW). (2005b). *Standards for Technology and Social Work Practice.* Retrieved from http://www.naswdc.org/practice/standards/NASWTechnologyStandards.pdf

National Institute of Standards and Technology (NIST). (2006). Guidelines for Media Sanitization (NIST Special Publication 800-88). Retrieved from http://csrc.nist.gov/publications/nistpubs/800-88/NISTSP800-88_with-errata.pdf

Nicastro, D. (2011, May 3). Large patient information breach list climbs. *HealthLeaders Media.* Retrieved from http://www.healthleadersmedia.com/content/TEC-265636/Large-Patient-Information-Breach-List-Climbs-to-265.html##

Nordmarken, N., & Zur, O. (2010). Home office: When the office is located at the home. Retrieved from http://www.zurinstitute.com/homeoffice.html

North Carolina Code, General Statutes § 8–53.3 (1998). Communications between psychologist and client or patient. Retrieved from http://www.ncga.state.nc.us/EnactedLegislation/Statutes/HTML/BySection/Chapter_8/GS_8-53.3.html

Nowell, D., & Spruill, J. (1993). If it's not absolutely confidential, will information be disclosed? *Professional Psychology: Research and Practice*, 24, 367–369.

Pabian, Y. L., Welfel, E., & Beebe, R. S. (2009). Psychologists' knowledge of their states' laws pertaining to Tarasoff-type situations. *Professional Psychology: Research and Practice*, 40, 8–14. DOI: 10.1037/a0014784

Paradise, L. V., & Kirby, P. C. (1990). Some perspectives on the legal liability of group counseling in private practice. *The Journal for Specialists in Group Work*, 15, 114–118.

Patten, C., Barnett, T., & Houlihan, D. (1991). Ethics in marital and family therapy: a review of the literature. *Professional Practice: Research and Practice*, 22, 171–175.

Patients' Bill of Rights. (1997). *Principles for the Provision of Mental Health and Substance Abuse Treatment Services.* (A joint initiative of mental health organizations). Brochure. Retrieved from http://www.apa.org/pubs/info/brochures/rights.aspx#

Pepper, R. S. (2003, March). Be it ever so humble … The controversial issue of psychotherapy groups in the home office setting. *Group*, 27(1), 41–52.

Pettifor, J. L., & Sawchuk, T. R. (2006). Psychologists' perceptions of ethically troubling incidents across international borders. *International Journal of Psychology*, 41, 216–225.

Pipes, R. B., Blevins, T., & Kluck, A. (2008). Confidentiality, ethics, and informed consent [Letter]. *American Psychologist*, 63, 623–624.

Pomerantz, A. M., & Handelsman, M. M. (2004). Informed consent revisited: An updated written question format. *Professional Psychology: Research and Practice*, 35, 201–205.

Pope, K. S., & Bajt, T. R. (1988). When laws and values conflict: A dilemma for psychologists. *American Psychologist*, 43, 828–829.

Pope, K. S., & Vasquez, M. J. T. (2005). *How to Survive & Thrive as a Therapist: Information, Ideas, & Resources for Psychologists in Practice.* Washington DC: American Psychological Association.

Pope, K. S., & Vasquez, M. J. T. (2011). *Ethics in Psychotherapy and Counseling: A Practical Guide* (4th ed.). Hoboken, NJ: John Wiley & Sons, Inc.

Pope, K. S., & Vetter, V. A. (1992). Ethical dilemmas encountered by members of the American Psychological Association: A national survey. *American Psychologist*, 47, 397–411.

Porfiri, L. T., & Resnick, R. J. (2000). *Law & Mental Health Professionals: Virginia.* Washington, DC: American Psychological Association.

Ragusea, S. A. (2002). A Professional Living Will for Psychologists. In L. VandeCreek & T. L. Jackson (Eds.), *Innovations in Clinical Practice: A Source Book* (pp. 301–305). Sarasota, FL: Professional Resource Press. Retrieved from www.mepa.org/docs/LivingWill.doc

Reamer, F. (2001, October). Documentation in social work: Evolving ethical and risk-management standards. *Social Work.* Retrieved from http://works.bepress.com/frederic_reamer/30/

Roback H. B., Moore R. F., Bloch F. S., & Shelton M. (1996). Confidentiality in group psychotherapy: Empirical findings and the law. *International Journal of Group Psychotherapy*, 46, 117–135.

Roback, H., Purdonn, S., Ochoa, E., & Bloch, F. (1993). Effects of professional affiliation on group therapists' confidentiality attitudes and behaviors. *Bulletin of the American Academy of Psychiatry and the Law*, 21(2) 147–153.

Robb, M. (2004). *Client Records: Keep or Toss?* NASW Insurance Trust. Retrieved from http://www.naswassurance.org/pdf/PP_Record_Retention.pdf

Robinson, D. J., & O'Neill, D. (2007). Access to health care records after death: Balancing confidentiality with appropriate disclosure. *Journal of the American Medical Association*, 297, 634–636. Retrieved from http://jama.ama-assn.org/cgi/content/full/297/6/634

Rubanowitz, D. E. (1987). Public attitudes toward psychotherapist-client confidentiality. *Professional Psychology: Research and Practice*, 18, 613–618.

Saks, E. R. (2011). *Informed Consent to Psychoanalysis: The Law, the Theory, and the Data.* University of Southern California Law School, Legal Studies Working Paper Series, (Paper 75), pp. 1–127. Retrieved from http://law.bepress.com/usclwps/lss/art75/

Salter, D. S., & Salter, B. R. (2012). Competence with diverse populations. In S. Knapp, M. Gottlieb, M. Handelsman, & L. VandeCreek (Eds.), *APA Handbook of Ethics in Psychology* (pp. 217–239). Washington DC: American Psychological Association. DOI:10.1037/13271-008.

Samstag, L. (2012, March). Introduction to the special section on ethical issues in clinical writing. *Psychotherapy*, 49(1), 1–2. DOI: 10.1037/a0027037

Sanbar, S. S. (2007). Medical Records: Paper and Electronic. In Sanbar, S. S. (Ed.), *Legal Medicine* (7th ed.). Philadelphia: Mosby.

Scarce, R. (2012, August 12). A law to protect scholars. *Chronicle of Higher Education*, 51(49), B-24. Retrieved from http://chronicle.com/article/A-Law-to-Protect-Scholars/2103/

Schank, J. A., & Skovholt, T. M. (1997). Dual-relationship dilemmas of rural and small-community psychologists. *Professional Psychology: Research and Practice*, 28, 44–49.

Schank, J. A., & Skovholt, T. M. (2005). *Ethical Practice in Small Communities: Challenges and Rewards for Psychologists.* Washington DC: American Psychological Association.

School Social Work Association of America. (2001). *School social workers and confidentiality.* Retrieved from http://sswaaorganization.org/indexd2ce.html?page=98

Sharkin, B. S. (1995). Strains on confidentiality in college-student psychotherapy: Entangled therapeutic relationships, incidental encounters, and third-party inquiries. *Professional Psychology: Research and Practice*, 26, 184–189.

Shuman, D. W., & Foote, W. (1999). *Jaffe v. Redmond's* impact: Life after the Supreme Court's recognition of a psychotherapist-patient privilege. *Professional Psychology: Research and Practice*, 30, 479–487

Shuman, D. W., Greenberg, S., Heilbrun, K., & Foote, W. E. (1998). An immodest proposal: Should treating mental health professionals be barred from testifying about their patients? *Behavioral Sciences and the Law*, 16, 509–523.

Sieck, B. C. (2012, March). Obtaining clinical writing informed consent versus using client disguise and recommendations for practice. *Psychotherapy*, 49(1), 3–11. DOI:10.1037/a0025059

Siegel, M. (1976, Fall). Confidentiality. *The Clinical Psychologist* [Newsletter of Division 12 of the American Psychological Association], 30, 23.

Smith, D. (1981). Unfinished business with informed consent procedures. *American Psychologist*, 36, 22–26.

Smith, T. S., McGuire, J. M., Abbott, D. W., & Blau, B. I. (1991). Clinical ethical decision making: An investigation of the rationales used to justify doing less than one believes one should. *Professional Psychology: Research and Practice*, 22, 235–239.

Somberg, D. R., Stone, G. L., & Claiborn, C. D. (1993). Informed consent: Therapists' beliefs and practices. *Professional Psychology: Research and Practice*, 24, 153–159.

Spragins, E. E., & Hager, M. (1997, June 30). Naked before the world: Will your medical secrets be safe in a new national databank? *Newsweek*, p. 84.

Strasburger, L. H., Gutheil, T. G., & Brodsky, A. (1997). On wearing two hats: Role conflict in serving as both psychotherapist and expert witness. *American Journal of Psychiatry*, 154, 448–456.

Stromberg, C. D., Haggarty, D. J., Leibenluft, R. F., McMillan, M. H., Mishkin, B., Rubin, B. L., & Trilling, H. R. (1988). *The Psychologist's Legal Handbook*. Washington DC: The Council for the National Register of Health Service Providers in Psychology.

Sullivan, T., Martin, W. L. Jr., & Handelsman, M. M. (1993). Practical benefits of an informed-consent procedure: An empirical investigation. *Professional Psychology: Research and Practice*, 24, 160–163.

Swidler & Berlin v. United States (1998), 524 U.S. 399.

Tarasoff v. Regents of the University of California. 13Cal.3d 177, 529 P.2d553 (1974, *vacated)*, 17 Cal.3d 425, 131 Cal. RPTR 14, 551 P.2d 34 (1976).

Thelen, M. H., Rodriquez, M. D., & Sprengelmeyer, P. (1994). Psychologists' beliefs concerning confidentiality with suicide, homicide, and child abuse. *American Journal of Psychotherapy*, 48,363–379.

Tracey, M. (1998, January/February). Be aware of malpractice risks when using electronic office devices. *National Psychologist*, 7(1), 17.

Traynor, M. (1997). Countering the excessive subpoena for scholarly research. Retrieved on September 18, 2009 from http://library.findlaw.com/1997/Oct/14/126469.html

United States Department of Health and Human Services (USDHHS). (1999). *Mental Health: A Report of the Surgeon General—Executive Summary*. Rockville, MD: U.S. Department of Health and Human Services, Substance Abuse and Mental Health Services Administration, Center for Mental Health Services, National Institutes of Health.

United States Department of Health and Human Services (USDHHS). (2003a). *Health Insurance Reform: Security Standards*. Retrieved from http://www.ncbi.nlm.nih.gov/pubmed/12596712

United States Department of Health and Human Services (USDHHS). (2003b). *Summary of the HIPAA Privacy Rule*. Retrieved from http://www.hhs.gov/ocr/privacy/hipaa/understanding/summary/privacysummary.pdf

United States Department of Health and Human Services (USDHHS). (2007). *Standards for Privacy of Individually Identifiable Health Information*. B. Definitions. (§§ 160.103 and 164.504). Retrieved from http://aspe.hhs.gov/admnsimp/nprm/pvc07.htm

United States Department of Health and Human Services (USDHHS). (2008). *Guidance to Render Unsecured Protected Health Information Unusable, Unreadable, or Indecipherable to Unauthorized Individuals*. Retrieved from http://www.hhs.gov/ocr/privacy/hipaa/administrative/breachnotificationrule/brguidance.html

United States Department of Health and Human Services (USDHHS). (2009). *Press Release: HHS Issues Rule Requiring Individuals Be Notified of Breaches of Their Health*

Information. Retrieved from http://www.hhs.gov/news/press/2009pres/08/20090819f.html

VandeCreek, L. (2008). Considering confidentiality within broader theoretical frameworks. (Commentary on Donner, 2008). *Professional Psychology: Research and Practice*, 39, 372–373. DOI: 10.1037/0735-7028.39.3.369

VandeCreek, L., Miars, R. D., & Herzog, C. E. (1987). Client anticipations and preferences for confidentiality of records. *Journal of Counseling Psychology*, 34, 62–67.

Vasquez, M. J. T. (1992). The psychologist as clinical supervisor: Promoting ethical practice. *Professional Psychology: Research and Practice*, 23, 196–202.

Vasquez, M. J. T. (1994). Implications of the 1992 ethics code for the practice of individual psychotherapy. *Professional Psychology: Research and Practice*, 25, 321–328.

Virginia Code, Statutes § 8.01–399. (2009). Communications between physicians [and clinical psychologists] and patients. Retrieved from http://leg1.state.va.us/cgi-bin/legp504.exe?000+cod+8.01-399

Virginia Code, Statutes § 8.01–400.2. (2005). Communications between certain mental health professionals and clients. Retrieved from http://leg1.state.va.us/cgi-bin/legp504.exe?000+cod+8.01-400.2

Virginia Code, Statutes § 23-9.2:3. (2008). Power of governing body of educational institution to establish rules and regulations Retrieved from http://leg1.state.va.us/cgi-bin/legp504.exe?000+cod+23-9.2C3

Virginia Code, Statutes §32.1–127.1:03. (2012). Health records privacy. Retrieved from http://leg1.state.va.us/cgi-bin/legp504.exe?000+cod+32.1–127.1C03

Virginia Psychological Association. (2009). *Applying Virginia's Legal Standards in Your Own Practice: Current Regulations and Their Implications.* Retrieved from http://www.vapsych.org/displaycommon.cfm?an=1&subarticlenbr=60

Virginia Supreme Court. (1997). Record #962068 *Fairfax Hospital v. Patricia Curtis*, October 31, 1997.

Walfish, S., & Ducey, B. B. (2007). Readability level of health insurance portability and accountability act notices of privacy practices used by psychologists in clinical practice. *Professional Psychology: Research and Practice*, 38, 203–207. DOI: 10.1037/0735-7028.38.2.203

Weeks, G. R., Odell, M., & Methven, S. (2005). *If Only I Had Known … Avoiding Common Mistakes in Couple Therapy*. New York: W. W. Norton.

Weithorn, L. A. (Ed.). (1987). *Psychology and Child Custody Determinations: Knowledge, Roles, and Expertise.* Lincoln: University of Nebraska Press.

Welch, B. (1998). Walking the documentation tightrope. *Insight: American Professional Agency*, Edition #2, 1998. Retrieved from http://americanprofessional.com/insight.htm

Welfel, E. R., Werth, J. L., & Benjamin, G.A. H. (2009). Introduction to the Duty to Protect. In J. L. Werth, E. R. Welfel, & G. A. H. Benjamin (Eds.), *The Duty to Protect: Ethical, Legal and Professional Considerations for Mental Health Professionals* (pp. 195–208). Washington DC: American Psychological Association.

Werth, J. L., Burke, C., & Burdash, R. J. (2002). Confidentiality in end-of-life and after-death situations. *Ethics & Behavior*, 12, 205–222. DOI: 10.1207/S15327019EB1203_1

Werth, J. L., & Richmond, J. M. (2009). End-of-Life Decisions and the Duty to Protect. In J. L. Werth, E. R. Welfel, & G. A. H. Benjamin (Eds.), *The Duty to Protect: Ethical,*

Legal And Professional Considerations for Mental Health Professionals (pp. 195–208). Washington DC: American Psychological Association.

Werth, E. R. Welfel, & G. A. H. Benjamin (Eds.). (2009). *The Duty to Protect: Ethical, Legal And Professional Considerations for Mental Health Professionals*. Washington DC: American Psychological Association.

Werth, J. L., Welfel, E. R., Benjamin, G. A. H., & Salacka, C. (2007, December). Duty to protect. *Monitor on Psychology*, 38(11), 4. Retrieved from http://www.apa.org/monitor/dec07/letters.html

Werth, J. S., Welfel, E. R., Benjamin, G. A. H., & Sales, B. D. (2009). Practice and Policy Responses to the Duty to Protect. In J. L. Werth, E. R. Welfel, & G. A. H. Benjamin (Eds.), *The Duty to Protect: Ethical, Legal And Professional Considerations for Mental Health Professionals* (pp. 249–261). Washington DC: American Psychological Association.

Woodhouse, S. S. (2012, March). Clinical writing: Additional ethical and practical issues. *Psychotherapy*, 49(1), 22–25. DOI: 10.1037/a0026965.

Woody, R. H. (1999). Domestic violations of confidentiality. *Professional Psychology: Research and Practice*, 30, 607–610.

Younggren, J. N. (2000). Is managed care really just another, unethical Model T? *The Counseling Psychologist*, 28, 253–262. DOI: 10.1177/0011000000282004 Retrieved from http://tcp.sagepub.com

Younggren, J. N., & Harris, E. A. (2008). Can you keep a secret? Confidentiality in psychotherapy. *Journal of Clinical Psychology: In Session*, 64, 589–600. DOI: 10.1002/jclp.20480

Zarit, J. M., & Zarit, S. H. (1996). Ethical Considerations in the Treatment of Older Adults. In S. H. Zarit & B. G. Knight (Eds.), *A Guide to Psychotherapy and Aging: Effective Clinical Interventions in a Life-Stage Context* (pp. 269–284). Washington, DC: American Psychological Association.

Zur, O. (2001). Out-of-office experience: When crossing office boundaries and engaging in dual relationships are clinically beneficial and ethically sound. *The Independent Practitioner*, 21(1), 96–100.

Zur, O. (2010). *Beyond the Office Walls: Home Visits, Celebrations, Adventure Therapy, Incidental Encounters and Other Encounters Outside the Office Walls.* Retrieved from http://www.zurinstitute.com/outofofficeexperiences.html.

Zur, O. (2012). *In-Home Therapy and Home Visits: Home-Based Mental Health.* Retrieved from http://www.zurinstitute.com/home_based_mental_health.html

AUTHOR INDEX

Page numbers in *italics* are located in the Notes

SUBJECT INDEX

Page numbers in *italics* are located in the Notes

CPSIA information can be obtained at www.ICGtesting.com
Printed in the USA
BVOW011537111212

307887BV00003B/3/P